An Introduction to
Financial Accounting

An Introduction to Financial Accounting

Colin Rickwood
Andrew Thomas

McGRAW-HILL BOOK COMPANY

London · New York · St Louis · San Francisco · Auckland · Bogotá
Caracas · Hamburg · Lisbon · Madrid · Mexico · Milan · Montreal
New Delhi · Panama · Paris · San Juan · São Paulo · Singapore
Sydney · Tokyo · Toronto

Published by
McGRAW-HILL Book Company Europe
Shoppenhangers Road, Maidenhead, Berkshire, SL6 2QL, England
Telephone 0628 23432
Fax 0628 770224

British Library Cataloguing in Publication Data
Rickwood, Colin, *1947–*
    An introduction to financial accounting.
    I. Title   II. Thomas, Andrew, *1948–*
    657.48
    ISBN 0-07-707443-2

Library of Congress Cataloging-in-Publication Data
Rickwood, Colin.
    An introduction to financial accounting/Colin Rickwood and Andrew Thomas.
        p.   cm.
    Includes bibliographical references and index.
    ISBN 0-07-707443-2: £14.95
        1. Accounting.   I. Thomas, Andrew, 1948– .   II. Title.
    HF5635.R55   1992   91-44885
    657—dc20   CIP

12345   HWV   95432

Typeset by Alden Multimedia Ltd

and printed and bound in Great Britain by BPCC Hazels Ltd. member of BPCC Ltd.

Contents

Preface

This book constitutes not only an introductory text for students taking a degree in accounting or business studies with a substantial element of accounting, but also covers the accounting syllabuses for Level 1 of the Chartered Association of Certified Accountants, the Preliminary and Intermediate examinations of the Association of Accounting Technicians, and the General Certificate of Secondary Education. Furthermore, the book provides a more than adequate coverage of the financial accounting content of the accounting syllabuses for Stage 1 of the Chartered Institute of Management Accountants and the General Certificate of Education at Advanced level of the Associated Examining Board and the Joint Matriculation Board. Its authorship links with *Advanced financial accounting*, by Samuels, Rickwood and Piper, make it a particularly suitable text for those intending to pursue more advanced study.

There are of course other texts that seek to provide an introduction to accounting, but this is not intended to be just one more. In writing this book, the authors have been concerned to ensure that the text matches the development of the student's understanding and competence in each area introduced. The particular structure and treatment of the material aims at meeting this concern, and users will find it valuable to bear in mind the approach adopted, which is set out in what follows.

A major aim in the approach is the provision of an appropriate balance between theory and the presentation of accounting methods. Each element in this balance is important. A proper understanding of accounting requires underpinning by an appreciation of its theoretical foundations. Although this may be readily recognized in the case of degree students, it is no less true of other students. Theory is often presented in textbooks in isolation, but this book integrates theory into the presentation of accounting methods. The other side of this balance, represented by the application of accounting, depends upon a thorough grasp of the mechanics of financial accounting. The book therefore examines in depth many of what are normally regarded as the basic aspects of accounting, such as the accounts of partnerships and clubs, particularly where this involves applications of important points of principle.

The structure of the book follows a proven pattern based on the authors' not inconsiderable experience of teaching at this level. Each chapter deals with a specific aspect of accounting, irrespective of how brief or lengthy this might be. This is intended to permit lecturers to choose that combination of chapters which fits their syllabus. However, it is important to appreciate that the order in which the chapters are presented is significant. There are also particular groupings of chapters, such as Chapters 6 and 8 which deal with books of prime entry, Chapters 11 and 12 that examine aspects of internal control and accuracy, and Chapters 19 and 20 which both involve a consideration of incomplete records.

The structure within each chapter also follows a deliberate pattern. These usually start by examining the purpose, theoretical foundation and practical relevance of the topic. This is followed by a description of the accounting methods and then comprehensive examples. A further unique feature of the book is that after most examples there is a series of notes.

These are intended to explain the familiar and more difficult aspects of the example in order that the reader is able to follow the example. The notes also provide guidance on further aspects of the topic that may be encountered in examination questions, such as alternative forms of wording.

Finally, the exercises at the end of each chapter are presented in a coherent progressive sequence. These start with a number of written questions designed to test understanding of terminology, legal requirements, theoretical foundations, etc. They are followed by mainly numerical questions that are presented in order of difficulty. The later examples are therefore often quite demanding. However, students should be able to answer these from reading the chapter. Moreover, the questions are not repetitive but have been selected because each tests some aspect of the topic not covered in a previous question. The student may be assured that the somewhat longer later questions have a deliberate purpose representing the most advanced aspects of the topic which they are likely to encounter. All users, especially lecturers, should also be aware that some questions are extensions of other questions in previous chapters. This is intended to provide a more comprehensive under-standing of the relationship between different topics in accounting, such as day books and cash books, provisions for depreciation and bad debts etc.

Since accounts are now frequently held in computers, a chapter is devoted to the implications of computerization. The aim has been to explain the possibilities that are opened up by the new technology, and to identify some of the changes in working practice which are required. The authors are indebted to Dr Andrew J. Hawker for writing this chapter. Dr Hawker is a lecturer in computing in the Department of Accounting at the University of Birmingham who has spent most of his working life in large industrial computer companies dealing with applications of computers to accounting.

The authors gratefully acknowledge the permission of the following bodies to repro-duce copies of their past examination questions: The Chartered Association of Certified Accountants (CACA); The Association of Accounting Technicians (AAT); The Associated Examining Board (AEB); and The Joint Matriculation Board (JMB).

Finally we wish to express our thanks to Mrs Karen Hanson for her patience and accuracy in the typing of the original manuscript.

1. The nature and functions of financial accounting

The nature and purposes of financial accounting

Financial accounting may be defined as the process of designing and operating an information system for collecting, measuring and recording business transactions, and summarizing and communicating the results of these transactions.

The first part of this definition, relating to collecting and recording business transactions, refers to double entry bookkeeping, which consists of maintaining a record of the money values of the transactions of a business. In many businesses this may be done mechanically or electronically using a computer. The second part of the definition, relating to communicating the results, refers to preparing final accounts and statements from the books of account (or any other system of recording) showing the profit earned during a given period and the financial state of affairs of a business at the end of that period.

These two functions of financial acconting may be broken down further as described below.

The recording and control of business transactions

This includes records of:

(a)   The amount of cash and cheques received, for what and from whom.
(b)   The amount of cash and cheques paid, for what and to whom. Records of money received and paid are kept so that the business knows how much money it has at any time.
(c)   Assets, expenses and goods purchased on credit. This is so that the business knows to whom it owes money and how much. These are referred to as creditors.
(d)   Assets and goods sold on credit. This is so that the business knows who owes it money and how much. These are referred to as debtors.

This function is often referred to as stewardship. The accountant has been traditionally regarded as the 'holder of the purse strings' and responsible for 'safeguarding' the assets of the business. The control aspect of this function includes ensuring that the correct amounts are paid to those entitled to them at the appropriate time, collecting the business's debts, safeguarding against fraud and misappropriation of goods or cash, etc.

To maintain accuracy in recording

Double entry bookkeeping is generally regarded as the most accurate method of bookkeeping, primarily because each transaction is entered in the books twice. This duplication, referred to as a form of 'internal check', highlights any errors.

To meet the requirements of the law

The law, in the form of the Companies Acts, states that companies must keep proper records of their transactions. There is no legislation that specifically requires sole traders or partnerships to keep records of their transactions. However, when the Inland Revenue makes a demand for income tax on self-employed persons, it usually asks for more than business proprietors would pay if they presented accounts showing their profit for the year. There is thus a financial incentive for sole traders and partnerships to maintain proper records. Furthermore, the Inland Revenue expects accounts to be kept. In addition any trader who does not keep proper records and goes bankrupt will find it more difficult to obtain discharge from bankruptcy.

To present final accounts to the owners of the business

These comprise a profit and loss account showing the amount of profit for the period and a balance sheet showing the financial position at the end of that period. The latter will include:

(a)   the amount of cash and money at the bank;
(b)   other assets that the business owns, such as goods for resale, vehicles, machinery etc.;
(c)   the debtors and creditors;
(d)   the amount of capital that has been invested in the business by its owner(s);
(e)   any money that has been borrowed by the business.

In the case of a sole trader, these final accounts show the owner his 'earnings' for the period and may be used to evaluate the profitability of the business. However, they are often primarily used to determine his tax liability. Final accounts perform similar functions in the case of companies. However, company final accounts are also designed to give information to third parties to enable them to evaluate the profitability and financial stability of the company. These include prospective shareholders, trade unions and employees, creditors and those who have lent the company money, government departments, and social pressure groups. This is discussed further below.

To present financial statements and reports to management

This enables them to plan and control their business activities. It includes the use of ratios to evaluate:

(a)   the profitability of the business;
(b)   the level of activity and productivity;
(c)   the solvency and liquidity position (i.e. whether the business will be able to pay its debts);
(d)   the efficiency of credit control procedures;
(e)   the efficiency of stock control procedures;
(f)   the effect of any loans on the business's profitability and financial stability.

The objectives of company accounts

As explained above, one of the main functions of financial accounting is the preparation of final accounts. These consist of a profit and loss account and a balance sheet. In the case of companies, the final accounts are often referred to as published accounts. These are sent to shareholders in the form of a pamphlet known as the annual report, corporate report or, in the USA, financial statements. It is therefore usual to discuss the objectives of company final accounts in terms of the functions of annual reports.

The function of annual reports is related to beliefs about the role of business organizations in society and their objectives. Up until about the mid-1970s the accountancy profession took the view that the primary objective of a business enterprise was to maximize the wealth of its shareholders. This was reinforced by disciplines such as economics that gave prominance to the classical theory of the firm. The function of annual reports was thus regarded as being to provide information about the profitability and financial position of a company to those with whom it has a capital contractual relationship, namely shareholders and loan creditors.

However, during the 1960s and early 1970s there was a swing in society's beliefs towards the idea that business enterprises exist for the benefit of the community as a whole. Similarly developments in disciplines such as economics and modern organization theory cast doubt on whether profit maximization was a meaningful description of business objectives. For example, Herbert Simon argues that business enterprises are 'satisficers'. Also, a survey of large UK companies undertaken by the accountancy profession found that 'the majority view of those replying to the survey seems to be that their primary objective is to make a profit for the benefit of a number of groups. It is not the majority view that the maximization of shareholder's profit is the primary objective.' Other respondents to this survey described their primary objective as being survival, or in terms of the service they provide.

It follows from this that enterprises are accountable to a number of different groups (e.g. employees, the public etc.), and that the function of annual reports is to provide each of them with information. This is the view taken by *The Corporate Report*[1] which is the UK accountancy profession's primary statement on the function/objective of annual reports, their users and the information that they need. It is not mandatory, but represents one of the most comprehensive pieces of published work in this area, and has probably led to a number of new developments in accounting practices and more recent UK statements on these matters.

During the 1980s there may have been a swing in society's beliefs back to an emphasis on the profit objective and shareholders as a result of the political philosophy known as 'enterprise culture'. There has also been relatively little legislation that gives other groups access to annual reports or provides for the disclosure of more information of a social or environmental nature. However, EC Directives on company law and other matters (e.g. employee participation) are likely to require greater disclosure. Furthermore, the privatization of government-owned enterprises and greater environmental awareness has probably resulted in more exposure of members of the public, such as small investors, to annual reports. This may lead to further developments in corporate reporting in the near future.

The 'basic philosophy' of *The Corporate Report* is reflected in the need for what is called 'public accountability':

there is an implicit responsibility to report publicly . . . incumbent on every entity whose size or format renders it significant; . . . we consider the responsibility to report publicly (referred to . . . as public accountability) is separate from and broader than the legal obligation to report and arises from the custodial role played in the community by economic entities; . . . they are involved in the maintenance of standards of life and the creation of wealth for and on behalf of the community.

The 'custodial role' of business enterprises refers to their function in creating wealth, maintaining the standard of living, and other considerations such as the quality of the environment. It follows from this notion of public accountability that the objective or function of annual reports is thus:

to communicate economic measurements of and information about the resources and performance of the reporting entity useful to those having reasonable rights to such information.

'Reasonable rights' is defined as follows:

A reasonable right to information exists where the activities of an organisation impinge or may impinge on the interest of a user group.

A similar study of the function of annual reports was undertaken in 1973 by the American Institute of Certified Public Accountants (AICPA); this is known as *The Objectives of Financial Statements*.[2] This document emphasizes the use to which the information is put:

The basic objective of financial statements is to provide information useful for making economic decisions.

It also regards annual reports as principally intended for those groups who only have access to limited information about the enterprise:

An objective of financial statements is to serve primarily those users who have limited authority, ability, or resources to obtain information and who rely on financial statements as their principal source of information about an enterprises economic activities.

The users of annual reports and their information needs

The users of annual reports identified in *The Corporate Report* are as follows:[1]

1. *The equity investor group* including existing and potential shareholders.
2. *The loan creditor group* including existing and potential holders of debentures and loan stock, and providers of short-term secured and unsecured loans and finance.
3. *The employee group* including existing, potential and past employees.
4. *The analyst–adviser group* including financial analysts and journalists, economists, statisticians, researchers, trade unions, stockbrokers and other providers of advisory services such as credit rating agencies.
5. *The business contact group* including customers, trade creditors and suppliers and in a different sense competitors, business rivals and those interested in mergers, amalgamations and takeovers.
6. *The government* including tax authorities, departments and agencies concerned with the supervision of commerce and industry, and local authorities.
7. *The public* including taxpayers, ratepayers, consumers and other community and special interest groups such as political parties, consumer and environmental protection societies and regional pressure groups.

Each of the above groups are said by *The Corporate Report* to have certain 'information needs'. These are described below in respect of each group of users.

The equity investor group

A basic premise in *The Corporate Report* is that 'investors require information to assist in reaching share trading decisions . . . and in reaching voting decisions at general meetings . . . . In particular investors will wish to make judgements concerning likely movements in share prices [and] likely levels of future dividend payments'. Similarly, the US *Objectives of Financial Statements* says that 'An objective of financial statements is to provide information useful to investors . . . for predicting potential cash flows to them'. Thus, according to *The Corporate Report* (p. 20) investors require information for the purpose of:

(a) Evaluating the performance of the entity and its management, and assessing the effectiveness of the entity in achieving its objectives.
(b) Assessing the economic stability and vulnerability of the reporting entity including its liquidity (i.e. whether it will have enough money to pay its debts), its present or future requirements for additional capital, and its ability to raise long- and short-term finance.
(c) Estimating the value of users' own or other users' present or prospective interests in or claims on the entity.
(d) Ascertaining the ownership and control of the entity.
(e) Estimating the future prospects of the entity, including its capacity to pay dividends and predicting future levels of investment.

Accountants have traditionally regarded published accounts as fulfilling two main functions: (1) stewardship, and (2) facilitating share trading and lending decisions. The concept of stewardship roughly corresponds with everyday usage of the word and refers to the directors' responsibility to account for the uses to which they have put the shareholders' investment. This is the one function of published accounts on which all accountants agree. *The Corporate Report* does not discuss this as such but rather emphasizes the share trading and decision making function of annual reports. However, it is debatable whether past data is likely to be useful in predicting future profits, dividends or share prices. The literature on efficient market theory suggests that the content of annual reports has little, if any, predictive value. Published accounts may therefore only perform a stewardship and feedback function.

The loan creditor group

According to *The Corporate Report* 'the information needs of loan creditors are similar in many respects to the needs of equity investors. If their securities are listed on a stock exchange they will have to make trading decisions'. However, certain information will be of particular relevance such as that relating to:

(a) The present and likely future cash position since this will determine whether the company will be able to pay the annual interest on loans and repay the monies borrowed as and when they become due.

(b)   The economic stability and vulnerability of the company in so far as this reflects the risk of possible default in repayment of monies borrowed by the company.

(c)   Prior claims on the company's assets in the event of it going into liquidation.

The employee group

The Corporate Report states that the rights of the employee group to information arises because 'the reporting entity has a responsibility for the future livelihood and prospects of its employees' (p. 21). Employees will require information to enable them to assess the security of employment and the prospects of promotion. They may also require information for the purpose of wage bargaining. Such information may relate to 'the ability of the employer to meet wage demands, management's intentions regarding employment levels, locations and working conditions, the pay, conditions and terms of employment of various groups of employees and the contributions made by employees in different divisions. In addition, employees are likely to be interested in indications of the position, progress and prospects of the employing enterprise as a whole and about individual establishments and bargaining units'. Many companies produce employee reports that usually contain a summary of the year's trading results in a simplified form. These are often also sent to shareholders with the annual report.

The analyst–advisor group

According to *The Corporate Report* 'the information needs of the analyst–advisor group are likely to be similar to the needs of the users who are being advised. For example, the information needs of stockbrokers are likely to be similar to the needs of investors and those of trade unions are likely to be similar to the needs of employees'. *The Corporate Report* also makes the point that this group, because of their expertise, will tend to demand more elaborate information than other groups.

The business contact group

This consists of the following groups:

(a)   *Customers.*   These may be concerned about the reporting entity's continued existence because of its importance as a source of supply, particularly where long-term contracts for the supply of goods have been entered into. Similarly, if the reporting entity is engaged in construction work, customers will wish to assess the likelihood of its being able to complete long-term contracts. In the case of manufactured goods, such as computers, vehicles etc., customers will be concerned about the reporting entity's continued existence because of its warranty obligations and the need for spare parts. Annual reports may thus be useful to customers in assessing the likelihood of the reporting entity's continued existence.

(b)   *Suppliers.*   Trade creditors will obviously want information relating to the reporting entity's ability to pay its debts. In addition, they would be concerned about the reporting entity's continued existence if it is a major customer. A supplier may also have to decide whether to increase its production capacity in order to meet the reporting entity's future demands.

(c) *Competitors and take-over bidders.* The rationale for competitors having a right to information is a little vague but seems to rest on the premise that inter-firm comparisons of performance and costs can facilitate improvements in efficiency. Similarly, given that mergers and take-overs of less efficient firms are in the public interest, a case can be made for the disclosure of information to potential bidders.

The government

The Corporate Report states that 'central and local government departments and agencies have a right to information as representatives of the public and other user groups'. The Inland Revenue and HM Customs & Excise have a statutory right to information about the reporting entity for the purpose of assessing its liability to taxation. Furthermore, the 'government needs information to estimate the effects of existing and proposed levies and other financial and economic measures, to estimate economic trends including balance and payment figures [and] to promote economic efficiency'.[1] In the UK most of this information is collected through special Government returns. However, in many other countries corporate reports perform this function.

The public

According to *The Corporate Report* the public has a right to information because of the custodial role that economic entities play in society and the impact they can have on the community and the environment:

> Such organisations, which exist with the general consent of the community, are afforded special legal and operational privileges, they compete for resources of manpower, materials and energy and they make use of community owned assets such as roads and harbours.

Some members of the public may be concerned about the employment policies of the reporting entity and therefore want information relating to local employment levels or discrimination in employment for example. Other members of the public may be interested in any plans that the reporting entity has that affect the environment, including issues relating to conservation and pollution. There are also a number of other matters of a political or moral nature that may be of particular concern to some sections of the community such as contributions to political organizations, pressure groups or charities, and whether the reporting entity is trading with countries having repressive political regimes. Some of this information must be disclosed under the Companies Acts (i.e. donations to political parties and charities) but *The Corporate Report* implies that the reporting entity has a responsibility to also make public any matters that might be regarded by the community as of general concern.

The regulatory framework of accounting

The regulatory framework of accounting is a general term used to describe the legislation and other rules that govern the content and format of company final accounts. There is no legislation or other regulations covering the final accounts of sole traders and partnerships. However, it is generally accepted that their accounts should closely follow the rules and regulations relating to companies since these are regarded as 'best practice'. There are three sources of rules and regulations governing the content and format of company final accounts, as follows:

1. The Companies Act with which all companies are required to comply.
2. The London Stock Exchange Admission of Securities to Listing regulations with which all companies whose shares are listed on The London Stock Exchange are expected to comply.
3. The accounting standards produced by the accountancy profession and financial reporting standards of the Accounting Standards Board with which all companies are expected to comply. These are discussed further below.

The UK accountancy profession comprises six major professional accountancy bodies as follows:
1. The Institute of Chartered Accountants in England and Wales (ICAEW)
2. The Institute of Chartered Accountants in Scotland (ICAS)
3. The Institute of Chartered Accountants in Ireland (ICAI)
4. The Chartered Association of Certified Accountants (CACA)
5. The Chartered Institute of Management Accountants (CIMA)
6. The Chartered Institute of Public Finance and Accountancy (CIPFA)

In 1970 the ICAEW set up the Accounting Standards Steering Committee (ASSC). Subsequently all the other above professional bodies became members of this committee. Its name was changed in 1975 to the Accounting Standards Committee (ASC). In 1990 the ASC was replaced by the Accounting Standards Board (ASB).

The ASC represented the six major professional accountancy bodies on matters relating to the form and content of company final accounts. It issued accounting standards known as Statements of Standard Accounting Practice (SSAP) with which company final accounts are still expected to comply. Each of these SSAPs specify how particular items or transactions are to be treated in the final accounts of companies.

The Accounting Standards Board (ASB) is continuing to perform the same function as the ASC, but is more independent of the professional accountancy bodies and has greater power to enforce accounting standards. Before the ASC could issue an SSAP, it required the approval of each of the six professional accountancy bodies. In contrast, the ASB can issue a Financial Reporting Standard without approval from any other body. The ASB has also established a Review Panel that is able to take companies to court under civil law where their final accounts contain a major breach of accounting standards.

References

1. Accounting Standards Steering Committee (1975). *The Corporate Report* (ICAEW).
2. American Institute of Certified Public Accountants (1973). *The Objectives of Financial Statements* (AICPA).

Exercises

1. Examine the nature of financial accounting.
2. Describe the main functions of financial accounting.

3. (a) What do you understand by the term 'stewardship' in financial accounting?
   (b) Describe the recording and control function of financial accounting.
   (c) Explain the role of financial accounting with regard to the presentation of final accounts.

4. (a) Explain the 'basic philosophy' of *The Corporate Report* and the notion of 'public accountability'.
   (b) What is the objective of corporate annual reports and what is meant by 'a reasonable right to information'?

5. (a) Which users of corporate annual reports are identified in *The Corporate Report*?
   (b) Describe the information needs of any two substantially different groups of users.

6. (a) Describe the sources of the rules and regulations that govern the content and format of company final accounts.
   (b) Outline the institutional framework by which the professional accountancy bodies have influenced the content and format of company final accounts during the last two decades.

2. The accounting equation and its components

The accounting entity

The fundamental objective of company accounts was stated very precisely by the Accounting Standards Committee[1] as 'to communicate economic measurements of, and information about, the resources and performance of the reporting entity useful to those having reasonable rights to such information'. This is an elegant statement which includes a reference to a critically important concept for accounting: 'the reporting entity'. Before we can go any further this entity concept must be clarified. Actually, the idea is really so basic that it might have passed the casual observer of accounting unnoticed. However, explicit recognition will help avoid many sources of potential confusion and set the foundation for the subsequent development of a structure for accounting processes.

At its simplest, the reporting or accounting entity is just the organizational unit which is the object of focus of the particular accounting process. It might be a particular company, club or business partnership which forms the entity, for example. Of course, we are used to hearing that a financial report relates to a specific organization, but now the organization is being called an entity.

However, the use of the word entity emphasizes the properties of being separate and discrete. Greater precision is demanded by accounting in deciding what is, and is not, part of the entity. Boundaries are being created to separate out the accounting entity. Realizing that these boundaries are necessary, even though they may be artificial, is the key to the entity concept. It becomes possible to accept that a business may be separate from its sole proprietor. When a local plumber buys tools to carry out his work, that action can be regarded as a purchase by the business, while when the same man buys a cinema ticket this would be seen as a personal purchase. In the same way, the salary paid to a company director is treated not as some internal transfer within a company but as a payment to an officer as a separate individual. In general, accounting sets up 'the business', 'the company' and 'the club' as entities which are artificial constructs, separate from their owners and employees as individuals.

At times this approach is shared with that of the law. In the UK, a company is a legal entity regarded, in law, as a separate personality and, correspondingly, the company is an accounting entity. By contrast, there may be no legal demarcation between an unincorporated business and its sole proprietor. The artificial nature of accounting entities has implications of its own, which are most obvious in the case of the single-owner, unincorporated business. The accountant might set up the business as an accounting entity, but this does not and cannot give it a legal existence which enables it, in the eyes of the law, to separately own property or other possessions, make contractual agreements or carry out transactions. What the accountant has created as separate is, in fact, just a part of the proprietor's domain so that anything that can be treated as being owned by the business actually belongs to the proprietor. The 'business' is simply a useful connector.

The balance sheet as an accounting equation

Accounting reflects the two-sided property of such a connector in the way it records and reports. Perhaps the most familiar form this takes is the *balance sheet*. This presents a financial equation which for the sole proprietorship shows that 'what the business owns is equal to what is owned by the proprietor'. In the form of an equation this would appear as:

Proprietor's ownership claims in the business = net resources possessed by the business

Special wording is used in balance sheets produced in practice and some explanation of these terms is useful.

The ownership claims are called *owner's equity* or *owner's capital*. The net resources themselves are analysed into the various elements which it comprises. The general term for the various possessions (which might include buildings, machinery, furniture etc.) is *assets*. The use of the word 'net' to describe the resources is to recognize that there are some amounts set against or to be deducted from the assets.

There are two major types of such deductions: provisions and liabilities. Liabilities represent claims by outsiders (as compared to the owners, whose claims are equity or capital) and may include such items as loans made to the business and amounts owed for goods supplied. As the name suggests, provisions are amounts *provided* to allow for liabilities which may be anticipated but not yet quantified, or for reductions in asset values. However, although there are a number of important matters to consider in relation to provisions, it will be entirely appropriate for present purposes to think of provisions as simply a special category of liability, and to postpone detailed attention until later. Chapters 11 and 12 are both particularly concerned with provisions.

Given that liabilities can be regarded as being negative in sign in relation to assets the accounting equation can now be stated in the form:

$$\text{Capital} = \text{Assets} - \text{Liabilities}$$

or alternatively

$$\text{Assets} = \text{Capital} + \text{Liabilities}$$

This is a fundamental equation and is a valuable basis from which to begin understanding the whole process of accounting. It sets out the balance sheet relationship which will hold at any point in time, although in practice a complete and detailed balance sheet may only be produced once in a period of a month or even a year. It is worth pointing out, then, that most accounting activity is concerned with individual transactions; nevertheless the balance sheet equation remains a focus towards which the activity is directed.

However, for now we will examine accounting simply in terms of balance sheets. Let us trace how this approach reflects the setting up of the plumbing business mentioned earlier.

Suppose Adam Bridgewater decided to start his business by opening a bank account for business transactions and depositing £2,000 into it on 1 July 19X1. The balance sheet equation would show owner's capital as being equal to cash at the bank, both being £2,000. There are a number of ways of presenting this: that used by companies usually adopts a so-called vertical approach placing capital vertically below net assets in the form:

Bridgewater (Plumber)
Balance sheet as at 1 July 19X1
Assets	£
Cash at bank	2,000
Capital	2,000

However, a side-by-side or horizontal presentation may illustrate more clearly the equation format. A question arises: on which side should assets be included? In practice there is considerable variation and it becomes a matter of convention. The most useful convention at this stage (and that given support by the 1981 and subsequent Companies Acts) is to show assets on the left-hand side, i.e.

Bridgewater (*Plumber*)
Balance sheet as at 1 July 19X1

Assets	£		£
Cash at bank	2,000	Capital	2,000

If on 2nd July 19X1 he draws out £800 cash and spends it all purchasing tools, then cash at bank will be decreased and a new asset, the tools, is introduced on the balance sheet.

Bridgewater (*Plumber*)
Balance sheet as at 2 July 19X1

Assets	£		£
Tools	800	Capital	2,000
Cash at bank	1,200		
	2,000		

In this case one asset is increased by exactly the same amount as another is decreased so that the accounting equation, Assets equals Capital plus Liabilities, continues to exist.

On 3 July he buys a range of plumbing accessories for £300 from the local storekeeper, but arranges to pay in the next few days. The arrangement is described as 'on credit'. The storekeeper becomes a creditor since he is now owed a debt of £300. There is no problem in maintaining the balance of the equation when including the effects of this transaction in the business balance sheet, since the new liability of £300 owed to the store exactly complements the £300 increase in assets represented by the accessories:

Bridgewater (*Plumber*)
Balance sheet as at 3 July 19X1

Assets	£		£
Tools	800	Capital	2,000
Accessories	300	Liability—creditor	300
Cash at bank	1,200		2,300
	2,300		

The manner in which the two components of the change in the balance sheet are complementary, so that the equality of the two sides remains intact, is worthy of note since it underlies the principles of double entry bookkeeping developed in Chapter 4. Another event in the life of this business offers further illustration. If the next day, Bridgewater pays the store the £300 to clear the outstanding debt this will decrease both the cash and the creditor—an asset and a liability—by the same amount giving:

Bridgewater (*Plumber*)
Balance sheet as at 4 July 19X1

Assets	£		£
Tools	800	Capital	2,000
Accessories	300		
Cash at bank	900		
	2,000		

The accounting equation and profit reporting

Drawing up a balance sheet after each of the number of transactions carried out every week in large corporations would be very time consuming and inefficient, and a business cannot be expected to do so. However, it is normal for even small businesses to produce a balance sheet once a year. Annual reporting has taken on a significance of its own for many reasons. A year's activity encompasses all the seasons and many statistics of economic and business performance are produced on this basis. Examples include annual inflation rates, annual interest rates, annual salaries, annual tax allowances and, not surprisingly, annual profits.

Bridgewater may be interested to see how his business has progressed in its first year. For him to be able to draw up a balance sheet he needs to know the amounts to include for assets and liabilities at that date. Suppose he obtains the following amounts relating to the position at the end of the day's trading on 30 June 19X2.

Assets of business: Building £5,000; stock of accessories £500; tools £1,100; cash at bank £200; trade debtors (amounts owed to the business by customers) £350.

Liabilities: bank loan £3,500; Creditors £450.

A number of changes and transactions are likely to have taken place during the year to produce this position, but these have not been tracked from balance sheet to balance sheet. The absence of a figure for capital will not prevent the balance sheet being drawn up given that it is the only missing figure in the accounting equation. So the balance sheet becomes:

Bridgewater (*Plumber*)
Balance sheet as at 30 June 19X2

Assets	£		£
Building	5,000	Bank loan	3,500
Tools	1,100	Creditors	450
Accessories	500	Total liabilities	3,950
Debtors	350	Capital (to balance)	3,200
Cash	200		7,150
	7,150		

Capital has been made to be the balancing item and by this means all balance sheets would inevitably balance. This inevitability is consistent with recognizing that the business is an entity which is an artificial creation. It cannot have any net ownership of its own. However, the capital figure at the end of the year is different to that at the beginning, and analysis and explanation of that change is needed to provide a more complete picture. In this case we see that the increase in the year given by the difference between opening and closing capital is £3,200 − £2,000 = £1,200. How could this have arisen?

One possible explanation is that Bridgewater paid some more money into the business. In this case let us decide that we know he did pay in a further £1,000. Of course, the opposite to paying in would be taking money out, so let us say that he took out £750 for personal use. The net affect will produce an increase of £1,000 − £750 = £250. The rest of the increase (i.e. £1,200 − £250 = £950) would be profit, i.e. increased capital generated by the business itself.

A simple example will illustrate how profit is able to generate increases in capital. A trader is able to start a small venture with £30 cash, equivalent to £30 capital. She uses the money to buy a bath. When she sells the bath for £40 she now has £40 cash and has increased capital by £10.

To provide a more useful definition of profit as increased capital, accounting has made use of explanations given by the economist Hicks,[2] to define profit as the maximum amount that could be withdrawn in a period from the business while leaving the capital intact. In the case of Bridgewater's business, the capital which is kept intact is the £2,000 figure for the start of the period. If he now took out the increase of £1,200 shown in the closing balance sheet this would represent a net withdrawal of £950, given that the money he has paid in exceeded what he had already taken out by £250. Measuring profit in relation to capital which is kept intact is commonly described as a capital maintenance approach, which forms one of the major pillars of profit measurement theory. It is implicit in all profit measurement approaches that will be drawn upon in this book.

The accounting period

The previous section commenced by recognizing the significance of annual reporting in assessing business performance. Profit is defined in terms of potential consumption 'in a period'. Although the use of a period of a year is no more than a convention—albeit a very useful one—the idea of periodic reporting is fundamental to present-day accounting. In relation to maintenance of capital, the second year of the plumbing business's performance will be measured in profit terms in relation to that year's opening capital, i.e. the £3,200 closing capital from year one. The approach adopted in accounting is an extension of the use of the entity concept. For accounting purposes, each complete period, usually of a year, is treated as a separate entity. It inherits as its opening balance sheet the closing balance sheet of the previous period.

Of course, cutting up business activities which run continuously into discrete periods introduces a number of new considerations, one of which is to ensure that the closing balance sheet from one period would be suitable to use as the opening balance sheet for the next.

One response which follows from the needs of periodic reporting is to classify items into two types—those that will be included in the closing balance sheet to be properly carried forward as part of the opening position of the new entity commencing next period, and those that are properly attributable to the period just finished.

An aspect of this has already been seen in the simple illustration of buying and selling a bath to make a profit. The transactions involved are all treated as being complete by the time the profit figure for the year is calculated. Details of the buying and selling transactions are not part of the next year's position except to the extent that they form an element contained within the total capital figure.

The approach which is being adopted here will be only briefly described now, it is taken up more fully in Chapter 10. It is known as the matching process. Sales associated with a particular period are recognized as the revenue of that period. From that revenue figure the expenditures used up in that period in creating those sales are matched against them. The aggregate sales plus the aggregate expenditures matched against them gives the profit for the year.

Expenditure of the type which is to be matched against the period's revenue and is used up in the period is identified as revenue expenditure, and this is distinguished from capital expenditure—that which represents amounts which it is appropriate to carry forward as part of the next year's opening balance sheet. Expenditure on tools, which represent the long-term equipment of the business, is capital expenditure and is carried forward from balance sheet to balance sheet. Rental expenditure on a building used during the year will be revenue expenditure—what it provides is used up in the period; the purchase of the building, however, would be capital expenditure, as it is entirely appropriate to represent ownership being carried forward from period to period.

Static and dynamic approaches to profit determination

The previous two sections have been describing two approaches to measuring profit in the accounts of businesses. The first can be identified as a comparative static approach. It computes profit through a comparison of the opening and closing capital positions adjusting these for additions and withdrawals of capital made by the owners during the year. Each balance sheet is a static representation of the elements of the accounting equation at a particular point in time.

The alternative is a more dynamic approach attempting to record increases and decreases in capital values throughout the period by recognizing the increases as revenue items and deducting from these the decreases or costs incurred in producing those revenues. By tracking the changes within a period the latter 'net production method' indicates the sources of profit.

Elements of the use and drawbacks of historic cost in accounting measurement

For accounting statements to be able to include amounts to represent the various assets and liabilities and to be able to aggregate these, it is necessary for a measurement unit to be established and a valuation model to be adopted. We have already been using a measurement unit, the £ sterling. Providing this represents a stable unit for expressing economic values, money measurement will be appropriate to accounting statements intended to reflect economic change and position of business entities.

The transaction price which is agreed in an arm's-length transaction when the asset or liability is originally acquired provides readily available objective valuations expressed in terms of monetary units of measurement. This is the major source of measurement utilized by historical cost accounting. Sales are recorded at the contracted sales value and purchases at the purchase price agreed. Measurement, then, involves recording transactions. When equipment is at first purchased, its value is included at the price paid for it. This approach has many strengths. It permits accounts to be produced by collecting information about the transactions entered—clearly a process which is commercially useful in tracking down what amounts have to be paid and collected and what cash balances should be left after making payments and collections. Amounts are determined 'automatically' by the transactions themselves rather than being left to the judgement and possible abuse of individuals. For these and other reasons this direct cost continues to be the predominant basis for accounting record keeping and reporting.

However, it is not without disadvantages. These arise largely because there is change over time in prices (both of individual items and as a result of inflation), for example, for goods and services in general. As a result, accounting reports based on historic costs may become unrealistic. Balance sheets will contain values for assets which are out of date, being based on prices when they were originally purchased, which may be several years ago; capital which is being maintained in the profit measurement process represents a value which is also out of date, both in terms of its value to the proprietors and owners, and in the capacity of the facilities it could provide for the business. The matching process becomes debased to the extent that sales may be made at prices which, although above the original purchase price of the item being sold, is below its current price. This would mean that a business might be reporting a profit on a sale even though this put it in the position where it was no longer able to buy the goods it owned prior to the sale.

These drawbacks must be borne in mind when, at a later stage, we consider the appraisal of accounts in Chapter 29. Attempts to address these drawbacks produce considerable complexity. As a result these will not be considered in any depth until the final chapter of this book and as part of more advanced texts.

Summary

Accounting may be perceived by many to be a mechanical process having little if any conceptual content. This chapter has been concerned to introduce at an early stage in the study of accounting some of the fundamentals which are needed to ensure the mechanics can be understood and developed through to more advanced study. The link between these ideas and the bookkeeping process which implements them remains to be made. This must be perceived as the processes are developed.

The first concept discussed was that of the accounting entity. It was seen to be a device, an artificial construct used to set the boundaries of the focus of attention of accounting. The artificial nature of the entity was reflected in the accounting equation, which showed it to be no more than a pivot between ownership claims and net resources. However, changes over time are seen to provide the basis upon which profit could be measured. This basis was related to measuring profit by matching costs against revenues. Historic cost measurement was briefly examined.

A number of technical terms have been introduced including owner's equity or owner's capital; assets; liabilities; capital maintenance; revenue and capital expenditure.

References

1. Accounting Standards Committee (1975). *The Corporate Report* (ICAEW), p. 28.
2. Hicks, J. R. (1946). *Value and Capital* (2nd edn), Clarendon Press, Oxford. Further discussion and references can be found in Chapter 1 of Samuels, J. M., Rickwood, C. P. and Piper, A. G. (1989). *Advanced Financial Accounting* (2nd edn), McGraw-Hill, Maidenhead.

Exercises

1. Identify what is meant by the entity concept in accounting. Explain the significance of the entity concept in period reporting.

2. Define and distinguish between the following:
   (a) assets and liabilities;
   (b) capital and revenue expenditure.

3. The position of a business at any time is represented by accountants in the balance sheet. Why is it that every business entity's position should 'balance'?

4. Explain briefly what is meant by the following terms: profit; capital and revenue expenditure; current and fixed assets.

5. J. Frank commenced business on 1 January 1989. His position was:

   Assets: land and buildings, £7,500; fixtures, £560; balance at bank, £1,740.
   Liabilities: loan on mortgage of land and buildings £4,000.

   He traded for a year, withdrawing £500 for his personal use and paying no additional capital. His position on 31 December 1989 was:

   Assets: land and buildings, £7,500; fixtures, £560; delivery van, £650; sundry debtors, £470; stock, £940; balance at bank, £1,050; cash in hand, £80.
   Liabilities: loan on mortage of land and buildings, £5,000; sundry creditors, £800.

   Calculate Frank's profit and loss for 1989.

3. Basic documentation and books of account

Basic documentation for cash and credit transactions

In accounting, a *cash transaction* is one where goods are paid for in cash or by cheque when they are received or delivered. A *credit transaction* is one where payment is made or received some time after delivery (normally in one instalment). This should not be confused with hire purchase transactions. Credit transactions are extremely common in many industries. The credit terms of most UK businesses are that goods which are delivered at any time during a given calendar month should be paid for by the end of the following calendar month.

Credit transactions often involve *trade discount*. This is a discount given by one trader to another. It is usually expressed as a percentage reduction of the recommended retail price of the goods, and is deducted in arriving at the amount the buyer is charged for the goods.

A large number of businesses also allow their customers *cash discount*. This is a reduction in the amount that the customer has to pay provided payment is made within a given period stipulated by the seller at the time of sale (e.g. $2\frac{1}{2}$ per cent or 5 per cent if paid in 10 days).

A cash transaction is recorded in the books of account from the receipt received if paid in cash, or from the cheque book stub if paid by cheque. A credit transaction, on the other hand, involves a number of documents, not all of which are recorded in the books of account. Figure 3.1 shows, in chronological order, the documents and procedures relating to a business transaction on credit, including who originates each document. Note that only the invoice, debit note, credit note and cheque are recorded in the books of account.

The main documents involved in a credit transaction are discussed below.

The invoice

The purpose of the invoice, which is sent by the seller, is primarily to inform the buyer how much is owed for the goods supplied. It is *not* a demand for payment. A specimen invoice is shown in Fig. 3.2. The information shown on an invoice consists of:

1. the name and address of the seller
2. the name and address of the buyer
3. the invoice and delivery note number of the seller (usually the same)
4. the date of the invoice
5. the address to which the goods were delivered
6. the buyer's order number
7. the quantity of goods sold
8. details of the goods supplied
9. the price per unit of each of the goods

Firm buying goods

Firm selling goods

Letter of enquiry

If this is acceptable: ← Sales quotation

Order → Check to see if goods are available. If so:

Space prepared for goods ← Advice note

Goods checked against delivery note and order ← Sent with goods — Delivery note

Checked against delivery note and order. → Invoice

If invoice is not correct.

Letter of complaint ← Looked into and if amount of invoice exceeds correct amount:

Checked against original invoice ← Credit note

If seller has undercharged buyer on invoice:

Checked against original invoice, delivery note and order ← Debit note

At end of the month some businesses send:

Checked against invoices, debit and credit notes, and if correct: ← Statement

Cheque → Paid into bank and if required by buyer:

← Receipt

Note that the documents are raised by the firm shown at the head of the column in which the document is shown. All of the documents are usually sent by post except where shown otherwise. The documents recorded in the buyer's and seller's books consist of those shown by a double lined box.

Figure 3.1 Inter-firm documentation for a credit transaction.

FROM: Trendy Gear Ltd
High Street
London

TO: Catalogue Times Ltd
Middlesex Street
London

INVOICE NO.:   38167
DATE: 30 January 19X5

Delivered to: 23 Oxford Road, London

No. of units	Details	Unit price	Total price
100	Dresses size 14, pattern No. 385	£6.50	£650
50	Leather bags, pattern No. 650	£3.00	£150
			£800
	Less: 25 per cent trade discount		£200
			£600
	Add: VAT at 17½ per cent		£105
			£705
	Tights unavailable—to follow later		

Date of Delivery: 30 January 19X5
Mode of Delivery: Our transport
Cash Discount Terms: 5 per cent monthly account
Your Order No.:   6382

Figure 3.2 An invoice.

10.   the total value of the invoice before value added tax (VAT)*
11.   the trade and cash discount
12.   VAT payable and the total value of the invoice including VAT
13.   when payment should be made
14.   the seller's terms of trade

The buyer checks the invoice against his order and the delivery note (or usually with a goods received note prepared by his receiving department). If correct, the invoice is then entered in the buyer's books. Similarly, a copy of the invoice would have been entered in the seller's books.

The debit note

A debit note is sent by the seller if he has undercharged the buyer on the invoice. It has basically the same layout and information as the invoice except that instead of details of

---

*Value added tax affects a large number of sales and purchase transactions which in turn must be incorporated in the recording of those transactions. Including VAT introduces little in the way of principles but some additional detail. In order to concentrate on the subject matter developed in this book VAT is recognized here but its treatment is then postponed to a later chapter.

the goods it shows details of the undercharge. It is recorded in the books of the seller and buyer in the same way as an invoice.

The credit note

A credit note may be sent by the seller for a number of reasons. These include:

1. the buyer has returned goods because they were not ordered, or they were the wrong type, quantity or quality, or are defective;
2. the seller has overcharged the buyer on the invoice. This may be due to an error in the unit price or calculations.

A credit note has basically the same layout and information as an invoice, except that instead of the details of the goods it will show the reason why it has been issued.

A credit note will be recorded in the books of the seller and buyer in a similar way to the invoice, except that the entries are the reverse. It is perhaps worth mentioning here the reason why this document is called a credit note. This is because it informs the buyer that his account in the books of the seller is being credited. Conversely, a debit note informs the buyer that his account in the seller's book is being debited. This is discussed in a later chapter in more depth.

A statement

As explained above, the most common terms of credit in the UK are that a buyer should pay for all the goods invoiced to him by the seller during a particular calendar month at the end of the following calendar month. The statement is a list of the invoices, debit notes and credit notes that the seller has sent to the buyer during a given calendar month, and thus shows how much the buyer owes the seller and when it should be paid. The statement is often a copy of the buyer's account in the seller's books. This is illustrated in Fig. 3.3. The layout shown is a mechanized system of bookkeeping.

Seller's name and address

Buyer's name and address

Month: January 19X5

Date of invoice	Invoice/ Credit note no.	Debits (amount of invoices and debit notes)	Credits (amount of credit notes and payments)	Balance
2 Jan	426	£23.12		£23.12
9 Jan	489	£16.24		£39.36
16 Jan	563	£52.91		£92.27
22 Jan	Cheque		£25.14	£67.13
25 Jan	1326		£6.00	£61.13
		Amount due on 28 February		£61.13

Cash discount terms: 5 per cent monthly

Figure 3.3 A statement.

The statement may be kept by the buyer for reference purposes or returned to the seller with the buyer's cheque. In either case neither the buyer nor the seller records the statement in their books. Not all businesses use statements.

The cheque

This is the most common form of payment in business because of its convenience and safety. Most cheques are crossed and therefore have to be paid into a bank account. This makes it possible to trace the cheque if stolen and fraudulently passed on to someone else. A crossed cheque may be paid into anyone's bank account unless the words 'account payee only' are written between the crossings, in which case it must be paid into the account of the person named on the cheque.

The information that must be shown on a cheque consists of:

1. the date;
2. the signature of the drawer (i.e. payer);
3. the name of the drawee (i.e. the bank at which the drawer has his account);
4. the name of the payee (i.e. who is to receive the money);
5. the words 'Pay . . . or Order the sum of . . . ;
6. the amount of money in figures and in words.

The bank account number of the drawer, the cheque and bank number is also shown on preprinted cheques.

Since there is only one copy of a cheque it is essential to write on the cheque stub or counterfoil who the cheque was paid to (i.e. the payee), the amount and what the payment was for. Without this information the books of account cannot be written up.

The bank paying-in book

The paying-in book provides a record of the cash and cheques received that have been paid into the business's bank account. The information shown on the bank paying-in book stub consists of:

1. the date;
2. the amounts paid in, from whom they were received, and to what they relate.

The receipt

The law requires the seller to give the buyer a receipt for goods which have been paid for in cash. However, there is no legal requirement to do so in the case of payments by cheque. A receipt must contain the following information:

1. the name of the payer;
2. the signature of the recipient;
3. the amount of money in figures and in words;
4. the date.

A receipt is only recorded in the books of account when it relates to cash receipts and payments.

Books of account

The main book of account in which all transactions are recorded is called the *ledger*. However, before a transaction is recorded in the ledger it must first be entered in a *book of prime entry*. These are designed to show more detail relating to each transaction than appears in the ledger. They also facilitate making entries in the ledger, in that transactions of the same type can be posted periodically in total rather than one at a time. Sometimes there are analysis columns in each book of prime entry in which are collected all those transactions relating to the same type of expenditure or income. A business may use up to nine books of prime entry, which consist of:

1. *The sales day book*, in which is recorded the sale on credit of those goods bought specifically for resale. It is written up from copies of sales invoices and debit notes retained by the seller. The amount entered in the sales day book is after deducting trade discount (but before deducting cash discount).
2. *The sales returns day book*, in which are recorded the credit notes sent to customers who returned goods bought on credit. It is written up from copies of credit notes retained by the seller.
3. *The purchases day book*, in which are recorded the invoices and debit notes received from suppliers for goods bought on credit for resale. The amount entered in the purchases day book is after deducting trade discount (but before deducting cash discount).
4. *The purchases returns day book*, in which are recorded the credit notes received from suppliers to whom goods bought on credit were returned.
5. *The petty cash book*, in which is recorded cash received and cash paid. This is written up from receipts (or petty cash vouchers where employees are reimbursed expenses).
6. *The cash book*, in which are recorded cheques received and cash paid into the bank and payments made by cheque. This is written up from the bank paying-in book and cheque book stubs.
7. *The bills receivable book*, in which are recorded bills of exchange received by the business. A bill of exchange can best be described as being similar to a post-dated cheque, except that instead of being written out by the person paying the money, it is prepared by the business to whom the money is owed and then signed by the debtor. When the period of credit given by the bill of exchange has expired, which is usually 30, 60 or 90 days, the creditor then presents the bill to the debtor's bank and receives payment.
8. *The bills payable book*, in which are recorded bills of exchange given to suppliers as payment.
9. *The journal*, in which are recorded any transactions that are not included in any of the other books of prime entry. At one time all entries were passed through the journal, but now it is primarily used for purchase and sale of fixed assets on credit, the correction of errors, opening entries in new sets of books and any remaining transfers. Fixed assets are items not bought specifically for resale, such as land and buildings, machinery, vehicles etc. The journal is written up from copies of the invoice.

Figure 3.4 provides a summary of the different books of prime entry, including the documents from which each is written up. Each of these books of prime entry is discussed in depth in later chapters.

Basic documents   *Books of prime entry*

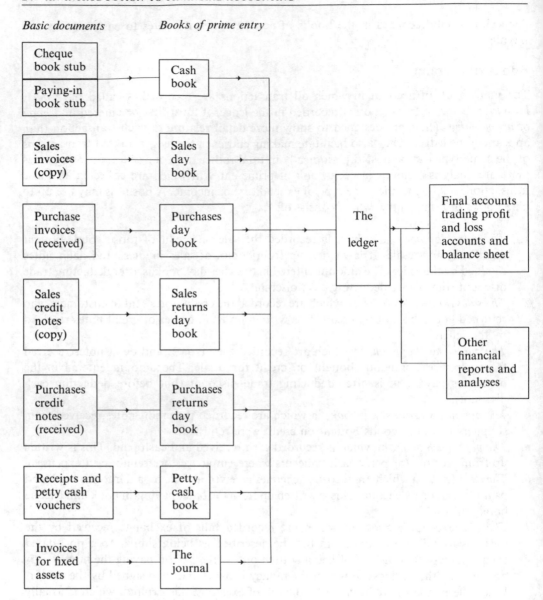

Figure 3.4 Books of account and related documents.

Exercises

1. Explain the difference between a cash transaction and a credit transaction.

2. Explain the difference between trade discount and cash discount.

3. Outline the purpose and content of: (a) an invoice; (b) a debit note; and (c) a credit note.

4. Explain the difference between an invoice and: (a) a statement; (b) a receipt.

5. List the books of prime entry with which you are familiar and briefly describe what each is intended to record, including the documents used to write them up.

6. Briefly describe the nature of a bill of exchange.

4.   The general ledger

The principles of double entry bookkeeping

Double entry bookkeeping is a systematic method of recording business transactions in a book called the ledger. Each page of the ledger is split into two halves, *the left half called the DEBIT side and the right half called the CREDIT side*. The ledger is divided into sections called accounts. In practice, each of these accounts is on separate pages.

The money value of each transaction is entered once on each side of the ledger in different accounts. For example, if we take one transaction such as the sale of goods for cash of £100 on the 6th January this would be recorded as follows:

		Debit				Credit		
Date	Details	Folio	Amount	Date	Details	Folio	Amount
			Cash account (page 1)					
6 Jan	Sales	p. 2	100					
			Sales account (page 2)					
				6 Jan	Cash	p. 1	100

The main purposes of this system are to provide a means of ascertaining the total amount of each type of income and expenditure, the value of the assets owned by the business (e.g. cash), and how much is owed to and by the business. For example, the cash account shows how much money the business has at any time. Also, when there are several transactions, the sales account will contain all the sales made during a period and thus it is possible to see at a glance the total sales for that period. Similarly, other accounts, such as wages, purchases, postage etc., will show the total amount spent on each of these types of expenses. The information is used to ascertain the profit or loss for a given period.

When the total amount of money on the debit side of an account is greater than that on the credit side, the account is said to have a *debit balance*. When the reverse is the case, the account is said to have a *credit balance. An account which contains a debit balance represents either an asset (such as cash) or an expense or loss. An account with a credit balance represents a liability, income (such as sales) or a gain.*

Ledger entries for cash transactions

When cash is received it is entered on the debit side of the cash account and credited to the account to which the transaction relates. When cash is paid out it is entered on the credit side of the cash account and on the debit side of the account to which the transaction relates. The same occurs with cheques received and paid, except that they are entered in an account called the bank account instead of the cash account.

When someone starts a business they usually put money into the business. This is debited to the cash or bank account (depending on whether it is cash or a cheque) and credited to a capital account. Money introduced at a later date by the proprietor as additional capital is treated in the same way. Any money withdrawn by the proprietor is credited in the cash or bank account (depending on whether it is cash or a cheque) and debited to a drawings account.

Sometimes businesses also borrow money. The amount received is debited to the cash or bank account (depending on whether it is cash or a cheque) and credited to an account in the name of the lender who is referred to as a loan creditor.

The ledger entries for various cash transactions are illustrated in Example 4.1.

Example 4.1
S. Baker started business on 1 January 19X0 as a grocer with a capital in cash of £1,000. She also borrowed £500 in cash from London Bank Ltd. Her transactions during January, which are all in cash, were as follows:

1 Jan	Paid one month's rent for the shop: £100
2 Jan	Bought fixtures and fittings for the shop: £300
8 Jan	Purchased goods for resale: £400
9 Jan	Paid £25 carriage inwards
10 Jan	Bought stationery for £50
15 Jan	Paid £200 in wages for shop assistant
20 Jan	Cash taken by S. Baker for her private use: £150
31 Jan	Cash takings for the month: £600

You are required to write up the accounts in the general ledger.

Debit			Credit		
Date	Details	Amount	Date	Details	Amount
Cash account					
19X0			19X0		
1 Jan	Capital	1,000	1 Jan	Rent	100
1 Jan	Loan—London Bank Ltd	500	2 Jan	Fixtures and fittings	300
31 Jan	Sales	600	8 Jan	Purchases	400
			9 Jan	Carriage inwards	25
			10 Jan	Stationery	50
			15 Jan	Wages	200
			20 Jan	Drawings	150
Capital					
			1 Jan	Cash	1,000

		Loan—London Bank		
		1 Jan Cash	500

		Sales	
		31 Jan Cash	600

Rent			
1 Jan Cash	100		

Fixtures and fittings			
2 Jan Cash	300		

Purchases			
8 Jan Cash	400		

Carriage inwards			
9 Jan Cash	25		

Stationery			
10 Jan Cash	50		

Wages			
15 Jan Cash	200		

Drawings			
20 Jan Cash	150		

Notes

1. The narrative in the details column of an account specifies the name of the account that contains the other entry for each transaction.
2. Carriage inwards refers to haulage costs relating to goods that this business has purchased and is responsible for transporting from the sellers' premises.

Ledger entries for credit transactions

The entries in the ledger for credit transactions are more complicated than those for cash transactions. This is because a credit transaction involves at least two (and sometimes three) events, each of which is recorded in double entry form. The first event consists of the purchase or sale of goods on credit as evidenced by an invoice. This invoice is recorded in the ledger as follows:

1 Feb   Sold goods on credit to AB Ltd for £500.

2 Feb   Purchased goods on credit from CD Ltd for £250.

The business or person to whom goods are sold on credit is referred to as a trade debtor. In the above example, AB Ltd is a debtor of the business whose books are being prepared. The term 'debtor' arises from the existence of an account in the seller's books which contains more on the debit side than on the credit side.

The business or person from whom goods are purchased on credit is referred to as a trade creditor. In the above example, CD Ltd is a creditor of the business whose books are being prepared. The term 'creditor' arises from the existence of an account in the purchaser's books which contains more on the credit side than on the debit side.

A second event which may occur when goods are bought and sold on credit is the return of goods. This can arise because some of the goods delivered were not ordered, or are defective, etc. When goods are returned the seller sends the buyer a credit note. This is recorded in the ledger as follows:

3 Feb   AB Ltd returned goods invoiced for £100.

	Sales returns		
	(inwards)		
3 Feb AB Ltd	100		

AB Ltd			
1 Feb Sales	500	3 Feb Sales returns	100

4 Feb   Returned goods to CD Ltd invoiced for £50.

Purchases returns
(outwards)

	4 Feb CD Ltd	50

CD Ltd

4 Feb Purchases returns	50	2 Feb Purchases	250

The debtor's and creditor's accounts thus show the amounts of money owed at any time.

The third event which occurs when goods are bought and sold on credit is the transfer of money in settlement of the debt. This is recorded in the ledger as follows:

5 Feb   Received a cheque from AB Ltd for £400.

Bank

5 Feb AB Ltd	400	

AB Ltd

1 Feb Sales	500	3 Feb Sales returns	100
		5 Feb Bank	400

6 Feb   Paid CD Ltd £200 by cheque.

Bank

	6 Feb CD Ltd	200

CD Ltd

4 Feb Purchases returns	50	2 Feb Purchases	250
6 Feb Bank	200		

An illustration of both credit and cheque transactions is shown in Example 4.2.

Example 4.2
E. Blue commenced business on 1 July 19X0 as a wholesale greengrocer with a capital in the bank of £2,000. His transactions during July were as follows:

1 July   Bought a second-hand van by cheque for £800
3 July   Paid tax and insurance on the van by cheque for £150
7 July   Purchased goods costing £250 on credit from A. Brown
11 July   Sold goods on credit to B. Green for £450
14 July   Paid carriage outwards by cheque amounting to £20
16 July   Returned goods to A. Brown of £50

18 July   Repairs to van paid by cheque: £30
20 July   B. Green returned goods of £75
23 July   Sent A. Brown a cheque for £140
26 July   Received a cheque from B. Green for £240
31 July   Paid telephone bill by cheque: £65
31 July   Paid electric bill by cheque: £45

You are required to write up the accounts in the general ledger.

Debit			Credit		
Date	Details	Amount	Date	Details	Amount

Bank account

19X0			19X0		
1 July	Capital	2,000	1 July	Vehicles	800
26 July	B. Green	240	3 July	Motor expenses	150
			14 July	Carriage outwards	20
			18 July	Motor expenses	30
			23 July	A. Brown	140
			31 July	Telephone and postage	65
			31 July	Light and heat	45

Capital

			1 July	Bank	2,000

Vehicles

1 July	Bank	800			

Motor expenses

3 July	Bank	150			
18 July	Bank	30			

Purchases

7 July	A. Brown	250			

A. Brown

16 July	Returns	50	7 July	Purchases	250
23 July	Bank	140			

Sales

			11 July	B. Green	450

B. Green

11 July	Sales	450	20 July	Returns		75
			26 July	Bank		240

Purchases returns
(outwards)

			16 July	A. Brown		50

Sales returns
(inwards)

20 July	B. Green	75	

Carriage outwards

14 July	Bank	20	

Telephone and
postage

31 July	Bank	65	

Light and heat

31 July	Bank	45	

Notes

1. The narrative in the details column of the expense accounts is 'bank' because the double entry is in the bank account.
2. Where there is more than one transaction relating to the same type of expenditure these are all entered in the same account (e.g. motor expenses). However, the purchase of a vehicle is shown in a different account from the running costs.
3. Lighting and heating expenses, such as coal, electricity, gas, heating oil etc., are usually all entered in an account called light and heat. The same principle is applied in the case of the telephone and postage account, the rent and rates account and the printing and stationery account.
4. Carriage outwards refers to haulage costs relating to goods that this business has sold and is responsible for delivering.
5. Sometimes a business pays cash into its bank account and at other times withdraws cash from its bank account. The ledger entries for these transactions are as follows:

   (a) Paying cash into the bank:
       Debit bank account
       Credit cash account
   (b) Withdrawing cash from a bank account:
       Debit cash account
       Credit bank account

A further related complication occurs where a business pays cash sales into its bank account. This can be treated as two transactions. The first being cash sales which are recorded as a debit in the cash account and a credit in the sales account. The second being the payment of this money into the bank which is recorded as in (a) above. Alternatively, where cash sales are banked on a regular basis, such as daily, the more common method of recording this is to simply debit the bank account and credit the sales account. There are thus no entries in the cash account.

Exercises

1. H. George commenced business as a wholesale butcher on 1 October 19X6 with a capital in cash of £5,000. Her transactions during October 19X6, which were all in cash, are as follows:

    1 Oct   Rent of shop: £200
    2 Oct   Purchases of goods: £970
    4 Oct   Bought fixtures and fittings: £1,250
    6 Oct   Borrowed £3,500 from S. Ring
    9 Oct   Purchased delivery van: £2,650
    12 Oct Sold goods for £1,810
    15 Oct Paid wages of £150
    18 Oct Purchases: £630
    19 Oct Drawings: £350
    21 Oct Petrol for van: £25
    22 Oct Printing costs: £65
    24 Oct Sales: £1,320
    25 Oct Repairs to van: £45
    27 Oct Wages: £250
    28 Oct Purchased stationery costing £35
    30 Oct Rates on shop: £400
    31 Oct Drawings: £175

    You are required to enter the above transactions in the ledger.

2. L. Johnson started business on 1 March 19X8 with a capital of £10,000 in a bank current/cheque account. During March 19X8 he made the following transactions:

    1 Mar   Paid £5,000 by cheque for a 10 year lease on a shop
    2 Mar   Bought office equipment by cheque at a cost of £1,400
    4 Mar   Bought goods costing £630 from E. Lamb on credit
    6 Mar   Paid postage of £35 by cheque
    9 Mar   Purchases by cheque: £420
    11 Mar Sold goods on credit to G. Lion for £880
    13 Mar Drawings by cheque: £250
    16 Mar Returned goods costing £180 to E. Lamb
    18 Mar Sold goods and received a cheque for £540 in payment
    20 Mar Paid telephone bill by cheque: £120
    22 Mar G. Lion returned goods invoiced at £310
    24 Mar Paid gas bill by cheque: £65
    26 Mar Sent E. Lamb a cheque for £230
    28 Mar Received a cheque for £280 from G. Lion
    30 Mar Paid electricity bill of £85 by cheque
    31 Mar Paid bank charges of £45

    You are required to enter the above transactions in the ledger.

3. N. Moss commenced business on 1 March 19X4 with a capital of £5,000 of which £1,000 was in cash and £4,000 in a bank current/cheque account. Her transactions during May were as follows:

1 May	Borrowed £2,000 from Birmingham Bank Ltd in the form of a cheque
2 May	Paid rent of £750 by cheque
5 May	Paid wages of £120 in cash
8 May	Purchased goods for £1,380 by cheque
10 May	Sold goods for £650 cash
12 May	Drawings in cash: £200
15 May	Bought goods on credit for £830 from S. Oak
18 May	Sold goods on credit for £1,250 to K. Heath
20 May	Bought shop fittings of £2,500 by cheque
23 May	Paid water rates of £325 in cash
25 May	Paid gas bill of £230 by cheque
27 May	Returned goods costing £310 to S. Oak
28 May	K. Heath returned goods with an invoice value of £480
29 May	N. Moss introduced further capital of a £3,000 cheque
30 May	Bought stationery of £90 in cash
31 May	Sent S. Oak a cheque for £300
31 May	Received a cheque for £500 from K. Heath

You are required to show the above transactions in the general ledger.

5. The balancing of accounts and the trial balance

The balancing of accounts

At the end of every accounting period it is necessary to balance each account in the ledger. This would have to be done at least annually, and more likely monthly.

The procedure for balancing an account is as follows:

1. Leave two lines under the last entry in the ledger account and draw parallel lines on the top and bottom of the next line in the amounts column on each side.
2. Add up each side of the ledger account and calculate the difference using a separate piece of paper.
3. If the amount of the debit side exceeds that on the credit side, enter the difference on the credit side immediately after the last entry on that side. Where the amount on the credit side exceeds that on the debit side, the difference should be entered on the debit side immediately after the last entry on that side. This should be described as the 'balance carried down' (c/d) and appear above the parallel lines. Enter the same figure on the opposite side below the parallel lines. This should be described as the 'balance brought down' (b/d).
4. Enter the total of each side of the ledger account between the parallel lines. These two figures should now be the same.

This is illustrated below using three accounts from the answer to Example 4.2.

Bank account

19X0			19X0			
1 July	Capital	2,000	1 July	Vehicle		800
26 July	B. Green	240	3 July	Motor expenses		150
			14 July	Carriage outwards		20
			18 July	Motor expenses		30
			23 July	A Brown		140
			31 July	Telephone		65
			31 July	Light and heat		45
			31 July	Balance	c/d	990
		2,240				2,240
1 Aug	Balance b/d	990				

A. Brown

16 July	Returns	50		7 July	Purchases		250
23 July	Bank	140					
31 July	Balance c/d	60					
		250					250
				1 Aug	Balance	b/d	60

B. Green

11 July	Sales	450		20 July	Returns		75
				26 July	Bank		240
				31 July	Balance	c/d	135
		450					450
1 Aug	Balance b/d	135					

If an account contains only one entry it is not necessary to calculate the balance. Where an account contains several entries all on the same side the balance may be entered as described above. However, in practice it is common to just enter a sub-total as follows:

Motor expenses

3 July	Bank	150
18 July	Bank	30
		180

If the total of each side of an account is the same there will be no balance and thus the total amount is simply entered between the parallel lines.

The purposes and preparation of a trial balance

The trial balance is neither a part of the ledger nor a book of prime entry (although it is often prepared on paper with the same ruling as the journal). It is a list of the balances in the ledger at the end of an accounting period, divided between those accounts with debit balances and those with credit balances. Since every transaction recorded in the ledger consists of both a debit and a credit entry, the total of the balances on each side should be the same. This is checked by entering on the trial balance the balance of each account in the ledger, and adding up each side.

The purposes of the trial balance may be summarized as follows:

1. To ascertain whether the total of the accounts with debit balances equals the total of the accounts with credit balances. If so, this proves that the same money value of each transaction has been entered on both sides of the ledger. It also proves the arithmetic accuracy of the ledger accounts. However, a trial balance can agree but there may still be errors in the ledger. For example, an amount may have been entered on the correct side but in the wrong account, or a transaction could have been completely omitted.
2. The trial balance is also used for the preparation of final accounts which show the profit or loss for the period and the assets and liabilities at the end of that period. In practice this is done in the form of an extended trial balance. This is discussed further in Chapter 14.

An illustration of the preparation of a trial balance is given in Example 5.1. The amounts are taken from the ledger in Example 4.2.

Example 5.1
E. Blue
Trial balance as at 31 July 19X0

Name of account	Debit	Credit
Bank	990	
Capital		2,000
Vehicles	800	
Motor expenses	180	
Purchases	250	
A. Brown		60
Sales		450
B. Green	135	
Purchases returns		50
Sales returns	75	
Carriage outwards	20	
Telephone and postage	65	
Light and heat	45	
	2,560	2,560

If a trial balance does not agree, students often fail to take a systematic approach to ascertaining the reason. It is therefore suggested that the following procedure be followed, which will minimize effort and time spent looking for the errors.

1. Recast the trial balance.
2. Check that no account has been omitted from the trial balance. This sometimes happens with the cash and bank balances as they are usually in separate books.

3.   Check that each amount entered in the trial balance is on the correct side. This is quick to do once you become familiar with the nature of different ledger accounts.
4.   Check to see that the amounts entered in the trial balance are the same as those shown in the ledger accounts.
5.   If the error has still not been found it will then be necessary to check all the entries in the ledger.

It is also worth noting that often in examinations no marks are given for correct trial balance totals. The student will therefore only lose marks for the error that caused it to disagree. Thus do not spend more than a few minutes trying to make a trial balance agree.

A further illustration of the preparation of a trial balance is given in Example 5.2. The data in the question would not be presented in this manner in practice, but the question is a useful way of testing your knowledge of which ledger accounts usually contain debit balances and which contain credit balances.

Example 5.2
The following is a list of the balances appearing in the general ledger of T. Wall at 30 September 19X0:

	£
Capital	32,890
Drawings	5,200
Loan from M. Head	10,000
Cash	510
Bank overdraft	1,720
Sales	45,600
Purchases	29,300
Returns inwards	3,800
Returns outwards	2,700
Carriage inwards	960
Carriage outwards	820
Trade debtors	7,390
Trade creditors	4,620
Land and buildings	26,000
Plant and machinery	13,500
Listed investments	4,800
Interest paid	1,200
Interest received	450
Rent received	630
Salaries	3,720
Repairs to buildings	810
Plant hire charges	360
Bank charges	240

You are required to prepare a trial balance.

T. Wall
Trial balance as at 30 September 19X0

Name of account	Debit	Credit
Capital		32,890
Drawings	5,200	
Loan from M. Head		10,000
Cash	510	
Bank overdraft		1,720
Sales		45,600
Purchases	29,300	
Returns inwards	3,800	
Returns outwards		2,700
Carriage inwards	960	
Carriage outwards	820	
Trade debtors	7,390	
Trade creditors		4,620
Land and buildings	26,000	
Plant and machinery	13,500	
Listed investments	4,800	
Interest paid	1,200	
Interest received		450
Rent received		630
Salaries	3,720	
Repairs to buildings	810	
Plant hire charges	360	
Bank charges	240	
	98,610	98,610

Notes

1. The cash account can only have a debit balance. However, the bank account may contain either a debit or a credit balance. A credit balance occurs where the business is overdrawn at the bank.
2. The items 'trade debtors' and 'trade creditors' are common in trial balances. These are the totals of the individual personal accounts of credit customers and suppliers respectively.
3. The item 'listed investments' refers to money invested in stocks and shares that are listed/quoted on the International Stock Exchange, London.

Types of errors that cause a trial balance to disagree

As explained above, one of the purposes of a trial balance is to ascertain whether the total of the debit balances in the ledger is the same as the total of the credit balances. The reason why this may not be the case is because of the existence of one or more of the following errors:

1. *Arithmetic errors*, such as the incorrect addition of the amounts on one side of an account, and/or in the calculation of a balance.
2. *Posting errors*. These may take three forms: (a) where a transaction has been entered on one side of the ledger but not on the other side; (b) where a transaction has been entered twice on the same side; (c) where the correct amount of transaction has been entered on one side of the ledger but the wrong amount has been entered on the other side. The most common errors of the latter type are of two forms: (i) where a zero is omitted from the end of an amount (for example, a transaction for 33,000 entered on one side of the ledger as 3,300), and (ii) *transposed figures* where the correct amount of a transaction has been entered on one side of the ledger but two or more of the figures have been reversed when the entry was made on the other side. For example, an amount of 323 entered on one side as 332. A difference of 9, 90, or other number divisible by 9 on the trial balance may indicate that there is a transposition error.

The first two types of error above have to be corrected by a one-sided ledger entry. The correction may be done by changing the figure to the correct amount. However, it is argued that the correction should take the form of another entry so that some record exists of the correction of the error. Furthermore, in practice it is frequently impractical to correct errors by simply changing a figure to the correct amount, since this usually also necessitates numerous other changes to subsequent totals and balances (e.g. an error in the bank account which occurred several months previously). Where an error is corrected by means of another entry it is essential that the details of the correction indicate where the original error is located.

An illustration of the types of error described above and their correction is given in Example 5.3.

Example 5.3
The following examples are shown in the same order as the types of error described above:

Error	*Correction*
(1) The debit side of the cash account has been overcast by £1,000 and this is reflected in the balance brought down	(1) Credit the cash account with £1,000
(2a) Cash purchases of £200 have been credited in the cash account but not entered in the purchases account	(2a) Debit the purchases account with £200
(2b) Rent paid of £50 has been credited in the cash account but also credited in error to the rent account	(2b) Debit the rent account with £100 (i.e. £50 × 2)

(2cii) Bank charges of £23 shown in the bank account have been debited to the bank charges account as £32

(2cii) Credit the bank charges account with £9

(3) The sales account shows a balance of £2,000 which has been entered on the trial balance as £200

(3) Delete the wrong figure on the trial balance and insert the correct amount

Exercises

1. Explain the main purposes of a trial balance.

2. Prepare a trial balance for Example 4.1.

3. Prepare a trial balance from your answer to Question 1 in Chapter 4.

4. Prepare a trial balance from your answer to Question 2 in Chapter 4.

5. Prepare a trial balance from your answer to Question 3 in Chapter 4.

6. The following is a list of balances in the ledger of C. Rick at 31 May 19X3:

	£
Cash at bank	2,368
Purchases	12,389
Sales	18,922
Wages and salaries	3,862
Rent and rates	504
Insurance	78
Motor expenses	664
Printing and stationery	216
Light and heat	166
General expenses	314
Premises	10,000
Motor vehicles	3,800
Fixtures and fittings	1,350
Debtors	3,896
Creditors	1,731
Cash in hand	482
Drawings	1,200
Capital	12,636
Bank loan	8,000

Prepare a trial balance.

7. The following is a list of balances in the general ledger of R. Keith at 30 June 19X2:

	£
Capital	39,980
Drawings	14,760
Loan—Bromsgrove Bank	20,000
Leasehold premises	52,500
Motor vehicles	13,650
Investment	4,980
Trade debtors	2,630
Trade creditors	1,910
Cash	460

Bank overdraft	3,620
Sales	81,640
Purchases	49,870
Returns outwards	960
Returns inwards	840
Carriage	390
Wages and salaries	5,610
Rent and rates	1,420
Light and heat	710
Telephone and postage	540
Printing and stationery	230
Bank interest	140
Interest received	620

Prepare a trial balance.

8. Describe the types of error that cause a trial balance to disagree.

9. A trial balance failed to agree. On investigation the following errors were found:

   (a) Wages of £250 have been credited in the cash account but no other entry has been made.
   (b) The credit side of the sales account has been undercast by £100 and this is reflected in the balance brought down.
   (c) Purchases of £198 shown in the purchases account have been entered in the creditors account as £189.
   (d) The drawings account contains a balance of £300, but this has been entered on the trial balance as £3,000
   (e) Bank interest received of £86 has been credited in the bank account and the interest received account.

   Describe the entries needed to correct the above errors.

6. Day books and the journal

Before a transaction is recorded in the ledger, it must first be entered in a book of prime entry. These are intended to facilitate the posting of the ledger, in that transactions of the same type are entered in the same book of prime entry which is periodically posted to the ledger in total (rather than one transaction at a time).

There are several books of prime entry. This chapter examines only those which are used to record credit transactions. These consist of: (1) the sales day book; (2) the purchases day book; (3) the sales returns day book; (4) the purchases returns day book; and (5) the journal. The transactions recorded in these books are as follows:

The sales day book

This is used to record the sale on credit of those goods bought specifically for resale. It is written up from copies of the sales invoices and debit notes retained by the seller. The amount entered in the sales day book is after deducting trade discount. At the end of each calendar month the total of the sales day book is credited to the sales account in the ledger and the amount of each invoice and debit note is debited to the individual debtors' accounts.

The purchases day book

This is used to record the purchase on credit of those goods bought specifically for resale. It is written up from the invoices and debit notes received from suppliers. The amount entered in the purchases day book is after deducting trade discount. At the end of each calendar month the total of the purchases day book is debited to the purchases account in the ledger and the amount of each invoice and debit note received is credited to the individual creditors' accounts.

The sales returns day book

This is used to record the credit notes sent to customers relating to goods they have returned or where they have been overcharged on the invoice. Note that the entry is made when a credit note has been issued, and not when the goods are returned or the amount of the invoice is queried. The sales returns day book is written up from copies of the credit notes retained by the seller. The amount shown in the sales returns day book is after deducting trade discount. At the end of each calendar month the total of the sales returns day book is debited to the sales returns account in the ledger and the amount of each credit note credited to the individual debtors' accounts.

The purchases returns day book

This is used to record the credit notes received from suppliers relating to goods returns or where there has been an overcharge on the invoice. Note that the entry is made when a credit note is received and not when the goods are returned or the amount of the invoice is queried. The purchases returns day book is written up from the credit notes received from suppliers. The amount entered in the purchases returns day book is after deducting trade discount. At the end of each calendar month the total of the purchases returns day book is credited to the purchases returns account in the ledger and the amount of each credit note received is debited to the individual creditors' accounts.

The journal

The journal is used to record a variety of things, most of which consist of accounting adjustments, such as the correction of errors, rather than transactions. However, the journal is also used to record transactions which are not appropriate to any other book of prime entry, the most common being the purchase and sale of fixed assets on credit. These are items not specifically bought for resale but to be used in the production and distribution of those goods normally sold by the business. Fixed assets are durable goods that usually last for several years and are normally kept by the business for more than one year. Examples include land and buildings, plant and machinery, motor vehicles, furniture, fixtures and fittings, office equipment etc.

Unlike the sales, purchases and returns day books, the journal has debit and credit columns. These are not a part of the double entry in the ledger. They are used to indicate what entries are going to be made in the ledger in respect of a given transaction or adjustment. Each entry in the journal consists of the name of the account which is to be debited (and the amount) and the name of the account that is to be credited (and the amount). The nature of the entry must also be explained in a narrative which always starts with the word 'being'. This is of particular importance because of the variety of entries that are made in the journal.

An illustration of the entries in the above five books of prime entry is given in Example 6.1.

Another use of the journal is referred to as opening entries. This is an entry to record the capital introduced into the business by the owner when it consists of assets in addition to cash and, possibly, liabilities. As the name implies, this entry usually occurs when the business is formed and the books are being opened. However, it is also used to record the take-over of another business. This is illustrated in Example 6.2.

Example 6.1
Bright Spark is an electrical goods wholesaler. The transactions during June 19X0, which are all on credit, were as follows:

1 June   Bought on credit from Lights Ltd various bulbs with a retail price of £1,000 and received 20 per cent trade discount
4 June   Sold goods on credit to Electrical Retailers Ltd for £500 and allowed then 10 per cent trade discount on this amount
8 June   Sent Electrical Retailers Ltd a credit note for goods returned that had a retail value of £300
10 June Sold goods on credit to Smith Retailers Ltd for £600 after deducting 40 per cent trade discount
12 June Purchased goods with a retail value of £1,000 from Switches Ltd who allowed us 30 per cent trade discount
15 June Purchased on credit from Cables Ltd goods costing £550

16 June   Sent Smith Retailers Ltd a credit note for goods returned which had a retail value of £100

18 June   Switches Ltd sent us a credit note for £300 in respect of goods returned

19 June   Received a credit note for goods returned to Lights Ltd that had a retail value of £250

25 June   Sold goods to General Retailers Ltd on credit for £250

27 June   Sent General Retailers Ltd a credit note for £50 to rectify an overcharge on their invoice

28 June   Sold goods on credit to Electrical Retailers Ltd at a price of £560

29 June   Purchased on credit a motor van from Brown Ltd which cost £800

30 June   Sold on credit to London Trading Co. some fixtures and fittings no longer required in the shop for £350. (Prior to this the business owned fixtures costing £1,000.)

You are required to make the necessary entries in the books of prime entry and general ledger.

Sales day book

Date	Name of debtor	Our invoice number	Folio	Amount £
19X0				
4 June	Electrical Retailers Ltd			450
10 June	Smith Retailers Ltd			600
25 June	General Retailers Ltd			250
28 June	Electrical Retailers Ltd			560
				£1,860

Sales returns day book

Date	Name of debtor	Our credit note number	Folio	Amount £
19X0				
8 June	Electrical Retailers Ltd			270
16 June	Smith Retailers Ltd			60
27 June	General Retailers Ltd			50
				£380

Purchases day book

Date	Name of creditor	Our ref. no. for supplier's invoice	Folio	Amount £
19X0				
1 June	Lights Ltd			800
12 June	Switches Ltd			700
15 June	Cables Ltd			550
				£2,050

Purchases returns day book

Date	Name of creditor	Our ref. no. for supplier's credit note	Folio	Amount £
19X0				
18 June	Switches Ltd			300
19 June	Lights Ltd			200
				£500

The ledger

	Debit				Credit	
Date	Details	Amount	Date	Details		Amount

Sales

			30 June	Total per sales day book		1,860

Electrical Retailers Ltd

Date	Details	Amount	Date	Details	Amount
4 June	Sales	450	8 June	Returns	270
28 June	Sales	560			

Smith Retailers Ltd

Date	Details	Amount	Date	Details	Amount
10 June	Sales	600	16 June	Returns	60

General Retailers Ltd

25 June	Sales	250	27 June	Returns	50

Sales returns

30 June	Total per sales returns day book	380

Purchases

30 June	Total per purchases day book	2,050

Lights Ltd

19 June	Returns	200	1 June	Purchases	800

Switches Ltd

18 June	Returns	300	12 June	Purchases	700

Cables Ltd

	15 June	Purchases	550

Purchases returns

	30 June	Total per purchases returns day book	500

Notes

1. The amount posted to the sales account is the total credit sales for the month as shown in the sales day book; the amounts entered in the debtors' accounts are the amounts of each invoice as shown in the sales day book.
2. The amount posted to the purchases account is the total credit purchases for the month as shown in the purchases day book; the amounts posted to the creditors' accounts are the amounts of the invoices as shown in the purchases day book.
3. The entries for returns are made in the same way. That is, the totals of the returns day books are entered in the returns accounts and the amount of each credit note is posted to the appropriate debtor's or creditor's account.

The journal

Date	Details (account in which the ledger entry is to be made)	Folio	Debit amount	Credit amount
19X0 29 June	Motor vehicles Dr to Brown Ltd Being purchased on credit of motor van reg. no. ABC123		800	800
30 June	London Trading Co. Dr to fixtures and fittings Being sale on credit of shop fittings		350	350

The ledger

Motor vehicles

29 June	Brown Ltd	800

Brown Ltd

		29 June Motor vehicles	800

Fixtures and fittings

1 June	Balance b/d	1,000	30 June	London Trading Co.	350
			30 June	Balance c/d	650
		1,000			1,000
1 July	Balance b/d	650			

London Trading Co.

30 June	Fixtures and fittings	350

Notes

1. The fixtures and fittings that were sold must obviously have already been owned by the business. Their cost is therefore included in the balance brought down on the debit side of the fixtures and fittings account along with the cost of other fixtures and fittings owned at that date.

2. The London Trading Co. is referred to as a sundry debtor and Brown Ltd as a sundry creditor.

Example 6.2

A. King went into business on 1 March 19X6 by taking over a firm owned by B. Wright. The purchase consideration was £47,500 which had been computed by valuing the assets and liabilities that were taken over as follows:

	£
Shop	30,000
Fixtures and fittings	12,500
Stock	4,600
Trade debtors	3,100
Trade creditors	2,700

You are required to show the opening entries in the journal of A. King.

The journal

Date	Details/account		Debit	Credit
19X0				
1 Mar	Land and buildings	Dr	30,000	
	Fixtures and fittings	Dr	12,500	
	Stock	Dr	4,600	
	Trade debtors	Dr	3,100	
	To trade creditors			2,700
	To capital			47,500
			50,200	50,200

Being assets and liabilities introduced
into business by owner from
takeover of an existing business

Notes

1. The ledger entries will consist of debiting and crediting the accounts shown above in the details column. In the case of debtors and creditors the amounts will be entered in the personal accounts of the individuals/firms concerned.
2. The capital of £47,500 is the difference between the total assets and liabilities brought into the business. This will be credited to the capital account.

Exercises

1. (a) Outline the purpose of those books of prime entry referred to as day books.
    (b) Describe the contents, and state which documents are used to write up each of the following:

    (i)   The sales day book;
    (ii) The purchases day book;
    (iii) The sales returns day book;
    (iv) The purchases returns day book.

2. (a) State two fundamentally different types of transactions/items that are recorded in the journal.
   (b) Describe how these two transactions are recorded in the journal.

3. B. Jones is in business as a food wholesaler. The following credit transactions took place during April 19X5:
   1 Apr Bought goods on credit from Brick Ltd for £725.
   2 Apr Sold goods on credit to Oak Ltd for £410.
   4 Apr Bought goods costing £315 from Stone Ltd on credit.
   7 Apr Sold goods on credit to Pine Ltd for £870.
   11 Apr Bought goods costing £520 from Slate Ltd on credit.
   15 Apr Sold goods to Lime Ltd for £630 on credit.
   17 Apr Bought goods on credit from Brick Ltd for £290.
   19 Apr Received a credit note for £120 from Brick Ltd.
   22 Apr Sent Oak Ltd a credit note for £220.
   24 Apr Stone Ltd sent us a credit note for £75 in respect of goods returned.
   27 Apr Sent Pine Ltd a credit note for £360.
   You are required to make the necessary entries in the books of prime entry and the general ledger.

4. B. Player buys and sells office furniture and equipment. During August 19X7 she had the following credit transactions:
   1 Aug Bought goods on credit from Disks Ltd which had a retail price of £1,000 and trade discount of 25 per cent.
   3 Aug Purchased goods with a retail price of £500 from Chairs Ltd who allowed 30 per cent trade discount.
   6 Aug Sold goods on credit to British Cars Ltd for £700 less 10 per cent trade discount.
   10 Aug Received a credit note from Desks Ltd in respect of goods returned which had a retail price of £300 and trade discount of 25 per cent.
   13 Aug Sold goods to London Beds Ltd on credit. These had a retail value of £800 and trade discount of 15 per cent.
   16 Aug Sent British Cars Ltd a credit note in respect of goods returned that were invoiced at a retail price of £300 less 10 per cent trade discount.
   18 Aug Purchased goods on credit from Cabinets Ltd that had a retail value of £900 and trade discount of 20 per cent.
   21 Aug Received a credit note from Chairs Ltd for goods returned that had a retail price of £200 and 30 per cent trade discount.
   23 Aug Sold goods on credit to English Carpets Ltd for £1,300 less 10 per cent trade discount.
   25 Aug Sent London Beds Ltd a credit note relating to an over charge of £100 in the retail value of those goods delivered on 13 August which carried trade discount of 15 per cent.
   You are required to make the necessary entries in the books of prime entry and the ledger.

5. Show the journal and ledger entries in respect of the following:
   (a) On 20 April 19X5 purchased on credit a machine not for resale from Black Ltd at a cost of £5,300.
   (b) On 23 April 19X5 sold on credit a motor vehicle for £3,600 to White Ltd. This had previously been used to deliver goods sold.
   (c) On 26 April 19X5 purchased some shop fittings for £480 on credit from Grey Ltd. These were not for resale.
   (d) On 28 April 19X5 sold on credit to Yellow Ltd for £270 a typewriter that had previously been used in the sales office.

6. W. Green decided to go into business as a building contractor on 1 August 19X8 by purchasing a firm owned by L. House. The purchase consideration was £96,000 which had been computed by valuing the assets and liabilities that were taken over as follows:

	£
Premises	55,000
Plant and machinery	23,000
Goods for resale	14,600
Trade debtors	6,300
Trade creditors	2,900

You are required to show the opening entries in the journal and ledger of W. Green.

7. The cash book

The pages of the cash book, like the ledger, are divided into two halves, the debit on the left and the credit on the right. A cash book can take one of three forms as follows:

1. A two-column cash book in which are recorded cash received and paid in one column on each side, and cheques received and paid in the other column on each side. This essentially combines and replaces the ledger accounts for cash and bank.
2. A two-column cash book in which are recorded cheques received and paid in one column on each side, and cash discount in the other column on each side (discussed further below).
3. A three-column cash book in which are recorded: (a) cash received and paid in one column on each side; (b) cheques received and paid in one column on each side; and (c) cash discount in the remaining column on each side (discussed further below).

In practice, cash received and paid is usually recorded in a separate petty cash book. Thus the cash book normally consists of a two-column cash book of type 2 above.

The two-column cash book

The two-column cash book is used to record receipts and payments by cheque. It is written up from the bank paying-in book and cheque book stubs. The cash book is used instead of a bank account in the ledger. This is because there are usually a large number of transactions involving the receipt and payment of cheques, and if these were recorded in a bank account in the ledger it would become cumbersome. Moreover it permits a division of labour in that one person can write up the cash book while another is working on the ledger. This also reduces the possibility of errors and provides a check on the work of the person who writes up the cash book where it is posted to the ledger by someone else.

In addition to being a book of prime entry, the cash book is also part of the double entry system. Thus, debits in this book are credited to an account in the ledger and no further entries are necessary. Similarly, credits in this book are debited to an account in the ledger and no further entries are necessary.

The two-column cash book gets its name from the existence of two columns on the debit side and two on the credit side. The additional column on the debit side is used to record the *cash discount allowed* to debtors and the extra column on the credit side is used to record the *cash discount received* from creditors. Both of these additional columns are, like the day books, memorandum columns in that each item entered in these columns requires both a debit and credit in the ledger.

Cash discount is a reduction given (in addition to trade discount) by the supplier of goods to a buyer if the latter pays for them within a period stipulated by the seller at the time of sale. Often in practice all goods supplied during a particular calendar month must be paid for by the end of the following calendar month if cash discount is to be obtained. Note that cash discount is not deducted on the invoice but is calculated from the amount shown on the invoice, and deducted at the time of payment.

Apart from the entries in these two additional columns, the cash book is written up in the same way as the bank account. A debit balance on the cash book represents the amount of money the business has in the bank. Unlike the cash account, the cash book may have a credit balance which means the business has an overdraft at the bank.

An illustration of the entries in the two-column cash book is given in Example 7.1.

Example 7.1
Using the answer to Example 6.1, enter the following transactions in a two-column cash book and write up the accounts in the general ledger.

Capital at 1 July £5,750
Bank balance at 1 July £4,750
Fixtures and fittings at 1 July £1,000

Bright Spark has the following cheque receipts and payments during July.

1 July	Cash sales paid into the bank: £625
3 July	Received a cheque for £70 for goods sold
4 July	Paid rent by cheque: £200
6 July	Received a cheque from the London Trading Co. for £350
8 July	Paid an electricity bill by cheque: £50
11 July	Sent Brown Ltd a cheque for £800
13 July	Bought a car which cost £1,000 and paid by cheque
16 July	The owner of Bright Spark paid into the business a cheque for £900 as additional capital
20 July	Paid wages of £150 by cheque
23 July	Purchases paid for by cheque: £670
24 July	The proprietor withdrew a cheque for £100
31 July	Paid Lights Ltd a cheque for their June account of £600 and they allowed us 5 per cent cash discount
31 July	Sent Switches Ltd a cheque for their June account of £400 and deducted $2\frac{1}{2}$ per cent cash discount
31 July	Paid Cables Ltd a cheque for £300 on account
31 July	Received from Smith Retailers Ltd a cheque for £525 after allowing them £15 cash discount
31 July	Received a cheque for £720 from Electrical Retailers Ltd in full settlement of their account, which amounted to £740
31 July	General Retailers Ltd paid £190 by cheque after deducting cash discount of £10 which was not allowed by us

As explained above, the cheques received and paid shown in the debit and credit amount columns are posted to the relevant ledger amounts in the normal manner. However, the amounts shown in the memorandum columns relating to the discount allowed and received require both a debit and credit entry in the ledger. In simple terms the entry for discount allowed is:

Debit   Discount allowed account
Credit   Debtor's personal account

The cash book

Debit side

Date	Details	Folio	Memo: Discount allowed	Debit amount
1 July	Balance	b/d		4,750
1 July	Sales			625
3 July	Sales			70
6 July	London Trading Co			350
16 July	Capital			900
23 July	Smith Retailers Ltd		15	525
31 July	Electrical Retailers Ltd		20	720
31 July	General Retailers Ltd			190
			35	8,130
1 Aug	Balance	b/d		3,900

Credit side

Date	Details	Folio	Cheque number	Memo: Discount received	Credit amount
4 July	Rent and rates		54301		200
8 July	Light and heat		2		50
11 July	Brown Ltd		3		800
13 July	Motor vehicles		4		1,000
20 July	Wages		5		150
23 July	Purchases		6		670
24 July	Drawings		7		100
31 July	Lights Ltd		8	30	570
31 July	Switches Ltd		9	10	390
31 July	Cables Ltd		10		300
31 July	Balance	c/d			3,900
				40	8,130

Similarly the entry for discount received is:

Debit   Creditor's personal account
Credit   Discount received account

This can be illustrated using just two of the personal accounts in the above example as follows:

Smith Retailers Ltd

10 June	Sales	600	16 June	Returns	60
			31 July	Bank	525
			31 July	Discount allowed	15
		600			600

Discount allowed

31 July	Smith Retailers	15

Lights Ltd

19 June	Returns	200	1 June	Purchases	800
31 July	Bank	570			
31 July	Discount received	30			
		800			800

Discount received

			31 July	Lights Ltd	30

However, entering each item of discount in the discount allowed and discount received accounts individually is inefficient, and defeats the main objective of the two-column cash book. The memorandum columns in the two-column cash book are intended to provide a means of ascertaining the total discount allowed and discount received for the period. The total of the memorandum discount allowed column is debited to the discount allowed account and the amount of each item of discount allowed is credited to the individual debtors' accounts. Similarly the total of the memorandum discount received column is credited to the discount received account and the amount of each item of discount received is debited to the individual creditors' accounts.

It can thus be seen that the memorandum discount columns in the cash book operate on the same principle, and perform the same function, as day books. That is, they facilitate the bulk posting of transactions to the ledger by aggregating items of the same type. However, since they are not a part of the double entry system, each item requires both a debit and credit entry in the ledger.

The proper ledger entries for discount allowed and discount received can now be illustrated by completing Example 7.1 using the answer to Example 6.1 as follows:

The ledger

Sales

30 June	Total per sales returns day book	380	30 June	Total per sales day book	1,860
			1 July	Bank	625
			3 July	Bank	70

London Trading Co.

30 June	Fixtures and fittings	350	6 July	Bank	350

Fixtures and Fittings

1 June	Balance b/d	1,000	30 June	London Trading Co.	350
			31 July	Balance c/d	650
		1,000			1,000
1 Aug	Balance b/d	650			

Capital

24 July	Bank–drawings	100	1 July	Balance b/d	5,750
31 July	Balance c/d	6,550	16 July	Bank–capital introduced	900
		6,650			6,650
			1 Aug	Balance b/d	6,550

Discount allowed

31 July	Total per cash book	35

Smith Retailers Ltd

10 June	Sales	600	16 June	Returns	60
			31 July	Bank	525
			31 July	Discount allowed	15
		600			600

Electrical Retailers Ltd

4 June	Sales	450	8 June	Returns	270
28 June	Sales	560	31 July	Bank	720
			31 July	Discount allowed	20
		1,010			1,010

General Retailers Ltd

25 June	Sales	250	27 June	Returns	50
			31 July	Bank	190
			31 July	Balance c/d	10
		250			250

1 Aug	Balance b/d	10			

Rent and Rates

4 July	Bank	200			

Light and Heat

8 July	Bank	50			

Brown Ltd

11 July	Bank	800	29 June	Motor vehicles	800

Motor vehicles

29 June	Brown Ltd	800	31 July	Balance c/d)	1,800
13 July	Bank	1,000			
		1,800			1,800
1 Aug	Balance b/d	1,800			

Wages

20 July	Bank	150			

Purchases

30 June	Total per Purchases	30	Total per		
		June	Purchases		
	Day Book	2,050		Returns Day Book	500
23 July	Bank	670			

Discount received

			31 July	Total per Cash Book	40

Lights Ltd

19 June	Returns	200	1 June	Purchases	800
31 July	Bank	570			
31 July	Discount received	30			
		800			800

Switches Ltd

18 June	Returns	300	12 June	Purchases	700
31 July	Bank	390			
31 July	Discount received	10			
		700			700

Cables Ltd

31 July	Bank	300	15 June	Purchases	550
31 July	Balance c/d	250			
		550			550
			1 Aug	Balance b/d	250

Notes

1. The personal accounts are usually balanced at the end of each month.
2. The entries in the purchases and sales accounts in respect of returns are an inferior alternative to having purchases returns and sales returns accounts.
3. The entry in the capital account in respect of drawings is an inferior alternative to having a drawings account.

The three-column cash book

The three-column cash book is not common in practice, but is sometimes required in examination questions. It can be seen as an extension of the two-column cash book described above. The additional column on each side is used to record cash received (debit side) and cash payments (credit side). These columns are intended to replace the cash account in the ledger. Thus the three-column cash book is used instead of the cash account and bank account in the ledger.

In addition to being a book of prime entry, the three-column cash book is also part of the double entry system. Thus entries in either the cash or bank columns require only one further entry in another ledger account on the opposite side.

The only additional complication that arises in the case of the three-column cash book concerns cash paid into the bank and cash withdrawn from the bank. At this point the reader may find it useful to refer back to Note 5 of Example 4.2 which explains the double entry for these items. The form which this takes in the three-column cash book is as follows:

(a)   Paying cash into the bank:

Debit   Bank account column
Credit   Cash account column

(b)   Withdrawing cash from the bank:

Debit   Cash account column
Credit   Bank account column

The three-column cash book is not common in practice because in most businesses cash received and paid is usually recorded in a separate petty cash book instead of a cash account. This is discussed further in the next chapter.

An illustration of the three-column cash book is given in Example 7.2.

Example 7.2

B. Andrews is in business as a motor factor and parts agent. The balances shown in her cash book at 1 December 19X2 were: bank, £1,630 and cash, £820. The following receipts and payments occurred during December 19X2:

2 Dec   Received a cheque for £1,000 from J. Sutcliffe as a loan repayable in five years
3 Dec   Purchased a personal computer for £1,210 and paid by cheque

Cash book for example 7.2

Date	Details	Memo: Discount allowed	Bank	Cash	Date	Details	Memo: Discount received	Bank	Cash
19X2					19X2				
1 Dec	Balance b/d	–	1,630	820	3 Dec	Office equipment		1,210	
2 Dec	J. Sutcliffe				4 Dec	Purchases			340
	–loan		1,000		5 Dec	Wages			150
6 Dec	Sales		480	160	8 Dec	Purchases		370	
9 Dec	Sales		280		12 Dec	Telephone		320	
11 Dec	Sales		200		15 Dec	Bank			200
15 Dec	Cash				17 Dec	Drawings		250	
20 Dec	Capital		500		18 Dec	Stationery			80
23 Dec	Bank			100	21 Dec	Rates		430	
26 Dec	A. Green	35	640		23 Dec	Cash		100	
28 Dec	J. Evans	45	860		25 Dec	K. Vale	40	530	
29 Dec	B. Court		920		27 Dec	M. Fenton	25	720	
					31 Dec	Balance c/d		2,580	310
		80	6,510	1,080			65	6,510	1,080
19X3									
1 Jan	Balance b/d	–	2,580	310					

57

4 Dec	Purchased in cash goods for resale costing £340
5 Dec	Paid wages of £150 in cash
6 Dec	Cash sales paid into bank: £480
8 Dec	Purchases by cheque: £370
9 Dec	Cash sales of £160
11 Dec	Cheque sales: £280
12 Dec	Paid telephone bill of £320 by cheque
15 Dec	Paid cash of £200 into bank
17 Dec	Drawings by cheque: £250
18 Dec	Bought stationery of £80 in cash
20 Dec	Introduced additional capital in the form of a cheque for £500
21 Dec	Paid water rates of £430 by cheque
23 Dec	Withdrew cash of £100 from the bank
25 Dec	Sent K. Vale a cheque for £530 after deducting cash discount of £40
26 Dec	Received a cheque for £640 from A. Green who deducted £35 cash discount
27 Dec	Paid M. Fenton £720 by cheque after deducting £25 cash discount
28 Dec	J. Evans sent us a cheque for £860 after deducting £45 cash discount
29 Dec	Received a cheque from B. Court for £920 who deducted £50 cash discount which we did not allow

You are required to enter the above transactions in a three-column cash book (see page 57).

Exercises

1. Describe the different forms of two- and three-column cash books with which you are familiar.

2. Describe the entries in the cash book and ledger in respect of discount allowed and discount received.

3. B. Jones is in business as a food wholesaler. The following receipts and payments by cheque took place during May 19X5:

1 May	Bank balance per cash book: £3,680
3 May	Introduced additional capital: £2,000
4 May	Sales by cheque: £840
7 May	Purchases by cheque: £510
10 May	Paid wages by cheque: £200
13 May	Paid rent by cheque: £360
15 May	Cash sales paid into bank: £490
18 May	Purchased shopfittings for £2,450
20 May	Paid gas bill of £180
23 May	Bought stationery by cheque: £70
26 May	Drawings by cheque: £250
31 May	Sent Brick Ltd a cheque for £850 after deducting £45 cash discount
31 May	Received a cheque from Oak Ltd for £160 after deducting £30 cash discount
31 May	Paid Stone Ltd £220 after deducting cash discount of £20
31 May	Pine Ltd sent us a cheque for £485 after deducing £25 cash discount
31 May	Sent Slate Ltd a cheque for £480 after deducting discount of £40. However, Slate Ltd did not allow the discount
31 May	Lime Ltd sent us a cheque for £575.

Show the entries in respect of the above in a two-column cash book.

4. (a)   Using your answers to Question 3 in Chapter 6 and Question 3 above, make the necessary entries in the general ledger given a balance on the capital account at 1 May 19X5 of £3,680; and

    (b)   Prepare a trial balance at 31 May 19X5.

5.   B. Player buys and sells office furniture and equipment. During September 19X7 the following receipts and payments occurred:

    1 Sept   Bank balance per cash book: £1,950
    1 Sept   Cash balance per cash book: £860
    3 Sept   Cash sales paid into bank: £470
    4 Sept   Cash purchases: £230
    6 Sept   Paid electricity bill of £510 by cheque
    9 Sept   Drew a cheque for £250 in respect of wages
    12 Sept   Cash sales: £290
    15 Sept   Paid £40 in cash for travelling expenses
    16 Sept   Paid water rates by cheque: £410
    19 Sept   Drawings in cash: £150
    20 Sept   Purchases by cheque: £320
    21 Sept   Paid postage of £30 in cash
    22 Sept   Paid cash of £350 into bank
    24 Sept   Introduced further capital of £500 by cheque
    25 Sept   Purchased a delivery vehicle for £2,500 and paid by cheque
    26 Sept   Received a cheque for £1,000 from B. Jones as a three-year loan
    27 Sept   Returned goods costing £170 and received a cash refund
    28 Sept   Paid tax and insurance on delivery vehicle of £280 in cash
    29 Sept   Withdrew cash of £180 from bank
    30 Sept   Received a cheque from British Cars Ltd for £350 after deducting £10 cash discount
    30 Sept   Received a cheque from London Beds Ltd for £580 after deducting £15 cash discount
    30 Sept   Paid Desks Ltd a cheque for £500 after deducting £25 cash discount
    30 Sept   Paid Chairs Ltd a cheque for £190 after deducting £20 cash discount
    30 Sept   Received a cheque from English Carpets Ltd for £1,100 after deducing £70 cash discount. However, this cash discount was not allowed.
    30 Sept   Paid Cabinets Ltd a cheque for £500 on account

Enter the above in a three-column cash book.

6.   Using your answers to Question 4 in Chapter 6 and Question 5 above:
    (a)   make the necessary entries in the ledger given a balance on the capital account at the 1 September 19X7 of £2,810; and
    (b)   prepare a trial balance at 30 September.

8.   The petty cash book

The petty cash book is used to record the receipt and payment of small amounts of cash. Any large amounts of cash received and cash takings are usually paid into the bank and thus recorded in the cash book. The petty cash book is written up from receipts and petty cash vouchers (where employees are reimbursed expenses).

   The petty cash book is used instead of a cash account in the ledger. This is because there are usually a large number of transactions in cash, and if these were recorded in a cash account in the ledger it would become cumbersome. Like the cash book, it also permits a division of labour and facilitates improved control. In addition to being a book of prime entry, the petty cash book is also part of the double entry system. Thus debits in this book are credited to an account in the ledger and no further entries are necessary. Similarly, credits in this book are debited to an account in the ledger and no further entries are necessary.

The columnar petty cash book

It is usual for a petty cash book to have analysis columns on the credit side. Each column relates to a particular type of expenditure, such as postage, stationery, travelling expenses, etc. These are intended to facilitate the posting of entries to the ledger. Every item of expenditure is entered both in the credit column and an appropriate analysis column. At the end of each calendar week or month the total of each column is debited to the relevant account in the ledger. Thus, instead of posting each transaction to the ledger separately, expenditure of the same type is collected together in analysis columns and the total for the period posted to the relevant ledger accounts.

The imprest system

Many firms also operate their petty cash on an imprest system. At the beginning of each period (week or month) the petty cashier has a fixed amount of cash referred to as a 'float'. At the end of each period (or the start of the next) the petty cashier is reimbursed the exact amount spent during the period, thus making the float up to its original amount. The reimbursement usually takes the form of a cheque drawn for cash. The amount of the petty cash float is determined by reference to the normal level of petty cash expenditure in each period.

The advantages of the imprest system are as follows:

1. It facilitates control of the total petty cash expenditure in each period as the petty cashier cannot spend more than the amount of the float except by applying to the management for an increase.
2. It deters theft of cash by the petty cashier since a large cash balance cannot be accumulated by drawing cash from the bank at irregular intervals.
3. The entries in the petty cash book are kept up to date because the cash expenditure is not reimbursed until the petty cash book is written up and the total amount of expenditure for the period is known.
4. It discourages the practice of loans and subs from petty cash since these would have to be accounted for at the end of the period, and in addition may result in insufficient cash to meet the necessary expenditure.

An illustration of a columnar petty cash book and the imprest system is shown in Example 8.1.

Example 8.1
A. Stone uses a columnar petty cash book to record his cash payments. He also operates an imprest system with a float of £150. During August 19X6 the cash transactions were as follows:

 1 Aug   Postage stamps: £5
 2 Aug   Cleaning materials: £13
 4 Aug   Telegram: £2
 5 Aug   Gratuity to delivery man: £4
 7 Aug   Tea, milk etc.: £1
 9 Aug   Rail fare: £11
10 Aug   Paper clips and pens: £6
13 Aug   Window cleaner: £10
18 Aug   Travelling expenses: £7
21 Aug   Envelopes: £3
22 Aug   Postage stamps: £9
24 Aug   Stationery: £14
27 Aug   Taxi fare: £12
28 Aug   Office cleaning: £8
31 Aug   Received reimbursement to make float up to £150

You are required to make the necessary entries in the petty cash book using appropriate analysis columns, and show the relevant ledger accounts.

The petty cash book

Debit   **Credit**

Amount £	Date	Details	Amount £	Postage £	Cleaning £	Stationery £	Travelling expenses £	Miscellaneous expenses £
	19X6							
b/d 150	1 Aug	Stamps	5	5				
	2 Aug	Materials	13		13			
	4 Aug	Telegram	2	2				
	5 Aug	Gratuity	4					4
	7 Aug	Tea and milk	1					1
	9 Aug	Rail fare	11				11	
	10 Aug	Clips and pens	6			6		
	13 Aug	Windows	10		10			
	18 Aug	Travelling	7				7	
	21 Aug	Envelopes	3			3		
	22 Aug	Stamps	9	9				
	24 Aug	Stationery	14			14		
	27 Aug	Taxi	12				12	
	28 Aug	Office	8		8			
105	31 Aug	Reimbursement	105	16	31	23	30	5
	31 Aug	Balance c/d	150					
255			255					
b/d 150	1 Sept							

In some firms the cash reimbursement is made at the beginning of the next period, in which case the entries are as follows:

Amount £	Date	Details	Amount £	Postage £	Cleaning £	Stationery £	Travelling expenses £	Miscellaneous expenses £
	31 Aug	Totals	105	16	31	23	30	5
	31 Aug	Balance c/d	45					
150			150					
b/d 45								
105	1 Sept	Reimbursement						
150								

The ledger

Telephone and postage

| 31 Aug | Total per PCB | 16 |

Cleaning

| 31 Aug | Total per PCB | 31 |

Printing and stationery

| 31 Aug | Total per PCB | 23 |

Travelling and entertaining

| 31 Aug | Total per PCB | 30 |

Miscellaneous expenses

| 31 Aug | Total per PCB | 5 |

Cash book

| | 31 Aug | Cash | 105 |

Notes

1. When designing a columnar petty cash book it is necessary first to decide on the appropriate number of analysis columns. This is done by identifying the number of different types of expenditure for which there is more than one transaction. In Example 8.1 there are four different types, namely postage, cleaning, stationery and travelling expenses. These four plus a column for miscellaneous expenses gives five columns. The headings for each of these columns should be the same as the name of the ledger account to which the total of the column will be posted.
2. The details column of the petty cash book is used to describe the nature of each transaction rather than the name of the ledger account containing the double entry ledger, since this is given at the head of the analysis column in which the item is entered.
3. The items entered in the miscellaneous expenses column often have to be entered in several different ledger accounts according to the nature of the transaction.
4. When cash is withdrawn from the bank to restore the float to its original amount the ledger entry consists of:

Debit petty cash book
Credit cash book (bank account)

5. When answering examination questions which contain cash and cheque items but do not specifically require a petty cash book, it is advisable to use a three-column cash book.

Exercises

1. (a) Describe the purpose and format of a columnar petty cash book.
   (b) Explain how you would determine the appropriate number of analysis columns.

2. (a) Describe how a petty cash imprest system operates.
   (b) Explain how such a system facilitates control.

3. C. Harlow has a petty cash book which is used to record his cash receipts and payments. This also incorporates an imprest system which has a float of £400. During February 19X2 the following cash transactions took place:

    1 Feb   Purchase: £31
    3 Feb   Wages: £28
    6 Feb   Petrol for delivery van: £9
    8 Feb   Bus fares: £3
    11 Feb   Pens and pencils: £8
    12 Feb   Payments for casual labour: £25
    14 Feb   Repairs to delivery van: £17
    16 Feb   Typing paper: £15
    19 Feb   Good for resale: £22
    20 Feb   Train fares: £12
    21 Feb   Repairs to premises: £35
    22 Feb   Postage stamps: £6
    23 Feb   Drawings: £20
    24 Feb   Taxi fares: £7
    25 Feb   Envelopes: £4
    26 Feb   Purchases: £18
    27 Feb   Wages: £30
    28 Feb   Petrol for delivery van: £14

   On 28 February 19X2 the cash float was restored to £400.
   Record the above in the petty cash book using appropriate analysis columns and make the necessary entries in the ledger.

4. The Oakhill Printing Co. Ltd operates its petty cash account on the imprest system. It is maintained at a figure of £80 on the first day of each month. At 30 April 19X7 the petty cash box held £19.37 in cash.
   During May 19X7, the following petty cash transactions arose:

19X7		£
1 May	Cash received to restore imprest	to be derived
1 May	Bus fares	0.41
2 May	Stationery	2.35
4 May	Bus fares	0.30
7 May	Postage stamps	1.70
7 May	Trade journal	0.95
8 May	Bus fares	0.64
11 May	Correcting fluid	1.29
12 May	Typewriter ribbons	5.42
14 May	Parcel postage	3.45
15 May	Paper clips	0.42
15 May	Newspapers	2.00
16 May	Photocopier repair	16.80
19 May	Postage stamps	1.50
20 May	Drawing pins	0.38
21 May	Train fare	5.40
22 May	Photocopier paper	5.63
23 May	Display decorations	3.07
23 May	Correcting fluid	1.14
25 May	Wrapping paper	0.78

27 May	String	0.61
27 May	Sellotape	0.75
27 May	Biro pens	0.46
28 May	Typewriter repair	13.66
30 May	Bus fares	2.09
1 June	Cash received to restore imprest	to be derived

Required:

Open and post the company's petty cash account for the period 1 May to 1 June 19X7 inclusive and balance the account at 30 May 19X7.

In order to facilitate the subsequent double entry postings, all items of expense appearing in the 'payments' column should then be analysed individually into suitably labelled expense columns.   (CACA)

9. The final accounts of sole traders

Final accounts consist of a profit and loss account and balance sheet. These are prepared at the end of a business's accounting year after the trial balance has been completed. Some businesses also produce final accounts half yearly, quarterly or even monthly. The purpose, structure and preparation of the profit and loss account and balance sheet are discussed below.

The purpose and structure of profit and loss accounts

The profit and loss account provides a summary of the results of a business's trading activities during a given accounting year. It shows the profit or loss for the year. The purpose of a profit and loss account is to enable users of accounts, such as the owner, to evaluate the performance of a business for a given accounting year. It may be used to determine the amount of taxation on the profit.

Chapter 2 explained that profit can be defined as the amount which could be taken out of a business as drawings in the case of a sole trader or partnership, or is available for distribution as dividends to shareholders in the case of a company, after maintaining the value of the capital of a business. Profit is not the same as an increase in the amount of money the business possesses. It is the result of applying certain accounting rules known as concepts and bases to the transactions of the business. These will be described in detail in the next chapter.

The basic format of a profit and loss account is as follows:

ABC

Profit and loss account for the year ended . . .

	£	£
Sales		X
Less: cost of sales		X
Gross profit		X
Less: other costs and expenses—		
Selling and distribution costs	X	
Administrative expenses	X	
Interest payable on loans	X	
		X
Net profit		X

In the accounts of sole traders and partnerships the actual composition of each of the above groupings of costs would be shown. Selling and distribution costs might consist of, for example, advertising expenditure, the wages of delivery van drivers, motor expenses including petrol and repairs etc. Administrative expenses usually comprise the salaries of office staff, rent and rates, light and heat, printing and stationery, telephone and postage etc. The published final accounts of companies contain a classification of costs similar to that shown above.

The purpose and structure of balance sheets

The balance sheet is a list of the assets and liabilities of a business at the end of a given accounting year. It therefore provides information about the resources of the reporting entity. This enables users of its accounts to evaluate its financial position—in particular whether the business is likely to be unable to pay its debts or whether it is likely to make a profit. The balance sheet is like a photograph of the financial state of affairs of a business at a specific point in time.

Balance sheets contain five groups of items as follows:

1. *Fixed assets*
   These are items not specifically bought for resale but to be used in the production and distribution of those goods normally sold by the business. Fixed assets are durable goods that usually last for several years, and are normally kept by a business for more than one accounting year. Examples of common fixed assets include land and buildings; plant and machinery; motor vehicles; office equipment; furniture and fixtures and fittings.
2. *Current assets*
   These are items that are normally kept by a business for less than one accounting year. Indeed, the composition of each type of current asset is usually continually changing. Examples include stocks, trade debtors, short-term investments, money in bank cheque account and cash.
3. *Current liabilities*
   These are debts owed by a business that are payable within one year (often considerably less) of the date of the balance sheet. Examples include trade creditors and bank overdrafts.
4. *Long-term liabilities*
   These are debts owed by a business that are not due until after one year (often much longer) from the date of the balance sheet. Examples include loans and mortgages.
5. *Capital*
   This refers to the amount of money invested in the business by the owner(s).

The structure of a balance sheet is shown in the diagram on page 68. Note that the items shown in an italic typeface are subtotals or totals which should be shown on the balance sheet:

$$ABC$$

Balance sheet as at . . .

Fixed assets

+

$$\left\{ \begin{array}{l} \text{Current assets} \\ -\,\text{Current liabilities} \\ =\ \textit{Net current assets} \end{array} \right\}$$

=

Total assets less current liabilities

−

Long term liabilities

=

Net assets

=

Capital

The gross profit: stock and the cost of sales

The first stage in the determination of the profit for the year involves calculating the gross profit. It is usually carried out in the profit and loss account. However, this part of the profit and loss account is sometimes presented as a separate account referred to as the *trading account*.

The gross profit for a given period is computed by subtracting the cost of goods sold/cost of sales from the sales revenue. It is important to appreciate that the cost of goods sold is not usually the same as the amount of purchases. This is because most businesses will have purchased goods that are unsold at the end of the accounting period. This is referred to as stock or inventory.

A manufacturing business will have a number of different types of stocks. However, for simplicity the following exposition is confined to non-manufacturing businesses whose stock consists of goods purchased for resale that have not undergone any further processing by the entity.

The cost of sales is determined by taking the cost of goods in stock at the end of the previous period, adding to this the cost of goods purchased during the current period, and subtracting the cost of goods unsold at the end of the current period. The cost of sales is then deducted from the sales revenue to give the gross profit. This is illustrated in Example 9.1.

Example 9.1
S. Mann, whose accounting year ends on the 30th April, buys and sells one type of aluminium engine head for sports cars. On the 1st May 19X9 there were 50 units in stock which had cost £100 each. During the subsequent accounting year he purchased a further 500 units at a cost of £100 each and sold 450 units at a price of £150 each. There were 100

units which cost £100 each that had not been sold at the 30th April 19X9. You are required to compute the gross profit for the year.

S. Mann

Trading account for the year ended 30 April 19X9

Units		£	£
450	Sales revenue		67,500
	Less: Cost of goods sold:		
50	Stock of goods at 1 May 19X8	5,000	
500	*Add*: goods purchased during the year	50,000	
550		55,000	
	Less: stock of goods at		
100	30th April 19X9	10,000	
450	Cost of sales		45,000
	Gross profit for the year		22,500

Notes

1. The numbers of units are not usually shown in the trading account. They have been included in the above to demonstrate that the cost of sales relates to the number of units that were sold.

The preparation of final accounts

The trading account

The trading account is an account in the ledger and is thus a part of the double entry system. It is used to ascertain the gross profit and is prepared by transferring the balances on the sales, purchases and returns accounts to the trading account. In addition certain entries are required in respect of stock. These are as follows:

1. Stock at the end of the previous period:
    Debit trading account
    Credit stock account
2. Stock at the end of the current period:
    Debit stock account
    Credit trading account

Note that the stock at the end of the previous period will be the stock at the start of the current period. The ledger entries in respect of stocks are illustrated below using the data in Example 9.1. Prior to the preparation of the trading account the ledger will appear as follows:

Sales

	19X9	
	30 Apr Balance b/d	67,500

Purchases

19X9		
30 Apr	Balance b/d	50,000

Stock

19X8		
30 Apr	Balance b/d	5,000

The trading account will then be prepared as follows:

Sales

19X9			19X9		
30 Apr	Trading a/c	67,500	30 Apr	Balance b/d	67,500

Purchases

19X9			19X9		
30 Apr	Balance b/d	50,000	30 Apr	Trading a/c	50,000

Stock

19X8			19X9		
30 Apr	Balance b/d	5,000	30 Apr	Trading a/c	5,000
19X9 30 Apr	Trading a/c	10,000			

S. Mann

Trading account for the year ending 30 April 19X9

	£		£
Stock at 1 May 19X8	5,000	Sales	67,500
Purchases	50,000	Stock at 30 April 19X9	10,000
Gross profit c/d	22,500		
	77,500		77,500
		Gross profit b/d	22,500

Notes

1. The gross profit is the difference between the two sides of the trading account and must be brought down to the opposite side of the account;
2. No dates are shown in the trading account since they appear as part of the heading of the account;

3. When the trading account is prepared in account form the stock at the end of the year may be shown as either a credit entry or deducted on the debit side as follows:

S. Mann

Trading account for the year ended 30 April 19X9

Opening stock	5,000	Sales	67,500
Add: purchases	50,000		
	55,000		
Less: Closing stock	10,000		
Cost of sales	45,000		
Gross profit c/d	22,500		
	67,500		67,500
		Gross profit b/d	22,500

This has the advantage of showing the cost of sales.

4. The trading account is an account in the ledger and thus part of the double entry system. However, when it is prepared for submission to the management, the owner(s) of a business or the Inland Revenue, it is often presented vertically as shown at the start of Example 9.1.
5. No entries other than those shown above (and the correction of errors) should be made in a stock account. It is not a continuous record of the value of stock.
6. The debit balance in the stock account on 30 April 19X8 was the result of an entry identical to that on 30 April 19X9.
7. The stock shown in a trial balance will always be that at the end of the previous year (and thus the opening stock of the year to which the trial balance relates).

The profit and loss account

The profit and loss account is an account in the ledger and thus a part of the double entry system. It is used to ascertain the net profit (or loss) for the year and is prepared in the same way as the trading account. That is, the balances on the income and expense accounts in the ledger are transferred to the profit and loss account by means of a double entry.

The balance sheet

The balance sheet is a list of the balances remaining in the ledger after the trading and profit and loss accounts have been prepared. In effect it is like a trial balance except that the balance sheet is presented using a different format. Note that the balances are not transferred to the balance sheet by means of a double entry.

In practice, and in examinations, it is usual to prepare final accounts from the information given in the trial balance. However, it is important to appreciate that the ledger entries described above also have to be done, although students are not normally expected to show them in their answer to examination questions.

An illustration of the preparation of final accounts, including the required ledger entries, is shown in Example 9.2.

Example 9.2

The following is the trial balance of A. Dillon at 31 March 19X0.

	Debit	Credit
Capital		42,140
Drawings	13,600	
Loan from S. Rodd		10,000
Bank	5,800	
Cash	460	
Sales		88,400
Purchases	46,300	
Sales returns	5,700	
Purchases returns		3,100
Stock at 1 April 19X9	8,500	
Carriage inwards	2,400	
Carriage outwards	1,600	
Trade debtors	15,300	
Trade creditors		7,200
Motor vehicles	23,100	
Fixtures and fittings	12,400	
Wages and salaries	6,800	
Rent	4,100	
Light and heat	3,200	
Telephone and postage	1,700	
Discount allowed	830	
Discount received		950
	151,790	151,790

The stock at 31 March 19X0 was valued at £9,800. The loan from S. Rodd is repayable on 1 January 19X4.

You are required to prepare the trading and profit and loss accounts and a balance sheet.

Sales

Trading a/c	88,400	Balance b/d	88,400

Sales returns

Balance b/d	5,700	Trading a/c	5,700

Purchases

Balance b/d	46,300	Trading a/c	46,300

Purchases returns

Trading a/c	3,100	Balance b/d	3,100

Stock

Balance b/d	8,500	Trading a/c	8,500
Trading a/c	9,800		

Carriage inwards

Balance b/d	2,400	Trading a/c	2,400

Carriage outwards

Balance b/d	1,600	Profit and loss a/c	1,600

Wages and salaries

Balance b/d	6,800	Profit and loss a/c	6,800

Rent

Balance b/d	4,100	Profit and loss a/c	4,100

Light and heat

Balance b/d	3,200	Profit and loss a/c	3,200

Telephone and postage

Balance b/d	1,700	Profit and loss a/c	1,700

Discount allowed

Balance b/d	830	Profit and loss a/c	830

Discount received

Profit and loss a/c	950	Balance b/d	950

Drawings

Balance b/d	13,600	Capital	13,600

Capital

Drawings	13,600	Balance b/d	42,140
Balance c/d	49,660	Profit for year	21,120
	63,260		63,260
		Balance b/d	49,660

All other accounts contain the balances shown in the trial balance.

A. Dillon

Trading and profit and loss accounts for the year ended 31 March 19X0

	£	£		£
Stock at 1 April 19X9		8,500	Sales	88,400
Purchases	46,300		*Less*: returns	5,700
Less: returns	3,100			82,700
	43,200			
Add: carriage inwards	2,400	45,600		
		54,100		
Less: stock at 31 March 19X0		9,800		
Cost of sales		44,300		
Gross profit c/d		38,400		
		82,700		82,700
Carriage outwards		1,600	Gross profit b/d	38,400
Wages and salaries		6,800	Discount received	950
Rent		4,100		
Light and heat		3,200		
Telephone and postage		1,700		
Discount allowed		830		
Net profit c/d		21,120		
		39,350		39,350
Capital a/c		21,120	Net profit b/d	21,120

A. Dillon

Balance sheet as at 31 March 19X0

Credit	£	Debit	£
Capital		*Fixed assets*	
Balance at 1 April 19X9	42,140	Motor vehicles	23,100
Add: profit for year	21,120	Fixtures and fittings	12,400
	63,260		35,500
Less: drawings	13,600	*Current assets*	
Balance at 31 March 19X0	49,660	Stock 9,800	
Long term liabilities		Debtors 15,300	
Loan from S. Rodd	10,000	Bank 5,800	
		Cash 460	
Current liabilities			31,360
Creditors	7,200		
	66,860		66,860

Notes

1. The gross profit is the difference between the two sides of the trading account and must be brought down to the opposite side of the profit and loss account.
2. The net profit is the difference between the two sides of the profit and loss account. This is brought down to the credit side of the profit and loss account and then transferred to the capital account by debiting the profit and loss account and crediting the capital account. The reason for this transfer is because the profit belongs to the owner and it increases the amount of capital he has invested in the business.
3. If the debit side of the profit and loss account exceeds the credit side this is shown as a net loss (carried down) on the credit side and debited to the capital account.
4. The balance on the drawings account at the end of the period must be transferred to the capital account.
5. Each of the transfers from the ledger accounts to the trading and profit and loss accounts should also be entered in the journal.
6. Notice that the debit balances remaining in the ledger after the profit and loss account has been prepared and are shown on the right-hand side of the balance sheet and the credit balances on the left-hand side. This may seem inconsistent with the debit and credit sides of the ledger being on the left and right respectively. However, it is a common approach in accounting. Like the trial balance, the total of each side of the balance sheet should be the same. That is, the total of the ledger accounts with debit balances should equal the total of the ledger accounts with credit balances. If this is not the case it indicates that an error has occurred in the preparation of the trading and profit and loss account (or the balance sheet).
7. The current assets in the balance sheet are shown in what is the reverse order of liquidity.
8. The current liabilities are sometimes shown on the balance sheet as a deduction from current assets.

9.   The entries on the balance sheet in respect of capital are a summary of the capital account in the ledger.

When the trading and profit and loss account and balance sheet are presented to the owner(s) of a business and the Inland Revenue it is common to use a vertical format. This is illustrated below using the data in Example 9.2.

A. Dillon

Trading and profit and loss accounts for the year ending 31 March 19X0

	£	£	£
Sales			88,400
Less: returns			5,700
			82,700
Less: Cost of sales—			
Stock at 1 April 19X9		8,500	
Add: Purchases	46,300		
Less: Returns	3,100	43,200	
Add: Carriage inwards		2,400	
		54,100	
Less: Stock at 31 March 19X0		9,800	
			44,300
Gross profit			38,400
Add: Discount received			950
			39,350
Less: Expenditure—			
Carriage outwards		1,600	
Wages and salaries		6,800	
Rent		4,100	
Light and heat		3,200	
Telephone and postage		1,700	
Discount allowed		830	18,230
Net profit for the year			21,120

Balance sheet as at 31 March 19X0	£	£
Fixed assets		
Motor vehicles		23,100
Fixtures and fittings		12,400
		35,500
Current assets		
Stock	9,800	
Debtors	15,300	
Bank	5,800	
Cash	460	
	31,360	
Less: *Current liabilities*		
Creditors	7,200	
Net current assets		24,160
Total assets less current liabilities		59,660
Less: *Long term liabilities*		
Loan from S. Rodd		10,000
Net assets		49,660
Capital		
Balance at 1 April 19X9		42,140
Add: Profit for year		21,120
		63,260
Less: Drawings		13,600
Balance at 31 March 19X0		49,660

Exercises

1. (a) Explain the purpose of a profit and loss account and a balance sheet.
    (b) Describe the structure of each.

2. Explain the relevance of stocks of goods for resale in the determination of the gross profit.

3. Explain each of the entries in the following stock account:

Stock

Trading account	4,600	Trading account	4,600
Trading account	6,300		

4. The following is the trial balance of R. Woods at 30 September 19X6:

	Debit	Credit
	£	£
Stock 1 October 19X5	2,368	
Purchases	12,389	
Sales		18,922
Salaries and wages	3,862	
Rent and rates	504	
Insurance	78	
Motor expenses	664	
Printing and stationery	216	
Light and heat	166	
General expenses	314	

Premises	5,000	
Motor vehicles	1,800	
Fixtures and fittings	350	
Debtors	3,896	
Creditors		1,731
Cash at bank	482	
Drawings	1,200	
Capital		12,636
	33,289	33,289

The stock at 30 September 19X6 is valued at £2,946.

You are required to prepare a trading and profit and loss account for the year ended 30 September 19X6 and a balance sheet at that date.

5.   On 31 December 19X3, the trial balance of Joytoys showed the following accounts and balances:

	Debit £	Credit £
Bank	500	
Capital		75,000
Bank loan		22,000
Inventory	12,000	
Purchases	108,000	
Sales		167,000
Rent, rates and insurance	15,000	
Plant and machinery at cost	70,000	
Office furniture and fittings at cost	24,000	
Discount allowed	1,600	
Bank interest	400	
Discount received		3,000
Wages and salaries	13,000	
Light and heat	9,000	
Drawings	10,000	
Returns outwards		4,000
Returns inwards	1,000	
Creditors		16,000
Debtors	22,500	
	£287,000	£287,000

You are given the following information:

1.   The inventory at 31 December 19X3 was valued at £19,500.
2.   The bank loan is repayable in 5 years' time.

You are required to prepare a trading and profit and loss account for the year ended 31 December 19X3, and a balance sheet at that date.

6.   The following is the trial balance of A. Evans as at 30 June 19X2.

	Debit £	Credit £
Capital		39,980
Drawings	14,760	
Loan—Solihull Bank		20,000
Leasehold premises	52,500	
Motor vehicles	13,650	
Investments	4,980	
Trade debtors	2,630	

	Debit	Credit
Trade creditors		1,910
Cash	460	
Bank overdraft		3,620
Sales		81,640
Purchases	49,870	
Returns outwards		960
Returns inwards	840	
Carriage	390	
Stock	5,610	
Rent and rates	1,420	
Light and heat	710	
Telephone and postage	540	
Printing and stationery	230	
Bank interest	140	
Interest received		620
	148,730	148,730

You are given the following additional information:

1. The stock at 30 June 19X2 has been valued at £4,920.
2. The bank loan is repayable on 1 June 19X5. *You are required to* prepare a trading and profit and loss account for the year ended 30 June 19X2 and a balance sheet as at that date.

7. The following is the trial balance of J. Peters as at 30 September 19X0.

	Debit	Credit
	£	£
Capital		32,890
Drawings	5,200	
Loan from A. Drew		10,000
Cash	510	
Bank overdraft		1,720
Sales		45,600
Purchases	29,300	
Returns inwards	3,800	
Returns outwards		2,700
Carriage inwards	960	
Carriage outwards	820	
Trade debtors	7,390	
Trade creditors		4,620
Land and buildings	26,000	
Plant and machinery	13,500	
Listed investments	4,800	
Interest paid	1,200	
Interest received		450
Rent received		630
Stock	3,720	
Repairs to buildings	810	
Plant hire charges	360	
Bank charges	240	
	98,610	98,610

Further information:

1. The stock at 30 September 19X0 was valued at £4,580.
2. The loan from A. Drew is repayable on 1 January 19X7.

You are required to prepare a trading and profit and loss account for the year ended 30 September 19X0 and a balance sheet at that date.

10. Accounting concepts, principles and conventions

An appreciation of the conceptual/theoretical foundations of financial accounting is fundamental to the understanding and interpretation of final accounts. This can be described as a set of rules, principles, postulates, conventions and methods. However, to avoid confusion, in 1971 the Accounting Standard Steering Committee (ASSC or ASC) issued Statement of Standard Accounting Practice No 2—Disclosure or Accounting Policies (SSAP2) which describes the conceptual foundations of accounting as comprising accounting concepts, accounting bases and accounting policies. These are discussed below.

Accounting concepts, bases and policies

The measurement of profit and the valuation of assets and liabilities involves a number of accounting concepts. These are defined in SSAP2 as 'broad basic assumptions which underlie the periodic financial accounts of business enterprises'.[1]

However, accounting concepts do not in themselves provide sufficient guidance as to how they should be applied. This requires the specification of accounting bases. These are defined in SSAP2 as 'the methods which have been developed for expressing or applying fundamental accounting concepts to financial transactions and items'.[1]

There are several different accounting bases which could be applied to a particular item or transaction. For example, should tools be treated as an expense or an asset? Each company has to choose that basis which is most appropriate in the circumstances. These are referred to as accounting policies, and are defined in SSAP2 as 'the specific accounting bases judged by business enterprises to be most appropriate to their circumstances and adopted by them for the purpose of preparing their financial accounts'.[1]

Various accounting bases and policies will be discussed in depth in subsequent chapters. This chapter examines the nature of certain accounting concepts and their implication for the preparation of final accounts.

Accounting concepts in SSAP2

There are a considerable number of accounting concepts, some of which were referred to earlier (see Chapter 2) such as the accounting/business entity concept, money/unit of measurement concept, etc. However, SSAP2 identifies what is described as four fundamental accounting concepts. These are explained below.

The going concern/continuity concept

The going concern concept refers to the assumption that an 'enterprise will continue in operational existence for the foreseeable future'. The implication of this is that assets will be valued at their historic cost and shown in the balance sheet at this value. It is assumed that the business will continue to operate over the remaining useful life of the assets. Similarly, monetary assets and liabilities, such as debtors and creditors, are shown in the balance sheet at the amount that will be received and paid in the ordinary course of business. However, if there is reason to believe that the entity will not be able to continue in business, the assets should be valued on a cessation basis. That is, at their net realizable value.

The consistency/comparability concept

The consistency concept dictates that there should be 'consistency of accounting treatment of like items within each accounting period and from one period to the next'.[1] For example, if certain types of tools and equipment are treated as fixed assets, then similar tools and equipment should be treated in the same way. Furthermore, the tools and equipment should also be treated as a fixed asset in subsequent years.

The purpose of this is to limit the possibility of misrepresentation, and to ensure that meaningful comparisons can be made between the results of different accounting periods. Judgements about a firm's performance and financial position depend to a large extent on the validity of comparisons. It is therefore essential that items and transactions of the same type are accounted for in the same way.

The accruals concept and the matching principle

According to SSAP2, under the accruals concept 'revenue and costs are accrued (that is, recognized as they are earned or incurred, not as money is received or paid), matched with one another so far as their relationship can be established or justifiably assumed, and dealt with in the profit & loss account of the period to which they relate'.[1]

The accruals concept is usually taken to include the matching principle. However, it can be argued that these are two separate assumptions. This is probably a useful premise for the purpose of the following explanation.

The matching principle is fundamental to the determination/identification of the point in time at which profits are deemed to occur. There is no natural or common-sense law about this. It is a convention which is generally accepted in accounting. The matching principle refers to the assumption that the cost of an item should be set against the revenue which it generates at the point in time when this arises. A classic example of the application of the matching principle is stock. Where goods are bought in one year but sold in the next, their cost is carried forward as goods in stock and set against the proceeds of sale in the year in which it occurs. This is expounded in SSAP9—Stocks and Long Term Contracts[3] as follows:

> The determination of profit for an accounting year requires the matching of costs with related revenues. (When costs) have been incurred in the expectation of future revenue, and when this will not arise until a later year it is appropriate to carry forward this cost to be matched with the revenue when it arises; the applicable concept is the matching of cost and revenue in the year in which the revenue arises rather than in the year in which the cost is incurred.

In terms of the calculation of the gross profit in the trading account, this process of carrying forward costs takes the form of the computation of the cost of sales. The cost is carried forward by being deducted from purchases in the form of the stock at the end of the year. It is brought forward to the following year in the form of the opening stock which is matched against the proceeds of sale by virtue of its being included in the cost of sales.

A more theoretical view of the matching principle is that it refers to ascertaining profit on the basis of a cause and effect relationship. Costs cause or give rise to certain effects which take the form of revenue. Matching is thus the determination of profit by attributing specific causes to particular effects at the point in time at which the effects occur.

The accruals concept may be further subdivided into the realization concept, accrued costs and prepayments. The realization or revenue recognition concept refers to the assumption that a sale is deemed to have taken place at that point in time at which the goods are delivered or services provided and not when the proceeds of sale are received. In practice this is normally taken to be the date on which the invoice is rendered. This is referred to in the above SSAP2 definition of the accruals concept as being the point in time at which revenue is 'earned'.

The accrued costs concept refers to the assumption that costs should be recognized as arising when they are incurred, and not as money is paid. That is, goods and services are deemed to have been purchased on the date they are received. This is referred to in the above SSAP2 definition of the accruals concept as being the point in time at which costs are 'incurred'. Thus services consumed for which no invoice has been received at the end of an accounting year (e.g. electricity, gas, telephone) are treated as a cost for that year, and the amount due as a liability.

Prepayments relate to services paid for in advance (e.g. rent, water rates, insurance, road tax) which have not been received at the end of an accounting year. These are treated as a cost of the following year and thus carried forward as an asset at the end of the current year. Accrued costs and prepayments are dealt with in depth in a later chapter.

The accruals concept and matching principle can be illustrated vividly by a simplified example. Suppose a business only had the following transactions:

15 Jan   purchased goods costing £100 on credit
15 Feb   paid for the goods purchased on 15 January
15 Mar   sold on credit for £150 the goods purchased on 15 January
15 Apr   received payment for the goods sold on 15 March

The accruals (and matching) concept dictates that:

1.   The cost of the goods was *incurred* in January
2.   The sales revenue was *earned* in March
3.   There is no profit or loss in January, February or April. The profit of £50 arose in March; the cost of the goods being carried forward as stock at the end of January and February.

The prudence/conservatism concept

The prudence concept is said to require that 'revenue and profits are not anticipated, but are recognised by inclusion in the profit and loss account only when realised in the form either of cash or of other assets the ultimate cash realisation of which can be assessed with reasonable certainty; provision is made for all known liabilities (expenses and losses) whether the amount of these is known with certainty or is a best estimate in the light of the information available'.[1]

It should be emphasized that the first part of this definition does not mean that sales revenue should only be recognized when the proceeds of sale are received in cash. The reference to 'other assets the ultimate cash realisation of which can be assessed with reasonable certainty' relates to debtors. Thus the prudence concept dictates that sales revenue should only be recognized in the profit and loss account if debtors are likely to pay their debts. This highlights an example of the application of the prudence concept which takes the form of a provision for bad debts. If it is anticipated that some debtors will default, the amount of this potential loss should be provided for in the profit and loss account and valuation of debtors in the balance sheet. Provisions for bad debts are examined in depth in Chapter 12.

Another example of the application of the prudence concept is the valuation of stock and work in progress at the lower of cost or net realizable value. Where the market or resale value of goods in stock has fallen below its cost, the amount of this reduction is taken into the trading account as a loss even though the goods have not been sold and the loss is as yet unrealized. In contrast, unrealized holding gains, such as an increase in the market value of buildings or investments are not recorded in the profit and loss account until the asset is sold.

A somewhat simpler but less valid description of the prudence concept is that it refers to the belief that it is better to report the lowest of the possible values of revenue and assets, and the highest of the possible values of costs and liabilities.

However, neither of the above explanations of the prudence concept make reference to what is probably its most contentious application, namely the decision whether to treat expenditure (such as advertising, research and development expenditure etc.) as an expense in the year it is incurred or as a fixed asset to be carried forward and set against future revenue in the form of depreciation. The prudence concept dictates that if the resulting future revenue cannot be assessed with reasonable certainty the expenditure should be treated as a cost in the profit and loss account of the year in which it is incurred (e.g. research expenditure). The criterion used in applying the prudence concept thus concerns whether future revenue can be 'assessed with reasonable certainty'. This refers to whether it is possible to estimate reasonably accurately each of the future years' revenue that will be generated as a result of the expenditure in question (e.g. advertising expenditure).

There are three main arguments which are usually cited as justifications for the prudence concept. First, it is necessary to compensate for the frequent over-optimism of managers in financial reporting. Second, overstating profits is potentially disastrous because it can lead to a reduction of capital. Third, it is the only practical way of dealing with uncertainty about potential revenues, costs, asset values and liabilities.

The prudence concept may be inconsistent with certain other accounting concepts. It is argued that the prudence concept conflicts with the consistency concept and results in a lack of comparability because there can be no uniform standards in its application. Furthermore, the prudence concept may conflict with the going concern concept. Taken to its extreme the prudence concept may be interpreted to mean that all assets ought to be valued at their lowest possible value; that is, at their net realizable value. However, the going concern concept dictates that assets should be shown in final accounts at their historic cost.

The prudence concept is also said to be inconsistent with the matching principle. This requires that certain costs such as development expenditure should be carried forward to future years as a fixed asset and matched with the sales revenue generated by this expenditure. However, the prudence concept dictates that if future revenues are difficult to predict accurately, costs such as development expenditure should be written off to the profit and loss account in the year in which they are incurred. SSAP2 states that where the matching principle/accruals concept is 'inconsistent with the prudence concept, the latter prevails'.[1]

Other accounting concepts and conventions

There are several other accounting concepts which are not contained in SSAP2. The most commonly cited are explained below.

Objectivity

The term objectivity implies that the information contained in final accounts should be objective and not subjective. This is a gross oversimplification in that much of the information in final accounts requires a subjective judgement by the preparer. For example, is advertising or development expenditure to be treated as an expense or a fixed asset; what is the net realizable value of stocks; which debtors may turn out to be bad debts, etc?

This is probably the reason why many pronouncements by professional accountancy bodies and other authors often refer to objectivity using another phrase. For example, the International Accounting Standard Committee (IASC) describes this as 'faithful representation' and 'neutrality'. Objectivity is also often commonly taken to include verifiability and freedom from prejudice or bias. One way of defining objectivity is thus as referring to the assumption that final accounts should be verifiable and neutral.

Verifiability has traditionally been interpreted to mean that there should be documentary evidence to support the items in the final accounts. Usually this takes the form of sales and purchases invoices, credit notes, invoices in respect of expenses and the purchase of fixed assets, bank statements etc. However, not all items in the final accounts are based on documentary evidence. Sometimes estimates (e.g. of bad debts and the net realizable value of stocks) have to be made. In this case the assumptions, available evidence and basis of measurement should be open to inspection and verification.

Neutrality is often linked with the idea that final accounts should be accurate, precise and unbiased. According to *The corporate report*, 'the information presented (in final accounts) should be objective or unbiased in that it should meet all proper user needs and neutral in that the perception of the measurer should not be biased towards the interest of any one user group'.[1] Similarly the IASC defines neutrality by arguing that 'financial statements are not neutral, if, by the selection or presentation of information, they influence the making of a decision or judgement in order to achieve a predetermined result or outcome'.[4]

It should be noted that objectivity must incorporate both verifiability and neutrality because, while an item in the final accounts may be based on verifiable documentary evidence, selection of the evidence could be biased. For example, it could be deliberately intended to over or understate profits and/or the value of assets. Conversely, an item which may be regarded as a legitimate asset should not be included in the final accounts because its measurement/valuation is too subjective and thus unverifiable (e.g. fixed assets for which there is not a well developed or readily available market).

The objectivity concept is obviously applied throughout the preparation of final accounts. However, there are a few contentious applications, mostly relating to certain types of intangible fixed assets known as non-purchased goodwill and brandnames. It is argued by the ASC that these should not be included on the balance sheet since their value cannot be determined objectively.

Finally, it is sometimes argued that there is an inconsistency between the objectivity and prudence concepts. The former demands freedom from the bias of interested parties whereas the latter is said to be a deliberate attempt to introduce bias in the form of understating profits and the value of net assets. However, this may be a misinterpretation of the concept of neutrality, which refers to not selecting measures that favour a particular group of users or give a predetermined outcome.

Materiality

The materiality concept provides guidance as to how a transaction or item of information should be classified in the final accounts and/or whether it should be disclosed separately rather than being aggregated with other similar items. This depends on whether the item is of a significant amount, relative to the size of the business. Whether or not a transaction or item is material or significant is generally taken to be a matter of professional judgement. In practice this is usually regarded as dependent on how large the amount is in relation to a business's total sales, the value of its assets, or other items of the same type. However, sometimes an item is taken as not being material simply because the absolute amount is small.

A common application of the materiality concept concerns whether an item of expenditure is to be regarded as a fixed asset. Where the amount is not material, the item would be treated as an expense even though it is expected to have a useful life of more than one accounting year and thus normally regarded as a fixed asset (e.g. relatively inexpensive tools and items of office equipment, fixtures and fittings, etc.)

Another common application of the materiality concept relates to the separate disclosure of certain items in final accounts. There are numerous references to materiality in the Companies Acts and Statements of Standard Accounting Practice which require the separate disclosure of items such as plant hire charges, rents receivable etc. where the amounts are material.

A related, but slightly different, way of explaining the materiality concept is in terms of the degree of aggregation of data in final accounts. The users of final accounts are unable to assimilate large amounts of detailed information. This necessitates considerable aggregation of data. The materiality concept provides guidance on what transactions are to be aggregated by virtue of it specifying which items should be disclosed separately.

Finally, another interpretation of the materiality concept concerns whether the disclosure of certain items is likely to influence decisions made by the users of final accounts. One criterion which can be used to decide if an item is material is whether or not it may be expected to influence the judgements, decisions or actions of users of final accounts. If this is expected to occur, then the item is said to be material and should be disclosed separately from other similar items. This interpretation of the materiality concept is found in the IASC definition of materiality as follows:

Information is material if its ommission or misstatement could influence the economic decisions of users taken on the basis of the financial statements. Materiality depends on the size of the item or error judged in the particular circumstances of its omission or misstatement. Thus, materiality provides a threshold or cut-off point rather than being a primary qualitative characteristic which information must have if it is to be useful.[4]

References

1.   Accounting Standards Steering Committee (1971). *Statement of Standard Accounting Practice 2—Disclosure of Accounting Policies* (ICAEW).
2.   *Accounting Standards Steering Committee (1975). The Corporate Report* (ICAEW).
3.   *Accounting Standards Steering Committee (1988). Statement of Standard Accounting Practice 9—Stocks and Long Term Contracts* (ICAEW).
4.   International Accounting Standards Committee (1989). *Framework for the Preparation and Presentation of Financial Statements* (IASC).

Exercises

1.   Explain the difference and interrelationship between accounting concepts, accounting bases and accounting policies.

2.   Explain each of the following accounting concepts including their implication for the preparation of final accounts:

     (a)   going concern
     (b)   consistency
     (c)   realization/revenue recognition.

3.   Explain fully the accruals concept and the matching principle. Give examples of its application in final accounts.

4.   Explain fully the prudence concept. Give examples of its application in final accounts.

5.   Discuss the assertion that the prudence concept is inconsistent with other accounting concepts and the matching principle.

6.   Explain each of the following accounting concepts including their implications for the preparation of final accounts:

     (a)   objectivity
     (b)   materiality

7.   An acquaintance of yours, H. Gee, has recently set up in business for the first time as a general dealer. The majority of his sales will be on credit to trade buyers but he will sell some goods to the public for cash. He is not sure at which point of the business cycle he can regard his cash and credit sales to have taken place.
     After seeking guidance on this matter from his friends, he is thoroughly confused by the conflicting advice he has received. Samples of the advice he has been given include:

     The sale takes place when:

     1.   you have bought goods which you know you should be able to sell easily
     2.   the customer places the order
     3.   you deliver the goods to the customer
     4.   you invoice the goods to the customer
     5.   the customer pays for the goods
     6.   the customer's cheque has been cleared by the bank.

     He now asks you to clarify the position for him.

     Required:

     (a)   Write notes for Gee, setting out, in as easily understood a manner as possible, the accounting conventions and principles which should generally be followed when recognizing sales revenue.
     (b)   Examine each of the statements 1–6 above and advise. Gee (stating your reasons) whether the method advocated is appropriate to the particular circumstances of his business.   (CACA)

8. 'If a business invests in shares, and the market value of the shares increases above cost then, until and unless the business sells them, no profit is made. If the business invests in stock for resale, and the market value of the stock falls below cost then the loss is recognized even though no sale has taken place'.

   'If a business undertakes an intensive advertising campaign which will probably result in increased sales (and profit) in succeeding years it will nevertheless usually write off the cost of the campaign in the year in which it is incurred'.

   Required:

   Explain the reasoning behind the application of accounting principles in situations such as these and discuss the effect on the usefulness of accounting information in relation to users' needs. (CACA)

9. On 20 December 19X7 your client paid £10,000 for an advertising campaign. The advertisements will be heard on local radio stations between 1 January and 31 January 19X8. Your client believes that as a result sales will increase by 60 per cent in 19X8 (over 19X7 levels) and by 40 per cent in 19X9 (over 19X7 levels). There will be no further benefits.

   Required:

   Write a memorandum to your client explaining your views on how this item should be treated in the accounts for the three years 19X7 to 19X9. Your answer should include explicit reference to at least *three* relevant traditional accounting conventions, and to the requirements of *two* classes of user of published financial accounts. (CACA)

10. One of your clients is a beef farmer. She informs you that the price of beef has fallen dramatically over the last few months and that she expects it to fall even further over the next three months. She therefore argues that the prudence concept should be applied to the valuation of her beef herd at the lower of cost or net realizable value; in this case at the latter value. She further asserts that this treatment is reasonable on the grounds that it will reduce her profit for tax purposes by the loss in value of her herd.

    One of your colleagues has advised you that this may be a misinterpretation of the prudence concept and could contravene the objectivity concept. Discuss.

11. One of your clients owns a garage and car sales business. He intends to bring into the business a veteran car which he inherited from his father. This will be kept in the car showroom and used in marketing and promotion. It will not be offered for sale.

    There is no well-developed or readily available market for this car but your client wants to bring it into the books as a fixed asset valued at £50,000 along with the other motor vehicles. You suspect that part of the motive for this to boost the value of assets on the balance sheet in order to obtain a loan from the bank.

    You are required to discuss whether including this in the final accounts is a contravention of the objectivity concept.

12. One of your clients has observed that in the final accounts you treat items of office equipment with a useful life of more than one year as expenses where they are relatively inexpensive whereas when they cost considerably more these are shown as fixed assets. She claims that this is a breach of the consistency concept and the matching principle.

    You are required to explain the justification for this apparent inconsistency in the treatment of office equipment and briefly discuss the assertion that is contradicts the consistency concept and the matching principle.

13. One of your clients is a building contractor who has asked you to prepare a set of final accounts which he intends to submit to his bank in support of an application for a loan to purchase some plant and machinery. He has noticed that you included in the profit and loss account an amount of £15,000 in respect of plant hire charges as a separate item from the costs of operating plant and machinery which amount to £20,000. Your client has suggested to you that these two items should be aggregated on the grounds of consistency.

    You are required to explain the justification for showing these two items separately.

11. Depreciation and fixed assets

The nature and types of fixed assets

Fixed assets are items not specifically bought for resale but to be used in the production or distribution of those goods normally sold by the business. They are durable goods that usually last for several years, and are normally kept by a business for more than one accounting year. However, as discussed in the previous chapter, expenditure on such items is only regarded as a fixed asset if it is of a material amount, as defined by the materiality concept. The Accounting Standards Committee (ASC) defines a fixed asset as 'an asset that: (a) is held by an enterprise for use in the production or supply of goods and services, for rental to others or for administrative purposes and may include items held for the maintenance or repair of such assets; and (b) has been acquired or constructed with the intention of being used on a continuing basis; and (c) is not intended for sale in the ordinary course of business'.

Money spent on fixed assets is referred to as capital expenditure. All other costs and expenses are referred to as revenue expenditure. The latter are entered in the profit and loss account of the year in which the costs are incurred.

Examples of tangible fixed assets include land and buildings; plant and machinery; motor vehicles; furniture, fixtures and fittings; office equipment (such as typewriters); and loose tools. Tools that are only expected to last for less than one year are referred to as consumable tools, and treated as revenue expenditure.

Fixed assets are classified as either tangible or intangible. An intangible fixed asset is defined by the ASC as 'a fixed asset that is non-monetary in nature and without physical substance'. Examples include goodwill, patents, brand names, trademarks and development costs. Goodwill usually arises in the balance sheet because at some time in the past the business has taken over, or been formed from, another business. The figure shown in the balance sheet for goodwill is the difference between the amount paid for that business and the value of its net assets. Goodwill is sometimes said to represent the potential future profits or sales arising from a business's reputation, location and existing customers. However, it is much more than this, in that it represents the advantages which are gained from taking over an existing business rather than building up a new business from scratch (e.g. not having to recruit staff, find premises, identify suppliers etc.). Goodwill is discussed in depth in Chapter 25.

Investments are also frequently included under the heading of fixed assets. These may consist of shares and/or debentures that are listed (quoted) on a stock exchange and unlisted securities. Investments should only be classified as a fixed asset where they are held on a long-term basis for the purpose of generating income. If this is not the case, investments should be treated as a current asset.

The valuation of fixed assets

The term 'valuation' refers to the amount at which assets are shown in the balance sheet. In historical cost accounting fixed assets are valued at their historic cost less the aggregate depreciation from the date of acquisition to the date of the balance sheet. The resulting figure is known as the written down value (WDV) or net book value. Depreciation is discussed below. Historic cost refers to the purchase price excluding value added tax. The historic cost of a fixed asset may also include a number of additional costs. The cost of land and buildings, for example, may include legal expenses, and the cost of any subsequent extensions and improvements (but not repairs and renewals). Similarly, the cost of machinery is taken to include delivery and installation charges. On the other hand, the cost of vehicles must exclude the first year's road tax and fuel where these have been included in the purchase price.

The nature of depreciation

The purchase of a fixed asset occurs in one year but the revenue generated from its use normally arises over a number of future years. This is referred to as its useful economic life. If the cost of fixed assets were treated as an expense in the profit and loss acount in the year of purchase this would probably result in an excessive loss in that year, and excessive profits in the years in which the revenue arose. This gives a misleading view of the profits and losses of each year and distorts comparisons over time. Thus the cost of a fixed asset is not treated as an expense in the year of purchase but rather carried forward and written off to the profit and loss account over the useful economic life of the asset in the form of depreciation. This is an application of the matching principle. According to the matching principle, that part of the cost of an asset which is 'used up' or 'consumed' in each year of the asset's useful economic life must be set against the revenue that this generates (in conjunction with other factors of production). That part of the cost of a fixed asset which is 'used up' or 'consumed' during an accounting period is referred to as depreciation. Thus depreciation may be defined as the allocation of the cost of a fixed asset over the accounting periods that comprise its useful economic life to the business according to some criterion regarding the amount which is 'used up' or 'consumed' in each of these periods.

SSAP12 defines depreciation as 'the measure of the wearing out, consumption or other reduction in the useful economic life of a fixed asset whether arising from use, effluxion of time or obsolescence through technological or market changes.[1] Obsolescence through technological change refers to where a new model of the asset which is significantly more efficient or performs additional functions comes onto the market. Obsolescence through market changes occurs when there is a substantial reduction in demand for the firm's product because of, for example, technological advances in competitors' products. Both of these causes of obsolescence usually result in a sudden relatively large decrease in value of the asset, particularly where it cannot be used for any other purpose.

Another common way of defining depreciation is that it refers to the permanent decrease in value of a fixed asset during a given accounting period. The Companies Act states that 'provisions for diminution in value shall be made in respect of any fixed asset which has diminished in value if the reduction in its value is expected to be permanent'. This conceptualization of depreciation leaves unanswered the question of what is meant by 'value'. Furthermore, many accountants would probably deny that the amount of depreciation shown in final accounts is a reflection of the loss in value of a fixed asset. They argue that accountants are not valuers, and that depreciation is simply the allocation of the cost of a fixed asset over its useful economic life to the business. There is no simple reconciliation of this schizophrenia which is said to arise from the dual purpose of depreciation as a means of measuring profit and valuing assets.

Depreciation can also be viewed as a provision for the replacement of fixed assets. The annual charge for depreciation in the profit and loss account represents a setting aside of some of the income so that over the useful life of the asset sufficient 'funds' are retained in the business to replace the asset.

However, it must be emphasized that no money is usually specifically set aside. Thus, when the time comes to replace the asset, the money needed to do so will not automatically be available. Furthermore, where depreciation is based on the historic cost of the asset the amount of funds set aside will be insufficient to provide for any increase in the replacement cost of the asset. This is discussed further in Chapter 33.

Finally, it should be noted that SSAP12 requires all tangible fixed assets except land and investments to be depreciated. This includes depreciating buildings. The reason is that although the market value of buildings at any point in time may exceed their historic cost, they nevertheless have a finite life and thus should be depreciated over their useful economic life.

Methods and bases of depreciation

A number of different methods have been developed for measuring depreciation each of which will give a different annual charge to the profit and loss account. There is no one method of depreciation that is superior to all others in all circumstances. The most appropriate method will depend on the type of asset and the extent to which it is used in each period:[1]

> There is a range of acceptable depreciation methods. Management should select the method regarded as most appropriate to the type of asset and its use in the business so as to allocate depreciation as fairly as possible to the periods expected to benefit from the asset's use.

The method/basis of depreciation that is chosen is referred to as one of the business's accounting policies, and should be applied consistently each year.

Whichever method is used to calculate depreciation, at least three data relating to the asset in question are needed: (1) the historic cost; (2) the length of the asset's expected useful economic life to the business; and (3) the estimated residual value of the asset at the end of its useful economic life. The useful life of an asset refers to the period which the business regards as being the most economical length of time to keep the particular asset. This will depend on a number of factors, such as the pattern of repair costs etc. The useful life of an asset may well be considerably shorter than its total life. Residual value refers to the estimated proceeds of sale at the end of the asset's useful life to the business. This is usually considerably more than its scrap value. It should be noted that both the useful life and the residual value have to be estimated when the asset is purchased.

The two most common methods of depreciation are the straight line and reducing balance methods. These are described below.

The straight line/fixed instalment method

Under this method the annual amount of depreciation which will be charged to the profit and loss account is computed as follows:

$$\frac{\text{Cost} - \text{Estimated residual value}}{\text{Estimated useful life in years}}$$

However, in practice, and in examination questions, the rate of depreciation is usually expressed as a percentage. The annual amount of depreciation is then calculated by applying the percentage to the cost of the asset.

This method gives the same charge for depreciation in each year of the asset's useful life. It is therefore most appropriate for assets which are depleted as a result of the passage of time (e.g. building, patents and trademarks). The method may also be suitable where the utilization of an asset is the same in each year.

The diminishing/reducing balance method

Under this method it is necessary to first compute the rate of depreciation as a percentage as follows:

$$100 - 100 \times \left(\frac{\text{Residual value}}{\text{Cost}} \right)^{\frac{1}{el}}$$

where el refers to the estimated useful life.

The annual amount of depreciation which will be charged to the profit and loss account is then computed thus:

$$\text{Rate of depreciation} \times \text{Written down value of asset}$$
$$\text{(at start of year)}$$

The written down value (WDV) of the asset refers to its cost less the aggregate depreciation of the asset since the date of acquisition. This method thus gives a decreasing annual charge for depreciation over the useful life of the asset. It is therefore most appropriate for fixed assets that deteriorate primarily as a result of usage where this is greater in the earlier years of their life (e.g. plant and machinery, motor vehicles, furniture and fittings, office equipment). However, this method may also be suitable even if the utilization is the same in each year. The logic behind this apparently inconsistent assertion involves taking into consideration the pattern of repair costs. These will be low in the earlier years of the asset's life and high in later years. Thus the decreasing annual amount of depreciation combined with the increasing repair costs will give a relatively constant combined annual charge in each year of the assets useful life which is said to reflect the constant annual usage.

The reducing balance method is also said to be a more realistic measure of the reduction in the market value of fixed assets, since this is likely to be greater in the earlier years of the asset's life than later years. However, it is highly questionable whether the written down value of a fixed asset is intended to be a reflection of its market value. A numerical example of the above methods of depreciation is given in Example 11.1.

Accounting for depreciation

The accounting entries in respect of the annual charge for depreciation are made after the trial balance has been extracted when the profit and loss account is being prepared. These consist of the following:

Debit   Depreciation expense account
Credit   Provision for depreciation account

The depreciation expense account is closed to profit and loss, i.e.

Debit   Profit and loss account
Credit   Depreciation expense account

The effect is to accummulate the provision while making a charge against profit and loss each year.

Example 11.1

D. McDonald has an accounting year ending on 31 December. On 1 January 19X1 he purchased a machine for £1,000 which has an expected useful life of three years and an estimated residual value of £343.

You are required to:

(a)   Calculate the amount of depreciation in each year of the asset's useful life using: (i) the straight line method; and (ii) the reducing balance method.
(b)   Show the journal and ledger entries relating to the purchase and the provision for depreciation in each year (using the amounts calculated from the straight line method).
(c)   Show the relevant entries on the balance sheet for 19X2 (using the amounts calculated from the straight line method).

(a)   The calculation of depreciation
(i)   The straight line method:

$$\text{Annual depreciation} = \frac{£1,000 - £343}{3} = £219 \text{ per annum}$$

(ii)   The reducing balance method:

$$\text{Rate} = 100 - \left[\left(\frac{343}{1,000} \right)^{1/3} \times 100 \right] = 100 - (\tfrac{7}{10} \times 100) = 30 \text{ per cent}$$

The annual amount of depreciation is calculated by applying this rate to the cost of the asset minus the aggregate depreciation of previous years (i.e. the written down value at the start of each year) as follows:

For 19X1:   30 per cent of £1,000 = £300
For 19X2:   30 per cent of (£1,000 − 300) = £210
For 19X3:   30 per cent of [£1,000 − (£300 + £210)] = £147

(b)   The ledger entries

Plant and machinery

19X1		
1 Jan	Bank	1,000

*Provision for depreciation on
plant and machinery*

19X1			19X1		
31 Dec	Balance c/d	219	31 Dec	Depreciation expense account	219
19X2			19X2		
31 Dec	Balance c/d	438	1 Jan	Balance b/d	219
			31 Dec	Depreciation expense account	219
		438			438
19X3			19X3		
31 Dec	Balance c/d	657	1 Jan	Balance c/d	438
			31 Dec	Depreciation expense account	219
		657			657
			19X4		
			1 Jan	Balance b/d	657

Depreciation expense account

19X1	Depreciation on plant	219		Profit and loss account	219
19X2	Depreciation on plant	219		Profit and loss account	219
19X3	Depreciation on plant	219		Profit and loss account	219

(c)   The journal entries

19X1
31 Dec	Depreciation on account	Dr	219	
	To provision for depreciation account			219

Being the charge for depreciation on
plant for 19X1

31 Dec	Profit and loss account	Dr	219	
	Depreciation expense			219

Being the entry to close off the depreciation
expense account at the year end

The entries for 19X2 and 19X3 would be exactly the same.

(d)   The balance sheet at 31 December 19X2 would appear as follows:

Fixed assets	Cost	Aggregate depreciation	WDV
Plant and machinery	1,000	438	562

Notes

1.   The entries on the balance sheet comprise the balance on the fixed asset account at the end of the year and the balance on the provision for depreciation account at the end of the year. The latter is referred to as the aggregate depreciation and is deducted from the historic cost to give the WDV, which is the only one of these three figures that enter into the computation of the total of the balance sheet.

Profits and losses on the disposal of fixed assets

Almost without exception, when an asset is sold at the end of (or during) its useful life the proceeds of sale differ from the estimated residual value (or written down book value if sold during its useful life). Where the proceeds are less than the written down value, this is referred to as a loss on sale. Where the proceeds are greater than the written down value this is referred to as a profit on sale. This can be illustrated using Example 11.1. Suppose the asset was sold on 31 December 19X3 for £400. The written down value is the difference between the cost of the asset and the aggregate depreciation up to the date of disposal. That is, £1,000 − £657 = £343. The profit (or loss) on sale is the difference between the proceeds of sale and the written down value of the asset. There is thus a profit on sale of £400 − £343 = £57.

The disposal of fixed assets and the resulting profit or loss on sale must be recorded in the ledger. The procedure is as follows:

1. Credit the proceeds of sale to the fixed asset account.
2. Transfer the aggregate depreciation up to the date of disposal from the provision for depreciation account to the fixed asset account.
3. A loss on sale should then be credited in the fixed asset account and debited to the profit and loss account. A profit on sale would be debited to the asset account and credited to the profit and loss account.

The effect of these entries is to eliminate the original cost of the asset from the fixed asset account. This is illustrated below using Example 11.1 and the additional data above.

The ledger entries

Provision for depreciation

19X3			19X3			
31 Dec	Plant and machinery	657	31 Dec	Balance	b/d	657

Plant and machinery

19X1			19X3		
1 Jan	Bank—purchase	1,000	31 Dec	Bank—proceeds of sale	400
			31 Dec	Provision for depreciation	657
19X3					
31 Dec	Profit and loss a/c —profit on sale	57	31 Dec	Profit and loss a/c (any loss on sale)	—
		1,057			1,057

Profit and loss account

Loss on sale of fixed assets	—	Profit on sale of plant and machinery	57

Before the above entries are made in the ledger the following journal entries are necessary:

The journal entries

19X3					
31 Dec	Provision for depreciation	Dr	657		
	To plant and machinery			657	
	Being the aggregate depreciation at the date of sale of the asset				

19X3					
31 Dec	Plant and machinery	Dr	57		
	To profit and loss account			57	
	Being the profit on sale of plant				

The depreciation charge on an asset in the years of acquisition and disposal

The previous example dealt with the highly unlikely situation of an asset being purchased and sold on the first and last day of an accounting year respectively. In practice, these transactions could occur on any day of the year. The way in which depreciation would then be computed depends on the usual practice of the business, or in examinations on what you are explicitly or implicitly instructed to do. Unless the question states otherwise, the depreciation must be calculated on a strict time basis for the period the asset is owned. In examination questions, assets tend to be purchased and sold on the first or last day of a calendar month for simplicity of calculation. It can be argued that in practice one should also calculate depreciation on a strict time basis. The charge for depreciation in the year of purchase would be as follows:

$$\frac{\text{Rate of}}{\text{depreciation}} \times \frac{\text{Cost of}}{\text{asset}} \times \frac{\text{Number of months (or days) between the date of purchase and the end of the accounting year in which the asset is purchased}}{12 \text{ (or 365)}}$$

The charge for depreciation in the year of sale would be as follows:

$$\frac{\text{Rate of}}{\text{depreciation}} \times \frac{\text{Cost of asset}}{\text{(or WDV)}} \times \frac{\text{Number of months (or days) between the start of the accounting year in which the asset is sold and the date of sale}}{12 \text{ (or 365)}}$$

In practice, to avoid these tedious calculations, some firms have a policy of charging a full year's depreciation in the year of purchase and none in the year of sale. There is little theoretical justification for this. Also, in examination questions, where the date of purchase or sale is not given, this is usually an indication to adopt this policy.

The accounting entries in respect of depreciation on acquisitions and disposals are illustrated in Example 11.2.

Example 11.2

P. Smith has an accounting year ending on 31 December. At the 31st December 1990 her ledger contained the following accounts:

	£
Motor vehicles	50,000
Provision for depreciation on vehicles	23,000

Vehicles are depreciated using the straight line method at a rate of 20 per cent per annum on a strict time basis.

The following transactions occurred during 1991:

Apr 1   Purchased a van for £5,000.

Aug 31   Sold a vehicle for £4,700. This cost £7,500 when it was bought on 31 July 1989.

Sept 30 Put one car in part exchange for another. The part exchange allowance on the old car was £4,100 and the balance of £3,900 was paid by cheque. The old car cost £10,000 when it was bought on 1 January 1989.

You are required to show the entries in the motor vehicles and provision for depreciation accounts in respect of the above for 1991.

Date of purchase	Details	Total depreciation on disposals	Depreciation charge for year ending 31 Dec 1991
		£	£
	Depreciation on disposals		
31 July 1989	For year ending 31/12/89:		
	20 per cent $\times$ 7,500 $\times$ 5/12	625	
	For year ending 31/12/90:		
	20 per cent $\times$ 7,500	1,500	
31 August 1991	For year ending 31/12/91:		
	20 per cent $\times$ 7,500 $\times$ 8/12	1,000	1,000
		3,125	
	Book value at 31/8/91:		
	7,500 $-$ 3,125 $=$ 4,375		
	Profit on sale:		
	4,700 $-$ 4,375 $=$ 325		
1 Jan 1989	For year ending 31/12/89:		
	20 per cent $\times$ 10,000	2,000	
	For year ending 31/12/90:		
	20 per cent $\times$ 10,000	2,000	
30 Sept 1991	For year ending 31/12/91:		
	20 per cent $\times$ 10,000 $\times$ 9/12	1,500	1,500
		5,500	
	Book value at 30/9/91:		
	10,000 $-$ 5,500 $=$ 4,500		
	Loss on sale		
	4,500 $-$ 4,100 $=$ 400		
	Depreciation on acquisitions		
1 Apr 1991	20 per cent $\times$ 5,000 $\times$ 9/12		750
30 Sept 1991	20 per cent $\times$ (3,900 + 4,100) $\times$ 3/12		400
	Depreciation on remainder		
	20 per cent $\times$ (50,000 $-$ 7,500 $-$ 10,000)		6,500
			10,150

Note

1. The 'depreciation on the remainder' of the plant is calculated on the plant owned at the end of the previous year that was not disposed of during the current year. Those items that were bought and sold during the year having already been depreciated in the previous calculations.

The ledger entries

Motor vehicles

1991			1991		
1 Jan	Balance b/d	50,000	31 Aug	Bank	4,700
1 Apr	Bank	5,000	31 Aug	Provision for depn.	3,125
31 Aug	Profit and loss a/c		30 Sept	Part exchange contra	4,100
	—profit on sale	325	30 Sept	Provision for depn.	5,500
30 Sept	Bank	3,900			
30 Sept	Part exchange		30 Sept	Profit and loss a/c	
	contra	4,100		—loss on sale	400
			31 Dec	Balance c/d	45,500
		63,325			63,325

1992		
1 Jan	Balance b/d	45,500

Provision for depreciation

1991			1991		
31 Aug	Vehicles	3,125	1 Jan	Balance b/d	23,000
30 Sept	Vehicles	5,500	31 Dec	Profit and loss a/c	10,150
31 Dec	Balance c/d	24,525			
		33,150			33,150
			1992		
			1 Jan	Balance b/d	24,525

Notes

1. When one asset is put in part exchange for another, the part exchange allowance is both debited and credited to the asset account and referred to as a contra. The credit entry represents the proceeds of sale of the old asset, and the debit entry represents a part payment for the new asset. The balance which has to be paid for the new asset in cash is debited to the asset account in the normal way. This together with the debit contra represents the total cost of the new asset.

2. The transfer from the provision for depreciation account to the fixed asset account relating to the aggregate depreciation on disposals must include the depreciation on disposals in respect of the current year. This therefore cannot be done until the total depreciation for the year has been ascertained. Thus all the entries in the provision for depreciation account are usually made at the end of the year after the trial balance has been prepared. It is important to note that this also means that any balance on a provision for depreciation account shown in a trial balance must relate to the balance at the end of the previous year.

3. There is another method of accounting for disposals which involves the use of a disposals account. Some examination questions explicitly require the use of a disposals account. Under this method, when a fixed asset is sold the cost of the asset is transferred from the fixed asset account to a fixed asset disposals account. The aggregate depreciation on the asset that has been sold, the proceeds of sale, and the profit or loss on sale are all entered in the disposals account instead of the fixed asset account. The provision for depreciation account contains the same entries whether a disposals account is used or not. The use of a disposals account is illustrated below, taking the information from Example 11.2.

Motor vehicles

1991			1991		
1 Jan	Balance b/d	50,000	31 Aug	Disposals account	7,500
1 Apr	Bank	5,000	31 Aug	Disposals account	10,000
30 Sept	Bank	3,900	31 Dec	Balance c/d	45,500
30 Sept	Disposals account				
	—part exchange	4,100			
		63,000			63,000

1992					
1 Jan	Balance b/d	45,500			

Motor vehicles disposals

1991			1991		
31 Aug	Motor vehicles	7,500	31 Aug	Bank	4,700
31 Aug	Profit and loss a/c		31 Aug	Provision for depn	3,125
	—profit on sale	325	30 Sept	Motor vehicles	
30 Sept	Motor vehicles	10,000		—part exchange	4,100
			30 Sept	Provision for depn	5,500
			30 Sept	Profit and loss a/c	
				—loss on sale	400
		17,825			17,825

There should never be a balance on the disposals account at the end of the year.

Reference

1. Accounting Standards Committee (1987). *Statement of Standard Accounting Practice 12—Accounting for Depreciation* (ICAEW).

Exercises

1. Examine the nature of fixed assets.

2. Explain the difference between capital expenditure and revenue expenditure.

3. What criteria would you use to decide whether expenditure should be classified as relating to a fixed asset?

4. Briefly explain the circumstances in which each of the following would be regarded as a fixed asset: (a) tools; (b) investments; and (c) development costs.

5. What is goodwill and how does it usually arise in a balance sheet?

6. Describe how fixed assets are valued in historical cost accounting.

7. Explain fully the nature of depreciation.

8. 'Depreciation is the loss in value of a fixed asset'. Discuss.

9. Describe the data needed in order to compute depreciation.

10. Describe two methods of depreciation including their effect on annual profits. In what circumstances might each of these be used and why?

11. 'Although the straight line method is the simplest to apply, it may not always be the most appropriate'. (ASC, SSAP12, 1987). Explain and discuss.

12. In the year to 31 December 19X9, Amy bought a new fixed asset and made the following payments in relation to it:

	£	£
Cost as per suppliers list	12,000	
Less: agreed discount	1,000	11,000
Delivery charge		100
Erection charge		200
Maintenance charge		300
Additional component to increase capacity		400
Replacement parts		250

Required:
(a) State and justify the cost figure which should be used as the basis for depreciation.
(b) What does depreciation do, and why is it necessary?
(c) Briefly explain, without numerical illustration, how the straight line and reducing balance methods of depreciation work. What different assumptions does each method make?
(d) Explain the term objectivity as used by accountants. To what extent is depreciation objective?
(e) It is common practice in published accounts in Germany to use the reducing balance method for a fixed asset in the early years of its life, and then to change to the straight line method as soon as this would give a higher annual charge. What do you think of this practice? Refer to relevant accounting conventions in your answer.   (CACA)

13. Pusher commenced business on 1 January 19X9 with two lorries—A and B. A cost £1,000 and B cost £1,600. On 3 March 19X0, A was written off in an accident and Pusher received £750 from the Insurance Company. This vehicle was replaced on 10 March 19X0 by C which cost £2,000.

  A full year's depreciation is charged in the year of acquisition and no depreciation charged in the year of disposal. .

(a) You are required to show the appropriate extracts from Pusher's balance sheet and profit and loss account for the three years to 31/12/X9, 31/12/X0 and 31/12/X1 assuming that

    (i)   the vehicles are depreciated at 20 per cent on the straight line method, and

    (ii) the vehicles are depreciated at 25 per cent on the reducing balance method.

(b) Comment briefly on the pros and cons of using the straight line and reducing balance methods of depreciation.

14. A. Black & Company Limited owned two machines which had been purchased on 1 October 1990, at a combined cost of £3,100 ex works. They were identical as regards size and capacity and had been erected and brought into use on 1 April 1991. The cost of transporting the two machines to the factory of A. Black & Company Limited was £130 and further expenditure for the installation of the two machines had been incurred totalling £590 for the foundations, and £180 for erection.

Provision for depreciation using the straight line method has been calculated from the date on which the machines started work, assuming a life of ten years for the machines. The first charge against profits was made at the end of the financial year, 30 September 1991.

One of the machines was sold on 31 March 1999 for £800 ex factory to H. Johnson. The work of dismantling the machine was undertaken by the staff of I. Sayer & Company Limited at a labour cost of £100. This machine was replaced on 1 May 1999, by one exactly similar in every way, which was purchased from R. Adams at a cost of £2,800, which covered delivery, erection on the site of the old machine, and the provision of adequate foundations. This new machine was brought into general operation on 1 July 1999.

You are required to show:

(a) the journal entries which should be made on 31 March and 1 May 1999, and

(b) how you would arrive at the amount of the provision for depreciation as regards the three machines for the year ended 30 September 1999.

NB. It is the practice of the company to charge depreciation on a *pro rata* time basis each year, and to operate a machinery disposal account where necessary.   (CACA)

15. Makers and Co. are a partnership with a small factory on the outskirts of London. They decide to erect an extension to their factory.

The following items appear in the trial balance of the firm, as at 31 December 19X9:

	£	£
Purchases	12,800	
Wages	16,400	
Hire of machinery	520	
Plant and machinery at cost to		
31 December 19X8	5,900	
Plant and machinery purchased during the year	2,540	
Plant and machinery sold during the year		
(cost in 19X0 £900; depreciation to		
31 December 19X8 £540)		160
Freehold premises at cost to 31 December 19X8	7,000	
(Land £3,000; Buildings £4,000)		
Freehold Land purchased during the year for a		
factory extension	2,800	
Provision for depreciation of plant and		
machinery at 31 December 19X8		2,400
Legal charges	80	

In the course of your examination of the books you ascertain that:

1. Building materials used in building the extension and costing £1,800 had been charged to the purchases account.

2. Wages paid to men engaged in building the extension amounted to £1,500 and had been charged to the wages account.

3. The hire charge was in respect of machinery used exclusively in the construction of the extension.

4. The legal charges, apart from £50 relating to debt collecting, were incurred in the purchase of the land.

It is decided that depreciation on plant and machinery is to be provided at $12\frac{1}{2}$ per cent on the closing book value.

You are required:

1. to write up the following ledger accounts:

    Factory extensions, Freehold premises, Plant and machinery, and Provisions for depreciation of plant and machinery, and

2. to show therefrom the particulars that should appear on the firm's balance sheet at 31 December 19X9.

(CACA)

16. Wexford Ltd, who prepare their accounts on 31 December each year, provide for depreciation of their vehicles by a reducing balance method, calculated as 25 per cent on the balance at the end of the year. Depreciation of plant is calculated on a straight line basis at 10 per cent per annum on cost; a full year's depreciation is charged in the year in which plant is acquired and none in the year of sale.

The balance sheet for 31 December 1992 showed:

	Vehicles £	Plant £
Original cost	25,060	96,920
Accumulated depreciation	14,560	50,120
Net book value	10,500	46,800

During the year ended 31 December 1993 the following transactions took place:

Purchases of vehicles	£4,750
Purchases of plant	£33,080

	Original cost £	Year of purchase	Proceeds of sale £
Sale of vehicle 1	3,200	1990	1,300
Sale of vehicle 2	4,800	1991	2,960
Sale of plant	40,000	1987	15,000

You are required to:

(a) present the ledger accounts relating to the purchases and sales of vehicles and plant for the year ended 31 December 1993; and
(b) show the journal entries for depreciation for the year.

17. The Balance Sheet of Beta Ltd as at 30 June 19X9 shows motor vehicles as follows:

	£
Motor Vehicles at cost	61,850
Less: Depreciation	32,426
Net Book Value	£29,424

Vehicles are depreciated on the straight line basis over a five year life. Depreciation is charged *pro rata* to time in the year of acquisition but no charge is made in the year of disposal. The disposal account is written up on the last day of each year.

During 19X9–X0 the following vehicle transactions took place:

30 Sept Purchased delivery van: £8,600
31 Oct   Purchased sales manager's car: £10,700
28 Feb   Purchased lorry: £4,000

The lorry was second-hand and originally cost £9,600.
Sales of vehicles:

31 Oct   Car   £300 originally cost £2,800
31 Dec   Tractor £540 originally cost £2,400
31 Mar   Van   £420 originally cost £1,900

The car was originally purchased 1 July 19X5, the tractor 30 November 19X6 and the van 1 April 19X7.
You are required to write up the accounts for vehicles, vehicle depreciation and vehicle disposals.

(CACA adapted)

12.   Bad debts and provisions for bad debts

The nature of and ledger entries for bad debts

When goods are sold on credit it sometimes transpires that the debtor is unwilling or unable to pay the amount owed. This is referred to as a bad or irrecoverable debt. The decision to treat a debt as bad is a matter of judgement. A debt may be regarded as irrecoverable for a number of reasons, such as being unable to trace the debtor, not worth taking the debtor to court, or the debtor is bankrupt. However, if a debtor is bankrupt this does not necessarily mean that the debt is irrecoverable. When a person is bankrupt his or her possessions are seized and sold in order to pay the creditors. Such payments are often made in instalments known as dividends. Frequently the dividends do not consist of the repayment of the whole of the debt. Thus when the 'final dividend' is received the remainder of the debt is irrecoverable.

When a debt is regarded as irrecoverable the entries in the ledger are as follows:

Debit: Bad debts account
Credit: Debtors account

Occasionally debts previously written off as bad are subsequently paid. When this happens the ledger entries are the reverse of the above, and the debtors account is credited with the money received in the normal way.

The nature of and ledger entries for provisions for bad debts

A provision is the setting aside of income to meet a known future liability or loss, the amount of which cannot be ascertained exactly, and is thus an estimate. An example would be a provision for damages payable resulting from a legal action where the verdict had gone against the business but the amount of the damages had not been fixed by the court at the end of the accounting year. If the damages had been fixed these would not be treated as a provision but as a liability. Another example of a provision is depreciation.

It should be noted that when accountants talk of setting aside income what they mean is that 'funds' are being retained in the business but not put into a separate bank account. The funds are automatically retained in the business by designating part of the income as a provision, since this reduces the profit which is available for withdrawal by the owner(s) of the business.

The need for a provision for bad/doubtful debts essentially arises because goods sold and recognized as sales revenue in one accounting year may not become known to be a bad debt until the following accounting year. Thus the profit of the year in which the goods are sold would be overstated by the amount of the bad debt. In order to adjust for this, a provision in respect of possible bad debts is created in the year of sale.

A provision for bad debts may consist of either a specific provision and/or a general provision. A specific provision involves ascertaining which particular debtors at the year end are unlikely to pay their debts. A general provision is an estimate of the total amount of bad debts computed using a percentage (based on previous years' figures) of the debtors at the end of the current year. Where both specific and general provision are made, the two amounts are added together and the total is entered in the ledger.

The accounting entries in respect of a provision for bad debts are made after the trial balance has been extracted when the profit and loss account is being prepared. The charge to the profit and loss account in each year consists of an amount necessary to increase or decrease the provision at the end of the previous year to the amount required at the end of the current year.

An increase in a provision always consists of:

Debit: Profit and loss account
Credit: Provision for bad debts account

A decrease in a provision is entered:

Debit: Provision for bad debts account
Credit: Profit and loss account

It is important to appreciate that any balance on a provision for bad debts account shown in a trial balance must therefore relate to the balance at the end of the previous year. The treatment of bad debts and provisions for bad debts is illustrated in Examples 12.1 and 12.2.

Example 12.1
A. Jones has an accounting year ending on 30 November. At 30 November 19X7 his ledger contained the following accounts:

	£
Trade debtors	20,000
Provision for bad debts	1,000

The trade debtors at 30 November 19X8 were £18,900. This includes an amount of £300 owed by F. Simons which was thought to be irrecoverable. It also includes amounts of £240 owed by C. Steven, £150 owed by M. Evans and £210 owed by A. Mitchell all of which are regarded as doubtful debts.

You have been instructed to make a provision for bad debts at 30 November 19X8. This should include a specific provision for debts regarded as doubtful and a general provision of 5 per cent of trade debtors.

Show the ledger entries in respect of the above and the relevant balance sheet extract.

Provision for bad debts at 30 November 19X8   £

Specific provision—C. Steven	240
M. Evans	150
A. Mitchell	210
	600

General provision—   900
  5 per cent × (£18,900 − £300 − £600)
                                                                          1,500

F. Simons

19X8			19X8		
30 Nov	Balance b/d	300	30 Nov	Bad debts	300

Bad debts

19X8			19X8		
30 Nov	F. Simons	300	30 Nov	Profit and loss a/c	300

Provision for bad debts

19X8			19X7		
30 Nov	Balance c/d	1,500	30 Nov	Balance b/d	1,000
			19X8		
			30 Nov	Profit and loss a/c	500
		1,500			1,500
			19X8		
			30 Nov	Balance b/d	1,500

Profit and loss account

Bad debts	300	
Provision for bad debts	500	

Balance sheet

Debtors (18,900–300)	18,600
Less: Provision for bad debts	1,500
	17,100

Notes

1. No entries are made in the accounts of those debtors which comprise the specific provision since these are only doubtful debts and thus not yet regarded as irrecoverable.
2. The balance carried down on the provision for bad debts account at the end of the year is always the amount of the new provision. The amount charged to the profit and loss account is the difference between the provision at the end of the current year and that at the end of the previous year. In this example the provision is increased from £1,000 to £1,500 by means of a credit to the provision for bad debts account of £500 and a corresponding debit to the profit and loss account.

3. In computing the amount of the general provision any bad debts and specific provisions must be deducted from the debtors. Otherwise the specific provision would be duplicated and a provision would be made for debts already written off as bad, which is clearly nonsense.
4. The bad debts written off must also be removed from debtors in preparing the balance sheet.
5. There is another method of accounting for bad debts and provisions for bad debts which essentially involves combining these two accounts. This is shown below.

(Provision for) bad debts

19X8			19X7		
30 Nov	F. Simons	300	30 Nov	Balance b/d	1,000
30 Nov	Balance b/d	1,500	19X8		
			30 Nov	Profit and loss a/c	800
		1,800			1,800
			19X8		
			30 Nov	Balance b/d	1,500

Profit and loss account

Bad debts	800

The combined charge to the profit and loss account for the year in respect of bad debts and the provision for bad debts is the difference between the two sides of the (provision for) bad debts account after inserting the amount of the provision at 30 November 19X8 as a balance carried down. The charge to the profit and loss account under both methods is always the same.

Example 12.2 (continuation of Example 12.1)
During the year ended 30 November 19X9 C. Steven was declared bankrupt and a first dividend of £140 was received from the trustee. M. Evans was also declared bankrupt and a first and final dividend of £30 was received from the trustee. A. Mitchell paid his debt in full. A further debt of £350 owed by R. Jackson that is included in the debtors at the 30 November 19X8 proved to be bad.

The trade debtors at 30 November 19X9 were £24,570. This figure is after recording all money received but does not take into account bad debts.

You have been instructed to make a provision for bad debts at 30 November 19X9. This should include a specific provision for doubtful debts and a general provision of 5 per cent of trade debtors.

Show the ledger entries in respect of the above and the relevant balance sheet extract.

Provision for bad debts at 30 November 19X9

	£
Specific provision—C. Steven (£240 − £140)	100
General provision—	1,200
5 per cent × (£24,570 − £120 − £350 − £100)	
	1,300

C. Steven

19X8			19X9		
30 Nov	Balance b/d	240	30 Nov	Bank	140
			30 Nov	Balance c/d	100
		240			240
19X9					
30 Nov	Balance b/d	100			

M. Evans

19X8			19X9		
30 Nov	Balance b/d	150	30 Nov	Bank	30
			30 Nov	Bad debts	120
		150			150

R. Jackson

19X8			19X9		
30 Nov	Balance b/d	350	30 Nov	Bad debts	350

Bad debts

19X9			19X9		
30 Nov	M. Evans	120	30 Nov	Profit and loss a/c	470
30 Nov	R. Jackson	350			
		470			470

Provision for bad debts

19X9			19X8		
30 Nov	Profit and loss a/c	200	30 Nov	Balance b/d	1,500
30 Nov	Balance c/d	1,300			
		1,500			1,500
			19X9		
			30 Nov	Balance b/d	1,300

Profit and loss account

	Bad debts	470		Provision for bad debts	200

Balance Sheet

Current assets	£	£
Debtors (£24,570 − £120 − £350)	24,100	
Less: Provision for bad debts	1,300	22,800

Alternative method
(Provision for) Bad debts

19X9			19X8		
30 Nov	M. Evans	120	30 Nov	Balance c/d	1,500
30 Nov	R. Jackson	350	19X9		
30 Nov	Balance c/d	1,300	30 Nov	Profit and loss a/c	270
		1,770			1,770
			19X9		
			30 Nov	Balance b/d	1,300

Notes

1. The amount due from M. Evans is written off as a bad debt because the final dividend in bankruptcy was declared, which means that no more money will be received in respect of this debt. However, the amount due from C. Steven is not written off as a bad debt, despite the fact that he was declared bankrupt, because further dividends are expected. Thus this debt is the subject of a specific provision in respect of the amount still outstanding.
2. No entries are required where a debt that was previously treated as a specific provision is subsequently paid as in the case of A. Mitchell.
3. The main method shown above which has separate bad debts and provision for bad debts accounts is the most common in practice. However, it is a short cut method which tends to obscure the logic behind provisions for bad debts, because it shows increases and decreases in the provision. The 'alternative method' shown above allows the logic to be demonstrated as follows. The bad debts for the year (£120 + £350 = £470) are set against the provision at the end of the previous year (£1500). Any under or over provision (1,500 + £470 = over provision of £1,030) is written back to the profit and loss account. The amount of the provision required at the end of the current year (£1,300) is then created in full by debiting the profit and loss account with this amount. This can be illustrated as follows:

(Provision for) bad debts

19X9			19X8		
30 Nov	M. Evans	120	30 Nov	Balance c/d	1,500
30 Nov	R. Jackson	350	19X9		
30 Nov	Profit and loss a/c		30 Nov	Profit and loss a/c	1,300
	over provision	1,030			
30 Nov	Balance c/d	1,300			
		2,800			2,800
			19X9		
			30 Nov	Balance b/d	1,300

The debit entry of £1,030 is the reversal of the over provision. The credit entry of £1,300 is the creation of the new provision. The net effect is the same as in the previous answer—a debit to the profit and loss account of £270 and a balance of the (provision for) bad debts account of £1,300. It should be stressed that nobody would prepare a (provision for) bad debts account in the manner shown immediately above. However, it serves to demonstrate that the underlying logic behind the provision for bad debts is essentially to shift the bad debts back into the year in which the goods were sold and at the same time provide for future losses in the form of doubtful debts.

Exercises

1. What do you understand by the term 'bad debts'? In what circumstances might a debt be treated as irrecoverable?

2. (a) Explain the nature of a provision, including how this differs from a liability.
    (b) Give one example of a provision other than provision for bad debts and depreciation.

3. (a) Explain the nature of a provision for bad debts.
    (b) Explain the difference between a specific and general provision for bad debts.

4. Examine the purpose and logic behind a provision for bad debts, with particular reference to the timing of profits and losses arising from credit sales.

5. A business has an accounting year ending on 31 July. It sells goods on credit and on the 31 July 19X1 had trade debtors of £15,680. This included debts of £410 due from A. Wall and £270 from B. Wood both of which were regarded as irrecoverable.
    The business has decided to create a provision for bad debts at 31 July 19X1 of 4 per cent of trade debtors. Previously there was no provision for bad debts.
    You are required to show the ledger entries in respect of the above bad debts and provision for bad debts.

6. B. Summers has an accounting year ending on 30 April. At 30 April 19X4 his ledger contained the following accounts.

	£
Trade debtors	25,000
Provision for doubtful debts	750

The trade debtors at 30 April 19X5 were £19,500. This includes £620 due from A. Winters and £880 from D. Spring both of which are thought to be irrecoverable.
    You have been instructed to make a provision for bad debts at 30 April 19X5 of 3 per cent of trade debtors.
    Show the ledger entries in respect of the bad debts and provision for bad debts.

7. The accounts for the year ended 30 November 19X7 of Springboard Limited included a provision for doubtful debts at that date of £900.00.
    During the year ended 30 November 19X8, the company received £500.00 from Peter Lyon towards the settlement of a debt of £700.00 which had been written off as irrecoverable by the company in 19X5. There is no evidence that Peter Lyon will be able to make any further payments to the company.
    Trade debtors at 30 November 19X8 amounted to £22,000.00, which includes the following debts it has now decided to write off as bad:

	£
Mary Leaf	800.00
Angus Way	300.00

In its accounts for the year ended 30 November 19X8, the company is to continue its policy of maintaining a provision for doubtful debts of 5% of debtors at the year end.
    Note: Bad debts written off or recovered are not to be recorded in the provision for doubtful debts account.

Required:
(a) Prepare the journal entry (or entries) in the books of the company necessitated by the receipt of £500.00 from Peter Lyon.

   Notes: 1. Journal entries should include narratives;
   2. For the purposes of this question, assume cash receipts are journalized.

(b) Prepare the provision for doubtful debts account in the books of the company for the year ended 30 November 19X8.

(c) The entry for debtors which will be included in the balance sheet as at 30 November 19X8 of the company. (AAT)

8. The following transactions are to be recorded. At the beginning of year 1 a provision for doubtful debts account is to be opened. It should show a provision of 2 per cent against debtors of £50,000. During the year bad debts of £2,345 are to be charged to the provision account. At the end of year 1 the bad debt provision is required to be 2 per cent against debtors of £60,000.

   In year 2 bad debts of £37 are to be charged against the account. At the end of year 2 a provision of 1 per cent against debtors of £70,000 is required.

   Required:
   Prepare provision for doubtful debts account for the two years. Show in the account the double entry for each item, and carry down the balance at the end of each year. (CACA adapted)

9. The balance sheet as at 31 December 19X5 of Zoom Products Limited included:

    Trade debtors　　　£85,360

    The account for the year ended 31 December 19X5 included a provision for doubtful debts at 31 December 19X5 of 3 per cent of the balance outstanding from debtors. During 19X6, the company's sales totalled £568,000, of which 90 per cent, in value, were on credit and £510,150 was received from credit customers in settlement of debts totalling £515,000. In addition, £3,000 was received from J. Dodds in settlement of a debt which had been written off as bad in 19X5; this receipt has been credited to J. Dodds account in the debtors' ledger

    On 30 December 19X6, the following outstanding debts were written off as bad:

J. White	£　600
K. Black	£2,000

    Entries relating to bad debts are passed through the provision for doubtful debts account whose balance at 31 December 19X6 is to be 3 per cent of the amount due to the company from debtors at that date.

    Required:
    (a) Write up the provision for doubtful debts accounts for the year ended 31 December 19X6, bringing down the balance at 1 January 19X7.
    (b) Prepare a computation of the amount to be shown as trade debtors in the company's balance sheet at 31 December 19X6. (AAT)

10. Because of their doubtful nature, P. Rudent instructed his accountants to make a specific provision in the accounts for the year ended 30 June 19X5 against the following debts:

	£
J. Black	28
C. Green	6
B. Grey	24
Fawn Ltd	20

    He also instructed that a general provision of 5 per cent for doubtful debts should be created on the other debtors, which at 30 June amounted to £8,000.

    No further business transactions were entered into with any of these debtors during the year ended 30 June 19X6, but an amount of £9 was received from J. Black's trustee in bankruptcy by way of a first dividend; a first and final dividend of £70 was received from the liquidator of Fawn Ltd and B. Grey paid his debt in full. A further debt of £95 due from S. White proved to be bad.

On 30 June 19X6 P. Rudent instructed his accountants to maintain the provision existing against C. Green's debt and to provide for the balance owing by J. Black, and to make further provision for debts owing to J. Blue £19 and R. Brown £15. The other debtors amounted to £7,500 and the accountants were instructed to make the provision for doubtful debts equal to 5 per cent of these debts.

Show what entries should be made in P. Rudent's nominal ledger to record these facts.   (CACA)

11. M. Shaft has an accounting year ending on 31 December. At 31 December 19X6 the ledger contained the following balances:

	£
Plant and machinery	30,000
Provision for depreciation on plant and machinery	12,500
Trade debtors	10,000
Provision for bad debts	1,260

The provision for bad debts consists of a general provision of £500 and specific provisions comprising: A. Bee £320; C. Dee £180; and F. Gee £260.

The following transactions occurred during 19X7:

31 Mar   Part exchanged one piece of plant for another. The part exchange allowance on the old plant was £4,000 and the balance of £1,000 was paid by cheque. The old plant cost £8,000 when it was purchased on 1 July 19X5.

30 Apr   A. Bee was declared bankrupt and a first dividend of £70 was received from the trustee.

15 June   A debt of £210 owed by J. Kay that is included in the debtors at 31 December 19X6 was found to be bad.

3 Aug   C. Dee paid his debt in full.

7 Oct   F. Gee was declared bankrupt and a first and final dividend of £110 was received from the trustee.

Plant and machinery is depreciated using the reducing balance method at a rate of 25 per cent per annum on a strict time basis. The trade debtors at 31 December 19X7 were £12,610. This figure is after recording all money received but does not take into account any of the above bad debts. The relevant specific provisions and a general provision for bad debts of 5 per cent should be maintained at 31 December 19X7.

You are required to:

(a) Show the ledger entries in respect of the above, including the charges to the profit and loss account and the balances at 31 December 19X7. Show your workings clearly and take all calculations to the nearest £.

(b) Briefly discuss the similarities between provisions for bad debts and depreciation with particular reference to the accounting concept(s) of which they are applications.

13. Prepayments and accruals

The nature of and ledger entries for accrued expenses

As discussed in Chapter 10, the accruals concept dictates that costs are recognized as they are incurred, not when money is paid. That is, goods and services are deemed to have been purchased on the date they are received. This gives rise to accrued expenses. These are *'creditors' in respect of services received which have not been paid for at the end of the accounting year*. Accrued expenses can obviously only occur where services are paid for in arrears, such as electricity, gas etc.

An accrual may comprise:

1. invoices received (for expenses) that have not been paid at the end of the accounting year, and/or
2. the value of services received for which an invoice has not been rendered at the end of the accounting year.

In the case of the latter, this requires an estimate to be made of the amount of the services consumed during the period between the date of the last invoice and the end of the accounting year. This may be based on any one of the following:

1. a meter reading taken at the end of the accounting year;
2. the amount consumed over a corresponding period of time during the current year;
3. the amount consumed during the same period of the previous year as adjusted for any increase in the unit price.

However, in practice final accounts are often not prepared until some time after the end of the accounting year. By that time the invoice covering the period in question is likely to have been received and can thus be used to ascertain the value of the services consumed during the relevant period.

Although accrued expenses are essentially creditors, rather than have a separate creditors' account it is usual to enter accruals in the relevant expense account. This consists of debiting the amount owing at the end of the year to the expense account as a balance *carried down* and crediting the same account as a balance *brought down*. Thus the amount that will be transferred to the profit and loss account consists of the amount paid during the year plus the accrual at the end of the year (less the accrual at the start of the year). This will reflect the total value of the services that have been received during the current accounting year. The balance brought down is entered on the balance sheet as a current liability. This is illustrated in Example 13.1.

Example 13.1
D. Spring has an accounting year ending on 31 December. The following amounts have been paid for electricity:

Date paid	Quarter ended	£
29 March 19X6	28 February 19X6	96
7 July 19X6	31 May 19X6	68
2 October 19X6	31 August 19X6	73
5 January 19X7	30 November 19X6	82
3 April 19X7	28 February 19X7	105

You are required to show the entries in the light and heat account for the year ended 31 December 19X6 and the relevant balance sheet extract.

Workings
Accrual at 1 Jan 19X6 = $\frac{1}{3} \times$ £96 = £32
Accrual at 31 Dec 19X6 = £82 + ($\frac{1}{3} \times$ £105 = £35) = £117

Light and heat

19X6				19X6		
29 Mar	Bank	96		1 Jan	Accrual b/d	32
7 July	Bank	68		31 Dec	Profit and loss a/c	322
2 Oct	Bank	73				
31 Dec	Accrual c/d	117				
		354				354
				19X7		
				1 Jan	Accrual b/d	117

Balance sheet as at 31 December 19X6

	£
Current liabilities	
Creditors and accrued expenses	117

Notes

1. The amount transferred to the profit and loss account is the difference between the two sides of the light and heat account after entering the accrual at the end of the year.

The nature of and ledger entries for prepaid expenses

The accruals concept also gives rise to prepaid expenses/prepayments. These can be described as *debtors in respect of services that have been paid for but not received at the end of the accounting year*. Prepayments can obviously only occur where services are paid for in advance, such as rent, water rates, road tax, insurance etc.

The amount of the prepayment is ascertained by determining on a time basis how much of the last payment made during the accounting year relates to the services that will be received in the following accounting year.

Although prepaid expenses are essentially debtors, rather than have a separate debtors' account it is usual to enter the prepayment in the relevant expense account. This consists of crediting the amount of the prepayment to the expense account as a balance *carried down* and debiting the same account as a balance *brought down*. Thus the amount that will be transferred to the profit and loss account consists of the amount paid during the year minus the prepayment at the end of the year (plus the prepayment at the start of the year). This will reflect the total value of the services that have been received during the current accounting year. The balance brought down is entered on the balance sheet as a current asset. This is illustrated in Example 13.2.

Example 13.2
M. Waters has an accounting year ending on 30th June. The following amounts have been paid as rent:

Date paid	Quarter ended	£
2 June 19X5	31 August 19X5	600
1 September 19X5	30 November 19X5	600
3 December 19X5	28 February 19X6	660
5 March 19X6	31 May 19X6	660
4 June 19X6	31 August 19X6	720

You are required to show the entries in the rent account for the year ended 30 June 19X6 and the relevant balance sheet extract.

Workings
Prepaid at 1 July 19X5 $= \frac{2}{3} \times £600 = £400$
Prepaid at 1 July 19X6 $= \frac{2}{3} \times £720 = £480$

Rent

19X5				19X5		
1 July	Prepayment b/d	400		30 June	Profit and loss	2,560
1 Sept	Bank	600		30 June	Prepayment c/d	480
3 Dec	Bank	660				
19X6						
5 Mar	Bank	660				
5 June	Bank	720				
		3,040				3,040

19X6		
1 July	Prepayment b/d	480

Balance sheet as at 30 June 19X6

Current assets
Debtors and Prepayments   480

Notes

1. The amount transferred to the profit and loss account is the difference between the two sides of the rent account after entering the prepayments at the end of the year.

Accruals and prepayments and the preparation of final accounts from the trial balance

The profit and loss account is usually prepared from the trial balance. This involves adjusting the amounts shown in the latter for any accruals and prepayments at the end of the accounting year. It is important to appreciate that because the trial balance is taken out at the end of the accounting year, the amounts shown in it include any accruals and prepayments at the end of the previous year. Thus, when preparing a profit and loss account from the trial balance, it is only necessary to add to the amount shown in the trial balance any accruals at the end of the accounting year and to subtract any prepayments.

Exercises

1. (a) Explain the nature of accrued and prepaid expenses.
   (b) Describe how the amount of each may be ascertained.

2. K. Wills has an accounting year ending on 31 December. The following amounts were paid in respect of rent and gas:

Expense	Date paid	Quarter ended	£
Rent	1 Nov 19X1	31 Jan 19X2	900
Rent	29 Jan 19X2	30 April 19X2	930
Gas	6 Mar 19X2	28 Feb 19X2	420
Rent	2 May 19X2	31 July 19X2	930
Gas	4 June 19X2	31 May 19X2	360
Rent	30 July 19X2	31 Oct 19X2	930
Gas	3 Sept 19X2	31 Aug 19X2	270
Rent	5 Nov 19X2	31 Jan 19X3	960
Gas	7 Dec 19X2	30 Nov 19X2	390
Gas	8 Mar 19X3	28 Feb 19X3	450

You are required to show the ledger entries in the rent and light and heat accounts for the year ended 31 December 19X2.

3. Oriel Ltd, whose financial year runs from 1 June to the following 31 May, maintains a combined rent and rates account in its ledger.

   Rent is fixed on a calendar year basis and is payable quarterly in advance. Rent was £2,400 for the year ended 31 December 19X8 and is £3,000 for the year ending 31 December 19X9.

   Oriel Ltd has made the following payments of rent by cheque:

Date	Amount	Details
19X8	£	
3 Jan	600	Quarter to 31 Mar 19X8
1 Apr	600	Quarter to 30 June 19X8
1 July	600	Quarter to 30 Sept 19X8
1 Oct	600	Quarter to 31 Dec 19X8
19X9		
3 Jan	750	Quarter to 31 Mar 19X9
1 Apr	750	Quarter to 30 June 19X9

Rates are assessed annually for the year from 1 April to the following 31 March and are payable in one lump sum by 30 September. The rates assessment was £2,040 for the year ended 31 March 19X9 and £2,280 for the year ending 31 March 19X9.

Oriel Ltd paid the rates for the year ended 31 March 19X9 by cheque on 30 September 19X8 and intends to pay the rates for the year ended 31 March 19X0 on 30 September 19X0.

Required:

(a)   Prepare the Rent and Rates Account for the year ended 31 May 19X9 only as it would appear in the ledger of Oriel Ltd.

(b)   Explain with particular reference to your answer to (a) the meaning of the term 'matching'.   (AAT)

4.   Munch Catering Ltd whose financial year runs from 1 December to the following 30 November maintains a 'Building occupancy costs' account in its general ledger. This account is used to record all payments in respect of rent, insurance and property taxes on the company's business premises.

Rent is fixed on a calendar year basis and is payable quarterly in advance. Rent was £1,800 for the year ended 31 December 19X9 and is £2,100 for the year ended 31 December 19X0.

Munch Catering Ltd has made the following payments of rent by cheque:

Date	Amount	Details
19X9	£	
29 Sept	450	Quarter to 31 Dec 19X9
29 Dec	525	Quarter to 31 Mar 19X0
19X0		
30 Mar	525	Quarter to 30 June 19X0
29 June	525	Quarter to 30 Sept 19X0
28 Sept	525	Quarter to 31 Dec 19X0

Munch Catering Ltd paid its building contents insurance premium of £547 for the year to 30 November 19X0 on 17 November 19X9. This policy was cancelled as from 31 May 19X0 and Munch Catering Ltd received a cheque for £150 as a rebate of premium on 21 June 19X0. A new buildings contents insurance policy was taken out with a different insurance company with effect from 1 June 19X0. The premium on this policy was £400 and this was paid in full by cheque by Munch Catering Ltd on 18 May 19X0.

Property taxes are assessed annually for the year from 1 April to the following 31 March and are payable in one lump sum by the 30 September. Munch Catering Ltd's assessment was £840 for the year to 31 March 19X0 and £1,680 for the year to 31 March 19X1.

Munch Catering Ltd paid the assessment for the year ended 31 March 19X0 by cheque on 2 October 19X0 and the assessment for the year ended 31 March 19X0 by cheque on 26 September 19X0.

Required:

Prepare the 'Building occupancy costs' account for the year ended 30 November 19X0 only as it would appear in the general ledger of Munch Catering Ltd.   (AAT)

5.   The ledger or RBD & Co included the following account balances:

	At 1 June 19X4	At 31 May 19X5
	£	£
Rents receivable: prepayments	463	517
Rent and rates payable		
prepayments	1,246	1,509
accruals	315	382
Creditors	5,258	4,720

During the year ended 31 May 19X5, the following transactions had risen:

	£
Rents received by cheque	4,058
Rent paid by cheque	7,491
Rates paid by cheque	2,805
Creditors paid by cheque	75,181
Discounts received from creditors	1,043
Purchases on credit	to be derived

Required:

Post and balance the appropriate accounts for the year ended 31 May 19X5, deriving the transfer entries to profit and loss account, where applicable.   (CACA adapted)

6. The balances on certain accounts of Foster Hardware Co. as at 1 April 19X1 were:

	£
Rent and rates payable—accruals	2,200
—prepayments	1,940
Rent receivable —prepayments	625
Vehicles (as cost)	10,540
Provision for depreciation of vehicles	4,720
During the financial year the business	
paid rent by cheque	5,200
paid rates by cheque	3,050
received cheque for rent of sub-let premises	960
traded in a vehicle—original cost	4,710
—accumulated depreciation	3,080
—part exchange allowance	1,100
paid balance of price of new vehicle by cheque	5,280
Closing balances as at 31 March 19X2 were:	
Rent and rates payable—accruals	2,370
—prepayments	1,880
Rents receivable —prepayments	680
Vehicles (at cost)	to be derived
Provision for depreciation of vehicles	3,890

Required:
Post and balance the appropriate accounts for the year ended 31 March 19X2, deriving the transfer entries to profit and loss account where applicable.   (CACA)

7. The trial balance of Snodgrass, a sole trader, at 1 January 19X8 is as follows:

	Dr £000	Cr £000
Capital		600
Fixed assets (net)	350	
Trade debtors	200	
Prepayments—rent	8	
—insurance	12	
Trade creditors		180
Accruals—electricity		9
—telephone		1
Stock	200	
Bank	20	
	790	790

The following information is given for the year:

	£000
Receipts from customers	1,000
Payments to suppliers	1,000
Payments for: rent	30
insurance	20
electricity	25
telephone	10
wages	100
Proprietor's personal expenses	50
Discounts allowed	8
Bad debts written off	3
Depreciation	50

At 31 December 19X8 the following balances are given:

	£000
Trade debtors	250
Prepayments—rent	10
—telephone	2
Trade creditors	160
Accruals—electricity	7
—insurance	6
Stock	230

Required:

Prepare a trading and profit and loss account for the year, and a balance sheet as at 31 December 19X8.   (CACA)

14. The preparation of final accounts from the trial balance

As explained in Chapter 9, final accounts are prepared after the trial balance has been produced and involves transferring the balance on various nominal accounts to the profit and loss account. In addition, the process of preparing final accounts involves a number of adjustments, some of which have been described in the last three chapters. These may be summarized as follows:

1. Accounting for stocks and work in progress
2. Provisions for depreciation
3. Provisions for bad debts
4. Accruals and prepayments
5. The correction of omissions and errors such as bad debts not written off during the year

Some further adjustments not addressed in the previous chapters are discussed below.

Stocks of tools, stationery and fuels

As explained in Chapter 11, loose tools are regarded as fixed assets, whereas consumable tools are designated as revenue expenditure. Thus any stocks of consumable tools, like stocks of stationery and fuel, are treated as current assets. However, irrespective of their classification, the accounting adjustments in respect of these items are essentially the same. That is, the value of the items in stock at the end of the accounting year is entered in the relevant ledger as a balance carried down on the credit side and as a balance brought down on the debit side. The difference between the two sides of the ledger account is then transferred to the profit and loss account in exactly the same way as with prepaid expenses. In the case of loose tools this is described as depreciation, which is referred to as having been computed using the revaluation method.

The principle which is applied to each of these items is as follows:

Stock at end of previous year at valuation
Add: purchase during the year
Less: stock at end of current year at valuation
= Charge to profit and loss account

The charge to the profit and loss account represents the value of stationery, fuel or tools that have been consumed during the year.

Adjustments for drawings

Drawings may take a number of forms in addition to cash. For example, it is common for the owner to take goods out of the business for his personal consumption. This requires an adjustment which may be done by either of two methods: (1) debit drawings and credit purchases with the *cost* of the goods to the business; or (2) debit drawings and credit sales where the goods are deemed to be taken at some other value such as the normal selling price.

Another form of drawings occurs where the business pays the owner's personal debts. A common example of this is taxation on the business profits. Sole traders and partnerships are not liable to taxation as such. It is the owner's personal liability and not that of the business. Therefore if taxation is paid by the business it must be treated as drawings. The ledger entry being to debit drawings and credit the cash book.

Goods on sale or return

Goods which have been sent to potential customers on sale or return or on approval must not be recorded as sales until actually sold. In the ledger, goods on sale or return at the end of an accounting year are included in stock at cost.

Sometimes, in examination questions, goods on sale or return are recorded as sales. This is an error and must be corrected by means of the following entries:

Debit sales account ⎫ with the selling
Credit trade debtors ⎬ price of the goods

Debit stock account ⎫ with the cost
Credit trading account ⎬ price of the goods

Note that the credit entry in the trading account takes the form of increasing the amount of the closing stock.

The extended trial balance

As explained above, the preparation of final accounts involves various adjustments. In the preceding three chapters these were described mainly in terms of the necessary ledger entries. However, in practice and in examinations final accounts are usually prepared from the trial balance, the ledger entries being done at some later date when the final accounts are completed.

Because the preparation of final accounts from the trial balance involves a large number of adjustments, in practice it is usual to make these adjustments using an extended trial balance. This may take a number of forms, but a useful approach is to set it up to comprise eight columns made up of four pairs as follows:

1. The trial balance debit side
2. The trial balance credit side
3. Adjustments to the debit side
4. Adjustments to the credit side

5. The profit and loss account debit side
6. The profit and loss account credit side
7. The balance sheet debit side
8. The balance sheet credit side

The first two columns are the normal trial balance. Columns 3 and 4 are used to make adjustments to the figures in the trial balance in respect of provisions for depreciation and bad debts, accruals and prepayments etc. Columns 5 and 6 are used to compute the amounts that will be entered in the profit and loss account. Columns 7 and 8 are used to ascertain the amounts that will be shown in the balance sheet.

Columns 3 and 4 relating to the adjustments are used like the journal in that items entered in these columns are intended to represent entries that will be made in the ledger. For example, one simple adjustment is the transfer of drawings to the capital account. This takes the form of an entry in the credit adjustment column on the line containing the balance on the drawings account with a corresponding entry in the debit adjustment column on the line containing the balance on the capital account in the trial balance.

Furthermore, adjustments may take the form of an entry in one of the adjustments columns and one of the profit and loss account columns. This is because the adjustment columns and the profit and loss account columns relate to entries that will be made in the ledger. However, no adjustments must be entered in the balance sheet columns because the balance sheet does not involve entries in the ledger.

The most common adjustments found in the extended trial balance are as follows:

1. *Provisions for depreciation*   Debit the profit and loss account column and credit the adjustment column on the line containing the balance on the provision for depreciation account in the trial balance.
2. *Provision for bad debts*   Debit the profit and loss account column and credit the adjustment column on the line containing the balance on the provision for bad debts account with any increase in the provision (opposite for any decrease).
3. *Accruals and prepayments*   Debit and credit the adjustment columns on the line relating to the expense in question.
4. *Stock at the start of the year*   Debit the profit and loss account column directly with the balance on the stock account in the trial balance.
5. *Stock at the end of the year*   Debit the adjustment column and credit the profit and loss account column to show the balance on the closing stock account.

After all the necessary adjustments have been made in the adjustment and profit and loss account columns, the amounts that will be entered in the profit and loss account and balance sheet columns can be ascertained. These are found by cross casting the amounts relating to each ledger account shown in the original trial balance. For example, if the original trial balance contained a rent account with a debit balance, any prepayment shown in the credit adjustment column would be deducted from this and the difference entered in the debit profit and loss account column. The prepayment shown in the debit adjustment column would also be extended across and entered in the debit balance sheet column. Expenses with accrued charges are treated in a similar way.

When all the amounts have been entered in the profit and loss account and balance sheet columns, the profit (or loss) can be computed in the normal manner as the difference between the two profit and loss account columns. The profit is entered in the profit and loss account debit column and the credit adjustment column. The latter is then extended into the balance sheet credit column and eventually added to the capital account balance.

When all the items in the trial balance have been extended across into the profit and loss account and balance sheet columns and the profit has been ascertained, the amounts in these columns are entered in the final version of the profit and loss account and balance sheet. An illustration of the use of the extended trial balance is given in Example 14.1.

Finally, it should be observed that although the extended trial balance is very common in practice, the time allocated to answering examination questions is unlikely to allow for full presentation of the extended trial balance, and this is rarely a requirement. Without the extended trial balance it becomes difficult to answer final accounts questions in a logical and comprehensive manner. Some students therefore find it helpful to make use of the trial balance printed on the question paper to save the task of copying this out. Adjustment columns can be drawn on the right hand side of the trial balance on the question paper, and the necessary adjustments can be made in rough form to permit the final accounts to be prepared in their answer book.

Example 14.1
T. King has an accounting year ending on 30 April. The following trial balance was prepared for the year ended 30 April 19X6:

	£	£
Capital		59,640
Drawings	7,600	
Bank overdraft		1,540
Cash	1,170	
Plant and machinery	87,000	
Provision for depreciation on plant		27,000
Sales		68,200
Purchases	42,160	
Debtors	15,200	
Creditors		12,700
Provision for bad debts		890
Bad debts	610	
Rent	4,200	
Light and heat	3,700	
Stationery	2.430	
Stock	5,900	
	169,970	169,970

You have been given the following additional information:

1. Plant and machinery is depreciated using the reducing balance method at a rate of 10 per cent per annum.
2. The provision for bad debts at 30 April 19X6 should be 5 per cent of debtors.
3. There is an accrual at 30 April 19X6 in respect of gas amounting to £580, and rent prepaid of £600.
4. Stock at 30 April 19X6 was £7,220.

T. King EXTENDED TRIAL BALANCE AS AT 30TH APRIL 19X6

	Trial balance		Adjustments		Profit and loss a/c		Balance sheet	
	DR	CR	DR	CR	DR	CR	DR	CR
Capital		59,640	7,600					52,040
Drawings	7,600			7,600				
Bank overdraft		1,540						1,540
Cash	1,170						1,170	
Plant and machinery	87,000						87,000	
Provision for depreciation on plant		27,000		6,000	6,000			33,000
Sales		68,200				68,200		
Purchases	42,160				42,160			
Debtors	15,200						15,200	
Creditors		12,700						12,700
Provision for bad debts		890	130			130		760
Bad debts	610				610			
Rent	4,200			600	3,600		600	
Light and heat	3,700		580		4,280			580
Stationery	2,430				2,430			
Stock at 1 May 19X5	5,900				5,900			
Stock at 30 April 19X6			7,220	7,220		7,220	7,220	
Profit				10,570	10,570			10,570
	169,970	169,970			75,550	75,550	118,790	118,790

123

You are required to prepare an extended trial balance at 30 April 19X6 and final accounts in vertical form.

Workings
1. Depreciation = 10 per cent × (£87,000 − £27,000) = £6,000
2. Provision for bad debts = (5 per cent × £15,200) − £890 = £130 decrease

T. King
Trading and profit and loss account for the year ended 30 April 19X6

	£	£
Sales		68,200
Less: Cost of Sales:		
Stock at 1 May 19X5	5,900	
Add: Purchases	42,160	
	48,060	
Less: Stock at 30 April 19X6	7,220	40,840
Gross profit		27,360
Add: Provision for bad debts released		130
		27,490
Less: Expenditure		
Rent	3,600	
Light and heat	4,280	
Stationery	2,430	
Bad debts	610	
Depreciation on plant	6,000	16,920
Net profit		10,570

Balance sheet as at 30 April 19X6

	£	£	£
Fixed assets	*Cost*	*Acc. Depn*	*WDV*
Plant and machinery	87,000	33,000	54,000
Current assets			
Prepayments		600	
Stock of goods		7,220	
Debtors	15,200		
Less: Provision for bad debts	760	14,440	
Cash		1,170	
23,430			
Less: Current liabilities			
Accruals	580		
Creditors	12,700		
Bank overdraft	1,540	14,820	
Net current assets			8,610
			62,610

Capital

Balance at 1 May 19X5	59,640
Add: Net profit	10,570
	70,210
Less: Drawings	7,600
Balance at 30 April 19X6	62,610

Exercises

1. The following is the trial balance of C. Jones as at 31 December 19X9.

	£	£
Capital account at 1/1/X9		22,607
Purchases	194,536	
Sales		263,675
Office wages and salaries	16,720	
Rent and rates	4,930	
Debtors	36,150	
Sundry expenses	2,071	
Bad debts written off	942	
Drawings	4,751	
Provision for doubtful debts		1,851
Cash at bank	1,408	
Creditors		17,154
Cash in hand	167	
Stock	41,062	
Motor car—cost	3,600	
—depreciation		1,050
	£306,337	£306,337

You are provided with the following additional information for the purposes of preparing the final accounts:

1. Closing stock has been valued at £49,678.
2. The rent of the premises is £3,200 per annum, payable half-yearly in advance on 31 March and 30 September.
3. Rates for the year ending 31 March 19X0 amounting to £744 were paid on 11 April 19X9.
4. Depreciation on the car is to be provided using the straight line method at a rate of 20 per cent per annum.
5. The provision for doubtful debts (£1,851) was the general provision which appeared in last year's accounts. During the current year, bad debts of £942 were written off against the accounts of specific customers. It has now been agreed that further debts amounting to £710 are to be written off against specific customers and closing provision is to be adjusted to 5 per cent of the revised debtors figure.
6. Wages and salaries to be accrued amount to £1,506.

You are required to prepare the trading and profit and loss account for the year ended 31 December 19X9, and the balance sheet as at 31 December 19X9. This should be done using an extended trial balance.

2. The following is the trial balance of J. Clark at 31 March 19X6:

	£	£
Capital		60,000
Drawings	5,600	

Purchases/sales	34,260	58,640
Returns inwards/outwards	3,260	2,140
Carriage inwards	730	
Carriage outwards	420	
Discount allowed/received	1,480	1,970
Plant and machinery at cost	11,350	
Provision for depreciation on plant		4,150
Motor vehicles	13,290	
Provision for depreciation on vehicles		2,790
Goodwill	5,000	
Quoted investments	6,470	
Freehold premises at cost	32,000	
Mortgage on premises		10,000
Interest paid/received	1,000	460
Stock	4,670	
Bank and cash	2,850	
Wages	7,180	
Rent and rates	4,300	
Provision for bad debts		530
Debtors/creditors	8,070	4,340
Light and heat	2,640	
Stationery	450	
	145,020	145,020

You are given the following additional information:

1. Goods on sale or return have been treated as sales. These cost £300 and were invoiced to the customer for £400.
2. The provision for bad debts is to be adjusted to 10 per cent of debtors.
3. At 31 March 19X6 there is electricity accrued of £130 and rates prepaid amounting to £210.
4. Stock at 31 March 19X6 was valued at £3,690.
5. During the year the proprietor has taken goods costing £350 from the business for his own use.
6. Depreciation on plant is 25 per cent on the reducing balance method and on vehicles 20 per cent by the same method.
7. Unrecorded in the ledger is the sale on credit on 1 July 19X5 for £485 of a motor vehicle bought on 1 January 19X4 for £1,000.
8. There are bad debts of £370 that have not been entered in the ledger.
9. There was a stock of stationery at 31 March 19X6 which cost £230.

You are required to prepare a trading and profit and loss account for the year and a balance sheet at the end of the year.

3. The following trial balance has been extracted from the ledger of Andrea Howell, a sole trader, as at 31 May 19X9, the end of her most recent financial year.

Andrea Howell
Trial balance as at 31 May 19X9

	Dr	Cr
	£	£
Property, at cost	90,000	
Equipment, at cost	57,500	
Provisions for depreciation (as at 1 June 19X8)		
—property		12,500
—equipment		32,500
Stock, as at 1 June 19X8	27,400	
Purchases	259,600	
Sales		405,000

Discounts allowed	3,370	
Discounts received		4,420
Wages and salaries	52,360	
Bad debts	1,720	
Loan interest	1,560	
Carriage out	5,310	
Other operating expenses	38,800	
Trade debtors	46,200	
Trade creditors		33,600
Provision for bad debts		280
Cash on hand	151	
Bank overdraft		14,500
Drawings	28,930	
13 per cent loan		12,000
Capital, as at 1 June 19X8		98,101
	612,901	612,901

The following additional information as at 31 May 19X9 is available:

1. Stock as at the close of business was valued at £25,900.
2. Depreciation for the year ended 31 May 19X9 has yet to be provided as follows:
   Property: 1% using the straight line method.
   Equipment: 15% using the straight line method.
3. Wages and salaries are accrued by £140.
4. 'Other operating expenses' include certain expenses prepaid by £500. Other expenses included under this heading are accrued by £200.
5. The provision for bad debts is to be adjusted so that it is 0.5 per cent of trade debtors as at 31 May 19X9.
6. 'Purchases' include goods valued at £1,040 which were withdrawn by Mrs Howell for her own personal use.

   Required:
   Prepare Mrs Howell's trading and profit and loss account for the year ended 31 May 19X9 and her balance sheet as at 31 May 19X9.   (AAT)

4. S. Trader carries on a merchanting business. The following balances have been extracted from his books on 30 September 19X1:

	£
Capital—S. Trader, at 1 October 19X0	24,239
Office furniture and equipment	1,440
Cash drawings—S. Trader	4,888
Stock on hand—1 October 19X0	14,972
Purchases	167,760
Sales	203,845
Rent	1,350
Light and heat	475
Insurance	304
Salaries	6,352
Stationery and printing	737
Telephone and postage	517
General expenses	2,044
Travellers' commission and expenses	9,925
Discounts allowed	517
Discounts received	955
Bad debts written off	331
Debtors	19,100
Creditors	8,162

Balance at bank to S. Trader's credit	6,603
Petty cash in hand	29
Provision for doubtful debts	143

The following further information is to be taken into account:

1. Stock on hand on 30 September 19X1 was valued at £12,972.
2. Provision is to be made for the following liabilities and accrued expenses as at 30 September 19X1: Rent £450; lighting and heating £136; travellers' commission and expenses £806; accountancy charges £252.
3. Provision for doubtful debts is to be raised to 3 per cent closing debtor balances.
4. Office furniture and equipment is to be depreciated by 10 per cent on book value.
5. Mr Trader had removed stock costing £112 for his own use during the year.

You are required to prepare:

(a) Trading and profit and loss accounts for the year ended 30 September 19X1 grouping the various expenses under suitable headings, and

(b) a balance sheet as at that date   (CACA)

5. F. Harrison is in business as a trader. A trial balance taken out as at 31 January 19X6 was as follows:

	£	£
Purchases	42,400	
Sales		50,240
Returns inwards and outwards	136	348
Salaries and wages	4,100	
Rent, rates and insurance	860	
Sundry expenses	750	
Bad debts	134	
Provision for doubtful debts at 1 February 19X5		280
Stock on hand at 1 February 19X5	13,630	
Fixtures and fittings:		
At 1 February 19X5	1,400	
Additions on 30 September 19X5	240	
Motor vehicles:		
At 1 February 19X5	920	
Sale of vehicle (book value at 1 February 19X5 £80)		120
Sundry debtors and creditors	4,610	3,852
Cash at bank and in hand	3,820	
F. Harrison Capital a/c—Balance at 1 February 19X5		20,760
F. Harrison drawings a/c	2,600	
	£75,600	£75,600

You are required to prepare trading and profit and loss accounts for the year ended 31 January 19X6, and draw up a balance sheet as on that date.

The following information is to be taken into account:

1. Included in sales are goods on sale or return which cost £240 and which have been charged out with profit added at 20 per cent of sale price.
2. Outstanding amount not entered in the books were: rent £36, sundry expenses £90.
3. Prepayments were: rates £60, insurance £10.
4. Stock on hand on 31 January 19X6 was valued at £15,450.
5. Provision for doubtful debts is to be £340.
6. Depreciation is to be provided for as follows: fixtures and fittings 10 per cent per annum, motor vehicles 25 per cent per annum.   (CACA)

6. S. Bullock, a farmer, makes up his accounts to 31 March each year. The trial balance extracted from his books as at 31 March 19X6 was as follows:

	£	£
Purchases—livestock, seeds, fertilizers, fodder etc.	19,016	
Wages and National Insurance	2,883	
Rent, rates, telephone and insurance	1,018	
Farrier and veterinary charges	34	
Carriage	1,011	
Motor and tractor running expenses	490	
Repairs—Farm buildings	673	
Implements	427	
Contracting for ploughing, spraying and combine work	308	
General expenses	527	
Bank charges	191	
Professional charges	44	
Sales		29,162
Motor vehicles and tractors—as at 1 April 19X5	1,383	
additions	605	
Implements—as at 1 April 19X5	2,518	
additions	514	
Valuation as at 1 April 19X5:		
Livestock, seeds, fertilizers, fodder etc.	14,232	
Tillages and growing crops	952	
Loan from wife		1,922
Minister bank		4,072
S. Bullock—Capital at 1 April 19X5		6,440
Current Account at 1 April 19X5		6,510
Drawings during the year	1,280	
	£48,106	£48,106

On 31 March 19X6:	£	£
Debtors and prepayments were:		
Livestock sales	1,365	
Motor Licences	68	
Liabilities were: Seeds and fertilizers		180
Rent, rates and telephone		50
Motor and tractor running expenses		40
Professional charges		127
Contracting		179
General expenses		54

Included in the above-mentioned figure of £50 is £15 for rent and this is payable for the March 19X6 quarter. In arriving at this figure the landlord has allowed a deduction of £235 for materials purchased for repairs to the farm buildings, which were carried out by S. Bullock, and is included in the 'Repairs to farm buildings' shown in the trial balance. In executing these repairs it was estimated that £125 labour costs were incurred and these were included in 'Wages and National Insurance'. This cost was to be borne by S. Bullock.

The valuation as at 31 March 19X6 was:

	£
Livestock, seeds, fertilizers, fodder etc.	12,336
Tillages and growing crops	898

Depreciation, calculated on the book value as at 31 March 19X6 is to be written off as follows:

Motor vehicles and tractors	25 per cent per annum
Implements	12½ per cent per annum

You are requested to prepare:

1. the profit and loss account for the year ended 31 March 19X6, and
2. the balance sheet as at that date.

(CACA)

15. Manufacturing accounts and the valuation of stocks

The main differences between the accounts of commercial and manufacturing businesses stem from the former buying goods for resale without further processing whereas the latter buy raw materials and components which are processed into finished goods to be sold. This makes it necessary for a manufacturing business to calculate the total factory cost of goods produced. The amount is computed in what is termed a manufacturing account and the result shown in place of 'purchases' in the trading account of a non-manufacturing business. Furthermore, the stocks in the trading account are the stock of finished goods unsold at the start and end of the accounting year. Apart from these differences the profit and loss account of a manufacturing business is the same as that of a commercial business, in that they both contain selling and distribution costs, administrative costs and financial charges (such as interest). The balance sheet is also the same, except that of a manufacturing business will also include a number of different categories of stock, which will be described later.

The classification of costs

One of the major differences between the accounts of a commercial and manufacturing business concerns the classification of costs. In a manufacturing business, costs are usually classified as either direct costs or indirect costs/overheads. Direct costs are those which can be traced to a particular product, and comprise direct materials, direct labour/wages and direct expenses. Overheads are costs which cannot be traced or attributed to a specific product.

Direct materials consist of any goods that form a part of the final product. These are composed of the raw materials and components which a manufacturing business turns into its finished product. In the case of, for example, a car manufacturer, one of its raw materials may be iron ore used to produce engines. However the material inputs do not just consist of raw materials. For example, some of the materials purchased by a car manufacturer may include steel, which is the finished product of another industry. Similarly, many companies find it cheaper to buy rather than manufacture parts of their finished product. For example, car manufacturers buy components such as tyres, lighting equipment etc. from outside suppliers. Thus direct materials consist of raw materials and various types of components that make up the final product.

Direct labour typically comprises the wages of those employees who physically work on the products or (say) push buttons that start machines that are used to produce the finished products. Wages paid to foremen, supervisors, cleaners, maintenance staff etc. are not direct wages.

Direct expenses are any costs that are directly attributed to a specific product. The most common direct expenses are royalties paid for the right to produce the finished product, the cost of any special drawings and sub-contracted work.

Indirect costs/overheads are those costs that cannot be traced or attributed to a particular product, and comprise factory/production/manufacturing overheads, selling and distribution overheads, and administrative overheads. Examples of factory overheads include the wages of supervisors, foremen, maintenance and cleaning staff, rent and rates, power, light and heat, consumable tools, repairs to plant, depreciation of plant etc.

Categories of stocks

A manufacturing business also differs from a commercial business in that it has a number of different categories of stocks as follows.

Direct materials

This is composed of raw materials and components that have been purchased but not put into production at the end of the accounting year.

Work in progress

This refers to goods which are not complete at the end of the accounting year.

Finished goods

This consists of goods that have been produced which are unsold at the end of the accounting year.

Purposes and preparation of a manufacturing account

As has already been mentioned, the main purpose of a manufacturing account is to calculate the factory cost of the products that have been completed during the accounting year. This replaces the purchases item in the trading account and thus must be done before the trading account can be prepared (after the trial balance has been completed). In calculating the cost of completed production it is usual to show the following in the manufacturing account in the order shown below.

1. *The direct material cost* of goods that have been put into production during the year. To calculate this it will be necessary to adjust the cost of purchases of direct materials for the opening and closing stocks thus:

   direct materials in stock at start of year
   add: purchases of direct materials during year
   less: direct materials in stock at end of year
   = cost of direct materials put into production during year

   It is also common to add any carriage inwards to the cost of purchases.

2. *The direct labour costs*
3. *The direct expenses*
4. *The prime cost of production*
    This is the sum of the direct materials, direct labour and direct expenses.
5. *The factory overheads*
6. *The total factory costs*
    This is the sum of the prime costs and the factory overheads.
7. *The factory cost of completed production*
    The total factory costs relate both to those products that have been completed during the year and those which are only partially completed at the end of the year. To arrive at the factory cost of completed production it is therefore necessary to make an adjustment for the opening and closing work in progress thus:

work in progress at start of year
add: total factory costs
less: work in progress at end of year
= factory cost of completed production

   The factory cost of completed production is transferred to the trading account in place of 'purchases' in a non-manufacturing business. The cost of sales is computed by adjusting the cost of completed production for the opening and closing stocks of finished goods thus:

stock of finished goods at start of year
add: factory cost of completed production
less: stock of finished goods at end of year
= cost of goods sold

An illustration of the preparation of a manufacturing account is shown in Example 15.1.

Example 15.1
The following information relating to the year ended 30 April 19X7 has been extracted from the books of A. Bush, a motor vehicle component manufacturer.

	£
Sales	298,000
Stocks of direct materials at 1 May 19X6	7,900
Stocks of direct materials at 30 April 19X7	6,200
Work in progress at 1 May 19X6	8,400
Work in progress at 30 April 19X7	9,600
Stocks of finished goods at 1 May 19X6	5,400
Stocks of finished goods at 30 April 19X7	6,800
Purchases of direct materials	68,400
Direct wages	52,800
Production supervisors' salaries	34,800
Sales staff salaries	41,700
Accounting staff salaries	38,200

Royalties paid for products produced under licence	17,500
Cost of power for machinery	9,200
Repairs to plant	6,700
Bad debts	5,100
Interest on bank loan	7,400
Depreciation on plant	18,600
Depreciation on delivery vehicles	13,200
Depreciation on accounting office equipment	11,500

Prepare manufacturing, trading and profit and loss accounts for the year ended 30 April 19X7, showing clearly the total direct/prime costs, manufacturing/factory costs, cost of completed production and cost of sales.

A. Bush
Manufacturing, trading and profit and loss accounts for the year ended 30 April 19X7

Direct materials:			
Stock at 1/5/X6	7,900	*Cost of completed*	
Add: purchases	68,400	*production* c/d	208,300
	76,300		
Less: Stock at 30/4/X7	6,200		
	70,100		
Direct wages	52,600		
Royalties	17,500		
Prime costs	140,200		
Factory overheads:			
Supervisors' salaries	34,800		
Power	9,200		
Repairs to plant	6,700		
Depreciation on plant	18,600		
Manufacturing costs	209,500		
Add: WIP at 1/5/X6	8,400		
	217,900		
Less: WIP at 30/4/X7	9,600		
	208,300		208,300
Finished goods:		Sales	298,000
Stock at 1/5/X6	5,400		
Add: cost of completed			
production b/d	208,300		
	213,700		
Less: stock at 30/4/X7	6,800		
Cost of sales	206,900		
Gross profit c/d	91,100		
	298,000		298,000

Selling and distribution costs:		Gross profit b/d	91,100
Sales staff salaries	41,700		
Depreciation on vehicles	13,200		
Bad debts	5,100		
Administrative costs:			
Staff salaries	38,200		
Depreciation on equipment	11,500		
Interest on loan	7,400	Net loss c/d	26,000
	117,100		117,100
Net loss b/d	26,000		

Manufacturing profits

In some businesses, manufactured goods are transferred from the factory to the warehouse at market prices, or an approximation thereof, in the form of cost plus a given percentage for profit. This is intended to represent the price that the warehouse would have to pay if it bought the goods from an external supplier, or the price the factory would receive if it sold the goods to an external customer. This is commonly referred to as the transfer price. The purpose of having internal transfer prices is said to be to make the managers in the factory and warehouse more aware of the impact of market forces, increase motivation and facilitate the evaluation of their performance.

The accounting entries are relatively straightforward. The figure for completed production carried down from the manufacturing account to the trading account will simply be at some transfer price or valuation other than cost. This gives rise to a manufacturing profit (or loss) which will be the difference between the two sides of the manufacturing account. The double entry for this profit (or loss) is to credit (or debit) the profit and loss account.

The valuation of finished goods and work in progress

The work in progress shown in the manufacturing account is usually valued at production/factory cost; that is, prime costs plus factory overheads. This is why the adjustment for the opening and closing work in progress is made after the total factory costs have been computed. Similarly, the finished goods stock shown in the trading account is normally valued at factory costs. This is consistent with the valuation of the completed production, which is also included in the trading account at factory cost. Thus neither the work in progress nor finished goods includes other overheads such as selling and distribution costs, administrative costs and interest. Sometimes work in progress is valued at prime cost; that is, excluding factory overheads. In this case the adjustment for work in progress must be made before the factory overheads in the manufacturing account.

The above assertions relating to the valuation of work in progress (WIP) and finished goods stock can be explained further by reference to Statement of Standard Accounting Practice 9—Stocks and Long Term Contracts.[1] This states that 'in order to match costs and revenue, costs of stocks should comprise that expenditure which has been incurred in the normal course of business in bringing the product or service to its present location and condition. This expenditure should include, in addition to cost of purchase (of direct materials), such costs of conversion as are appropriate to the location and condition. Costs of conversion comprises: (a) costs which are specifically attributable to units of production, i.e. direct labour, direct expenses and sub-contracted work; (b) production overheads. Note that this specifically excludes selling, distribution and administrative overheads.

Finally, it is important to consider that sometimes goods in stock may have to be sold at a price which is below their cost. If there are goods in stock at the end of a given accounting year which are expected to result in a loss, those goods should be valued and entered in the accounts at their expected proceeds of sale and not their cost. This is an application of the prudence concept in that a potential loss is being recognized in the accounts before it is realized. SSAP9 therefore dictates that 'stocks normally need to be stated at cost, or, if lower, at net realisable value. The comparison of cost and net realisable value needs to be made in respect of each item of stock separately. Net realisable value is the estimated proceeds from the sale of items of stock (and WIP) less all further costs to completion and less all costs to be incurred in marketing, selling and distributing directly related to the items in question'.[1]

The identification of the cost of stock

In the case of both manufacturing and non-manufacturing business the determination of the cost/purchase price of goods in stock often presents a major problem. It is frequently not possible to identify the particular batch(es) of goods that were purchased which are in stock at the end of the year. This is referred to as fungible stock, which means substantially indistinguishable goods. In these circumstances it is necessary to make an *assumption* about the cost of goods in stock. There are a number of possible assumptions, but the most reasonable assumption will depend on the type of goods involved, the procedure for handling the receipt and sale of stocks, prices etc. According to SSAP9, the most appropriate assumption is one which 'provides a fair approximation to the expenditure actually incurred'.[1] This is discussed further below.

Most large businesses operate what is called a perpetual inventory system, which includes a stores ledger containing an account for each type of good that is purchased. The stores ledger accounts are used to record the quantities and prices of goods purchased, the quantities and cost of goods sold (or issued to production in the case of direct materials), and thus the balance and cost of goods in stock after each receipt and sale. However, this system also requires an assumption or decision about the cost of goods in stock, and thus the cost of goods that were sold.

As explained above, there are a number of possible assumptions, or what are referred to as bases/methods of identifying/pricing the cost of stock. The bases make assumptions about the flow of items in stock. These flow assumptions are not selected as a result of the actual way in which stock is used but in order to reflect a particular view of the economic effects of stock usage in accounts. Three common approaches are 'first in, first out' (FIFO)', 'last in, first out' (LIFO) and average unit cost (AUC).

These assume, respectively that (i) the oldest stock is used first, (ii) the more recent stock is used first, and (iii) stock used should be charged at the average cost of all the particular type of item in stock.

In some aspects, the last of these represents a compromise between the other two. It becomes arithmetically more complicated than the former and is not considered in detail here. FIFO and LIFO are described below using Example 15.2. In order to appreciate fully the nature of the problem, the reader may find it advantageous to attempt Part (b) before proceeding further. Note that an answer which claims it cannot be done is not acceptable. It must be done!

Example 15.2

P. Easton commenced business on 1 January 19X1 as a dealer in scrap iron. The following purchases and sales were made during the year:

Jan	Purchased 40 tonnes at £5 per tonne
Feb	Purchased 50 tonnes at £6 per tonne
Mar	Sold 30 tonnes at £10 per tonne
Apr	Purchased 70 tonnes at £7 per tonne
May	Sold 80 tonnes at £15 per tonne

You are required to prepare:

(a) a perpetual inventory record of the quantities and values of goods purchased, sold and stock; and

(b) a trading account showing the gross profit for the six months to 30 June 19X1 given that the above are the only purchases and sales.

State any assumptions that you make.

1. *First in, first out (FIFO)*

The FIFO assumption is that the goods sold are those which have been in stock for the longest time. The stock is therefore composed of the most recent purchases that make up the quantity in stock, and the cost of stock is the price paid for these. Given the FIFO assumption, the answer to Example 15.2 will be as follows:

Stores ledger account

Date	Purchases			Cost of sales			Stock		
	Units	Price	Value	Units	Price	Value	Units	Price	Value
Jan	40	5	200				40	5	200
Feb	50	6	300				40	5	200
							50	6	300
							90		500
Mar				30	5	150	10	5	50
							50	6	300
							60		350

Apr	70	7	490				10	5	50
							50	6	300
							70	7	490
							130		840
May				10	5	50			
				50	6	300			
				20	7	140	50	7	350
				80		490			
	160		990	110		640	50		350

P. Easton
Trading account for the six months ended 30 June 19X1

	£	£
Sales: 30 tonnes @ £10	300	
80 tonnes @ £15	1,200	1,500
Less: Cost of sales—		
Purchases	990	
Less: Stock at 30 June 19X1	350	640
Gross profit		860

The FIFO method is based on the premise that the physical movement of goods over time will have this sequence of events, particularly where they are perishable. The use of the first in, first out method is favoured by SSAP9, and the Inland Revenue.

2. *Last in, first out (LIFO)*

The LIFO assumption is that the goods sold are those which have been in stock for the shortest time. The stock is therefore composed of those goods which have been held for the longest time, and the cost of stock is the price paid for these. Given the LIFO assumption, the answer to Example 15.2 will be as follows:

Stores ledger account

Date	Purchases			Cost of sales			Stock		
	Units	Price	Value	Units	Price	Value	Units	Price	Value
Jan	40	5	200				40	5	200
Feb	50	5	300				50	6	300
							40	5	200
							90		500
Mar				30	6	180	20	6	120
							40	5	200
							60		320

Date	Receipts qty	Receipts price	Receipts value	Issues qty	Issues price	Issues value	Balance qty	Balance price	Balance value
Apr	70	7	490				70	7	490
							20	6	120
							40	5	200
							130		810
May				70	7	490	10	6	60
				10	6	60	40	5	200
				80		550	50	5	260
							50		260
	160		990	110		730	50		260

Average unit cost

Under this approach the cost of stock issued in March would be calculated as 30 units out of the total of 90 units costing a total of $(40 \times £5) + (50 \times £5) = £500$, i.e. $(30/90) \times £500 = £167$.

The remaining stock of 60 units would be valued at $£500 - £167 = £333$.

The cost of the May issues would be $(80/130) \times (£333 + £490) = £506$.

The closing stock would be valued at $(£333 + £490) - £506 = £317$.

FIFO and LIFO compared

Clearly each of these methods of calculating the cost of stock results in different values for stock and profit. In times of constantly rising prices, FIFO will give a higher figure of profits and value of stock than LIFO to the extent that it matches older, lower costs against revenues. A business should choose whichever method is appropriate to its particular circumstances and apply this consistently in order that meaningful comparisons can be made.

FIFO is by far the most common method used in practice in the UK because it is favoured by SSAP9 and the Inland Revenue. However, some businesses and accountants still advocate the use of LIFO on the grounds that this gives a more realistic figure of profit in times of rising prices. The valuation of stocks is a controversial issue in accounting, and is one of the areas most open to deliberate manipulation. The debate is further accentuated by the fact that the Companies Act and the International Accounting Standards Committee (IASC) permit the use of either FIFO or LIFO. It remains to be seen whether the courts in the UK will insist on the use of those methods favoured by SSAP9, such as FIFO.

Reference

1.   Accounting Standards Committee (1988). *Statement of Standard Accounting Practice 9—Stocks and Long Term Contracts* (ICAEW).

Exercises

1. (a) Explain the difference between direct costs and overheads.
   (b) Describe the different types of direct costs and overheads found in a manufacturing business.

2. Describe the different categories of stocks normally held by a manufacturing business.

3. (a) Explain the main purpose of a manufacturing account.
   (b) Describe the structure and main groups of costs found in a manufacturing account.

4. (a) Explain the difference between the total factory cost of production and the factory cost of completed production.
   (b) What is the justification for adjusting the total factory cost for work in progress rather than, say, the total prime/direct cost?

5. Work in progress and finished goods stocks should be valued at the cost of purchase and conversion. Explain.

6. Explain the circumstances in which stocks might be shown in the accounts at a value different from their historic cost.

7. Explain fully the basis on which finished goods stock and work in progress should be valued in final accounts.

8. Explain how the matching principle and the accruals concept are applied to the valuation of stocks.

9. (a) What is a perpetual inventory system?
   (b) Describe two methods of calculating the cost of fungible stocks.
   (c) Explain the circumstances in which each of these methods may be justifiable.

10. 'In selecting a method of calculating the cost of stock, management should ensure that the method chosen bears a reasonable relationship to actual costs. Methods such as . . . LIFO do not usually bear such a relationship' (ASC, SSAP9). Discuss.

11. The trial balance extracted at 30 April 19X4 from the books of Upton Upholstery, a furniture manufacturer, is given below:

	£	£
Factory machinery at cost	28,000	
Factory machinery depreciation 1/5/X3		5,000
Office equipment	2,000	
Office equipment depreciation 1/5/X3		800
Trade debtors and creditors	15,000	16,000
Cash and bank	2,300	
Bank loan		11,000
Stocks 1/5/X3—Raw materials	4,000	
Incomplete production	16,400	
Finished goods	9,000	
Carriage inwards	1,200	
Carriage outwards	700	
Purchases—raw material	84,000	
Light and heat	3,000	
Rent and rates	6,600	
Direct factory wages	19,900	
Office wages	5,200	
Sales commision to selling agents	1,400	
Sales of finished goods		140,000
Capital account		35,000
Drawings	9,100	
	£207,800	£207,800

Notes
1. At 30 April 19X4, accrued direct factory wages amounted to £600 and office wages £100; rent paid included £600 paid on 20 January 19X4, for the period 1 January to 30 June 19X4.
2. Records showed that, at the year end, stock values were as follows: raw materials £5,400; incomplete production £17,000; finished goods £8,000.
3. Depreciation should be allowed for factory machinery on the straight line method over seven years, and office equipment on the reducing balance method at 25 per cent p.a.

4. A provision of £1,000 should be made for doubtful debts.
5. Light and heat should be apportioned between the factory and office in the ratio 4 : 1 respectively; rent and rates in the ratio 3 : 1 respectively.

You are required to prepare manufacturing, trading and profit and loss accounts for the year ended 30 April 19X4 and a balance sheet at that date.

12. From the following information prepare manufacturing, trading and profit and loss accounts for the year ended 31 December 19X9. Show clearly the prime cost, factory cost of completed production, cost of sales, gross profit, administrative overheads, selling and distribution overheads and net profit.

	£
Stock of raw materials at 1 Jan 19X9	2,453
Work in progress valued at factory cost at 1 Jan 19X9	1,617
Stock of finished goods at 1 Jan 19X9	3,.968
Purchases of raw materials	47,693
Purchases of finished goods	367
Raw materials returned to suppliers	4,921
Carriage outwards	487
Carriage inwards	683
Direct wages	23,649
Administrative salaries	10,889
Supervisors' wages	5,617
Royalties payable	7,500
Electricity used in factory	2,334
Light and heat for administrative offices	998
Sales staff salaries and commission	8,600
Bad debts	726
Discount received	2,310
Discount allowed	1,515
Depreciation—plant	13,400
—delivery vehicles	3,700
—office fixtures and furniture	1,900
Rent and rates (factory $\frac{3}{4}$, office $\frac{1}{4}$)	4,800
Delivery expenses	593
Postage and telephone	714
Printing and stationery	363
Proceeds from the sale of scrap metal	199
Interest payable on loan	3,000
Bank charges	100
Insurance on plant	1,750
Advertising	625
Repairs to plant	917
Sales	145,433

Purchases of raw materials include £2,093, and direct wages £549, for materials and work done in constructing an extension to the factory.

Stock of raw materials at 31 Dec 19X9	3,987
Work in progress valued at factory cost at 31 Dec 19X9	2,700
Stock of finished goods at 31 Dec 19X9	5,666

13. W. Wagner, a manufacturer, provided the following information for the year ended 31 August 19X0:

Stocks at 1 September 19X9	£
Raw materials	25,000
Work in progress	25,900
Finished goods	26,600
Raw materials purchased	176,600
Factory general expenses	14,800

Direct wages	86,900
Repairs to plant and machinery	9,900
Factory lighting and heating	20,010
Carriage inwards	1,910
Carriage outwards	2,500
Sales	320,000
Raw materials returned	7,800
Factory maintenance wages	19,000
Administrative expenses	30,000
Selling and distribution expenses	15,100
Plant and machinery at cost	178,000
Freehold land and buildings at cost	160,000
Provision for depreciation on plant and machinery (at 1 September 19X9)	80,000

Additional information:

1. Amounts owing at 31 August 19X0:

	£
Direct wages	4,800
Factory heating and lighting	1,500

2. Depreciation on plant and machinery is to be provided at 10 per cent per annum on cost. There were no sales or purchases of plant and machinery during the year.

3. Stocks at 31 August 19X0:

	£
Raw materials	30,000
Work in progress	17,800
Finished goods	35,090

The raw materials are valued at cost, the work in progress at factory cost, whilst the stock of finished goods is valued at the factory transfer price.

4. All manufactured goods are transferred to the warehouse at factory cost plus 10 per cent.

5. Other balances at 31 August 19X0:

	£
Trade debtors	26,000
Trade creditors	38,000

Required:
(a) A manufacturing account for the year ended 31 August 19X0.
(b) A trading and profit and loss account for the year ended 31 August 19X0.
(c) Comment on Wagner's current year manufacturing profitablity.   (AEB adapted)

14. Zacotex Ltd, a manufacturer, produced the following financial information for the year ended 31 March 19X9.

	£
Raw material purchases	250,000
Direct labour	100,000
Direct expenses	80,900
Indirect factory labour	16,000
Factory maintenance costs	9,700
Machine repairs	11,500
Sales of finished goods during the year	788,100
Stocks at 1 April 19X8:	
Raw materials	65,000
Finished goods	48,000
Work in progress	52,500

Other factory overhead	14,500
Factory heating and lighting	19,000
Factory rates	11,500
Administration expenses	22,000
Selling and distribution expenses	36,800

Additional information:

1. The stocks held at 31 March 19X9 were:

Raw materials	£51,400
Finished goods	£53,800
Work in progress	£41,000

NB: Raw materials are valued at cost; finished goods at factory cost; work in progress at factory cost.
Of the raw materials held in stock at 31 March 19X9, £15,000 had suffered flood damage and it was estimated that they could only be sold for £2,500.
The remaining raw material stock could only be sold on the open market at cost less 10 per cent.
2. One quarter of the administration expenses are to be allocated to the factory.
3. The raw materials purchases figure for the year includes a charge for carriage inwards. On 31 March 19X9 a credit note for £1550 was received in respect of a carriage inwards overcharge. No adjustment had been made for this amount.
4. Expenses in arrear at 31 March 19X9 were:

	£
Direct labour	6,600
Machine repairs	1,700
Selling and distribution expenses	4,900

5. Plant and machinery at 1 April 19X8:

	£
At cost	250,000
Aggregate depreciation	75,000

During the year an obsolete machine (cost £30,000, depreciation to date £8,000) was sold as scrap for £5,000.
On 1 October 19X8 new machinery was purchased for £70,000 with an installation charge of £8,000.
The company depreciates its plant and machinery at 10 per cent per annum on cost on all items in company ownership at the end of the accounting year. Items purchased during the year are allocated a full year's depreciation charge.
6. An analysis of the sales of finished goods revealed the following:

	£
Goods sold for cash	105,000
Goods sold on credit	623,100
Goods sold on sale or return: returned	25,000
Goods sold on sale or return: retained	
and invoice confirmed	35,000
	788,100

7. On 1 April 19X8 the company arranged a long term loan of £250,000 at a fixed rate of interest of 11 per cent per annum. No provision had been made for the payment of the interest.

Required:

For the year ended 31 March 19X9:
(a)   a manufacturing account showing prime cost and factory cost of goods produced
(b)   a trading and profit and loss account.   (AEB adapted)

15. On 1 April 19X5, Modern Dwellings Ltd commenced business as builders and contractors. It expended £14,000 on the purchase of six acres of land with the intention of dividing the land into plots and buildings 72 houses thereon.

During the year ended 31 March 19X6 roads and drains were constructed for the project at a total cost of £8,320.

Building was commenced, and on 31 March 19X6, 30 houses had been completed and eight were in course of construction.

During the year the outlay on houses was as follows:

Materials etc.	£36,000
Labour and sub-contracting	£45,000

The value of the work in progress on the uncompleted houses at 31 March 19X6 amounted to £8,500, being calculated on the actual cost of materials, labour and sub-contracting to date.

During the year, 24 houses had been sold, realizing £80,000.

Prepare a trading account for the year ended 31 March 19X6. It can be assumed that the plots on which the 72 houses are to be built are all of equal size and value.   (CACA)

16. After stocktaking for the year ended 31 May 19X5 had taken place, the closing stock of Cobden Ltd was aggregated to a figure of £87,612.

During the course of the audit which followed, the undernoted facts were discovered:

1. Some goods stored outside had been included at their normal cost price of £570. They had, however, deteriorated and would require an estimated £120 to be spent to restore them to their original condition, after which they could be sold for £800.
2. Some goods had been damaged and were now unsaleable. They could, however, be sold for £110 as spares after repairs estimated at £40 had been carried out. They had originally cost £200.
3. One stock sheet had been over-added by £126 and another under-added by £72.
4. Cobden Ltd had received goods costing £2,010 during the last week of May 19X5 but because the invoices did not arrive until June 19X5, they have not been included in stock.
5. A stock sheet total of £1,234 had been transferred to the summary sheet as £1,24.
6. Invoices totalling £638 arrived during the last week of May 19X5 (and were included in purchases and in creditors) but, because of transport delays, the goods did not arrive until late June 19X5 and were not included in closing stock.
7. Portable generators on hire from another company at a charge of £347 were included, at this figure, in stock.
8. Free samples sent to Cobden Ltd by various suppliers had been included in stock at the catalogue price of £63.
9. Goods costing £418 sent to customers on a sale or return basis had been included in stock by Cobden Ltd at their selling price, £602.
10. Goods sent on a sale or return basis to Cobden Ltd had been included in stock at the amount payable (£267) if retained. No decision to retain had been made.

Required:

Using such of the above information as is relevant, prepare a schedule amending the stock figure as at 31 May 19X5. State your reason for each amendment or for not making an amendment.   (CACA)

17. Your company sells, for £275 each unit, a product which it purchases from several different manufacturers, all charging different prices. The manufacturers deliver at the beginning of each week throughout each month. The following details relate to the month of February.

	Quantity	Cost each £	Sales (units)
Opening stock	10	145	
Deliveries: Week 1	20	150	15
Week 2	34	165	33
Week 3	50	145	35
Week 4	30	175	39

From the above data you are required to:

(a) prepare stock records detailing and values using the following pricing techniques:

    (i) last in, fast out (LIFO);
    (ii) first in, first out (FIFO).

(b) prepare trading accounts using each of the stock pricing methods in (a) above and showing the gross profit for each method.
(c) compare the results of your calculations and state the advantages and disadvantages of FIFO and LIFO pricing methods in times of inflation. (JMB adapted)

18. A businessman started trading with a capital in cash of £6,000 which he placed in the business bank account at the outset.

His transactions, none of which were on credit, were as follows (in date sequence) for the first accounting period. All takings were banked immediately and all suppliers were paid by cheque. He traded in only one line of merchandise.

	Purchases		Sales	
Quantity	Price per unit		Quantity	Price per unit
No.	£		No.	£
1,200	1.00			
1,000	1.05		800	1.70
600	1.10		600	1.90
900	1.20		1,100	2.00
800	1.25		1,300	2.00
700	1.30		400	2.05

In addition he incurred expenses amounting to £1,740, of which he still owed £570 at the end of the period.

Required:
Prepare separately using both the FIFO (first in, first out) and the LIFO (last in, first out) methods of stock valuation:

(a) a statement of cost of sales for the period; and
(b) a balance sheet at the end of the period.

Note: Workings are an integral part of the answer and must be shown. (CACA)

16. The bank reconciliation statement

The purpose of preparing a bank reconciliation statement is to ascertain whether or not the balance shown in the cash book is correct by comparing it with that shown on the bank statement/passbook supplied by the bank. In practice, these two figures are rarely the same because of errors, omissions and the timing of bank deposits and cheque payments.

The bank reconciliation is not done in a book of account and thus is not a part of the double entry system. It must be prepared at least yearly before the final accounts are compiled. Because most businesses usually have a large number of cheque transactions they often prepare a bank reconciliation statement either monthly or at least quarterly.

The first step in the preparation of a bank reconciliation involves identifying payments, and sometimes receipts, that are on the bank statement but which have not been entered in the cash book. Such payments may include cheques dishonoured, bank charges and interest, standing orders for hire purchase instalments, insurance premiums, loan interest etc. Occasionally, receipts such as interest and dividends received by credit transfer are also found to be on the bank statement but not in the cash book. When these omissions of receipts and payments occur the remedy is obviously to enter them in the cash book and compute a new balance. However, in examination questions the student is sometimes required to build them into the bank reconciliation statement instead.

In addition to the above omissions there are nearly always also receipts and payments in the cash book which at the date of the reconciliation have not yet been entered by the bank on the bank statement. These consist of:

1. Cheques and cash received that have been paid into the bank and entered in the cash book but which have not *yet* been credited on the bank statement.
2. Cheques drawn that have been sent to the payee and entered in the cash book but which have not *yet* been presented to our bank for payment or which have not *yet* passed through the bank clearing system and thus do not appear on the bank statement.

Example 6.1 shows the procedure involved in preparing a bank reconciliation statement.

Example 16.1
The following is the cash book of J. Alton for the month of June 19X5.

Cash book

19X5			19X5		
1 June	Balance b/d	1,000	2 June	D. Cat	240
11 June	A. Hand	370	13 June	E. Dog	490
16 June	B. Leg	510	22 June	F. Bird	750
24 June	C. Arm	620	30 June	Balance c/d	1,200
30 June	Cash	180			
		2,680			2,680

The following is the statement of J. Alton received from his bank:

Bank statement

Date	Details	Debit	Credit	Balance
19X5				
1 June	Balance			1,000
5 June	D. Cat	240		760
15 June	A. Hand		370	1,130
18 June	E. Dog	490		640
20 June	Dividend received		160	800
21 June	B. Leg		510	1,310
30 June	Bank charges	75	510	1,235

In practice bank statements do not usually show the names of the people from whom cheques were received and paid. It is therefore necessary to identify the payments by means of the cheque number. However, the use of names simplifies the example for ease of understanding. The procedure is essentially the same.

The first step is to tick all those items which appear in both the cash book and on the bank statement during the month of June. A note is then made of the items which are unticked as follows:

1. Cheques and cash paid into the bank and entered in the cash book but not credited on the bank statement by 30 June 19X5 = C. Arm £620 + Cash £180 = £800.
2. Cheques drawn and entered in the cash book not presented for payment by 30 June 19X5 = F. Bird £750.
3. Amounts received by credit transfer shown on the bank statement not entered in the cash book = Dividends £160.
4. Standing orders and other payments shown on the bank statement not entered in the cash book = Bank charges £75.

Clearly Items 1 and 2 above will eventually appear on the bank statement in a later month. Items 3 and 4 must be entered in the cash book. However, the purpose of the bank reconciliation statement is to ascertain whether the difference between the balance in the cash book at 30 June 19X5 of £1,200 and that shown on the bank statement at the same date of £1,235 is explained by the above list of unticked items. Alternatively, are there other errors or omissions that need to be investigated?

The bank reconciliation statement will appear as follows:

J. Alton
Bank reconciliation statement as at 30 June 19X5

	£	£
Balance per cash book		1,200
Add: Dividends received not entered in cash book	160	
Cheques not yet presented	750	910
		2,110
Less: Bank charges not entered in cash book	75	
Amounts not yet credited	800	875
Balance per bank statement		1,235

It can thus be seen that since the above statement reconciles the difference between the balances in the cash book and on the bank statement, there are unlikely to be any further errors or omissions.

Notes

1. The dividends received are added to the cash book balance because it is lower than the bank statement balance as a result of this omission. Also it will increase by this amount when the dividends are entered in the cash book.
2. The bank charges are deducted from the cash book balance because the bank statement balance has been reduced by this amount but the cash book balance has not. Also, the cash book balance will decrease by this amount when the bank charges are entered in the cash book.
3. The cheques not yet presented are added to the cash book balance because it has been reduced by this amount whereas the bank statement balance has not.
4. The amounts not yet credited are deducted from the cash book balance because it has been increased by this amount whereas the bank statement balance has not.

Sometimes in examination questions the student is not given the cash book balance. In this case the bank reconciliation statement is prepared in reverse order as follows:

	£	£
Balance per bank statement		1,235
Add: Amounts not yet credited	800	
Payments on bank statement not in the cash book	75	875
		2,110
Less: Cheques not yet presented	750	
Receipts on bank statement not in the cash book	160	910
= Balance per cash book		1,200

An alternative method of dealing with bank reconciliations is to amend the cash book for any errors and omissions, and only include in the bank reconciliation statement those items which constitute timing differences. This is illustrated in Example 16.2, along with some other items frequently found in examination questions.

Example 16.2

The following is a summary from the cash book of Shopping Ltd for March 19X8:

Cash book

Opening balance b/d	5,610	Payments	41,890
Receipts	37,480	Closing balance c/d	1,200
	43,090		43,090

When checking the cash book against the bank statement the following discrepancies were found:

1. Bank charges of £80 shown in the bank statement have not been entered in the cash book

2. The bank has debited a cheque for £370 in error to the company's account
3. Cheques totalling £960 have not yet been presented to the bank for payment
4. Dividends received of £420 have been credited on the bank statement but not recorded in the cash book
5. There are cheques received of £4,840 which are entered in the cash book but not yet credited to the company's account by the bank
6. A cheque for £170 has been returned by the bank marked 'refer to drawer' but no entry relating to this has been made in the books
7. The opening balance in the cash book should have been £6,510 and not £5,610
8. The bank statement shows that there is an overdraft at 31 March 19X8 of £1,980

You are required to:

(a) make the entries necessary to correct the cash book; and
(b) prepare a bank reconciliation statement as at 31 March 19X8.

Cash book

Balance b/d	1,200	Bank charges	80
Dividends	420	Refer to drawer	170
Error in balance	900	Balance c/d	2,270
	2,520		2,520
Balance b/d	2,270		

Shopping Ltd
Bank reconciliation statement as at 31 March 19X8

	£	£
Balance per cash book		2,270
Add: Cheques not yet presented		960
		3,230
Less: Amounts not yet credited	4,840	
Cheque debited in error	370	5,210
Balance per bank statement (overdrawn)		1,980

Notes

1. The cheque debited in error is shown in the bank reconciliation statement rather than the cash book because it will presumably be corrected on the bank statement in due course and thus not affect the cash book.
2. Sometimes in examination questions the cash book contains a credit (i.e. overdrawn) balance. In this case, the bank reconciliation statement is prepared by reversing the additions and subtractions which are made when there is a favourable cash book balance. The bank reconciliation statement will thus appear as follows:

   Balance per cash book (credit/overdrawn)
   Add: Amounts not yet credited
   Less: Cheques not yet presented
   = Balance per bank statement

Alternatively if the cash book balance is not given in the question and the bank statement contains an overdrawn balance, the bank reconciliation statement would be prepared as follows:

Balance per bank statement (debit/overdrawn)
Add: Cheques not yet presented
Less: Amounts not yet credited
= Balance per cash book

Exercises

1. Explain the purpose of a bank reconciliation statement.

2. Describe the procedures involved in the collection of the data needed to prepare a bank reconciliation statement.

3. The following is a summary from the cash book of the Rosie Company Limited for October 19X7:

Cash book

	£		£
Opening balance b/d	1,407	Payments	15,520
Receipts	15,073	Closing balance c/f	960
	£16,480		£16,480

On investigation you discover that:

1. Bank charges of £35 shown on the bank statement have not been entered in the cash book.
2. A cheque drawn for £47 has been entered in error as a receipt.
3. A cheque for £18 has been returned by the bank marked 'refer to drawer', but it has not been written back in the cash book.
4. An error of transposition has occurred in that the opening balance in the cash book should have been carried down as £1,470.
5. Three cheques paid to suppliers for £214, £370 and £30 have not yet been presented to the bank.
6. The last page of the paying-in book shows a deposit of £1,542 which has not yet been credited to the account by the bank.
7. The bank has debited a cheque for £72 in error to the company's account.
8. The bank statement shows an overdrawn balance of £124.

You are required to:
(a) show what adjustments you would make in the cash book; and
(b) prepare a bank reconciliation statement as at 31 October 19X7.   (CACA)

4. The following is a summary of the cash book of Grow Ltd for March 19X9:

Cash book

Opening balance b/d	4,120	Payments	46,560
Receipts	45,320	Closing balance c/d	2,880
	49,440		49,440

On investigation you discover that at 31 March 19X9:

1. The last page of the paying-in book shows a deposit of £1,904 which has not yet been credited by the bank.
2. Two cheques paid to suppliers for £642 and £1,200 have not yet been presented to the bank.
3. Dividends received of £189 are shown on the bank statement but not entered in the cash book.

4.   Bank charges of £105 shown on the bank statement have not been entered in the cash book.
5.   A cheque for £54 has been returned by the bank marked 'refer to drawer', but it has not been written back in the cash book.
6.   A cheque drawn for £141 has benn entered in error as a receipt in the cash book.
7.   The bank has debited a cheque for £216 in error to the company's account.

You are required to:
(a)   show the adjustments that should be made in the cash book; and
(b)   prepare a bank reconciliation statement at 31 March 19X9.

5.   On 15 May 19X8, Mrs Lake received her monthly bank statement for the month ended 30 April 19X8. The bank statement contained the following details:

Mrs Lake
Statement of account with Smith Ltd
(* Balance indicates account is overdrawn)

Date	Particulars	Payments	Receipts	Balance
		£	£	£
1 Apr	Balance			1,053.29
2 Apr	236127	210.70		842.59
3 Apr	Bank Giro Credit		192.35	1,034.94
6 Apr	236126	15.21		1,019.73
6 Apr	Charges	12.80		1,006.93
9 Apr	236129	43.82		963.11
10 Apr	427519	19.47		943.64
12 Apr	236128	111.70		831.94
17 Apr	Standing Order	32.52		799.42
20 Apr	Sundry Credit		249.50	1,048.92
23 Apr	236130	77.87		971.05
23 Apr	236132	59.09		911.96
25 Apr	Bank Giro Credit		21.47	933.43
27 Apr	Sundry Credit		304.20	1,237.63
30 Apr	236133	71.18		1,166.45

For the corresponding period, Mrs Lake's own records contained the following bank account:

Date	Detail	£	Date	Detail	Cheque No.	£
1 Apr	Balance	827.38	5 Apr	Purchases	128	111.70
2 Apr	Sales	192.35	10 Apr	Electricity	129	43.82
18 Apr	Sales	249.50	16 Apr	Purchases	130	87.77
24 Apr	Sales	304.20	18 Apr	Rent	131	30.00
30 Apr	Sales	192.80	20 Apr	Purchases	132	59.09
			25 Apr	Purchases	133	71.18
			30 Apr	Wages	134	52.27
			30 Apr	Balance		1,310.40
		£1,766.23				£1,766.23

Required:
(a)   Prepare a statement reconciling the balance at 30 April as given by the bank statement to the balance at 30 April as stated in the bank account.
(b)   Explain briefly which items in your bank reconciliation statement would require further investigation.

(CACA)

6. A young and inexperienced bookkeeper is having great difficulty in producing a bank reconciliation statement at 31 December. He gives you his attempt to produce a summarized cash book, and also the bank statement received for the month of December. These are shown below. You may assume that the bank statement is correct. You may also assume that the trial balance at 1 January did indeed show a bank overdraft of £7,000.12.

Cash book summary–draft

	£	£	£	
1 Jan				
Opening overdraft		7000.12	35,000.34	payments Jan–Nov
Jan–Nov receipts	39,500.54			
Add: discounts	500.02			
				balance 30 Nov
		40,000.56	12,000.34	
		47,000.68	47,000.68	
1 Dec		12,000.34		payments Dec Cheque No.
Dec Receipts	178.19		37.14	7654
	121.27		192.79	7655
	14.92		5,000.00	7656
	16.88		123.45	7657
		329.26	678.90	7658
			1.47	7659
Dec Receipts	3,100.00		19.84	7660
	171.23		10.66	7661
	1,198.17	4,469.40	10,734.75	Balance c/d
		16,799.00	16,799.00	
31 Dec balance		10,734.75		

Bank statement—December 31

Withdrawals	£	Deposits £	Balance	£
			1 Dec	800.00
7650	300.00	178.19		
7653	191.91	121.27		
7654	37.14	14.92		
8751	1,111.11	16.88		
7656	5,000.00	3,100.00		
7655	129.79	171.23		
7658	678.90	1,198.17		
Standing order	50.00	117.98		
7659	1.47			
7661	10.66			
Bank charges	80.00		31 Dec	3,472.34

Required:
(a) A corrected cash book summary and a reconciliation of the balance on this revised summary with the bank statement balance as at 31 December, as far as you are able.
(b) A brief note as to the likely cause of any remaining difference.   (CACA)

7. The balance sheet and profit and loss account of Faults Ltd, show the following two items:

Bank balance—Overdrawn	£3,620
Profit and loss account—Trading profit for year	£23,175

However, the balance as shown on the bank statement does not agree with the balance as shown in the cash book. Your investigation of this matter reveals the following differences, and additional information:

1. Cheque payments entered in the cash book but not presented to the bank until after the year end—£3,138.
2. Bankings entered in the cash book but not credited by the bank until after the year end—£425.
3. Cheques for £35 and £140 received from customers were returned by the bank as dishonoured, but no entries concerning these events have been made in the cash book.
4. Items shown on bank statements but not entered in the cash book:

   Bank charges, £245.
   Standing order—Hire purchase repayments on purchase of motor car 12 @ £36.
   Standing order—Being quarterly rent of warehouse, £125, due on each quarter day.
   Dividend received on investment, £90.

5. The cheques were returned by the bank for the following reasons: the £35 cheque requires an additional signature and should be honoured in due course; the £140 cheque was unpaid due to the bankruptcy of the drawer and should be treated as a bad debt.
6. The hire purchase repayments of £36 represent £30 capital and £6 interest.
7. A cheque for £45 received from a customer in settlement of his account had been entered in the cash book as £450 on the payments side, analysed to the purchases ledger column and later posted.

You are required to prepare:

(a) a statement reconciling the cash book balance with the bank statement, and
(b) a statement showing the effect of the alterations on the trading profit   (CACA adapted)

17. Control accounts

Up until this point it has been assumed that the books of account include a single general ledger. However, in practice it is usual for this to be split into at least three different ledgers, consisting of the following:

1. *A sales/debtors ledger* which contains all the personal accounts of debtors;
2. *A purchases/creditors ledger* which contains all the personal accounts of creditors;
3. *An impersonal ledger* which contains all the other accounts. These comprise the nominal (i.e. sales, purchases, wages and expense) accounts, and other assets and liabilities.

It is also usual for the impersonal ledger to contain a sales/debtors ledger control account and a purchases/creditors ledger control account (sometimes also referred to as total accounts). These control accounts contain *in total* the entries that are made in the personal ledgers, and are normally written up monthly from the total of the relevant books of prime entry. For example, in the case of credit sales, the individual invoices shown in the sales day book are entered in each of the debtors personal accounts in the sales ledger, and the total sales for the month as per the sales day book is debited to the debtors control account in the impersonal ledger and credited to the sales account.

Where an impersonal ledger contains debtors and creditors control accounts these constitute part of the double entry and therefore enter into the trial balance which would be prepared for the impersonal ledger alone. In these circumstances the sales and purchases ledgers are outside the double entry system and are thus not entered in the trial balance.

A simple illustration of the preparation of control accounts is shown in Example 17.1.

Example 17.1
The books of Copper Tree Ltd include three ledgers comprising an impersonal ledger, debtors ledger and creditors ledger. The impersonal ledger contains debtors ledger and creditors ledger control accounts as part of the double entry.

The following information relates to the accounting year ended 30 June 19X8:

	£
Debtors ledger control account balance on 1 July 19X7 (debit)	5,740
Creditors ledger control account balance on 1 July 19X7 (credit)	6,830
Sales	42,910
Purchases	38,620
Cheques received from debtors	21,760
Cheques paid to creditors	19,340
Returns outwards	8,670
Returns inwards	7,840
Carriage outwards	1,920

Carriage inwards	2,130
Discount received	4,560
Discount allowed	3,980
Bills of exchange payable	5,130
Bills of exchange receivable	9,720
Bad debts	1,640
Provision for bad debts	2,380
Amounts due from customers as shown by debtors ledger, transferred to creditors ledger	950
Cash received in respect of a debit balance on a creditors ledger account	810

You are required to prepare the debtors ledger and creditors ledger control accounts.

Debtors ledger control

Balance b/d	5,740	Bank	21,760
Sales	42,910	Returns inwards	7,840
		Discount allowed	3,980
		Bills receivable	9,720
		Bad debts	1,640
		Transfer to creditors	950
		Balance c/d	2,760
	48,650		48,650
Balance b/d	2,760		

Creditors ledger control

Bank	19,340	Balance b/d	6,830
Returns outwards	8,670	Purchases	38,620
Discount received	4,560	Cash	810
Bills payable	5,130		
Transfer from debtors	950		
Balance c/d	7,610		
	46,260		46,260
		Balance b/d	7,610

Notes

1. Carriage inwards, carriage outwards and provisions for bad debts are not entered in the control accounts since they do not appear in the individual debtors or creditors accounts in the personal ledgers.
2. The transfer of £950 between the debtors and creditors control accounts is intended to reflect the total of the transfers between the debtors and creditors ledgers during the year. These usually occur where the business buys and sells goods to the same firm. Thus instead of exchanging cheques, the amount due as shown in the debtors ledger is set against the amount owed as shown in the creditors ledger (or vice versa depending on which is the smaller).

3. The cash received of £810 in respect of a debit balance on a creditors ledger account is credited to the creditors account and the creditors control account. A debit balance in the creditors ledger usually arises because a supplier has been overpaid as a result of either duplicating a payment or paying for goods that are the subject of a credit note. The cash received is a refund to correct the previous overpayment.

4. Bills of exchange were explained briefly at the end of Chapter 3. The most relevant characteristics are that bills of exchange are a method of payment where the business which owes the money signs a document undertaking to make payment after the expiry of a specified period of time (usually 30, 60 or 90 days). This document is referred to as a bill of exchange receivable in the case of a debtor, and a bill of exchange payable in the case of a creditor. The essential point is that in the debtors and creditors personal accounts the debt is treated as paid on the date the bill of exchange is signed (and not when the money is actually received or paid which is at a later date). The same therefore applies in the control accounts.

5. The balances carried down on the control accounts at the end of the period are the difference between the two sides of the accounts.

Purposes of control accounts

The main purpose of a control account is to provide a check on the accuracy of the ledger to which it relates. Since the entries in the control account are the same (in total) as those in the ledger to which it relates, the balance on the control account should equal the total of a list of balances of the individual personal accounts contained in the ledger. If the balance on the control account is the same as the list of balances, this proves that the ledger is arithmetically accurate and that all the items in the books of prime entry have been entered in the ledger on the correct side.

The main function of control accounts is therefore to facilitate the location of errors highlighted in the trial balance by pinpointing the personal ledger in which these errors are likely to be found. Furthermore, the existence of control accounts is likely to deter fraud and the misappropriation of funds since it is usually prepared by the accountant as a check on the clerk who is responsible for the personal ledger. Finally, control accounts facilitate the preparation of (monthly or quarterly) final accounts since the total values of debtors and creditors are immediately available.

The use of control accounts in the location of errors is illustrated in Example 17.2.

Example 17.2
The books of C. Hand Ltd include three ledgers comprising an impersonal ledger, debtors ledger and creditors ledger. The impersonal ledger contains debtors ledger and creditors ledger control accounts as part of the double entry.

The following information relates to the accounting year ended 30 April 19X8:

	£
Debtors ledger control account	
balance on 1 May 19X7 (debit)	8,460
Cheques received from debtors	27,690
Sales	47,320

Returns outwards	12,860
Returns inwards	7,170
Carriage inwards	3,940
Bills receivable	8,650
Bills payable	4,560
Discount received	5,710
Discount allowed	2,830
Provision for bad debts	1,420
Bad debts	970
Proceeds of bills receivable discounted	6,150
Amounts due from customers as shown by debtors ledger transferred to creditors ledger	830
Total of balances in debtors ledger on 30 April 19X8	8,460

(a) You are required to prepare the debtors ledger control account for the year ended 30 April 19X8

(b) After the preparation of the control account the following errors were identified:

(i) The total of the sales returns day book had been over-cast by £360;

(ii) Cash received of £225 has been entered on the wrong side of a debtors personal account;

(iii) The total of the discount allowed column in the cash book is shown as £2,830 when it should be £3,820;

(iv) Sales of £2,000 have been entered in the sales day book as £200 in error.

Prepare a statement showing the amended balances on the debtors ledger and the debtors ledger control account. Compute the amount of any remaining undetected error.

(a) Debtors ledger control

Balance b/d	8,460		Bank	27,690
Sales	47,320		Returns inwards	7,170
			Bills receivable	8,650
			Discount allowed	2,830
			Bad debts	970
			Transfer to creditors	830
			Balance c/d	7,640
	55,780			55,780

Balance b/d	7,640	

(b) Debtors ledger

	£
Original balances	8,460
Add: sales error	1,800
Less: cash received posted to wrong side of debtors account (£225 × 2)	450
Amended balance	9,810

Debtors ledger control account

Original balance		7,640
Add: returns over-cast	360	
sales error	1,800	2,160
		9,800
Less: discount allowed under-cast		990
Amended balance		8,810

Undetected error = £9,810 − £8,810 = £1,000

Notes

1. The returns outwards, carriage inward, bills payable, discount received and provision for bad debts are not entered in the debtors ledger control account. The proceeds of bills of exchange receivable whether discounted or not should also not be entered in the debtors ledger control account. As explained above, the entry in the control account in respect of bills receivable of £8,650 is made when the bills were signed as accepted by the debtor and not when the proceeds are received. This is dealt with in a separate account shown below.

Bills receivable

Debtors control	8,650	Bank	6,150
		Balance c/d	2,500
	8,650		8,650
Balance b/d	2,500		

2. The difference of £1,000 between the amended balances on the debtors ledger and the debtors ledger control account indicates that there are still one or more errors in the debtors ledger and/or the debtors ledger control account.

Alternative systems

Sometimes in practice, control accounts are not part of the double entry in the impersonal ledger. Instead they are prepared on a loose sheet of paper and are thus purely memoranda. The entries still consist of totals from the appropriate day books and other books of prime entry. However, in this case the impersonal and personal ledgers must be taken together to produce a trial balance. The values of debtors and creditors in such a trial balance are therefore a list of the balances in the relevant personal ledger.

Exercises

1. Explain the main purposes of control accounts.

2. The following information has been extracted from the books of a trader at 1 July 19X6:

	£
Amount owing by debtors	40,000
Amount owing to creditors	31,200

The transactions during the year ended 30 June 19X7 were as follows:

Returns inwards	15,750
Returns outwards	8,660
Discount received	3,187
Discount allowed	5,443
Sales	386,829
Purchases	222,954
Bad debts written off	3,400
Cheques received from customers	230,040
Cheques paid to suppliers	108,999

You are required to write up the sales ledger control account and the purchase ledger control account for the year ended 30 June 19X7.

3. The following particulars relating to the year ended 31 March 19X9 have been extracted from the books of a trader.

	£
Debtors ledger control account balance on 1 April 19X8 (debit)	7,182
Sales	69,104
Cash received from debtors including proceeds of bills discounted	62,079
Discounts allowed	1,846
Discounts received	1,461
Returns inwards	983
Returns outwards	627
Bills receivable accepted by debtors £3,243 discounted for	2,950
Bad debts written off	593
Cash paid in respect of a credit balance on a debtors ledger account	66
Amounts due from customers as shown by debtors ledger transferred to creditors ledger	303
Interest charged on overdue account to debtors ledger	10
Credit balance on debtors ledger control account on 31 March 19X9	42

Prepare the debtors ledger control account for the year ended 31 March 19X9, using relevant figures selected from the data shown above. (CACA)

4. The books of Trader Ltd include three ledgers comprising an impersonal ledger, debtors ledger and creditors ledger. The impersonal ledger contains debtors ledger and creditors ledger control accounts as part of the double entry.
    The following information relates to the month of January 19X1:

Debtors control account balance on 1 January 19X1	4,200 debit
Debtors control account balance on 1 January 19X1	300 credit
Creditors control account balance on 1 January 19X1	250 debit
Creditors control account balance on 1 January 19X1	6,150 credit
Credit sales for the month	23,000
Credit purchases for the month	21,500
Returns inward	750
Returns outward	450
Carriage inwards	25
Carriage outwards	15
Cheques received from debtors	16,250
Cheques paid to creditors	19,800
Discount allowed	525
Discount received	325
Irrecoverable debts	670
Provision for bad debts	400

Cheques received from debtors, dishonoured	1,850
Bills of exchange payable, accepted by us	4,500
Bills of exchange receivable, accepted by debtors	5,300
Bad debts recovered	230
Cash received from bills receivable	4,850
Debtors balances set against accounts in the creditors ledger	930
Cash paid on bills payable	3,700
Interest charged on overdue debts	120
Allowances received	280
Allowances given	340
Debtors control account balance on 31 January 19X1	240 credit
Creditors control account balance on 31 January 19X1	420 debit

You are required to prepare the debtors ledger and creditors ledger control accounts for January 19X1.

5. The following particulars relating to the year ended 31 March 19X7, have been extracted from the books of Ball and Chain Ltd. All sales have been recorded in personal accounts in the debtors ledger, and the debtors ledger control account is part of the double entry in the impersonal ledger.

	£
Debtors ledger control account balance on 1 April 19X6 (debit)	14,364
Sales	138,208
Cheques received from debtors including bad debts recovered of £84	118,258
Discounts allowed	3,692
Discounts received	2,922
Returns inwards	1,966
Returns outwards	1,254
Bills receivable	6,486
Bad debts written off	1,186
Provision for bad debts	1,800
Cash paid in respect of a credit balance on a debtors ledger account	132
Amounts due from customers as shown by debtors ledger transferred to creditors ledger	606
Interest charged on overdue account to debtors ledger	20
Total of balances in debtors ledger on 31 March 19X7 (debit)	20,914

(a) Prepare the debtors ledger control account for the year ended 31 March 19X7 using relevant figures selected from the data shown above.

(b) Subsequently the following errors have been discovered:

(i) The total of the sales day book has been under-cast by £1,000.

(ii) An entry of £125 in the returns inwards book has been entered on the wrong side of the debtors personal account.

(iii) Discount allowed of £50 had been entered correctly in a debtors personal account but no other entries have been made in the books.

(iv) A cheque for £3,400 from a debtor had been entered correctly in the cash book but has been posted to the debtors personal account as £4,300.

Prepare a statement showing the amended balances on the debtors ledger and the debtors ledger control account.

6. The books of K. Wills include three ledgers comprising the impersonal ledger, debtors ledger and creditors ledger. The impersonal ledger contains debtors ledger and creditors ledger control accounts as part of the double entry.

The following information relates to the accounting year ended 30 June 19X9:

	£
Debtors ledger control account balance on 1 July 19X8 (debit)	17,220
Creditors ledger control account balance on 1 July 19X8 (credit)	20,490
Cheques received from debtors	45,280
Cheques paid to creditors	38,020

Sales	98,730
Purchases	85,860
Returns outwards	16,010
Returns inwards	18,520
Bills of exchange payable	21,390
Bills of exchange receivable	29,160
Discount received	7,680
Discount allowed	6,940
Bad debts	4,920
Cash received in respect of a debit balance on a creditors ledger account	2,430
Amounts due from customers as shown by debtors ledger, transferred to creditors ledger	2,850
Total of balances in creditors ledger on 30 June 19X9 (credit)	20,700

(a)   You are required to prepare the debtors ledger and creditors ledger control accounts.

(b)   After the preparation of the above control accounts the following errors were discovered:

   (i)   The total of the purchases day book has been over-cast by £500;
   (ii)   Returns outwards of £180 have been entered on the wrong side of the personal account concerned;
   (iii) Discount received of £120 has been entered correctly in the appropriate personal account but is shown in the cash book as £210;
   (iv)   A cheque paid for £340 had been entered correctly in the cash book but has been posted to the creditors personal account as £3,400.

You are required to prepare a statement showing the amended balances on the creditors ledger and the creditors ledger control account. Compute the amount of any remaining undetected error.

7.   The following figures relating to the year ended 31 March 19X8 have been extracted from the books of a manufacturer:

	£
Total of sales ledger balances as per list	8,300
Total of bought ledger balances as per list	1,270
Balances on sales ledger control account	8,160
Balances on bought ledger control account	1,302

The balances on the control accounts, as shown above, have been included in the trial balance and in this trial balance the total of the credit balances exceeded the total of the debit balances by £58.

Subsequently, the following errors have been discovered:

1.   goods returned by a customer to the value of £10 have been entered on the wrong side of his personal account;
2.   the total of the sales day book for the month of March had been under-cast by £80;
3.   the total of the purchases for the month of March had been correctly shown as £633 in the bought day book and control account, but incorrectly posted to the purchased account as £635;
4.   an allowance of £10 made by a supplier because of a slight defect in the goods supplied had been correctly entered in the personal account concerned, but no other entries had been made in the books;
5.   a credit balance of £22, on a supplier's personal account had been overlooked and therefore did not appear in the list of bought ledger balances.

An undetected error still remained in the books after the discovery of the above-mentioned errors.

You are required to:

(a)   prepare a statement showing the amended totals of the balances on the sales and bought ledgers and the amended balances on each of the control accounts assuming that the errors discovered have been corrected;
(b)   calculate the amount of undetected error and to state where in the books you consider such error is to be found.   (CACA)

8. Fox and Company maintain control accounts, in respect of both the sales ledger and purchase ledger, within their nominal ledger. On 31 December 19X1 the net total of the balances extracted from the sales ledger amounted to £9,870, which figure did not agree with the balance shown on the sales ledger control account. An examination of the books disclosed the following errors and omissions, which when rectified resulted in the corrected net total of the sales ledger balances agreeing with the amended balance of the control account.

1. £240 standing to the credit of Rice's account in the purchase ledger had been transferred to his account in the sales ledger, but no entries had been made in the control accounts in respect of this transfer.
2. Debit balances of £42 in the sales ledger had been extracted as credit balances when the balances were listed at 31 December 19X1.
3. £8,675, a month's total in the sales day book, had been posted to the control account as £8,765, although posted correctly to the sales account.
4. A balance of £428 owing by Stone had been written off to bad debts as irrecoverable, but no entry had been made in the control account.
5. Entries on the debit side of Hay's account in the sales ledger had been under-cast by £100.
6. The following sales ledger balances had been omitted from the list of balances at 31 December 19X1 —debits £536, credits £37.
7. The sale of goods to Croft amounting to £60 had been dealt with correctly and debited to his account. Croft had returned such goods as not being up to standard and the only treatment accorded thereto was the crossing out of the original entry in Croft's account.
8. £22 allowed to Field as discount had been correctly recorded and posted. Subsequently this discount had been disallowed and a like amount had been entered in the discounts received column in the cash book and posted to Field's account in the purchase ledger and included in the total of discounts received.

You are required to:

1. give the journal entries, where necessary, to rectify these errors and omissions, and, if no journal entry is necessary, to state how they should be rectified; and
2. prepare the sales ledger control account showing the balance before and after rectification has been made, and reconcile the balance carried forward on this account with the total of balances extracted from the sales ledger.   (CACA)

18. Errors and suspense accounts

As explained in Chapter 5, one of the main purposes of the trial balance is to check the accuracy of a ledger. If a trial balance agrees this indicates that:

1. there are no arithmetic errors in the ledger accounts; and
2. every transaction recorded in the ledger has been entered once on each side.

   However, there can still be errors in the ledger that do not cause a trial balance to disagree. These are explained below.

Types of error which do not cause a trial balance to disagree

Error of principle

This refers to when a transaction has been entered on both sides of the ledger but one of the entries is in the wrong *class/type* of account. That is, for example, an expense that has been debited to an asset account in error (or vice versa), or income being credited to a liability account in error (or vice versa).

Error of commission

This refers to when a transaction has been entered on both sides of the ledger and in the correct *class/type* of account but in the wrong account; for example, stationery entered in the purchases account in error.

Error of omission

This refers to where a transaction has not been recorded anywhere in the books of account.

Error of original/prime entry

This refers to when the wrong amount has been entered in a book of prime entry. That is, the amount entered in the book of prime entry is different from that shown on the original document. This will mean that the wrong amount has been entered on both sides of the ledger. For example, a sales invoice for £980 entered in the sales day book as £890 will result in both the sales and debtors accounts containing a figure of £890 instead of £980.

Compensating errors

A compensating error is two separate errors which are totally unrelated to each other except that they are both of the same amount. Each of these two errors are not of the four types above but rather would individually cause a trial balance to disagree.

Double posting error

This refers to where the correct amount has been entered in a day book (of prime entry) but the wrong amount is shown on both sides of the ledger. Another type of double posting error can be said to have occurred when the correct amount of a transaction has been entered on the wrong side of both of the accounts to which it has been posted.

Illustrations of these errors and their correction are shown in Example 18.1. The errors are presented in the same order as the above list.

Example 18.1

State the title of each of the following errors and show the journal entries needed for their correction.

1. Plant that was acquired at a cost of £5,000 has been credited in the cash book but debited to the purchases account in error.
2. The purchase of consumable tools for £80 has been debited to the repairs account in error.
3. Bank charges of £27 shown on the bank statement have not been entered in the cash book.
4. A purchase invoice received from A. Creditor for £1,000 has been entered in the purchases day book as £100.
5. Wages paid of £40 have not been posted to the wages account, and the debit side of the purchases account has been over-cast by £40.
6. Rent received of £400 has been entered in both the cash book and the ledger as rent paid.

The journal

1.	Plant and machinery	Dr	5,000	
	To purchases account			5,000
	Being correction of error of principle			
2.	Consumable tools	Dr	80	
	To repairs account			80
	Being correction of error of commission			
3.	Bank charges	Dr	27	
	To cash book			27
	Being correction of error of omission			
4.	Purchases account	Dr	900	
	To A. Creditor/creditors control			900
	Being correction of error of prime entry (no correction of purchases day book is necessary)			

| 5. | Wages account | Dr | 40 | |
| | To purchases account | | | 40 |

Being correction of compensating error
—wages not posted and purchases
account over-cast

6.	Cast book	Dr	800	
	To rent payable account			400
	To rent receivable account			400

Being correction of rent receivable
of £400 entered as rent payable

Suspense accounts

Suspense accounts are used for two purposes as follows:

1. Recording undefined transactions. That is, where money is received or paid but there is no record of what it relates to, the amount would be entered in the cash book and posted to a suspense account. When the nature of the transaction is known, the amount is transferred from the suspense account to the appropriate account.
2. To record any difference on a trial balance and thus make it agree. If a trial balance fails to agree by a relatively small amount and the error(s) cannot be found quickly, the difference is inserted in the trial balance (to make it agree) and in a suspense account. The entry in the suspense account must be on the same side of the ledger as the entry in the trial balance. At a later date when the error(s) are located they are corrected by means of an entry in the suspense account and the other in the account containing the error. This correction through the suspense account is necessary because the original entry in the suspense account (which made the trial balance agree) in effect corrected all the errors in total. Thus the correction must effectively be moved from the suspense account to the account that contains the error.

An illustration of the use of suspense accounts is given in Example 18.2.

Example 18.2
A trial balance failed to agree because the debit side exceeds the credit side by £2,509. A suspense account has been opened into which the difference is entered. Subsequently the following errors were identified:

1. The debit side of the cash book has been over-cast by £1,000.
2. Goods bought by cheque for £200 have been credited in the cash book but not entered in the purchases account.
3. Rent paid of £50 has been credited in the cash book but also credited in error to the rent account.
4. Car repairs of £23 shown in the cash book have been debited to the motor expenses account as £32 in error.
5. The sales account contains a balance of £2,000 but this has been entered in the trial balance as £200.

You are required to prepare the journal entries needed to correct the above errors and show the entries in the suspense account.

Suspense account

Cash book	1,000	Difference on trial balance	2,509
Motor expenses	9	Purchases	200
Extraction error on sales	1,800	Rent	100
	2,809		2,809

The journal

Suspense account	Dr	1,000	
Cash book			1,000

Being correction of arithmetic error

Purchases account	Dr	200	
Suspense account			200

Being correction of posting error

Rent account	Dr	100	
Suspense account			100

Being correction of posting error (£50 × 2)

Suspense account	Dr	9	
Motor expenses			9

Being correction of transposed figures

Suspense account	Dr	1,800	
Trial balance (no ledger entry)			1,800

Being correction of extraction error

Notes

1. It should be noted that only errors of the type which cause a trial balance to disagree are corrected by means of an entry in the suspense account; that is, arithmetic and posting errors described in Chapter 5. This is clearly because errors which cause a trial balance to disagree give rise to the original entry in the suspense account.
2. The correction of errors via a suspense account always involves a double entry, with one exception. This relates to the correction of extraction errors, such as item 5 above, where the only entry is in the suspense account. A useful way of working out whether the entry in the suspense account is a debit or credit is to imagine what entry is needed to correct the trial balance; the entry in the suspense account will be on the opposite side of the ledger.
3. Sometimes in examination questions and in practice the errors which have been identified are not the only errors. Obviously in this case there will still be a balance on the suspense account after the known errors have been corrected. This shows the amount of the remaining errors.

Exercises

1. Describe the types of errors that:

   (a) cause a trial balance to disagree,
   (b) do not cause a trial balance to disagree.

2. Describe the two main uses of a suspense account.

3. The draft trial balance of Regent Ltd as at 31 May 19X8 agreed. The business proceeded with the preparation of the draft final accounts and these showed a profit of £305,660. However, a subsequent audit revealed the following errors:

   1. Bank charges of £56 had been omitted from the cash book.
   2. The purchases journal had been over-cast by £400.
   3. The sales journal had been under-cast by £100.
   4. An invoice for £127 received from Alpha Ltd had been entered into the purchases journal as £217. (This is quite independent of the error made in the purchases journal referred to above.)
   5. It is now considered prudent to write off the balance of £88 on P. Shadey's account as bad.
   6. An invoice from Caring Garages Ltd for £550 in respect of servicing Regent Ltd's motor vehicles had been posted to the debit of motor vehicles account.
   7. Depreciation of 10 per cent per annum has been provided for on motor vehicles inclusive of the £550 invoice referred to in point 6 above.

Regent Ltd maintains control accounts for debtors and creditors in its general ledger. Individual accounts for debtors and creditors are maintained on a memorandum basis only.

Required
(a) Prepare journal entries to show how the above errors would be corrected. (Note: dates and narratives not required.)
(b) What is the profit for the year after correcting the above errors?   (AAT)

4. When preparing a trial balance the bookkeeper found it disagreed by £600, the credit side being that much greater than the debit side. The difference was entered in a suspense account. The following errors were subsequently found:

   1. A cheque for £32 for electricity was entered in the cash book but not posted to the ledger.
   2. The debit side of the wages account is over-cast by £28.
   3. There is a debit in the rent account of £198 which should be £918.
   4. The purchase of a van for £300 has been posted to the debit side of the purchases account in error.
   5. A cheque received from A. Watt for £80 has been credited to A. Watson's account in error.
   6. The sale of some old loose tools for £100 had been credited to sales account in error.
   7. An amount of £17 paid for postage stamps has been entered in the carriage outwards account in error.
   8. Bank interest of £41 shown on the bank statement has not been entered in the books.
   9. An amount of £9 for stationery has been entered in the cash book but not posted to the stationery account. Cash sales of £43 are entered correctly in the cash book but posted to the sales account as £34.
   10. A credit sale to A. Bloggs of £120 was entered in the sales day book as £12.
   11. A credit balance of £62 shown in the discount received account has been entered on the debit side of the trial balance.

   You are required to prepare the journal entries necessary to correct the above errors and show the suspense account.

5. At the end of January 19X0 a trial balance extracted from the ledger of Gerald Ltd did not balance and a suspense account was opened for the amount of the difference. Subsequently the following matters came to light:

   1. £234 had been received during January from a debtor who owed £240. No entry has been made for the £6 outstanding but it is now decided to treat it as cash discount.
   2. Returns to suppliers during January were correctly posted individually to personal accounts but were incorrectly totalled. The total, overstated by £100, was posted to the returns account.

3. A bank statement drawn up to 31 January 19X0 showed a credit balance of £120 while the balance of the bank account in the trial balance was an overdraft of £87. The difference was found on reconciliation to comprise:

   (i) a direct debit for the annual subscription to a trade association, £70, for which no entry had been made in the books of account.
   (ii) entry in the bank account for payment to a supplier shown as £230 instead of £320.
   (iii) unpresented cheques on 31 January totalled £327.
   (iv) the remainder of the difference was due to an addition error in the bank account.

4. A cheque for £163 was received during January in full settlement of a debt which was written off in the previous financial year. It was correctly entered in the bank account but not posted elsewhere, pending instructions.
5. A debtor's account with a balance of £180 had been taken out of the loose-leaf ledger when a query was investigated and not replaced at the time the trial balance was extracted.
6. A credit note for £5 sent to a customer in respect of an allowance had been posted to the wrong side of the customer's personal account.

   Required:
   Show what correcting entries need to be made in the ledge accounts in respect of these matters. Set out your answer as follows:

Item	Account(s) to be debited £	Account(s) to be credited £

(CACA adapted)

6. Chi Knitwear Ltd is an old-fashioned firm with a handwritten set of books. A trial balance is extracted at the end of each month, and a profit and loss account and balance sheet are computed. This month however the trial balance will not balance, the credits exceeding debits by £1,536.

   You are asked to help and after inspection of the ledgers discover the following errors.

   1. A balance of £87 on a debtors account has been omitted from the schedule of debtors, the total of which was entered as debtors in the trial balance.
   2. A small piece of machinery purchased for £1,200 had been written off to repairs.
   3. The receipts side of the cash book had been under-cast by £720.
   4. The total of one page of the sales day book had been carried forward as £8,154, whereas the correct amount was £8,514.
   5. A credit note for £179 received from a supplier had been posted to the wrong side of his account.
   6. An electricity bill in the sum of £152, not yet accrued for, is discovered in a filing tray.
   7. Mr Smith, whose past debts to the company had been the subject of a provision, at last paid £731 to clear his account. His personal account has been credited but the cheque has not yet passed through the cash book.

   You are required to:

   (a) write up the suspense account to clear the difference, and
   (b) state the effect on the accounts of correcting each error. (CACA)

7. The draft final accounts of RST Ltd for the year ended 30 April 19X5 showed a net profit for the year after tax of £78,263.
   During the subsequent audit, the following errors and omissions were discovered. At the draft stage a suspense account had been opened to record the net difference.

   (a) Trade debtors were shown as £55,210. However:

      (i) bad debts of £610 had not been written off;
      (ii) the existing provision for doubtful debtors, £1,300 should have been adjusted to 2 per cent of debtors;
      (iii) a provision of 2 per cent for discounts on debtors should have been raised.

(b)　Rates of £491 which had been prepaid at 30 April 19X4 had not been brought down on the rates account as an opening balance.

(c)　A vehicle held as a fixed asset, which had originally cost £8,100 and for which £5,280 had been provided as depreciation, had been sold for £1,350. The proceeds had been correctly debited to bank but had been credited to sales. No transfers had been made to disposals account.

(d)　Credit purchases of £1,762 had been correctly debited to purchases account but had been credited to the supplier's account as £1,672.

(e)　A piece of equipment costing £9,800 and acquired on 1 May 19X4 for use in the business had been debited to purchases account. (The company depreciates equipment at 20 per cent per annum on cost.)

(f)　Items valued at £2,171 had been completely omitted from the closing stock figure.

(g)　At 30 April 19X5 an accrual of £543 for electricity charges and an insurance prepayment of £162 had been omitted.

(h)　The credit side of the wages account had been under-added by £100 before the balance on the account had been determined.

Required:
Using relevant information from that given above:

(a)　prepare a statement correcting the draft net profit after tax;

(b)　post and balance the suspense account. (Note: The opening balance of this account has not been given and must be derived.)
　　　　　　　　　　　　　　　　　　　　　　　　　　　　　　　　　　　　　(CACA)

8.　Miscup showed a difference on their trial balance of £14,650. This was posted to a suspense account so that the accounts for the year ended 31 March 19X9 could be prepared. The following balance sheet was produced:

Miscup
Balance sheet as at 31 March 19X9

	£		Cost £	Depreciation £	Net £
		Fixed assets			
Capital	125,000	Freehold premises	60,000	—	60,000
Profit for the year	33,500	Motor vehicles	25,000	11,935	13,065
	158,500	Fixtures and fittings	1,500	750	750
			86,500	12,685	73,815
		Current assets			
		Stocks	75,410		
		Debtors	37,140		
		Cash in hand	75		
Current liabilities					112,625
					186,440
Trade creditors and accrued charges	£ 41,360				
Bank overdraft	1,230	Suspense account			14,650
	42,590				
	£201,090				£201,090

On checking the books to eliminate the suspense account you find the following errors:

1.　The debit side of the cash book is under-cast by £10,000.

2.　A credit item of £5,000 in the cash book on account of a new building has not been posted to the nominal ledger.

3.　The purchases day book had been summarized for posting to the nominal ledger but an item of purchases of £100 had been entered in the summary as £1,000 and a further transport charge of £450 had been entered as £45.

4. An item of rent received, £45, was posted twice to the nominal ledger from the cash book.
5. The debit side of the debtors control account was under-cast by £100.
6. On reconciling the bank statement with the cash book it was discovered that bank charges of £3,250 had not been entered in the cash book.
7. Depreciation of motor vehicles was undercharged by £500.
8. Stocks were undervalued by £1,250.
9. Suppliers' invoices totalling £2,110 for goods included in stock, had been omitted from the books.

You are required to show:

(a) the journal entries necessary to eliminate the balance on the suspense account, and
(b) the balance sheet of Miscup as at 31 March 19X9, after correcting all the above errors.   (CACA)

19. Single entry and incomplete records

Incomplete records is a general term given to a situation where the transactions of a business have not been recorded in double entry form (or using a mechanized accounting or computer system). There is no legislation which requires bodies sole (i.e. sole traders or partnerships) to keep records in double entry form. Furthermore, it is often too expensive for small businesses to maintain a complete system of double entry bookkeeping. In addition, many small businesses claim to have little practical use for any records other than how much money they have, and the amounts of debtors and creditors. Many sole traders are usually able to remember, without records, what fixed assets they own, and frequently claim to know roughly how much profit they are making. However, their concept of profit often differs from that of the accountant, since many traders neglect to take into account certain costs, such as depreciation, when calculating what they regard as profit. In the case of small businesses the accountant is therefore usually engaged not to write up the books, but to ascertain the profit of the business for tax purposes. Often, but not always, a balance sheet is also prepared.

In practice there are three different forms of incomplete records:

1. *Incomplete records of revenue income and expenditure* That is, there are no basic documents or records of revenue income and expenditure, or the records are inadequate. This situation usually arises where the books and documents have been accidentally destroyed (e.g. in a fire) or the owner failed to keep proper records. In these circumstances it is not possible to construct a trading and profit and loss account. However, it may still be possible to ascertain the profit for the period provided there is information available relating to the assets and liabilities of the business at the start and end of the relevant period.
2. *Single entry* This term is used to describe a situation where the business transactions have only been entered in a book of prime entry, usually a cash book, and not in the ledger. However, one would also expect to be able to obtain documents or information relating to the value of fixed assets, stocks, debtors, creditors, accruals, prepayments and any long-term liabilities. Given that this is available, it would be possible to prepare a trading and profit and loss account and balance sheet.
3. *Incomplete single entry* This term may be used to describe a variation on point 2 above where there are no books of account (or these are incomplete) but the receipts and payments can be ascertained from the bank statements and/or supporting documents. In this case it would be necessary to produce a cash book summary from the information given on the bank statements. The final accounts will then be prepared from this cash book summary together with the supporting documents and information referred to in point 2 above.

The procedure for preparing final accounts from the above three different forms of incomplete records is described below.

Incomplete records of revenue income and expenditure

As explained above, in these circumstances it is not possible to construct a trading and profit and loss account. However, it may still be possible to ascertain the profit for the relevant period provided that the information to prepare a balance sheet at the start and end of the period is available.

The profit (or loss) is found by calculating the difference between the net asset value of the business at the start and end of the year as shown by the two balance sheets. The logic behind this computation is that an increase in net assets can only come from two sources, either additional capital introduced by the owner or profits generated from the sale of goods and/or other assets. This is illustrated below.

Balance sheet as at 1 January 19X1

Capital	20,000	Assets	25,000
		Less: liabilities	5,000
	20,000	Net assets	20,000

Balance sheet as at 31 December 19X1

Capital	30,000	Assets	38,000
		Less: liabilities	8,000
	30,000	Net assets	30,000

Ignoring the possibility of additional capital introduced during the year, this business has a profit for the year of £30,000 − £20,000 = £10,000. This is computed by ascertaining the increase in either the net assets or the capital. Both must give the same answer. Any decrease in net assets or capital will mean there has been a loss for the year.

However, part of the increase in net assets and capital may be due to additional capital being introduced during the year of say £3,000. In this case the profit for the year is that part of the increase in net assets and capital which is not the result of additional capital introduced during the year thus:

	£
Net assets/capital at end of year	30,000
Less: net assets/capital at start of year	20,000
Increase in capital	10,000
Less: capital introduced	3,000
Profit for the year	7,000

Alternatively the owner of the business may have made drawings during the year. These will reduce the capital and net assets. In this case the profit for the year is the increase in net assets/capital plus the drawings for the year.

In sum, profits (or losses) are reflected in an increase (or decrease) in the net asset value of a business over a given period. The net asset value corresponds to the capital. The profit or loss can thus be ascertained by computing the change in capital over the year and adjusting this for any capital introduced and/or drawings during the year. This is presented in the form of a statement, as shown below. Notice that this statement is simply a reordering of the entries normally shown in the capital account of a sole trader as presented in the balance sheet.

Statement of profit or loss for the year ended . . .

		£
Capital at end of current year		—
Less: Capital at end of previous year		—
Increase in capital		—
Add: Drawings during the year including any goods taken by the proprietor for his own use		—
Less: Capital introduced during the year either in the form of cash or any other asset		—
Profit for the year		—

Before this statement can be prepared it is necessary to calculate the capital at the end of the current year and at the end of the previous year. This is done by preparing a balance sheet at each of these dates. These are referred to as a statement of affairs. This is illustrated in Example 19.1.

Example 19.1

A. Ferry has been in business for the last 10 years as an electrical retailer, and has asked you to compute her profit for the year ended 31 December 19X8.

She has no business bank account and kept no records of her income and expenditure apart from the purchase and sale of fixed assets, stock, debtors and creditors, and a running cash balance. She has been able to give you the following information relating to her affairs:

1. At 31 December 19X8 the business owns freehold land and buildings used as a shop and workshop. This cost £10,000 on 1 July 19X2.
2. During the year ended 31 December 19X8 the business owned the following vehicles:

Date of purchase	Cost	Date of sale	Proceeds
31 Mar 19X5	£1,000	31 Oct 19X8	£625
1 May 19X6	£1,200	unsold at 31 Dec 19X8	
1 July 19X8	£2,000	unsold at 31 Dec 19X8	

You estimate that the above vehicles have a useful working life of five years and no residual value. In previous years these have been depreciated using the straight line method.

3. During the year ended 31 December 19X8 the owner has put £5,280 in cash into the business and taken out £15,900 as drawings.
4. Amounts outstanding at:

	31 Dec 19X7	31 Dec 19X8
	£	£
Debtors	865	645
Creditors	390	480
Accruals	35	20
Prepayments	40	25

Included in debtors at 31 December 19X8 are doubtful debts of £85.
5. Stocks have been valued at £565 on 31 December 19X7, and £760 on 31 December 19X8. The latter amount includes a television which cost £60 and was worthless at that date due to it having been accidentally damaged beyond repair.
6. The cash balances at 31 December 19X7 and 19X8 were £285 and £165, respectively.

You are required to calculate the profit for the year ended 31 December 19X8, showing clearly your workings.

Workings

	£	£
Motor vehicles owned at 31 December 19X7		
Purchased 31/3/X5		1,000
Purchased 1/5/X6		1,200
Total cost		2,200
Depreciation using the fixed instalment method		
20 per cent × £1,000 × 2 years 9 months	550	
20 per cent × £1,200 × 1 year 8 months	400	
		950
Written down value at 31 Dec 19X7		1,250

	£	£
Motor vehicles owned at 31 December 19X8		
Purchased 1/5/X6		1,200
Purchased 1/7/X8		2,000
Total cost		3,200
Depreciation using the fixed instalment method		
20 per cent × £1,200 × 2 years 8 months	640	
20 per cent × £2,000 × 6 months	200	
		950
Written down value at 31 Dec 19X8		2,360

A. Ferry

Statement of affairs as at 31 December 19X7

	£		£
Capital	12,580	Freehold land and builings	10,000
Accruals	35	Motor vehicles	1,250
Creditors	390	Stock	565
		Debtors	865
		Prepayments	40
		Cash	285
	13,005		13,005

A. Ferry

Statement of Affairs as at 31 December 19X8

	£	£		£	£
Capital		13,310	*Fixed assets*		10,000
			Freehold land & buildings at cost		
Current liabilities			Motor vehicles at cost	3,200	
Accruals	20		*Less*: Aggregate		
Creditors	480	500	depreciation	840	2,360
					12,360
			Current assets		
			Prepayments		25
			Stock (760 − 60)		700
			Debtors	645	
			Less: Provision for doubtful debts	85	560
			Cash		165
					1,450
		13,810			13,810

A. Ferry

Statement of profit for the year ended 31 December 19X8

	£
Capital at 31 December 19X8	13,310
Less: Capital at 31 December 19X7	12,580
	730
Add: Drawings	15,900
	16,630
Less: Capital introduced	5,280
Net profit for the year	11,350

Notes

1. There is no need to compute the profit or loss on disposals of fixed assets since this will automatically be reflected in the increase in net assets/capital. However, it is necessary to compute the written down value (or possibly market values) of fixed assets at the end of each year as shown in the workings in order to prepare the statement of affairs.
2. The stock at 31 December 19X8 excludes the cost of the television that was damaged beyond repair of £60.
3. Doubtful debts have been provided for by reducing the amount of debtors at 31 December 19X8.
4. The amounts for capital in the statements of affairs are the difference between the two sides of these balance sheets.
5. It is usual to treat the statement of affairs at the end of the previous year as workings not requiring any formal presentation. However, the statement of affairs at the end of the current year should contain the usual headings and subtotals and be in a form presentable to the owner and other interested parties such as the Inland Revenue.

Single entry

As explained above single entry refers to the situation where a business has some record of its receipts and payments, fixed assets, stocks, debtors, creditors, accruals, prepayments and long-term liabilities. However, these records are not in double entry form and usually consist of just a cash book.

   One possibility is for the accountant to complete the records by posting the receipts and payments to the appropriate accounts in the ledger either in full or summarized form. The final accounts are then prepared from the trial balance in the normal way. This is common in practice. However, in very small businesses this may be too expensive and/or impractical. In this case the final accounts are prepared directly from the cash book or a summary thereof, and the appropriate adjustments made for debtors, creditors, provisions, accruals, prepayments, etc. Examination questions on this topic also usually take the same form. An illustration of this treatment of single entry records is given in Example 19.2. Because of the importance and length of the workings, the procedure for answering the question is presented as a series of steps. These are well worth memorizing as a model for answering such questions.

Example 19.2
The following is the balance sheet of L. Cook at 31 December 19X5.

	£		£
		Freehold land and buildings	
Capital	19,240	at cost	12,500
Trade creditors	2,610	Motor vehicles (cost £5,000)	2,900
Electricity accrued	30	Rates prepaid	60
		Stock of goods for resale	1,650
		Trade debtors	3,270
		Bank	1,500
	21,880		21,880

The only book kept by Cook is a cash book, a summary of which for the year ended 31 December 19X6 has been prepared as follows:

	£		£
Balance b/d	1,500	Rates	140
Cash takings banked	4,460	Salaries	2,820
Cheques from debtors	15,930	Electricity	185
Additional capital	500	Bank charges	10
		Motor expenses	655
		Payments to creditors	16,680
		Stationery	230
		Sundry expenses	40
		Balance c/d	1,630
	22,390		22,390

From the supporting documents it has been ascertained that:

1. The following amounts have been paid from the cash takings before they were banked:

Drawings	£22,000
Purchases	£ 560
Petrol	£ 85
Repairs to buildings	£ 490

2. Cook has taken goods out of the business for his own use that cost £265.
3. Motor vehicles have been depreciated in past years at 20 per cent per annum by the reducing balance method.
4. Stock at 31 December 19X6 was valued at £1,960.
5. The trade debtors and trade creditors outstanding at the end of the year are £2,920 and £2,860 respectively.
6. At 31 December 19X6 there are rates prepaid of £70 and electricity accrued of £45. You expect to charge Cook £100 for your services.

Prepare a trading and profit and loss account for the year ended 31 December 19X6 and a balance sheet at that date. Present your answer in vertical form and show all your workings clearly.

Workings/procedure

1. If necessary prepare a statement of affairs as at the end of the previous year to ascertain the capital at that date.
2. If necessary prepare a summarized cash book to ascertain the balance at the end of the year and the total amounts received and spent on each type of income and expenditure, and assets.

3. (a) Compute the net credit purchases by preparing a creditors control account as follows:

Creditors control

19X6			19X6		
31 Dec	Bank	16,680	1 Jan	Balance b/d	2,610
31 Dec	Balance c/d	2,860	31 Dec	Net purchases	16,930
		19,540			19,540

The net purchases figure is the difference between the two sides.
(b) Compute the cash and cheque purchases and then the total purchases:

$$\text{Total purchases} = £560 + £16,930 = £17,490$$

4. (a) Compute the net credit sales by preparing a debtors control account as follows:
Debtors control

19X6			19X6		
1 Jan	Balance b/d	3,270	31 Dec	Bank	15,930
31 Dec	Net sales	15,580	31 Dec	Balance c/d	2,920
		18,850			18,850

The net purchases figure is the difference between the two sides.
(b) Compute the cash and cheque sales and then the total sales:

$$\text{Cash sales} = £4,460 + £22,000 + £560 + £85 + £490 = £27,595$$

$$\text{Total sales} = £27,595 + £15,580 = £43,175$$

Note that sometimes the computations in (a) and (b) have to be combined. This is necessary when the cash and/or cheque sales are not given separately from the cheques received from debtors. In this case the total cash and cheques received in respect of sales are credited to the control account. The sample principle would also have to be used in the case of purchases when cash and/or cheque purchases are not given separately from cheques paid to creditors.

5. Compute the charges to the profit and loss account for those expenses with accruals and prepayments by preparing the relevant ledger accounts. Alternatively, in examinations this may be shown as workings in the profit and loss account.

Light and heat

19X6			19X6		
31 Dec	Bank	185	1 Jan	Balance b/d	30
31 Dec	Accrual c/d	45	31 Dec	Profit and loss a/c	200
		230			230

Rates

19X6			19X6		
1 Jan	Prepayment b/d	60	31 Dec	Profit and loss a/c	130
31 Dec	Bank	140	31 Dec	Prepayment c/d	70
		200			200

6. Prepare the final accounts, remembering to add together any cheque and cash expenditure of the same type (e.g. motor expenses in this example), and make any other necessary adjustments in respect of provisions for depreciation and bad debts etc.

L. Cook

Trading and profit and loss account for the year ended 31 December 19X6

	£	£
Sales		43,175
Less: Cost of sales—		
Stock at 1 Jan 19X6	1,650	
Add: Purchases (17,490 − 265)	17,225	
	18,875	
Less: Stock at 31 Dec 19X6	1,960	16,915
Gross profit		26,260
Less: Expenditure—	2,820	
Salaries		
Rates (60 + 140 − 70)	130	
Motor expenses (655 + 85)	740	
Light and heat (185 + 45 − 30)	200	
Repairs to buildings	490	
Stationery	230	
Accountancy fees	100	
Depreciation on vehicles (20 per cent × 2,900	580	
Sundry expenses	40	
Bank charges	10	5,340
Net profit		20,920

Balance sheet as at 31 December 19X6

Fixed assets	*Cost*	*Agg. Depn.*	*WDV*
Freehold land and builings	12,500	—	12,500
Motor vehicles	5,000	2,680	2,320
	17,500	2,680	14,820

Current assets	£	£	£
Stock		1,960	
Trade debtors		2,920	
Prepayments		70	
Bank		1,630	
		6,580	
Current liabilities			
Trade creditors	2,860		
Accruals (45 + 100)	145	3,005	
Net current assets			3,575
Net assets			18,395
Capital			
Balance at 1 Jan 19X6			19,240
Add: Capital introduced			500
Net profit			20,920
			40,660
Less: Drawings (22,000 + 265)			22,265
Balance at 31 Dec 19X6			18,395

Notes

1. The goods taken by the proprietor for his own use should be added to drawings and deducted from purchases (rather than added to sales) since the question gives their cost.

Exercises

1. Describe the different forms of incomplete records with which you are familiar.

2. The following is the balance sheet of Round Music as at 30 June 19X4:

	£		£
Capital	42,770	Plant	31,000
Creditors	5,640	Stock	9,720
Accruals	90	Debtors	6,810
		Prepayments	150
		Bank	820
	48,500		48,500

During the year ended 30 June 19X5 there was a fire which destroyed the books of account and supporting documents. However, from questioning the proprietor you have been able to obtain the following information:

1. The plant at 30 June 19X4 cost £50,000 and has been depreciated at 10 per cent per annum by the fixed instalment method on a strict time basis. Additional plant was purchased on the 1 April 19X5 at a cost of £20,000. Plant costing £10,000 on 1 January 19X2 was sold on 1 October 19X4 for £4,450.
2. Stock at 30 June 19X5 was valued at £8,630. This includes goods costing £1,120 that are worthless because of fire damage.
3. Debtors and creditors at 30 June 19X5 were £6,120 and £3,480 respectively. Debtors include doubtful debts of £310.

4. Accruals and prepayments at 30 June 19X5 were £130 and £80 respectively.
5. There was a bank overdraft at 30 June 19X5 of £1,430.
6. During the year the business had borrowed £7,000 from Lickey Bank which was repayable on 1 January 19X8.
7. During the year the owner introduced additional capital of £5,000 and made drawings of £18,500 by cheque. The proprietor also took goods costing £750 from the business for his own use.

You are required to compute the profit for the year ended 30 June 19X5 and prepare a balance sheet at that date. Present your answer in vertical form showing clearly the cost of fixed assets and the aggregate depreciation.

3. Jane Grimes, retail fruit and vegetable merchant, does not keep a full set of accounting records. However, the following information has been produced from the business's records:
1. Summary of the bank account for the year ended 31 Augst 19X8:

	£		£
1 Sept 19X7 balance brought forward	1,970	Payments to suppliers	72,000
Receipts from trade debtors	96,000	Purchase of motor van (E471 KBR)	13,000
Sale of private yacht	20,000	Rent and rates	2,600
Sale of motor van (A123 BWA)	2,100	Wages	15,100
		Motor vehicle expenses	3,350
		Postages and stationery	1,360
		Drawings	9,200
		Repairs and renewals	650
		Insurances	800
		31 Aug 19X8 balance carried forward	2,010
	£120,070		£120,070

1 Sept 19X8

Balance brought forward   £2,010

2. Assets and liabilities, other than balance at bank:

As at	1 Sept 19X7	31 Aug 19X8
	£	£
Trade creditors	4,700	2,590
Trade debtors	7,320	9,500
Rent and rates accruals	200	260
Motor vans: A123 BWA—At cost	10,000	—
Provision for depn.	8,000	—
E471 KBR—At cost	—	13,000
Provision for depn.	—	To be determined
Stock in trade	4,900	5,900
Insurances prepaid	160	200

3. All receipts are banked and all payments are made from the business bank account.
4. A trade debt of £300 owing by Peter Blunt and included in the trade debtors at 31 August 19X8 (see 2 above), is to be written off as a bad debt.
5. It is Jane Grimes' policy to provide depreciation at the rate of 20 per cent on the cost of motor vans held at the end of each financial year; no depreciation is provided in the year of sale or disposal of a motor van.
6. Discounts received during the year ended 31 August 19X8 from trade creditors amounted to £1,100.

Required:
(a) Prepare Jane Grime's trading and profit and loss account for the year ended 31 August 19X8.
(b) Prepare Jane Grime's balance sheet as at 31 August 19X8.   (AAT)

4. The following is the balance sheet of A. Fox at 31 July 19X8.

	£		£
Capital	48,480	Freehold land and buildings (at cost)	35,000
Creditors	5,220	Fixtures and fittings (cost £10,000)	5,800
Electricity accrued	60	Stock	3,300
		Debtors	6,540
		Bank	3,000
		Telephone prepaid	120
	53,760		53,760

The only book kept by A. Fox is a cash book in which all transactions passed through the bank account are recorded. A summary of the cash book for the year ended 31 July 19X9 has been prepared as follows:

	£		£
Balance b/d	3,000	Wages	5,640
Cash takings		Telephone	280
banked	18,920	Electricity	370
Cheques from		Motor expenses	1,810
debtors	31,860	Payments to creditors	33,360
Additional		Printing	560
capital	1,000	Purchases	4,500
		Balance c/d	8,260
	54,780		54,780

From the supporting documents it has been ascertained that:

(i) The following amounts have been paid from the cash takings before they were banked:

Drawings	£4,000
Purchases	£1,120
Car repairs	£ 980
Window cleaning	£ 170

(ii) Stock at 31 July 19X9 was valued at £3,920.
(iii) At 31 July 19X9 there are telephone charges prepaid of £140 and electricity accrued of £290.
(iv) The trade debtors and trade creditors outstanding at the end of the year are £5,840 and £5,720 respectively.
(v) Fox has taken goods out of the business for his own use that cost £530.
(vi) Fixtures and fittings have been depreciated in past years at 20 per cent per annum by the reducing balance method.

You are required to prepare a trading and profit and loss account for the year ended 31 July 19X9 and a balance sheet at that date. Present your answer in vertical form.

5. Miss Fitt owns a retail shop. The trading and profit and loss account and balance sheet are prepared annually by you from records consisting of a bank statement and a file of unpaid suppliers and outstanding debtors. The following balances were shown on her balance sheet at 1 January 19X8:

	£
Shop creditors	245
Shop fittings (cost £250) at written down value	200
Stock in hand	475
Debtors	50
Cash at bank	110
Cash float in till	10

The following is a summary of her bank statement for the year ended 31 December 19X8:

	£
Takings banked	6,983
Payments to suppliers	6,290
Rent of premises to 31 December 19X8	400
A. Smith—shopfitters	85
Advertising in local newspaper	50
Sundry expenses	38

You obtain the following additional information:

1. Takings are banked daily and all suppliers are paid by cheque, but Miss Fitt keeps £15 per week for herself, and pays her assistants £11 per week out of the takings.
2. The work done by A. Smith was for new shelving and repairs to existing fittings. The cost of new shelves was estimated at £50.
3. The cash float in the till was considered insufficient and raised to £15
4. Miss Fitt took £75 worth of goods for her own use without payment.
5. Your charges will be £25 for preparing the accounts.
6. The outstanding accounts file shows £230 due to suppliers, £10 due in respect of sundry expenses, and £85 outstanding debtors.
7. Depreciation on shop fittings is provided at 10 per cent on cost, a full year's charge being made in year of purchase.
8. Stock in hand at 31 December 19X8 was £710.

You are required to prepare Miss Fitt's trading and profit and loss account for the year ended 31 December 19X8, and her balance sheet as at that date. (CACA)

6. A year ago, you prepared accounts for A. Wilson, a retailer. His closing position was then:

Balance sheet at 31 March 19X0

	£	£
Delivery van (cost £4,800 in May 19X8)		2,880
Stock		6,410
Debtors (£1,196 less provision £72)		1,124
Owing from Askard Ltd		196
		10,610
Bank balance	70	
Trade creditors	2,094	
Accountant's fee	120	
Provision for legal claim	600	2,884
Wilson's capital		£7,726

Mr Wilson does not keep full records (despite your advice) and once again you have to use what information is available to prepare his accounts to 31 March 19X1. The most reliable evidence is a summary of the bank statements for the year. It shows:

	£	£
Balance at 1 April 19X0 (overdraft)		(70)
Cash and cheques from customers		33,100
Cheques from Askard Ltd		7,840
		40,870
Less cheques drawn for:		
Wilson's personal expenses	7,400	
Van—tax, insurance, repairs	440	
Rent, rates and general expenses	2,940	
Cash register	400	

Accountant's fee	120	
Trade creditors	28,284	
Legal claim settled	460	40,044
Balance at 31 March 19X1		826

For some of the sales Askard credit cards are accepted. Askard Ltd charges 2 per cent commission. At the end of the year the amount outstanding from Askard Ltd was £294.

Some other sales are on credit terms. Wilson keeps copies of the sales invoices in a box until they are settled. Those still in the 'unpaid' box at 31 March 19X1 totalled £1,652 which included one for £136 outstanding for four months—otherwise they were all less than two months old. Wilson thinks he allowed cash discounts of about £150 during the year. The debt of £72 outstanding at the beginning of the year for which a provision was made was never paid.

The amount of cash and cheques received from credit customers and from cash sales was all paid into the bank except that some cash payments were made first. These were estimated as:

	£
Part-time assistance	840
Petrol for van	800
Miscellaneous expenses	200
Wilson's drawings	2,000

Invoices from suppliers of goods outstanding of the year end totalled £2,420. Closing stock was estimated at £7,090 (cost price) and your fee has been agreed at £200. It has been agreed with the Inspector of Taxes that £440 of the van expenses should be treated as Wilson's private expenses.

Required:
Prepare the profit and loss account for Wilson's business for the year to 31 March 19X1 and a balance sheet at that date.   (CACA)

7. David Denton set up in business as a plumber a year ago, and he has asked you to act as his accountant. His instructions to you are in the form of the following letter.

Dear Henry,
I was pleased when you agreed to act as my accountant and look forward to your first visit to check my records. The proposed fee of £250 p.a. is acceptable. I regret that the paperwork for the work done during the year is incomplete. I started my business on 1 January last, and put £6,500 into a business bank account on that date. I brought my van into the firm at that time, and reckon that it was worth £3,600 then. I think it will last another three years after the end of the first year of business use.

I have drawn £90 per week from the business bank account during the year. In my trade it is difficult to take a holiday, but my wife managed to get away for a while. The travel agent's bill for £280 was paid out of the business account. I bought the lease of the yard and office for £6,500. The lease has ten years to run, and the rent is only £300 a year payable in advance on the anniversary of the date of purchase, which was 1 April. I borrowed £4,000 on that day from Aunt Jane to help pay for the lease. I have agreed to pay her 10 per cent interest per annum, but have been too busy to do anything about this yet.

I was lucky enough to meet Miss Prism shortly before I set up on my own, and she has worked for me as an office organizer right from the start. She is paid a salary of £3,000 per annum. All the bills for the year have been carefully preserved in a tool box, and we analysed them last week. The materials I have bought cost me £9,600, but I reckon there was £580-worth left in the yard on 31 December. I have not paid for them all yet; I think we owed £714 to the suppliers on 31 December. I was surprised to see that I had spent £4,800 on plumbing equipment, but it should last me five years or so. Electricity bills received up to 30 September came to £1,122; but motor expenses were £912, and general expenses £1,349 for the year. The insurance premium for the year to 31 March next was £800. All these have been paid by cheque but Miss Prism has lost the rate demand. I expect the Local Authority will send a reminder soon since I have not yet paid. I seem to remember that rates came to £180 for the year to 31 March next.

Miss Prism sent out bills to my customers for work done, but some of them are very slow to pay. Altogether the charges made were £29,863, but only £25,613 had been received by 31 December. Miss Prism thinks that 10 per cent of the remaining bills are not likely to be paid. Other customers for jobs too small to bill have paid £3,418 in cash for work done, but I only managed to bank £2,600 of this money. I used £400 of the difference to pay the family's grocery bills, and Miss Prism used the rest for general expenses, except for £123 which was left over in a drawer in the office on 31 December.

Kind regards,
Yours sincerely,
David.

You are required to draw up a profit and loss account for the year ended 31 December, and a balance sheet as at that date.   (CACA)

20.   The final accounts of clubs

A club is an organization whose primary objective is to provide a service to its members (e.g. sports and social clubs) and/or some section of the community (e.g. senior citizens). Its main aim is therefore not to earn a profit but often simply to break even. Thus in the final accounts of clubs the profit and loss account is replaced with an *income and expenditure account*. Any difference between the income and expenditure for the year is referred to as a surplus or deficit (i.e. not a profit or loss). The income and expenditure account is prepared using the same principles as the profit and loss account, namely the matching and accrual of revenue income and expenditure. However, the contents differ in that income will take the form of subscriptions, entrance fees from sports activities, surpluses on a bar, dances, raffles, gaming machines, annual dinners etc.

Another major difference between clubs and business enterprises is that clubs are usually managed by voluntary officers. Members of the club therefore frequently expect them to provide an account of the money that has been received and the way in which it has been spent. Thus the final accounts of clubs often include a *receipts and payments account*. This is simply a summary of the cash book showing the opening and closing cash and bank balances and the total amounts received and spent on each type of income and expenditure, assets etc.

Many clubs are quite small and may have few, if any, assets and liabilities other than cash. It therefore serves little purpose to prepare a balance sheet, particularly if a receipts and payments account has been produced. However, some clubs are relatively large. In this case the final accounts should include a *balance sheet*. It will take the same form as for business enterprises with one major difference which is that the capital account is replaced by an *accumulated/general fund*. This is an accumulation of previous years' surpluses (less deficits) of income over expenditure, and represents the net worth of the club. Unlike the capital account of business enterprises, there cannot be capital introduced or drawings against the accumulated fund. The only other significant difference between the balance sheet of a business enterprise and that of a club is that the latter also contains subscriptions in arrears and subscriptions in advance. These are examined further later.

Although clubs are not primarily trading organizations they frequently engage in certain activities that are intended to make a profit/surplus as a way of raising additional funds or subsidizing other functions, for example, the sale of drinks and snacks, gaming machines, raffles, dances etc. Where these involve material amounts of money it is usual to compute the profit or loss on the activity in a separate account such as a *bar trading account*. Similarly, where the amounts are less significant it is usual to also compute the profit or loss (e.g. on a dance) and show this as a separate item in the income and expenditure account.

Annual subscriptions

Many clubs require their members to pay an annual subscription. These are usually accounted for on an accruals basis, that is, applying the accruals concept. This means that

185

the amount which is credited to the income and expenditure account in respect of subscriptions is the amount due for the year, irrespective of whether this has all been received.

The application of the accruals concept gives rise to subscriptions in arrear and subscriptions in advance in the final accounts. Where some members have not paid their subscriptions at the end of a given accounting year these are referred to as subscriptions in arrear, and treated as debtors. Where some members have paid their subscriptions for the following accounting year these are referred to as subscriptions in advance, and treated as creditors.

However, as in the case of accrued and prepaid expenses, debtors and creditors in respect of subscriptions are not entered in separate personal accounts. Instead, these are recorded in the subscriptions account. Subscriptions in arrear are entered in the subscriptions account as a balance carried down on the credit side and a balance brought down on the debit side. Subscriptions in advance are entered in the subscriptions account as a balance carried down on the debit side and a balance brought down on the credit side. Thus subscriptions in arrear are shown on the balance sheet as a current asset and subscriptions in advance are shown as a current liability.

Sometimes subscriptions are recorded in the income and expenditure account on a strict cash received basis and not an accruals basis. In this case there will not be any subscriptions in arrear or advance in the final accounts. This is said to be an application of the prudence concept. It is sometimes justified on the grounds that members, unlike other debtors, are more likely to fail to pay subscriptions in arrear, and clubs are unlikely to take legal or other action to force payment. However, the use of the cash received basis is not common in examination questions and should only be applied where specifically required.

The preparation of final accounts of clubs

It is common to find that the books of account of a club have been kept on a *single entry* basis. This means that the procedure to be followed in the preparation of the final accounts will be as described in the previous chapter. This is illustrated in Example 20.1 below.

Example 20.1
City Football Club has the following assets and liabilities at 1 July 19X7: freehold land and buildings at a cost £50,000; equipment at WDV £12,000; grass mower at cost £135; bar creditors £1,380; subscriptions in advance £190; subscriptions in arrear £105; bar stocks £2,340; rates in advance £240; electricity accrued £85.

A summary of the receipts and payments during the year ended 30 June 19X8 is as follows:

	£		£
Bank balance at 1 July 19X7	695	Rates	490
Bar takings banked	5,430	Electricity	255
Subscriptions received	3,610	Purchase of new	520
Sale of dance tickets	685	grass mower	
Gate money received	8,490	Bar steward's wages	2,200
		Bar creditors	4,980
		Band for dance	490
		Postage and telephone	310
		Printing and stationery	175
		Bank balance at	
		30 June 19X8	9,490
	18,910		18,910

You are given the following additional information:

1. Bar stocks at 30 June 19X8, £2,560.
2. Bar creditors at 30 June 19X8 £980.
3. Rates paid include £400 for the six months to the 30 September 19X8.
4. Electricity in arrear at 30 June 19X8 £70.
5. Subscriptions in arrear at 30 June 19X8 £95.
6. Subscriptions in advance at 30 June 19X8 £115
7. The following amounts have been paid from bar takings before they were banked: sundry expenses £25, bar purchases £235, office salaries £1,200, stationery £45, and travelling expenses £140.
8. The new grass mower was purchased by putting in part exchange the old one, for which the trade in value was £180.
9. Depreciation on the equipment is 20 per cent p.a. using the reducing balance method. No depreciation is charged on the grass mower.

You are required to prepare:

(a) a bar trading account for the year ended 30 June 19X8.
(b) an income and expenditure account for the year ended 30 June 19X8.
(c) a balance sheet as at 30 June 19X8.

Show clearly all your workings.

Workings/procedure

1. If necessary prepare a statement of affairs as at the end of the previous year in order to ascertain the accumulated/general fund.

City Football Club
Statement of affairs as at 30 June 19X7

Fixed assets	£	£	£
Freehold land and buildings at cost			50,000
Equipment at WDV			12,200
Grass mower at cost			135
			62,335
Current assets			
Payments in advance		240	
Stock		2,340	
Subscriptions in arrear		695	
		3,380	
Less: current liabilities			
Accrued expenses	85		
Creditors	1,380		
Subscriptions in advance	190	1,655	
			1,725
Accumulated fund at 30 June 19X7			64,060

2. If necessary prepare a receipts and payments account for the year in order to ascertain the bank and cash balance at the end of the year and the total amounts received and spent on each type of income and expenditure, and on assets.
3. (a) Compute the net credit bar purchases by preparing a creditors control account:

Creditors control

19X8				19X7		
30 June	Bank	4,980		1 July	Balance b/d	1,380
30 June	Balance c/d	980		19X8		
				June 30	Net purchases	4,580
		5,960				5,960

The figure for net purchases is the difference between the two sides.

(b) Compute the cash and cheque bar purchases and then the total bar purchases:

$$\text{Total purchases} = £235 + £4,580 = £4,815$$

4. (a) Compute and net credit bar sales if any by preparing a debtors control account.
   (b) Compute the cash and cheque bar sales and then the total bar sales:

$$\text{Cash and total sales} = £5,430 + £25 + £235 + £1,200 + £45 + £140$$
$$= £7,075$$

5. Ascertain the profit or loss on any other trading activities (e.g. catering, raffles, gaming machines etc.), and social functions (e.g. dances, annual dinner etc.):

$$\text{Profit on dance} = £685 - £490 = £195$$

6. Ascertain the income for the year in respect of subscriptions by preparing the ledger account. Alternatively, in examinations this may be shown as workings in the income and expenditure account.

Subscriptions

19X7			19X7		
1 July	Subs in arrear b/d	105	1 July	Subs in advance b/d	190
19X8			19X8		
30 June	Subs for year	3,675	30 June	Bank	3,610
30 June	Subs in advance c/d	115	30 June	Subs in arrear c/d	95
		3,895			3,895

The figure for subs for the year of £3,675 is the difference between the two sides. It is credited to the income and expenditure account.

7. Compute the expenditure for the year in respect to those expenses with accruals and prepayments by preparing the relevant ledger accounts. Alternatively, in examinations this may be shown as workings in the income and expenditure account:

Rates

19X7			19X8		
1 July	Prepayment b/d	240	30 June	Income and expenditure a/c	530
19X8					
30 June	Bank	490	30 June	Prepayment c/d	200
		730			730

Light and heat

19X8			19X7		
30 June	Bank	255	1 July	Accrual b/d	85
			19X8		
30 June	Accrual c/d	70	30 June	Income and expenditure a/c	240
		325			325

8. Ascertain the depreciation charges for the year and any profit or loss on the sale of fixed assets:

$$\text{Depreciation on equipment} = 20 \text{ per cent} \times £12,200 = £2,440$$

$$\text{Profit on sale of grass mower} = £180 - £135 = £45$$

9. Prepare the bar trading account, income and expenditure account and balance sheet remembering to add together any cheque and cash expenditure of the same type (e.g. stationery) and make any other necessary adjustments.

City Football Club

Bar trading account for the year ended 30 June 19X8

	£	£
Sales		7,075
Less: Cost of sales —		
Stock at 1 July 19X7	2,340	
Add: purchases	4,815	
	7,155	
Less: stock at 30 June 19X8	2,560	
	4,595	
Other bar costs —		
Steward's wages	2,200	6,795
Profit on bar		£ 280

City Football Club

Income and expenditure account for the year ended 30 June 19X8

	£	£
Income		
Gate receipts		8,490
Subscriptions		3,675
Profit on bar		280
Surplus on dance		195
Profit on sale of fixed assets		45
		12,685
Less: Expenditure		
Rates (490 + 240 − 200)	530	
Light and heat (255 + 70 − 85)	240	
Postage and telephone	310	
Printing and stationery (175 + 45)	220	
Sundry expenses	25	
Office salaries	1,200	
Travelling expenses	140	
Depreciation on equipment	2,440	5,105
Excess of income over expenditure		7,580

City Football Club

Balance sheet as at 30 June 19X8

Fixed assets	£	£
Freehold land and buildings at cost		50,000
Equipment at WDV	12,200	
Less: depreciation	2,440	9,760
Grass mower (520 + 180)		700
		60,460

	£	£	£
From page 190			60,460
Current assets			
Prepayments		200	
Stock		2,560	
Subscriptions in arrear		95	
Bank		9,490	
		12,345	
Less: current liabilities			
Accruals	70		
Subscriptions in advance	115		
Creditors	980	1,165	11,180
			71,640
Accumulated fund			
Balance at 30 June 19X7			64,060
Add: Excess of income over			
expenditure for the year			7,580
Balance at 30 June 19X8			71,640

Special items

As seen above, clubs have a variety of different forms of income, many of which are not found in business enterprises. Some of these are not common in practice but provide examples that examiners can use to test important principles. Those most frequently encountered in examinations are discussed below.

Donations, bequests and gifts

Small donations, bequests and gifts in the form of money are credited to the income and expenditure account. Donations and gifts in the form of domestic goods (such as furniture for the clubhouse or old clothes for resale) with a relative small value are not usually recorded in the income and expenditure account (until they are sold, when just the sale is recorded).

However, where donations of money or other assets are of a material amount (i.e. large in relation to the size of the club's normal income), the generally accepted best practice is to credit such items direct to the accumulated fund instead of the income and expenditure account. This is because it would probably be misleading to credit the income and expenditure account with large amounts of income which is of a non-recurring nature. Members might be misled into thinking that the resulting surplus for the year was likely to be repeated in future years and thus could be used to cover additional recurring expenditure or reduced bar prices! The corresponding debit entry would be in the receipts and payments account in the case of money, or to the relevant asset account where the donation or bequest takes some other form, such as land, buildings, paintings etc. In the latter case the amount entered in the accounts would be a valuation.

Membership/entrance fees

Clubs which have valuable assets that are in great demand, such as golf and other sports facilities, often require new members to pay an entry or joining fee (in addition to the annual subscription). To treat this as income for the year in which it was received by crediting the income and expenditure account would be a breach of the matching principle, the reason being that this fee is in the nature of a prepayment by the member for services which the club is obliged to provide over his/her period of membership, which is usually several years.

Such fees are referred to as deferred income, and the matching principle dictates that these should be credited to the income and expenditure account over the number of years which the club expects to have to provide the member with its services. Clearly the decision relating to the length of this period is highly subjective. One possibility is the average number of years that people remain a member of the club. However, in practice a more arbitrary period may be selected depending on the nature of the club's services and the size of the membership fee.

The accounting entries in respect of joining fees are thus to credit these to a deferred income account, and each year to transfer a given proportion (e.g. 10 per cent if to be spread over 10 years) to the income and expenditure account. The balance on the deferred income account is shown on the balance sheet after (and separate from) the accumulated fund.

Life membership subscriptions

Instead of paying an annual subscription some clubs permit their members to make a once-only payment which entitles them to membership for life. These are referred to as life membership subscriptions and, like entrance fees above, are in the nature of a prepayment by the member for services that the club is obliged to provide over the remainder of his/her life. They must therefore not be credited to the income and expenditure account as income of the year they are received.

Life membership subscriptions are a form of deferred income, and the matching principle dictates that they be spread over the number of years which the club expects to have to provide the life member with its services. Clearly the decision relating to the length of this period is highly subjective. One possibility is the average number of years between people becoming life members and their death. However, in practice a more arbitrary period may be selected depending on the nature of the clubs services. For example, the period may be considerably longer for a golf club or social club than an athletics club or senior citizens club, since the period of life membership of the latter is restricted by physical and age constraints.

The accounting entries in respect of life membership subscriptions are thus to credit these to a deferred income account, and each year to transfer a given proportion (e.g. 5 per cent if to be spread over 20 years) to the income and expenditure account. The balance on the deferred income account is shown on the balance sheet after (and separate from) the accumulated fund.

There is, however, an alternative treatment of life membership subscriptions which is an application of the prudence concept rather than the matching principle. This dictates that because the period of membership cannot be predicted with reasonable certainty, the income should not be recognized until the member dies. Thus all the life membership subscriptions are credited to a fund account, and when a member dies his/her subscription is transferred to the accumulated fund (or possibly the income and expenditure account).

The life membership subscription fund account is shown in the balance sheet just below the accumulated fund and separate from any items that have been treated as deferred income, such as membership/entrance fees. This method of treating life membership subscriptions would be adopted in examination questions that do not give any indication of the length of time over which these should be credited to income, and which give details of how many life members died during the accounting year.

Prize funds

Some clubs give prizes or other monetary awards to their members and/or other people that they wish to honour or assist for educational reasons. These are frequently financed from a separate fund, which may have been created by the club or from money that was donated for the express purpose of making the award. When the fund is set up the money donated for this purpose is invested in securities which provide some sort of income. This often takes the form of government stocks carrying a fixed rate of interest. The prizes or awards are usually paid out of the interest received and not the original donation, which remains invested.

The accounting entries for prize funds can be confusing partly because they involve two related accounts. The first is a prize fund account which appears on the balance sheet along with other funds such as the accumulated fund and any life membership subscription fund. The other is a prize fund investment account which is usually treated as a fixed asset. When the fund is set up, the money set aside or donated for this purpose is debited to the prize fund investment account and credited to the prize fund account.

When income is received from the prize fund investments this is debited in the receipts and payments account and credited to the prize fund account. When the prizes are awarded the amounts are credited in the receipts and payments account and debited to the prize fund account. This is illustrated in Example 20.2 below.

Example 20.2
Parkview plc donated £10,000 to the City Club on 31 December 19X0. It was agreed that the annual income from this is to be used to make a grant to members' children for educational purposes. The donation was invested in 10 per cent Government Stock on 1 January 19X1. The annual income of £1,000 was received on 31 December 19X1 and this was given to J. Smith as a grant on 1 January 19X2.

Show how this would be recorded in the ledger of City Club.

Receipts and payments

19X0			19X1		
31 Dec	Grant fund—		1 Jan	Grant fund	
	Parkview donation	10,000		investments	10,000
19X1			19X2		
31 Dec	Grant fund—		1 Jan	Grant fund—	
	interest	1,000		J. Smith	1,000

Grant fund investments

19X1		
1 Jan	Bank	10,000

Parkview grant fund

19X2			19X0		
1 Jan	Bank	1,000	31 Dec	Bank	10,000
			19X1		
			31 Dec	Bank	1,000

Notes

1. The balance on the grant fund at the end of each accounting year is normally the same as that on the grant fund investment account. However, as in the above example, these may differ because of time lags between the receipt of investment income and the payment of the grant.

Exercises

1. Explain the difference between the receipts and payments account and an income and expenditure account.

2. Explain the nature of an accumulated fund in the balance sheet of a club.

3. Describe the entries in the accounts of a club for each of the following and explain the justification for each treatment:

   (a) Donation of second-hand clothing for resale.
   (b) A gift of a large amount of cash.
   (c) A bequest of premises to be used as a clubhouse.

4. Describe two possible methods of accounting for each of the following in the accounts of clubs and explain the theoretical/conceptual justification for each method:

   (a) Membership/entrance fees
   (b) Life membership subscriptions.

5. Explain the nature and accounting entries in respect of prize funds in the accounts of clubs.

6. The secretary of the Woodland Hockey Club gives you the following summary of his cash book for the year ended 31 May 19X9:

	£		£
Balances at commencement of year:		Rent	234
At bank	63	Printing and stationery	18
In hand	10	Affiliation fees	12
Subscriptions:		Captain's and secretary's	
Supporters	150	expenses	37
Supporters 19X9–X0 season	20	Refreshments for	
Fees per game	170	visiting teams	61
Annual social	134	Annual social	102
		Equipment purchased	26
		Balance at close of	
		year: At bank	49
		In hand	8
	£547		£547

The secretary also gives you the following information:

	31 May 19X8 £	31 May 19X9 £
Amounts due to the club:		
Supporter's subscriptions	14	12
Fees per game	78	53
Re annual social	6	—
Amounts owing by the club:		
Rent	72	54
Printing	—	3
Secretary's expenses	4	8
Refreshments	13	12

On 31 May 19X8 the club's equipment appeared in the books at £150. It is desired that 12 per cent be written off the book value of the equipment as it appears on 31 May 19X9.
   You are required to:

1. Show your computation of the club's accumulated fund as on 31 May 19X8.
2. Prepare the income and expenditure account showing the result for the year ended 31 May 19X9, and the balance sheet as on that date.   (CACA)

7. The treasurer of the Senior Social Club has prepared the following summary of the club's receipts and payments for the year ended 30 November 19X0.

Senior Social Club
Receipts and payments account for the year ended 30 November 19X0

	£		£
Cash and bank balances b/f	810	Secretarial expenses	685
Members' subscriptions	4,250	Rent	2,500
Donations	1,480	Visiting speakers'	
Sales of competition		expenses	1,466
tickets	1,126	Donations to charities	380
		Prizes for competitions	550
		Purchase of equipment	1,220
		Stationery and printing	469
		Balance c/f	396
	7,666		7,666

On 1 December 19X9 the club owned equipment which had cost £3,650 and which was valued at £2,190. The club's equipment as at 30 November 19X0 (inclusive of any purchases during the year) was valued at £1,947.

The following additional information is available:

As at...	1 December 19X9 £	30 November 19X0 £
Stocks of prizes	86	108
Owing to suppliers of prizes	314	507
Subscriptions in arrears	240	580
Subscriptions in advance	65	105

Required:

(a) Calculate the value of the accumulated fund of the club as at 1 December 19X9.

(b) Prepare a subscriptions account for the year ended 30 November 19X0 showing clearly the amount to be transferred to the club's income and expenditure account for the year.

(c) Prepare a statement showing the surplus or deficit made by the club on competitions for the year ended 30 November 19X0.

(d) Prepare the club's balance sheet as at 30 November 19X0.   (AAT)

8. The Elite Bowling and Social Club prepares its annual accounts to 31 October. The following receipts and payments account has been prepared by the treasurer:

	£		£
Cash in hand, 31 Oct 19X7	10	Bar purchases	1,885
Balances at bank, 31 Oct 19X7		Wages	306
Current account	263	Rent and rates	184
Deposit account	585	Lighting and heating	143
Spectators entrance fees	54	New mower (less allowance	
Subscriptions: to 31/10/X7.	30	for old one £40)	120
to 31/10/X8.	574	General expenses	132
to 31/10/X9.	44	Catering purchases	80
Bar takings	2,285	Additional furniture	460
Deposit account interest	26	Cash in hand at 31/10/X8.	8
Catering receipts	120	Balances at bank, 31/10/X8.	
		Current account	176
		Deposit account	497
	£3,991		£3,991

The following information is also supplied:

1. The book values of the fixed assets on 31 October 19X7 were: furniture, fixtures and fittings £396 (cost £440) and mower £20 (cost £120).

2. The current assets and liabilities were as follows:

	31 Oct 19X7	31 Oct 19X8
	£	£
Bar stock at cost	209	178
Amount owed to the brewery for		
bar purchases	186	248
Due for rent and rates	12	26
Due for lighting and heating	9	11
Subscriptions in arrear	30	50

3. During the year the steward commenced to provide light refreshments at the bar and it has been agreed that in the annual accounts provision should be made for the payment to him of a bonus of 40 per cent of the gross profit arising from this catering venture.

4. Depreciation to furniture, fixtures and fittings is to be provided at a rate of 10 per cent on cost. No depreciation is to be provided on the new mower, but a full year on the new furniture.

You are required to prepare:

(a) a statement showing the general fund of the club as on 31 October 19X7;

(b) an income and expenditure account for the year ended 31 October 19X8 (showing separately gross profit on bar sales and catering); and

(c) a balance sheet as at 31 October 19X8.   (CACA)

9. The following receipts and payments account for the year ended 31 October 19X0 has been prepared from the current account bank statements of the Country Cousins Sports Club:

19X9		£	19X0		£
1 Nov	Balance b/f	1,700	31 Oct	Clubhouse:	
19X0				Rates and	
31 Oct	Subscriptions	8,600		insurance	380
	Bar takings	13,800		Decorations and	
	Donations	1,168		repairs	910
	Annual dinner—			Annual dinner—	
	Sale of tickets	470		Catering	650
				Bar purchases	9,200
				Stationery and	
				printing	248
				New sports	
				equipment	2,463
				Hire of films	89
				Warden's salary	4,700
				Petty cash	94
				Balance c/f	7,004
		£25,738			£25,738

The following additional information has been given:

At 31 October	19X9	19X0
	£	£
Clubhouse, at cost	15,000	15,000
Bar stocks, at cost	1,840	2,360
Petty cash float	30	10
Bank deposit account	600	730
Subscriptions received in advance	210	360
Creditors for bar supplies	2,400	1,900

It has been decided to provide for depreciation annually on the clubhouse at the rate of 10 per cent of cost and on the new sports equipment at the rate of $33\frac{1}{3}$ per cent of cost.

The petty cash float is used exclusively for postages.

The only entry in the bank deposit account during the year ended 31 October 19X0 concerns interest.

One quarter of the warden's salary and one half of the clubhouse costs, including depreciation, are to be apportioned to the bar.

The donations received during the year ended 31 October 19X0 are for the new coaching bursary fund, which will be utilized for the provision of training facilities for promising young sportsmen and sportswomen. It is expected to make the first award during 19X1.

Required:
(a) An account showing the profit or loss for the year ended 31 October 19X0 on the operation of the bar.
(b) An income and expenditure account for the year ended 31 October 19X0 and a balance sheet at that date for the Country Cousins Sports Club.   (CACA)

10. The treasurer of a club has given you the following account of its activities during the year ended 30 June 19X8.

Receipts		*Payments*	
	£		£
Bank balance at 1/7/X7 (including £75 received during the year ended 30/6/X7 on the prize fund investments)	390	Additional billiard table with accessories bought 1/7/X7	300
		Repairs to billiard tables	50

Annual subscriptions		Purchases for bar	3,680
(including £20 relating		Steward's wages and	
to previous year)	340	expenses	400
Life membership subscriptions		Rates	140
(5 @ £16)	80	Lighting and heating	72
Sundry lettings	180	Cleaning and laundry	138
Bar receipts	4,590	Sundry expenses	80
Receipts for billiards	275	Prizes awarded for previous year from	
Gifts from members	3,500	income available at 1/7/X7	75
Income from £1,500 5 per cent		Repayment of mortgage of	
defence bonds allocated specifically		5 per cent 30/6/X8 with	
for a prize fund	75	interest for two years	4,400
		Bank balance at 30/6/X8	95
	£9,430		£9,430

You are also given the following information:

1. The freehold building, owned and occupied by the club, was purchased for £6,000 many years ago.
2. On 1 July 19X2, the club acquired six billiard tables for which they paid £1,200, and it is considered that the tables have a life of twelve years.
3. The bar stock at 1 July 19X7 was £150 and at 30 June 19X8 £180.
4. Annual subscriptions outstanding from members at 30 June 19X8 amounted to £10.
5. On 1 July 19X7 there were 25 life members who had paid subscriptions of £16 each. During the year ended 30 June 19X8 three of these members had died.

You are required to prepare an income and expenditure account and balance sheet showing clearly how you have treated the subscriptions of life members and the prize fund. (CACA)

11. The Dohray Amateur Musical Society has a treasurer who is responsible for receipts and payments which he records in cash and bank books. Periodically, these books are handed over to the firm of certified accountants which employs you.

   One of your tasks is to prepare the final accounts of the society. As a preliminary step, you have prepared the receipts and payments account (rounded to the nearest £1) for the year ended 31 May 19X5. This is shown below, together with the explanatory notes which the treasurer has supplied to enable you to understand the nature of some of the items.

Dohray Amateur Musical Society receipts and payments account for the year ended 31 May 19X5

Receipts	Cash £	Bank £	Payments	Cash £	Bank £
Opening balances	31	309	Creditors: trade		
Debtors: members			fixed assets (note 4)		
joining fees (note 1)	190	160	musical instruments		522
annual subscriptions			trophies		83
(note 2)	285	70	Creditors: trade		
Annual concert (note 3)			purchases for resale		
takings	1,791		(note 4)		
Sales of goods (note 4)			sheet music		118
sheet music	140		musical instruments		336
musical instruments	287		Annual concert (note 3)		
Prize moneys (note 7)	190		hall booking fees		490
Sponsorship grant			printing of publicity		
(note 5)		300	posters		112
Refreshment sales	113		hire of professional		
Raffle profits	64		soloists		236

PAC grants (note 6)			musicians	174
revenue	100		adjudication fees	50
capital	400		Musical festivals (note 7)	
Transfers from cash a/c	2,910		entrance fees	250
			hire of buses	281
			Honoraria (note 8)	
			secretary	150
			treasurer	100
			RMFC affiliation fee	
			(note 9)	72
			Rent of society's premises	
			(note 10)	510
			Refreshment purchases	72
			Bank charges	42
			Sundry expenses	60
			Transfers to bank a/c	2,910
			Closing balances c/d	49	723
	3,091	4,249		3,091	4,249

Explanatory notes supplied by the treasurer

1. On joining the society, members pay a non-returnable fee of £10 (before 1 June 19X2, the fee had been £5). It has been found from experience that, on average, members remain in the society for five years. On this basis, one fifth of each joining fee is credited to income and expenditure account each year.

   New members statistics are:

During year ended 31 May	Number of new members	Joining fees suspense at 31 May 19X4
	No.	£
19X1	20	20
19X2	24	48
19X3	32	192
19X4	27	216
19X5	35	Nil
		£476

2. Annual subscriptions are due on 1 June each year. It is the society's policy to credit these to income and expenditure account on an actual receipts basis, not an accruals basis. However, if subscriptions are received in advance, the amounts are credited to income and expenditure account for the year for which they are paid.
3. The society's major money raising event is its annual public concert. This is given in a large hall which the society hires. The society also hires professional musicians and soloists and has to pay the fees of the adjudicators (judges).
4. The society buys trophies (silver bowls and shields) to present to the winners of the individual musical items at the annual concert. It also buys musical instruments some of which are for use by the members and others for resale to the members. Musical scores and sheets are also bought for resale to the members.
5. A local building company has given a grant to the society for a period of three years in return for publicity. This sponsorship grant was received in full on 1 June 19X4 and is being credited to income and expenditure account in equal instalments in each of the three years to 31 May 19X7.
6. The Performing Arts Council (PAC) has awarded the society an annual grant towards the running costs. In addition the PAC makes capital grants. The society's policy is to hold capital grants in suspense and to release each year's grant to income and expenditure account over a period of five years,

from the year of grant onwards. At 31 May 19X4 capital grants held in suspense were analysed as follows:

In respect of year ended 31 May	Capital grants suspense £
19X1	30
19X2	70
19X3	120
19X4	120
	£340

7. Throughout the year, the society competes at various musical festivals. Cash prizes won by individual members are retained by the society and credited to income and expenditure account in order to reduce the cost of attending the festivals.

8. The offices of secretary and treasurer are unpaid, but the society gives each of them an *ex gratia* (honorary) cash award, termed an honorarium.

9. In order to participate in the musical festivals, the society has to be affiliated to the Regional Musical Festival Committee (RMFC). The annual fee, which has remained the same for a number of years, is paid on 1 March in each year.

10. The society pays rent for its premises. The rental, which is inclusive of rates, heating, lighting, cleaning etc. is reviewed annually on 31 March. The payment shown in the receipts and payments account represents quarterly payments in advance, as follows:

	Payment £
19X4	
30 June	120
30 September	120
31 December	120
19X5	
31 March	150
	£510

Further information was supplied by the treasurer as follows:

	19X4 £	19X5 £
1. Creditors at 31 May		
Fixed assets		
musical instruments	79	119
trophies	23	13
Purchases for resale		
sheet music	14	20
musical instruments	45	39
2. Subscriptions		
Payments in advance included in the actual receipts for the year	30	40
3. Stocks at 31 May		
Goods for resale		
sheet music	31	52
musical instruments	70	94
Refreshments	not brought into account on the grounds that it is not material in amount	

4. Fixed assets (at cost) at 31 May
     Musical instruments   1,378   ⎰ to be
     Trophies   247   ⎱ derived

    There were no fixed asset disposals during the year

5. Provision for depreciation at 31 May
     Musical instruments   704   ⎰ to be
     Trophies   96   ⎱ derived

Depreciation is calculated on the cost of these assets at the end of the financial year. The straight line method is employed using the following assumed asset lives.

    Musical instruments   5 years
    Trophies   10 years

    The Society had been formed on 1 June 19X0.

Required:

Prepare for the Dohray Amateur Musical Society:

(a) The Income and Expenditure account for the year ended 31 May 19X5; showing the surplus or deficit on each of the activities:

    Annual concert
    Musical festivals,
    Sales of goods; and

(b) the balance sheet at that date.

Note: Workings are an integral part of the answer and must be shown.   (CACA)

21. Accounting for hire purchase transactions

Asset purchase, by an exchange of cash for the asset presents a simple case of capital expenditure readily recorded by the double entry system. Hire purchase agreements and instalments sales provide the buyer with the opportunity of making payments over an extended period. This effectively provides some of the finance to make the payment for the purchase, repaying this over time. The legal position relating to these transactions varies. This book is not concerned with the detailed legal considerations necessary to classify specific arrangements. The general features can be set out.

Under a hire purchase contract an asset is supplied to the purchaser under an agreement for the purchaser to make a given number of periodic payments, the last of which results in transfer of ownership from the supplier to the purchaser. Although legal title remains with the suplier until this last payment, the hirer is granted uninterrupted use of the asset.

In an instalment credit sale a series of periodic payments are again to be made. However, legal title passes when the asset is delivered, although the supplier may have rights to repossession in cases of default.

The economic effects of both hire purchase and instalment credit sales are very similar and this is reflected in the accounting treatment. Even though hire purchase assets are not owned in strict legal form the substance of the agreement gives the purchaser comparable rights to ownership, so the transaction is treated as if a sale has taken place and the hirer is regarded as a buyer by including the assets in the balance sheet. This chapter will consider the entries made to record these types of transaction in the buyer's books. The transactions are more complex than outright purchase for two related reasons.

First, it is recognized that the payments made comprise amounts both for the supply of the asset and for the financing costs. One would expect to pay more when deferring payment over an extended period, equivalent to the interest that would be paid had the sum deferred been borrowed. It would be inconsistent if two businesses buying the same asset, one as a cash purchase and one on hire purchase, recorded the purchase at differing amounts, given that the difference related to financing rather than properties of the asset. The cash price represents a capital expenditure; interest is a revenue expenditure and needs to be separated.

The second matter to be addressed is that where the contract extends over more than one accounting period, interest must be spread over the periods on an appropriate basis for periodic reporting. The accruals concept and matching principles set out in Chapter 10 arise again.

Dividing up the hire purchase payments

Splitting the total payments into the capital and revenue expenditure elements is relatively straightforward given the disclosure of the cash purchase price. The difference between the sum of any initial down payment plus the agreed instalments and the cash purchase price represents the interest element.

For example, an asset, say a computer, which has a cash price of £6,000, is purchased for a down payment of £1,900 plus five annual instalments of £1,000 paid at the end of each year. Total interest is (£1,900 + 5 × £1,000) − £6,000 = £900. Spreading the interest payments over the five years is less simple. Supplying businesses might be liable to quote nominal percentage rates but these do not represent the equivalent interest that is being charged. A nominal rate may be quoted as 3 per cent, calculated as:

$$\frac{\text{interest}}{\text{capital}} \div \text{number of years i.e. } \frac{900}{6,000} \div 5 = 3 \text{ per cent}$$

The actual (effective) interest rate will be much higher because the amount of finance will be reducing due to the repayments being made. Even if the average of the initial £6,000 and final zero amount is taken, the rate of 6 per cent understates the effective rate.

Identifying the effective rate requires the use of annuity calculations, possibly using tables. This is not considered in this book. However, the supplier may provide the result of this calculation. In this case the rate is very close to 7 per cent. Given this information, it is possible to analyse the payments over the life of the agreement as follows:

	Year 1 £	Year 2 £	Year 3 £	Year 4 £	Year 5 £	Sum £
Outstanding finance—initial	6,000	4,100	3,387	2,624	1,808	
Repayment at start of year	1,900	713	763	816	873	
Balance for year	4,100	3,387	2,624	1,808	935	
Interest at 7 per cent for year	287	237	184	127	65	900
Capital repayment at year end	713	763	816	873	935	4,100
Instalments	1,000	1,000	1,000	1,000	1,000	5,000

As a method for approximating the annuity calculations, the Rule of 78 (sum of the years' digits) method may be used. This is a relatively simple method of apportioning the interest over the life in declining amounts. In this case it is a five year agreement and the sum of the years' digits is 5 + 4 + 3 + 2 + 1 = 15. The interest is allocated over the five years in the proportions 5:4:3:2:1, so the first year allocation will be [5 ÷ (5 + 4 + 3 + 2 + 1)] × £900 = £300. Over the five years, we get:

	Year 1 £	Year 2 £	Year 3 £	Year 4 £	Year 5 £	Sum £
Interest	300	240	180	120	60	900
Capital repayment	700	760	820	880	940	4,100

The similarity of the results can be seen.

Accounting entries in the buyer's books

Two basic approaches can be used to make the entries. The two are not fundamentally different, but differ in the information retained within the double entry system.

The first method which follows is, perhaps, the simplest:

Initial entries

	Debit	Credit
Cash price of the asset	Asset	Supplier
Initial down payment	Supplier	Cash

On payment of instalment

Payment made	Supplier	Cash

At the end of each accounting period

Interest (as calculated by annuity or rule of 78)	Hire purchase interest (expense) (closed to Profit and loss)	Supplier
Annual depreciation on asset	Profit and loss	Provision for depreciation

Using the example of the computer and employing the annuity method of interest apportionment and straight line depreciation over an eight year life, the relevant ledger accounts will show for the first year:

Computer at cost

1/1	HP Supplier	6,000

HP supplier

			1/1	Computer	6,000
1/1	Cash	1,900	31/12	HP interest	287
31/12	Cash	1,000			
	c/fwd	3,387			
		6,287			6,287
				b/fwd	3,387

HP interest (expense)

31/12	HP supplier	287	31/12	Profit and loss	287

Accumulated depreciation

			31/12	Profit and loss	750

The second method presents the position of the supplier more clearly. Here the total liability to make payments to the supplier is recognized at the start rather than being added in as amounts accrue, like the £287 in the first year. However, recognition that the interest element is not yet due is given by creating a deferred interest account and transferring amounts to the interest expense account each year.

The initial entries are	*Debit*	*Credit*
Total payments due to the supplier		
Cash price of the asset	Asset	
Balance being total interest	Deferred interest	
On payment of instalment		
Payment made	Supplier	Cash
At end of each accounting period		
Interest (as calculated)	HP interest (expense)	Deferred interest
Annual depreciation on asset	Profit and loss	Provision for depreciation

For the example these are shown as:

	£	£
At start		
Dr Computer	6,000	
Cr HP supplier		6,900
Dr Deferred interest	900	
On down payment		
Dr HP supplier	1,900	
Cr Cash		1,900
At year end		
Dr HP supplier	1,000	
Cr Cash		1,000
Dr Interest (expense)	287	
Cr Deferred interest		287
Dr Profit and loss (depreciation)	750	
Cr Accumulated depreciation		750

The Companies Act gives support for the treatment as an asset and does not allow the balance on the asset account to be reduced by offsetting this by the balance on the HP supplier's account.

Exercise

1. On 3 January, 19X1, Pulsford (Machinists) acquired machinery from Lawrence Ltd, under a hire purchase agreement extending over three years. The agreement required them to make an initial deposit of £31,600, followed by three annual payments of £31,000 to be made by 31 December each year, commencing 19X1.

    The cash price of the machinery is £34,000 and Lawrence Ltd inform Pulsford that the terms represent an effective rate of interest of 12 per cent.

    Required:
    Show the entries that will record the transactions resulting from the hire purchase agreement, assuming that Pulsford make all payments when due, using:
    (a)   the annuity method; and
    (b)   the Rule of 78 to allocate interest.

22. Investment accounts

The activities of businesses extend not only to manufacturing and the supply of goods and services but also to external investment in the shares of companies and various forms of loan stock, including debentures and government stock. The accounts which record these investments may have the appearance of being different and complex. However, the accounting involved is just an application of the accruals and prepayments approach introduced in Chapter 10 and applied in detail in Chapter 13. A particular layout is shown which is intended to achieve two aims: clarify the accruals approach by separating the revenue (income) and capital elements of entries; keep a record of the number of units of shares or stock owned. As a result, investment ledgers will be presented with three columns.

1. The first column records the nominal value of the security held–the nominal values of securities are fixed when they are issued so, even if the market prices fluctuate, nominal values will remain constant unless the investing business disposes of some or acquires additional units of the security. Although not part of the double entry, this column provides a useful running total indicating the quantity of units held.
2. The second column records the income elements–typically interest is paid on debentures and government stock at particular dates. Interest represents income and payment does not produce any change in the nominal value of the security held.
3. The third column records the capital value of the security and, with the income column, is part of the double entry accounting. However, where capital values are recorded at cost, this column will only contain adjusting entries to record disposing or acquiring securities.

Purchase and sale of fixed interest securities

Interest is usually fixed on the issue of a security as a fixed percentage of the nominal value, payable at predetermined dates, often half yearly or quarterly. Consider the example of 8 per cent government stock, interest payable on 30 June and 31 December. Government stock prices are usually quoted at the price for £100 nominal value of the stock. These prices will vary in the market but, say, on 29 June 19X1 the 8 per cent stock is priced at 84 (i.e. to buy £100 nominal, a purchaser would pay £84). The interest payable on £100 nominal at the end of every June and December would be £4 (i.e. half of 8 per cent of the *nominal* value).

A business buying £25,000 of the stock would pay 84 × £25,000 ÷ 100 = £21,000. The next day, interest would be payable of 4 × £25,000 ÷ 100 = £1,000. The company would know this when it bought the stock, so it was effectively paying £20,000 for the capital element of the stock plus £1,000 for interest it was about to receive. Provided no other factors in the market changed, the market price of the stock would be expected to fall, as soon as the interest is paid, by £1,000 to £20,000. One can see that recognizing the £1,000 in this way is an application of the accruals principle.

A security purchased to include interest due at the next payment date is described as *cum interest* (cum. int.) and similarly shares purchased which include the right to a dividend that has been declared are known as cum. div. In fact, a time must be set when the lists of owners entitled to interest (or dividends) are finalized, so that those making the payment can identify who to pay. This point in time will normally be at the close of trading on a particular day before the payment is due. It is very important if you are buying to be sure about entitlement to interest (or dividend) so, to make this clear, the description changes. Loan stock becomes *ex interest* and shares *ex div.* when they are traded without entitlement to a forthcoming payment. Thus when a share goes ex div. a fall in price is to be expected. In the absence of either the cum.- or ex- description, it is assumed that a security would be cum. int. (or cum. div.).

The sudden change in price when stock goes ex interest gives a clear indication of the income element. Of course, understanding of accruals procedures would indicate that transactions at intermediate dates also include income components. Using the same 8 per cent stock, purchase at 31 March at 78 includes an accrual of three months' interest which, on £25,000 nominal, would be £25,000 × 8 per cent ÷ 4 = £500.

The total amount paid is 78 × £25,000 ÷ £19,500 which would be split £500 to income, £19,000 to capital. Sales follow similar principles. If £9,000 nominal were sold on 30 April (one month later) at 88, this would include four months' interest, amounting to $\frac{4}{12}$ × 8 per cent × £9,000 = £240. The total amount realized would be £7,920, split £240 income, £7,680 capital. Given that £19,000 was originally paid for the capital content of the stock, £9,000 nominal would have cost $\frac{9}{25}$ of £19,000 i.e. £6,840 on a *pro rata* basis. A profit on sale has been made of £840.

On 30 June, half year's interest of £640 would be received.

These transactions would be recorded in the investment account as follows:

8 per cent government stock payable 30 June and 31 December

19X1		Nominal £	Income £	Capital £			Nominal £	Income £	Capital £
31/3	Cash purchase at 78	25,000	500	19,000					
					30/4	Cash—sale at 88	9,000	240	7,680
					30/6	Cash—½ yr's interest on £16,000		640	

Year-end entries

At the year end, the investment account must be closed off. To the extent that each accounting year is treated as a separate entity, the recording is comparable to sale by the year just finished and purchase by the year just starting. Accrued income must be recognized. If the business has an accounting year end at 30 September, three months' interest is accrued. If there are no further sales or purchases a cash payment the following 31 December will comprise interest for the three months from the previous accounting year and for the three months to 31 December. The entries for 19X1 and 19X2 will then appear as follows:

8 per cent government stock payable 30 June and 31 December

19X1/2		Nominal £	Income £	Capital £			Nominal £	Income £	Capital £
31/3	Cash purchase at 78	25,000	500	19,000					
					30/4	Cash— sale at 88	9,000	240	7,680
30/9	Profit and loss—profit on sale of interest			840[1]	30/6	Cash— ½ yr's interest on £16,000		640	
30/9	Profit and loss— investment income		700[2]		30/9	c/fwd $\frac{16}{25}$ c/fwd 3 months' accrued interest on £16,000	16,000	320	12,160
		25,000	1,200	19,840			25,000	1,200	19,840
b/fwd	19X1/2	16,000	32	12,160	30/6	Cash— ½ yr's interest		640	
					30/6	Cash— ½ yr's interest		640	
30/9	Profit and loss investment income		1,280		30/9	c/fwd c/fwd 3 months' interest	16,000	320	12,160
		16,000	320	12,160			16,000	1,600	12,160
b/fwd	19X2/3	16,000	320	12,160					

Note the following:

1. the profit on the sale has been identified as the balancing item
2. the investment income in the first year is made up as follows:

On £25,000 from 31/3/X1 to 30/4/X1	£166.67	
On £16,000 from 1/5/X1 to 30/9/X1	533.33	
	£700.00	

Investment in shares

In the case of shares, dividend levels are not fixed until they are declared. As a result it is not appropriate to accrue dividends until the declaration is made, and when this is recognized, the full amount is recorded with no apportionment on a time basis.

Discussion of the nature of shares and their issue is presented in Chapters 26 and 27, where different types of issue will be considered. Any issue increasing the nominal value will need to be reflected in the investment account.

Exercise

1. Lane Ltd, which has a year end at 30 September, bought 34,000 of 6 per cent government stock at 78 on 1 May 19X0. Interest is paid half yearly on 1 January and 1 July.
    The company sold 33,000 of the stock on 1 December at 76 ex interest.

Required:
Show the ledger account for the stock to 30 September, 19X1.

23. Departmental and branch accounts

As organizations grow it becomes useful to divide up their operations. When businesses form separate departments, they will want to see how well each of those separate units are performing. You are probably familiar with departmental stores. Here, a range of different activities are each run as sub-businesses within the whole organization. The store's management will be concerned to know how well the store is performing as a whole, but will find it useful to have information about the performance of the individual departments. Its significance may be increased by delegation of responsibilities to department heads.

Delegation of responsibilities is clearly necessary when operations become geographically more spread, as in the case of a retail chain store. With each separate branch of the business operating from separate and possibly distant locations, considerable responsibility must be delegated to the local manager. Accounting can contribute to the management of such organizations by providing information which not only gives indications of the separate performances but also provides some degree of control.

We have already seen that it is useful to separate some of the activities of an organization in reporting its results in Chapter 20. Here, bar trading operations were separately identified within the accounts of a club. These ideas are extended in this chapter, which examines how accounting can be adapted to increasing levels of delegation, starting with simple departmental division, moving to branches, where, although the head office maintains the accounts, the branch is responsible for its stocks, and concluding with branches which maintain their own self-contained accounting systems. Understanding the accounting methods which are used is valuable in a number of more advanced topics. Large public companies typically consist of many separately identified companies each with their own accounting ledgers but owned by a common parent. The principles developed in branch accounts are applied in extended form to deal with the complexity of such groups of companies, particularly in the combining of individual company statements to form consolidated accounts.

Departmental analysis

Where it is decided to produce separate profit and loss results for each trading department within a business, in addition to identifying the sales for each unit and tracking costs which are specifically identifiable to the departments, it is necessary to apportion (i.e. divide up on the basis of ratios) the untraceable overhead costs. No matter how carefully the apportionment ratios are selected, they will depend on the exercise of judgement, and to that extent are arbitrary. The basis should be chosen to attempt to reflect the extra cost likely to be caused by the particular department or, failing that, the benefits the department receives. A simple example making use of the context of the departmenal store will be used to illustrate the preparation of departmental accounts.

Example 23.1

Status Stores run three departments, clothing, footwear and stationery. For accounting purposes departmental accounts are to be prepared, apportioning building costs (rent etc.) on the basis of floor space occupied and office administration in proportion to gross profit. The following information has been extracted from the store's accounts for the year ended 31 December 19X1:

	Clothing £	Footwear £	Stationery £
Sales	47,000	27,000	26,000
Purchases	23,000	16,000	10,500
Wages	2,500	1,800	2,100
Stocks at 1 Jan 19X1	6,000	1,000	500
at 31 Dec 19X1	4,000	2,000	1,000
Floor space ratio	3	2	1

Rent, rates, lighting, heating and building maintenance (all departments)	£13,800
Administration and office salaries etc.	£20,000

Trading accounts can be prepared for each department:

	Clothing £	£	Footwear £	£	Stationery £	£
Sales		47,000		27,000		26,000
Less cost of sales:						
opening stock	6,000		1,000		500	
Add purchases	23,000		16,000		10,500	
	29,000		17,000		11,000	
Less closing stock	4,000	25,000	2,000	15,000	1,000	10,000
Gross profit		22,000		12,000		16,000

Traceable costs can be deducted from the resulting gross profit:

Less wages		2,500	2,100	1,800
Departmental surplus		19,500	9,900	14,200

Building and administration overheads must be apportioned and deducted to complete the statement:

Building costs (3:2:1)	6,900		4,600		2,300	
Administration (22:12:16)	8,800	15,700	4,800	9,400	6,400	8,700
Departmental profit		3,800		500		5,500

To illustrate the dependence of the result upon choice of ratios, let us consider the impact of changing the basis of apportioning administration costs from gross profit to turnover.

Departmental surpluses would remain unchanged:

	Clothing		Footwear		Stationery	
	£	£	£	£	£	£
Surplus		19,500		9,900		14,200
Less: Building costs	6,900		4,600		2,300	
Administration						
(47:27:26)	9,400	16,300	5,400	10,000	5,200	7,500
Revised profit		3,200	loss	(100)		6,700

Although the total profit remains at £9,800, each department's results have altered and footwear has changed from profit to loss. Of course, this is unlikely to infer that closing the footwear department now will increase overall profit. All we can identify is that such action would eliminate the £9,900 departmental surplus. If no reduction in building and administration costs resulted, then, continuing existing operations in clothing and stationery would produce an overall loss. Clearly the departmental statements should not be used directly in shut-down decisions. The analysis of profit and loss to show departmental results would not normally be extended to analysis of balance sheets.

Integrated branches

This will usually refer to accounting systems in which a single set of accounts is used to record the activities of an organization in such a way as to provide control over the stock and sales receipts of its branches.

If a branch handles very small numbers of stock units, individual items could be tracked to maintain control. However, when the numbers increase and there is a regular replenishment of stock it becomes useful to control these in aggregate. Control is facilitated when branches are not allowed to purchase their own stock but are supplied from headquarters or by suppliers on headquarters' orders. Two forms of accounting to fulfil this need are common. Both share the same basis, which acts as a control for stock levels and sales receipts simultaneously by valuing stock items at selling price. We can track stock in this way for example:

		£
	Opening stock at selling price	300
plus	Deliveries at selling price	2,000
		2,300
	Sales at selling price	1,800
equals	Closing stock at selling price	£500

These figures can be verified to complete the control process: **opening stock** by a physical count (stocktake); **deliveries** are made only from headquarters or from suppliers on the basis of orders from headquarters, records can be maintained at headquarters; **sales** receipts are confirmed by amounts shown as banked by the branch. A stocktake which provides **closing stock** also gives the opening stock value for next period.

The first form of system uses a two-column branch stock account, the extra column being used for control purposes only, so that it represents a memorandum column rather than part of the actual double entry system. In the memorandum column all amounts are recorded at selling price. It is possible to consider sales on credit and returns of sales within this system, as the following example shows.

The amounts given below represent the records from the transactions of the village branch of a retail business for April 19X1.

	£		£
Opening Stock (at cost)	1,800	Cash sales	2,600
Debtors	1,800	Credit sales	5,500
Goods received from head office		Returns to head office	
at cost	4,860	at cost	300
Goods returned by credit		Bad debts (agreed by	
customers	420	head office)	110
		Discounts allowed	
Cash received from debtors	5,900	(as above)	400
		Closing stock at cost	480

All goods are sold at cost plus a third. These will be included in the ledger accounts.

Branch stock account

	Memo	£		Memo	£
Stock b/fwd	2,400	1,800	Cash Sales	2,600	2,600
Goods from head office	6,480	4,860	Credit Sales—debtors	5,500	5,500
Customer returns	420		Returns to head office	520	390
Bad debts		420			
Discounts allowed		400	Closing stock c/fwd	640	480
Branch profit transferred			Deficiency (balancing item)	40	
to head office		1,380			
	9,300	8,970		9,300	8,970
Stock b/fwd	640	480			

Goods to branch account

	£		£
Branch stock—returns	390	Branch stock—depn.	4,860
Trading elimination from			
head office cost of sales	4,470		
	4,860		4,860

A memo column at selling price is included in a branch stock account, which is similar to a trading account.

Branch debtors

b/fwd	1,800	Returns	420
Branch stock—sales	5,500	Cash	5,900
		Bad debts	110
		Discounts allowed	400
		c/fwd	470
	7,300		7,300
b/fwd	470		

Cash

Branch debtors	5,900
Branch banking	2,600
	8,500

The deficiency of £40 is identified at selling price representing £30 at cost. This may be considered sufficiently small to be allowable, given that minor losses due to breakages etc. occur.

The profit for the branch could have been calculated another way once the deficiency is established. Given the constant mark-up, the gross profit on sales of £2,600 plus £5,500 less £420 returns is:

$$(2,600 + 5,500 - 420) \times 25 \text{ per cent} = £1,920$$

Bad debts, discounts and the cost of the deficiency must be deducted from this:

$$1,920 - 110 - 400 - 30 = £1,380$$

The second approach integrates the memorandum entries into the double entry system by recognizing that trading profit can be calculated as an element of sales.

At the beginning of this section the relationships between stocks, deliveries and sales, all at selling price, was set out. This can be rearranged as:

Sales *equals* opening stock (at SP) *plus* deliveries (at SP) less closing stock (at SP)

The profit elements can be rearranged as:

Profit on sales *equals* profit on sale of opening stock *plus* profit on sale deliveries *less* profit not yet realized on closing stock

Numerically, if sales are made at cost plus 25 per cent (i.e. profit = 20 per cent of sales) the profit calculation can be shown in parallel to the usual cost of sales statement:

	At selling prices		Showing stock and deliveries at cost		Profit elements	
	£	£	£	£	£	£
Sales		1,800		1,800		360
Less opening stock	300		240		60	
Plus deliveries	2,000		1,600		400	
	2,300		1,840		460	
Less closing stock	500	1,800	400	1,440	100	
		—		360		360

The trading profit figure calculated by the familiar sales less cost of sales approach is identical to that produced by the mark-up on sales or the mark-up on stock movements included in the cost of sales. Note that any profit included in the closing stock when valued at selling price must be eliminated. Since the stock has not yet been sold, this profit would be unrealized. The integrated system records the profit elements in a branch stock mark-up account. Thus, using the earlier example of the village branch results for April 19X1, the following ledger accounts would be produced:

Branch stock mark-up

Returns to head office	130	Unrealized profit b/fwd	600
Unrealized profit c/fwd	160	Goods from head office	1,620
Branch trading surplus to			
Profit and loss	1,930		
	2,220		2,220
		b/fwd	160

Branch stock (at selling price)

Stock b/fwd	2,400	Cash sales	2,600
Goods from head office	6,480	Credit sales	5,500
Customer returns	420	Returns to head office	520
		Stock c/fwd	640
		Deficiency (to branch surplus)	40
	9,300		9,300

Branch debtors and cash accounts are unchanged. The opening stock, shown as £2,400 at selling price, is brought forward together with £600 unrealized profit. Similarly, the mark-up of £1,620 on the delivery of £4,860 is included in the branch stock as £6,480 at selling price.

The surplus must be reduced by bad debts, discounts and stock losses. Note, however, that in this approach, profit was taken on the items of lost stock when received from the head office and has not been carried forward with closing stock. As a result stock losses must be eliminated at selling prices to produce the branch profit for the month:

	£	£
Trading surplus from branch stock mark-up account		1,930
Less: bad debts	110	
discounts allowed	400	
stock losses at selling price	40	550
Branch profit transferred to HO trading account		1,380

As with departmental analysis, no balance sheets are produced on a branch basis, although amounts carried forward for debtors, stock (at cost after deducting mark-up carried forward) etc. will contribute to the total business statements.

Separate branch ledgers

Where the branches are of sufficient size, it may be that each branch maintains its own ledgers. The resulting task for accounting is to be able to combine these ledgers to produce accounting statements for the business as a whole. Combining in this way becomes increasingly complex as the number of separate ledgers expands, so it would be unusual for this approach to be applied to businesses with numerous small branches.

Under this approach, head office finances branch operations and its position as 'owner' means that all profits produced by the branch 'belong to' the head office. However, commission on the profit is often paid to branch management.

Head office can allow the branch to trade in an independent manner purchasing goods for resale both through head office and direct from suppliers. where goods are transferred from head office to the branch at above cost (to enable head office to earn some part of the profit on these items when sold), any unrealized profit should be eliminated in the calculation of the total business profit and loss. It would be unacceptable for a business to buy an item, say a car, for £5,000 and decide to transfer it to its branch at £8,000 so that it could claim to have made a profit of £3,000! No profit has been realized until the car is sold to an external customer. Unrealized profit may be identified in goods in stock at branch or goods in transit (i.e. sent from head office but not yet received at branch).

In this approach a business with a single branch will maintain two sets of books for accounting purposes: one set for head office; one set for the branch. Initially they are treated as two entities. Although there may be many individual transactions between the two component entities, the head office is regarded as the supplier of capital and its investment in the branch will be represented in the branch books by the credit balance on an account known as the 'head office current account'. Of course, there will be an equivalent account in the head office books representing the head offices investment labelled 'branch current account' which may be expected to have a debit balance.

It follows that, once all outstanding matters have been sorted out and reflected in the accounts, the two current accounts should be equal but opposite in sign. Thus when combining the accounts of the branch and head office it will be possible to eliminate the current accounts, since they cancel out. The combined business cannot have a current account balance in itself! However, we will have to give some attention to getting 'outstanding matters . . . sorted out and reflected in the accounts'. Initially the current accounts can differ for a number of reasons: there may be goods or cash shown as sent in one set of books but not received in the other; or there may be profit earned at the branch to be transferred to the head office. Having properly reflected all outstanding matters in the two sets of books, the current accounts can then be eliminated and the balances added together to form the combined accounts. A worked example will illustrate this.

Example 23.2

Bell, who runs a shop in Bradford selling high quality knitwear, has appointed Wheeler to operate a branch in Hull. All goods are purchased by the head office at Bradford and those sent to Hull are invoiced at cost plus 25 per cent. Wheeler is to receive a commission of 20 per cent of the net profits of the Hull branch before charging salaries.

The trial balances at 31 December 19X4 were as follows:

	Head Office £	£	Branch £	£
Capital account		34,000		
Salaries	9,000		9,000	
Fixtures at written down value	15,000		10,000	
Stock at cost 31/12/X3	7,000			
Stock at invoiced value 31/12/X3			7,500	
Sales		50,000		35,000
Purchases	42,000			
Goods to branch at invoiced prices		20,000	17,500	
Branch and head office current account	19,500			17,000
Expenses	12,000		6,500	
Provision for unrealized profit		1,500		
Creditors		1,000		
Cash in hand and at bank	2,000		1,500	
	£106,500	£106,500	£52,000	£52,000

Account is to be taken of the following:

1. Stock at the shop at 31/12/X4 amounted to £8,500 at cost at Bradford and £10,000 at invoiced prices at Hull.
2. Goods with an invoice value of £2,500 were sent from the head office but still in transit at 31/12/X4.
3. Depreciation is to be charged at 20 per cent of the written down value of fixtures.

A trading profit and loss account for the head office, branch and the business as a whole, is to be prepared showing the calculation of commission and the Branch Current account.

Note the following: first, the provision for unrealized profit in the head office account which represents profit in the opening stock, i.e. at 31/12/X3. Stock at invoiced prices of £7,500 includes £1,500 mark-up. Second, the current accounts do not agree. They must be adjusted before balance sheets can be combined. All adjustments for goods and cash in transit are made in the head office books.

In head office books:

Branch current account

b/fwd	19,500	Goods in transit	2,500
		c/fwd	17,000
	19,500		19,500
c/fwd	17,000		

The goods in transit will be regarded as part of head office stocks. Although they have an invoiced value of £2,500, eliminating the unrealized profit gives a cost of £2,000. Total closing stocks at Bradford will be £8,500 plus £2,000 goods in transit, i.e. £10,500. The provision for unrealized stock will need to be adjusted to a fifth of the £10,000 stock at Hull i.e. £2,000, and increase of £500. Combined stocks are then: £10,500 (Bradford) plus £10,000 (Hull) less £2,000 (provision) equals £18,500. The profit and loss accounts for head office, branch and combined business can then be calculated showing transfers as internal sales of the head office on the one hand, and purchases of the branch on the other, but eliminated in the combined accounts.

Solution

	Head Office		Branch		Combined	
	£	£	£	£	£	£
Sales—external		50,000		35,000		85,000
internal		17,500		—		—
		67,500				
Opening stock	7,000		7,500		13,000	
Purchases/transfers	42,000		17,500		42,000	
	49,000		25,000		55,000	
Closing stock	10,500		10,000		18,500	
		38,500	15,000			36,500
Gross profit		29,000		20,000		48,500
Expenses	12,000		6,500		18,500	
Depreciation	3,000		2,000		5,000	
		15,000		8,500		23,500
Profit before commission and salaries		14,000		11,500		25,000
Salary		9,000	9,000		18,000	
Commission			2,300	11,300	2,300	20,300
		5,000				
Less: addition to provision for unrealized profit		500				
Profit		4,500		200		4,700

The branch profit of £200 must be transferred to head office. this will be effected by debiting the branch current account in the head office books and crediting the head office current account in the branch books by £200, giving a balance in both of £17,200 and total profits of £4,500 + £200 = £4,700, all of which is retained.

The balance sheets can now be prepared:

	Head office	Branch	Combined
	£	£	£
Capital b/fwd	34,000		34,000
Add: retained profit	4,700		4,700
HO account	38,700	17,200	38,700
Fixtures	15,000	10,000	25,000
Depreciation	3,000	2,000	5,000
	12,000	8,000	20,000

Stocks	10,500			
Provision for unrealized profit	2,000	8,500	10,000	18,500
Cash		2,000	1,500	3,500
		22,500	19,500	42,000
Creditors (including commission)		1,000	2,300	3,300
		21,500		
Branch account	17,200			
		£38,700	£17,200	£38,700

Exercises

1. Mighty Bytes buy computer games and sell them at a mark-up of 25 per cent on cost through two outlets; their main store and a branch which was opened on 1 September 1984. On 31 August 1985, the trial balance presented below was prepared:

	£	£
Capital		117,000
Balance at bank	18,000	
Cash received from branch		153,000
Purchases	440,000	
Head office expenses	49,000	
Branch salaries	16,000	
Head office sales		325,000
Head office premises	25,000	
—depreciation		5,000
Branch premises	20,000	
Stock (head office) at cost at 1 September 19X4	32,000	
	600,000	600,000

The following items have not been dealt with:

1. Goods sent to branch: £215,000 at selling price.
2. Stocktaking at 31 August 19X5 showed no losses at head office and stock at branch £43,000 at selling price.
3. Branch expenses of £14,000 were paid out of branch takings before remitting cash to head office.
4. Cash in hand at branch at 31 August 19X5: £3,000.
5. Depreciation is to be provided on a straight line basis at 10 per cent on the cost of premises.

You are required to:

(a) calculate the profit or loss for the branch for the year ended 31 August 1985; and
(b) prepare a trading and profit and loss account for Mighty Bytes for the same year, and a balance sheet at the year end.

2. Supaspend Ltd run a retail store which has two departments. For each department a branch stock account and a branch mark-up account are maintained. All goods are purchased for the company by the chief buyer. Goods supplied to departments are recorded in the branch stock account at the normal selling price, which

is calculated by adding a mark-up on cost of 33⅓ per cent for the Fashions Department and 50 per cent for the Luxuries Department.

On 1 January 19X2 the stock in the Fashions Department was valued at £8,400 at selling price, and that in the Luxuries Department at £12,000.

During 19X2 the following took place:

	Fashions	Luxuries
Purchases (at cost)	£35,400	£54,000
Sales (before adjusting for returns)	£48,000	£89,500
Customers returned goods for which a full refund was made.	£1,200	£1,800

These goods were in perfect condition and returned to the departmental stock (at selling price).

Goods originally costing £1,800 included in the purchases for Luxuries were later transferred to the Fashions Department.

The Fashions Department purchases included a batch of faulty skirts which had been charged in the branch stock account at £1,600. These were returned to the supplier and a refund was made to the company.

Stocktaking at 31 December 1982 revealed that there were no goods missing in the Fashions Department, although goods priced for sale at £900 had been damaged and had to be sold as waste for £100.

The closing stock at 31 December 1982 in the Luxuries Department amounted to £7,200 at selling price. It was not uncommon for there to be shoplifting of these goods and a loss of 1 per cent of sales was considered tolerable.

Required:

Prepare, for each department for the year ended 31 December 1982, a memorandum stock account, a memorandum mark-up account and a computation of departmental profits.

3. Bentley Arts Shops which had operated in the retail trade from a head office in the city centre, opened a branch renting premises in a major suburb on 1 May 1986. All purchases continue to be made by the head office, goods sent to the branch being charged out at selling price, which is cost plus 50 per cent. The head office only sells to cash customers but the branch sells to some customers on account. Certain expenses are met directly by the branch out of cash receipts and the branch holds a small cash float remitting any remaining cash to the head office regularly.

The branch keeps a sales ledger and maintains essential records. The head office operates an integrated system of accounting for its own activities but has not yet dealt with matters relating to the branch given below:

1. Goods sent to the branch at selling price: £105,000
2. Branch expenses of £5,000 were paid out of branch takings before remitting cash to head office
3. Cash remitted to head office: £65,000
4. Cash in hand on 30 April 19X7: £2,000
5. Debtors outstanding at 30 April 19X7: £12,000
6. Depreciation is to be provided on branch fixtures and fittings at 25 per cent on cost.

Before dealing with the above the following trial balance as at 30 April 19X7 was prepared:

	£	£
Proprietor's capital		46,000
Head office premises	25,000	
—depreciation		9,000
Head office—sales		114,000
Purchases	147,000	
Head office stock at cost on 1 May 19X6	13,000	
Head office expenses	16,000	
Branch rent, salaries and expenses	10,000	
Branch fixtures and fittings	8,000	
Cash received from branch		56,000
Balance at bank	6,000	
	225,000	225,000

You determine that stocktaking at the close of trading on 30 April 19X7 had shown that no stock had been lost at the head office and that the stock at the branch amounted to £18,000 at selling prices. Any stock unaccounted for at the branch will be considered normal pilferage. On 5 May 1987 the head office received £9,000, which the branch had sent on 30 April 19X7.

You are required to:

(a) write up the branch stock account, calculating the selling price of stock lost through pilferage;
(b) calculate the profit for Bentley for the year ended 30 April 19X7; and
(c) present a balance sheet for the business at that date.

24. The final accounts of partnerships

The law and characteristics of partnerships

For a number of commercial reasons, it may be mutually advantageous for two or more people to form a partnership. The Partnership Act 1890 defines a partnership as 'the relation which subsists between persons carrying on business in common with a view of profit'. It cannot have less than two partners and, at one time, the Act set a limit of 20 partners. However, with the introduction of the Companies Act 1967 this maximum has been relaxed in the case of a number of professional firms, such as accountants, solicitors etc.

Since partnerships are not able to limit their liability to creditors and other members of the public, there is no need for any special legislation to protect these groups. Thus partners are largely free to make whatever agreements between themselves that they wish to cover their mutual relationships. The powers and rights of the partners between themselves are governed by any written agreement they may make. This is referred to as the 'articles or deed of partnership'. It is important for partners to reach an agreement on matters such as the following:

1. the capital to be introduced by each partner;
2. the sharing of profits and losses;
3. partners' drawings;
4. the preparation and audit of accounts;
5. the dissolution of the partnership;
6. the resolution of disputes.

In the absence of any partnership agreement, or if the agreement is silent on any of the items 1–6 above or the following matters, a partnership is subject to the provisions of the Partnership Act 1890, which includes the following:

1. Each partner has unlimited liability. That is, if the debts of the partnership cannot be paid because the business has insufficient assets to do so, the creditors have recourse to the private property of the individual partners. The partners are said to be jointly and severally liable for the debts of the firm and therefore a creditor may sue the partnership or any individual partner.
2. Voting powers. In the ordinary day-to-day running of a partnership individual partners often make routine business decisions without consulting the other partners. At the other extreme, certain fundamental decisions, such as to change the type of business the partnership is engaged in, or the admission of a new partner, require the consent of all the partners. Other major decisions are supposed to be determined by a majority vote. Each partner has one vote. However, a partnership deed may specify some other distribution of voting power.

3. Every partner may take part in the management of the business. However, some partnership agreements provide for certain partners to be sleeping or limited partners. Neither of these normally take part in the management of the business.
4. Every partner is entitled to access to the books and papers of the partnership. This includes sleeping and limited partners.
5. Each partner is an agent of the partnership and can thus sign contracts on behalf of the partnership, which will then be legally bound to honour them.
6. A new partner can only be admitted to the partnership if all the existing partners give their consent. However, a partnership deed may specify otherwise.
7. A partnership will be dissolved by:
   (a) any partner giving notice to the other partner(s) of his intention to leave the partnership;
   (b) the death of a partner.

The sharing of profits between the partners

Consider the following situation. A and B enter into partnership; A is to work full-time in the business while B will only spend a few hours each week on partnership business; B is to put into the business £10,000 as capital whereas A is to contribute capital of only £1,000. You are asked by A and B to suggest how the profits might be shared so as to recompense A for working more hours than B in the business, and to compensate B for having put into the business (and therefore at risk) substantially more capital than A.

The way this is normally done is to give each partner a prior share of the profits as: (1) *a salary* related to the amount of the time each devotes to the business; and (2) *interest on the capital* each invests. The remaining profit can then be divided between the partners according to whatever they agree is fair. This might be equally, since both have already been compensated for the unequal time and capital they contribute.

Another aspect of sharing partnership profits concerns *interest on drawings*. This is intended to compensate one partner for having annual drawings that are less than the other partner(s) and thus penalize those partners who have greater drawings. Interest on drawings will relate to the period from the date of the drawings to the end of the accounting year in which the drawings took place.

If there is no agreement between the partners concerning how profits and losses should be shared, section 24 of the Partnership Act 1890 would be applied which states that:

1. profits and losses are to be shared equally between the partners;
2. no partner will receive a salary or interest on capital, or be charged interest on drawings;
3. any loans made by a partner to the business (as distinct from capital introduced) will be entitled to interest at the rate of 5 per cent per annum.

Capital and current accounts

In the accounts of sole traders there would be a capital account and usually a drawing account. In the books of a partnership there will be:

1. *A capital account* for each partner. Unlike the capital account of a sole trader, this will only contain the original capital put into the business plus any further capital introduced during the life of the business.
2. A *current account* for each partner, in which is entered:

    (a) drawings of money or goods taken by the partner for his or her own use (debit);
    (b) interest charged on drawings (debit);
    (c) interest on loans to the partnership (credit);
    (d) salary (credit);
    (e) interest on capital (credit);
    (f) the partner's share of profit or loss.

There may also be a *drawings account* in which all goods or money taken by the partner during the year are entered instead of putting them in the partner's current account. However, at the end of the year this is transferred to the partner's current account. Note also that current accounts are sometimes labelled drawings accounts.

The partner's capital accounts are shown on the balance sheet in the same place as that of a sole trader. Underneath these are entered the balances on the partner's current accounts at the end of the year (unless an account has a debit balance in which case it should be entered after the net current assets).

The profit and loss appropriation account

In partnership final accounts the profit and loss account contains exactly the same entries as that of a sole trader.

After the profit and loss account has been prepared, the profit for the year is carried down to a profit and loss appropriation account in which is shown the sharing of profits between the partners. The basis for sharing may include partners' salaries, interest on capital and interest on drawings, as well as the division of any remaining amount in some agreed portion. The latter is often referred to as the residual profits. The appropriation account is a part of the double entry in the ledger and as a general rule it is worth remembering that the double entry for each item in the appropriation account is on the opposite side of the relevant partner's current account. The contents of the profit and loss appropriation account are illustrated in Example 24.1.

Example 24.1
Bonnie and Clyde are in partnership sharing profits in the ratio 2:1. From the following you are required to prepare the profit and loss appropriation account for the year ended 31 December 19X8 and show the relevant items in the balance sheet at that date.

	Bonnie	Clyde
	£	£
Capital at 31 December 19X7	100,000	80,000
Current account balances at 31 December 19X7	16,340	28,290
Drawings—1 April 19X8	4,000	8,000
31 August 19X8	6,000	9,000
30 September 19X8	8,000	—
Salaries	20,000 p.a.	25,000 p.a.
Interest on capital	10 per cent p.a.	10 per cent p.a.
Interest on drawings	5 per cent p.a.	5 per cent p.a.

Clyde introduced additional capital of £10,000 in cash on 1 January 19X8 and Bonnie lent the business £20,000 on 30 June 19X8. The profit of the year ended 31 December 19X8 was £78,700.

Before dividing the profit between the partners, the partners' capital accounts need to be adjusted. These ledger accounts are often prepared in columnar form as follows:

Capital account

Bonnie	Clyde			Bonnie	Clyde
£	£	19X8		£	£
		1 Jan	Balance b/d	100,000	80,000
		1 Jan	Bank		10,000
					90,000

The loan from Bonnie is not entered in his capital account but rather in a separate loan account, which constitutes a long-term liability.

Next it may be useful to prepare a schedule which shows the division of the profits as follows:

	Bonnie	Clyde	Total
	£	£	£
Profit for 19X8			78,700
Loan interest ($\frac{6}{12}$ × 5 per cent × £20,000)	500	—	(500)
Partners' salaries	20,000	25,000	(45,000)
Interest on capital:			
10 per cent × £100,000	10,000	—	—
10 per cent × £90,000	—	9,000	(19,000)
	30,500	34,000	14,200
Interest on drawings (see note)	(350)	(450)	800
	30,150	33,550	15,000
Balance of profits (residual profits) shared 2 : 1	10,000	5,000	(15,000)
Totals	40,150	38,550	—

Notes

1.   The interest on partners' loans is computed using the rate of 5 per cent per annum specified in the Partnership Act 1890, unless you are told that some other rate has been agreed by the partners.
2.   The interest on capital is computed using the balance on the partners' capital account and not the current account, unless you are told the contrary. Note also that in this example the balance on the capital account at the end of the year can be used because the additional capital was introduced at the start of the year. Where additional capital is introduced at some other date it will be necessary to compute the interest on a strict time basis.

3. The interest on drawings is calculated on a monthly basis as follows:

$Bonnie$ $\frac{9}{12}$ × 5 per cent × 4000 = 150

$\frac{4}{12}$ × 5 per cent × 6000 = 100

$\frac{3}{12}$ × 5 per cent × 8000 = $\underline{100}$

$\overline{\underline{350}}$

$Clyde$ $\frac{9}{12}$ × 5 per cent × 8000 = 300

$\frac{4}{12}$ × 5 per cent × 9000 = $\underline{150}$

$\overline{\underline{450}}$

4. The sum of the total of each column in the above schedule should always equal the profit for the year (i.e. £40,150 + £38,550 = £78,700; £30,150 + £33,550 + £15,000 = £78,700 etc.)

The entries in the appropriation account can now be made. Although the total for each partner could be entered from the schedule, for a fuller presentation the separate elements are all shown below:

Bonnie and Clyde

Profit and loss appropriation account for the year ended 31 December 19X8

	£	£		£	£
			Net profit for year b/d		78,700
			Interest on drawings—		
Loan interest–Bonnie			Bonnie	350	
(6/12 × 5 per cent × £20,000)			Clyde	450	800
		500			
Salaries—Bonnie	20,000				
Clyde	25,000	45,000			
Interest on capital—					
Bonnie					
(10 per cent × £100,000)	10,000				
Clyde					
(10 per cent × £90,000)	9,000	19,000			
Share of profit—					
Bonnie	10,000				
Clyde	5,000	15,000			
		79,500			79,500

The double entry for the items in the appropriation accounts is in the partners' current accounts, which are also usually prepared in columnar form as follows:

Current accounts

	Bonnie £	*Clyde* £		*Bonnie* £	*Clyde* £
Drawings	18,000	17,000	Balance b/d	16,340	28,290
Interest on drawings	350	450	Loan interest	500	—
Balance c/d	38,490	49,840	Salaries	20,000	25,000
			Interest on capital	10,000	9,000
			Share of profit	10,000	5,000
	56,840	67,290		56,840	67,290
			Balance b/d	38,490	49,840

The relevant balances will then be included in the balance sheet thus:

Bonnie and Clyde

Balance sheet as at 31 December 19X8

	£	£
Capital		
Bonnie		100,000
Clyde		90,000
		190,000
Current accounts		
Bonnie	38,490	
Clyde	49,840	88,330
Loan—Bonnie		20,000

Sometimes these are shown on the balance sheet in columnar form as follows:

	£ *Bonnie*	£ *Clyde*	£ *Total*
Capital	100,000	90,000	190,000
Current accounts	38,490	49,840	88,330
	138,490	139,840	278,330
Loan—Bonnie			20,000

Notes

1. Where money has actually been paid to the partners which is described as salaries this must be treated as drawings and not included in the profit and loss account as wages and salaries. It may, however, be interpreted as indicating that the partners wish to give themselves a prior share of profits in the form of a salary. In this case the amounts paid must still be treated as drawings but an equivalent amount is entered in the appropriation account as salaries, as described above.

2. Additional capital introduced during the year may include assets other than cash. This would usually be entitled to interest on capital from the date the assets were introduced until the end of the year in question (and subsequent years).
3. Interest is usually only charged on cash and cheque drawings and not on goods taken by the partners for their own use.
4. Losses would be shared in the same ratio as profit. If, in the case of Example 24.1, the profit for the year had been only £55,000 the schedule of division of profits would be as follows:

	Bonnie £	Clyde £	Total £
Profit for year			55,000
Loan interest	500	—	(500)
Salaries	20,000	25,000	(45,000)
Interest on capital	10,000	9,000	(19,000)
	30,500	34,000	(9,500)
Interest on drawings	(350)	(450)	800
	30,150	33,550	(8,700)
Loss shared 2 : 1	(5,800)	(2,900)	8,700
	24,350	30,650	—

Note that loan interest, salaries, interest on capital and interest on drawings are all given even if there is a net loss for the year (i.e. before the appropriation). Salaries etc. simply increase the amount of the residual loss.

Partners' commission

Some partnership businesses are departmentalized, with each of the departments being managed by a different partner. In such circumstances it is common for partners' salaries to take the form of an agreed commission expressed as a percentage of the profit of their department. This necessitates the preparation of a trading account for each department which normally takes the form of a columnar trading account containing columns on both the debit and credit sides for each department. Computing the profits of each partner's department is done in the same way as departmental accounts, discussed in Chapter 23. Having ascertained the profit of each department the partner's commission can be calculated and accounted for in exactly the same way as partners' salaries.

A guaranteed share of profit

Some partnership agreements include a clause guaranteeing that if a particular partner's share of profit in any year is below some agreed figure, then all or certain other partners will make it up to the guaranteed amount from their share of profit. The amount by which the actual share of profit falls short of the guaranteed amount is usually shared (i.e. made up) by the other partners in their profit sharing ratio. Such a guarantee is fairly common in professional firms as an enticement to an employee to become a partner while at the same time being guaranteed an amount equal to the employee's existing remuneration. The guaranteed amount may include or exclude the partner's interest on capital and/or salary, but in the absence of information to the contrary it is usually taken to be the residual profit share that is guaranteed.

If, in the amended Example 24.1, when profits are only £55,000, Bonnie was guaranteed a share of residual profit of at least £2,000, the profit sharing schedule would appear as follows:

	Bonnie £	Clyde £	Total £
Profit for year	—	—	55,000
Salaries, interest on loans and capital	30,150	33,550	63,700
Share of losses	2,000	(10,700)	(8,700)
	32,150	22,850	—

Exercises

1. (a) Define a partnership.
    (b) What are the legal limits on the number of partners?
    (c) Outline the principal matters normally found in the articles or deed of partnership.

2. Describe the main characteristics of a partnership.

3. If there is no partnership agreement the provisions of the Partnership Act 1890 apply. List the main provisions of this Act with regard to the rights of partners between themselves, including the sharing of profits or losses.

4. Explain each of the following in the context of partnership profit sharing:
    (a) partners' salaries,
    (b) interest on capital,
    (c) interest on drawings,
    (d) residual profit.

5. Lane and Hill have decided to form a partnership. Lane is to contribute £150,000 as capital and Hill £20,000. Hill is to work full-time in the business and Lane one day a week. Because Hill has no other income, she anticipates making drawings of £1,000 per month from the partnership. Lane expects to make drawings of about £1,000 per quarter.
    You have been asked to advise the partners on how to share profits in such a way as to compensate each of them for their unequal contributions of capital and labour and withdrawals.

6. Explain the difference between each of the following ledger accounts in the books of a partnership:
    (a) capital account,
    (b) current account,
    (c) drawings account.

7. Clayton and Hammond are in partnership sharing profits and losses equally. The partnership agreement provides for annual salaries of Clayton: £17,000 and Hammond: £13,000. It also provides for interest on capital of 8 per cent per annum and interest on drawings of 4 per cent per annum.
    You are given the following additional information:

	Clayton £	Hammond £
Capital at 1 July 19X5	90,000	60,000
Current account at 1 July 19X5	16,850	9,470
Drawings—1 Oct 19X5	3,000	2,000
1 Mar 19X6	5,000	1,000
Capital introduced—1 Nov 19X5	10,000	—
Loan by Hammond—1 Apr 19X6	—	20,000

The profit shown in the profit and loss account for the year ended 30 June 19X6 was £67,500. You are required to prepare the profit and loss appropriation account, capital and current accounts.

8. Light and Dark are in partnership sharing profits and losses in the ratio 7 : 3 respectively. The following information has been taken from the partnership records for the financial year ended 31 May 19X9:
   Partners' capital accounts, balances as at 1 June 19X8:

Light	£200,000
Dark	£140,000

   Partners' current accounts, balances as at 1 June 19X8:

Light	£15,000 Cr
Dark	£13,000 Cr

   During the year ended 31 May 19X9 the partners made the following drawings from the partnership bank account:

Light	£10,000 on 31 August 19X8
	£10,000 on 30 November 19X8
	£10,000 on 28 February 19X9
	£10,000 on 31 May 19X9
Dark	£7,000 on 31 August 19X8
	£7,000 on 30 November 19X8
	£7,000 on 28 February 19X9
	£7,000 on 31 May 19X9

   Interest is to be charged on drawings at the rate of 12 per cent per annum. Interest is allowed on capital accounts and credit balances on current accounts at the rate of 12 per cent per annum. Dark is to be allowed a salary of £15,000 per annum.
   The net profit of the partnership for the year ended 31 May 19X9 is £102,940.

   Required:
   (a) A computation of the amount of interest chargeable on each partner's drawings for the year ended 31 May 19X9.
   (b) The partnership appropriation account for the year ended 31 May 19X9.
   (c) A computation of the balance on each partner's current account as at 31 May 19X9. (AAT)

9. The partnership of Sewell, Grange and Jones has just completed its first year in business. The partnership agreement stipulates that profits should be apportioned in the ratio of Sewell 3, Grange 2 and Jones 1 after allowing interest on capital at 12 per cent per annum and crediting Sewell with a salary of £15,000.
   The following information relates to their first financial year which ended on 31 October 19X0.

   1. The partners introduced the following amounts as capital on 1 November 19X9:

	£
Sewell	50,000
Grange	40,000
Jones	20,000

   2. Cash drawings during the year were:

	£
Sewell	3,900
Grange	4,500
Jones	2,400

   3. The draft profit and loss account for the year showed a net trading profit of £61,720.
   4. Included in the motor expenses account for the year was a bill for £300 which related to Grange's private motoring expenses.

5. No entries had been made in the accounts to record the following:
   (a) As a result of a cash flow problem during April, Grange invested a further £10,000 as capital with effect from 1 May 19X0, and on the same date Jones brought into the business additional items of equipment at an agreed valuation of £6,000. In addition, in order to settle a debt Jones had privately undertaken some work for Foster, a creditor of the partnership. Foster accepted the work as full settlement of the £2,000 the partnership owed her for materials.
   (b) Sewell had accepted a holiday provided by Miller, a debtor of the partnership. The holiday which was valued at £1,000 was accepted in full settlement of a debt of £2,500 that Miller owed to the partnership and that he was unable to pay.
   (c) Each partner had taken goods for his own use during the year at cost as follows:

	£
Sewell	1,400
Grange	2,100
Jones	2,100

Note: It is the policy of the firm to depreciate equipment at the rate of 10 per cent per annum based on the cost of equipment held at the end of each financial year.

Required:

(a) The profit and loss appropriation account for the year ended 31 October 19X0 showing clearly the corrected net trading profit of the first year's trading.
(b) The capital and current accounts of Sewell, Grange and Jones for the year ended 31 October 19X0.
                                                                                (AEB)

10. The following is the trial balance of Peace and Quiet, grocers, as at 31 December 19X8.

	£	£
Capital: Peace		10,000
Capital: Quiet		5,000
Current account: Peace		1,280
Current account: Quiet		3,640
Purchases/sales	45,620	69,830
Debtors/creditors	1,210	4,360
Leasehold shop at cost	18,000	
Equipment at cost	8,500	
Depreciation on equipment		1,200
Shop assistants salaries	5,320	
Light and heat	1,850	
Stationery	320	
Bank interest and charges	45	
Stock	6,630	
Bank	3,815	
Drawings—Peace 1 May 19X8	2,200	
—Quiet 1 Sept 19X8	1,800	
	95,310	95,310

Additional information:

1. The stock at 31 December 19X8 was valued at £5,970.
2. There is electricity accrued at the end of the year of £60.
3. Stationery unused at 31 December 19X8 was valued at £50.
4. The equipment is depreciated at 10 per cent p.a. on the reducing balance method.
5. There is a partnership deed which says that each partner is to be credited with interest on capital at 10 per cent per annum; salaries of £6,200 per annum for Peace and £4,800 per annum for Quiet; interest on drawings of 8 per cent p.a. The remainder of the profit is to be divided equally between the partners.

6.   Included in the capital of Peace is capital introduced of £1,000 on 1 April 19X8 and a loan to the partnership of £2,000 on 1 October 19X8.

You are required to prepare the profit and loss account and appropriation account for the year and a balance sheet at the 31 December 19X8.

11.   Peter and Paul, whose year end is the 30 June, are in business as food wholesalers. Their partnership deed states that:

(a)   profits and losses are to be shared equally;
(b)   salaries are Peter £20,000 per annum and Paul £18,000 per annum;
(c)   interest on capital of 10 per cent is allowed;
(d)   interest on drawings of 5 per cent is charged;
(e)   interest on loans from partners is given at the rate shown in the Partnership Act 1890.

The trial balance as at 30 June 19X8 is as follows:

	£	£
Capital—Peter		100,000
Paul		80,000
Current accounts—Peter	804	
Paul		21,080
Loan at 1 July 19X7—Peter		12,000
Freehold premises at cost	115,000	
Plant and machinery at cost	77,000	
Provision for depreciation on plant		22,800
Motor vehicles at cost	36,500	
Provision for depreciation on vehicles		12,480
Loose tools at 1 July 19X7	1,253	
Stock	6,734	
Debtors	4,478	
Creditors		3,954
Bank	7,697	
Electricity accrued at 1 July 19X7		58
Paid for electricity	3,428	
Purchases	19,868	
Sales		56,332
Warehouse wages	23,500	
Rates	5,169	
Postage and telephone	4,257	
Printing and stationery	2,134	
Provision for bad debts		216
Selling expenses	1,098	
	308,920	308,920

You also ascertain the following:

1.   Stock at 30 June 19X8 is £8,264.
2.   Depreciation by the straight line method is 10 per cent per annum on plant and machinery and 20 per cent per annum on motor vehicles. The latter are used by the administrative staff. The revaluation method of depreciation is used for loose tools. These have a value at 30 June 19X8 of £927.
3.   Included in wages are drawings of £6,000 by Peter on 1 March 19X8 and £8,000 by Paul on 1 October 19X7.
4.   The provision for bad debts at 30 June 19X8 is to be £180.
5.   Debtors include bad debts of £240.
6.   Sales include goods costing £160 which are on sale or return. The selling price of these is £200.
7.   Electricity accrued at 30 June 19X8 amounts to £82.
8.   Rates prepaid at 30 June 19X8 are £34.

You are required to prepare a profit and loss account for the year ended 30 June 19X8 and a balance sheet at that date. Present your answer in vertical form.

12. Simon, Wilson and Dillon are in partnership. The following trial balance has been prepared on 31 December 19X9:

	£	£
Capital accounts—Simon		35,000
—Wilson		25,000
—Dillon		10,000
Current accounts—Simon		5,600
—Wilson		4,800
—Dillon	1,800	
Freehold land and buildings	65,000	
Stock	34,900	
Bank	10,100	
Delivery vehicles at cost	30,000	
Provision for depreciation on vehicles		18,000
Goodwill at cost	11,000	
8 per cent mortgage on premises		40,000
Salesmen's salaries	19,480	
Debtors control account	28,000	
Creditors control account		25,000
Unquoted investments	6,720	
Loose tools at valuation	1,200	
Sales		130,000
Investment income		800
Returns	400	600
Purchases	64,000	
Rates	12,100	
Motor expenses	2,800	
Provision for bad debts		400
Mortgage interest paid	1,600	
Printing and stationery	1,100	
Extension to premises	5,000	
	£295,200	£295,200

You are also given the following additional information:

1. The stock at 31 December 19X9 was valued at £31. 0.
2. There is investment income accrued at 31 December 19X9 of £320.
3. The stock of stationery at 31 December 19X9 was £170.
4. At the same date there were motor expenses accrued of £240 and rates paid in advance of £160.
5. The provision for bad debts at 31 December 19X9 is to be adjusted to 2 per cent of the trade debtors.
6. Mortgage interest accrued should be provided for at the end of the year.
7. Depreciation on vehicles, on a strict time basis, is 10 per cent per annum using the straight line method.
8. The loose tools in stock at 31 December 19X9 were valued at £960.
9. The following errors have been found:

    (a) unrecorded in the ledger is the sale of a delivery vehicle on credit on 1 November 19X9 for £1,900. This vehicle cost £2,400 when it was purchased on 1st April 19X7;
    (b) bad debts for this year of £2,000 have not been written off;
    (c) bank charges of £130 have been omitted from the books.

Simon and Dillon are to be allocated salaries of £15,000 and £10,000 per annum respectively. All partners will be entitled to interest on capital of 10 per cent per annum. The remaining profit or loss is shared between Simon, Wilson and Dillon in the ratio of 2:2:1 respectively.

You are required to prepare in vertical form a profit and loss account and appropriation account for the year ended 31 December 19X9 and a balance sheet at that date.

13. A, B, C and D were partners in a garage business comprising (i) petrol sales, (ii) repairs and servicing and (iii) second-hand car dealing. A was responsible for petrol sales, B for repairs and servicing and C for second-hand car deals, while D acted purely in an advisory capacity.

The partnership agreement provided the following:

(i)   Interest on fixed capital at 10 per cent per annum.
(ii) Each working partner to receive commission of 10 per cent of the gross profit of that partners' own department.
(iii) Profits were shared as follows: A: 2/10, B: 3/10, C: 3/10, D: 2/10.
(iv) Accounts to be made up annually to 30 September.

A trial balance extracted from the books at 30 September 19X8 showed the following balances:

		Dr £	Cr £
A	Capital account		3,500
	Current account		1,350
	Drawings account	6,000	
B	Capital account		7,500
	Current account		7,500
	Drawings account	13,250	
C	Capital account		6,500
	Current account		5,500
	Drawings account	10,500	
D	Capital account		12,500
	Current account		2,150
	Drawings account	3,500	
Freehold premises at cost		25,000	
Goodwill at cost		10,000	
Servicing tools and equipment at cost		9,000	
Servicing tools and equipment—accumulated depreciation to 1 October 19X7			1,350
Bank balance			10,105
Stocks at 1 October 19X7—Petrol		950	
	Spares	525	
	Second-hand cars	6,350	
Debtors		4,350	
Cash in hand		125	
Creditors			2,350
Sales—Petrol			68,650
	Servicing and Repairs	86,750	
	Cars	156,000	
Purchases—Petrol		58,500	
	Spares	51,650	
	Second-hand cars	118,530	
Wages—Forecourt attendants		5,570	
	Mechanics	31,350	
	Car sales staff	8,550	
	Office personnel	1,850	
Rates		2,500	
Office expenses		1,800	
Heating and lighting		550	
Advertising		775	
Bank interest		350	
		£371,705	£371,705

The following additional information is obtained:

1. Stocks at 30 September 19X8

	£
Petrol	1,050
Spares	475
Second-hand cars	9,680

2. Depreciation on tools and equipment is to be provided at 5 per cent per annum by the straight line method.
3. Your fees for preparation of the accounts will be £175.
4. The service department did work valued at £11,300 on the second-hand cars.
5. The service department used old cars valued at £550 for spare parts in services and repairs.

You are required to prepare:

(a) Trading and profit and loss account for the year ended 30 September 19X8.
(b) Balance sheet at 30 September 19X8.
(c) Partners' current accounts in columnar form for the year.   (CACA)

14. (a) When accounting for the relationship of partners *inter se*, the partnership agreement provides the rules which in the first instance are to be applied.
      What information would you expect to find in a partnership agreement to provide such rules, and what should you do if the agreement fails to deal with any aspect of the partnership relationship which affects the accounts?
    (b) A, B and C are in partnership, agreeing to share profits in the ratio 4 : 2 : 1. They have also agreed to allow interest on capital at 8 per cent per annum; a salary to C of £5,000 per annum; and to charge interest on drawings made in advance of the year end at a rate of 10 per cent per annum.

      A has guaranteed B a minimum annual income of £6,500, gross of interest on drawings.
      The balance sheet as at 30 June 19X9 disclosed the following:

		£	£
Capitals	A	50,000	
	B	30,000	
	C	10,000	90,000
Current accounts	A	2,630	
	B	521	
	C	(418)	
			2,733
Loan account	A		15,000
	Net capital employed		£107,733

Drawings during the year were: A £6,400; B £3,100; C £2,000.
Net Trading Profit for the year to 30 June 19X0 was £24,750.
You are required to prepare the current accounts for the partners as at 30 June 19X0.   (CACA)

15. Brick, Stone and Breeze carry on a manufacturing business in partnership, sharing profits and losses: Brick one half, Stone one third and Breeze one sixth. It is agreed that the minimum annual share of profit to be credited to Breeze is to be £2,200, and any deficiency between this figure and her true share of the profits is to be borne by the other two partners in the ratio that they share profits. No interest is to be allowed or charged on partners' capital or current accounts.

The trial balance of the firm as on 30 June 19X0, was as follows:

	£	£
Stock on 1 July 19X9	7,400	
Purchases	39,100	
Manufacturing wages	8,600	
Salaries	5,670	
Rates, telephone and insurance	1,744	
Incidental trade expenses	710	
Repairs and renewals	1,250	
Cash discounts allowed	280	
Cash discounts received		500
Office expenses	3,586	
Carriage inwards	660	
Carriage outwards	850	
Professional charges	500	
Sales		69,770
Provision for doubtful debts as at 1 July 19X9		400
Provision for depreciation as at 1 July 19X9:		
Machinery and plant		2,500
Motor vehicles		1,300
Capital accounts:		
Brick		9,000
Stone		5,000
Breeze		4,000
Current accounts as at 1 July 19X9:		
Brick		1,900
Stone	500	
Breeze		400
Freehold buildings, at cost	9,800	
Machinery and plant, at cost	8,200	
Motor vehicles, at cost	2,500	
Bank balance	750	
Sales ledger balances	7,000	
Bought ledger balances		4,330
	£99,100	£99,100

The following information is given to you:

1. An amount of £3,000 for goods sent out on sale or return, has been included in sales. These goods were charged out to customers at cost plus 25 per cent and they were still in the customers' hands on 30 June 19X0, unsold.
2. Included in the item, repairs and renewals, is an amount of £820 for an extension to the factory.
3. Telephone and insurance paid in advance amounted to £424 and £42 was owing in respect of a trade expense.
4. A debt of £80 has turned out to be bad and is to be written off and the provision for doubtful debts is to be increased to £520.
5. Provision for depreciation on machinery and plant and on motor vehicles is to be made at the rate of 10 per cent and 20 per cent annum respectively on the cost.
6. The value of the stock on hand on 30 June 19X0 was £7,238.
7. Each month Brick has drawn £55, Stone £45 and Breeze £20, and the amounts have been included in salaries.

You are required to prepare:

(a) the trading and profit and loss account for the year ended 30 June 19X0;
(b) to write up the partners' current accounts, in columnar form, for the year; and
(c) to draw up the balance sheet as on 30 June 19X0.   (CACA)

16. A. Cherry owned a farmhouse and land, the latter being used by him and his sons, Tom and Leo, in carrying on a fruit and poultry business in partnership. The partnership agreement stipulated that the father should take one sixth of the profits, such to be not less than £1,200 per annum, the sons sharing the remainder equally.

The following are extracts from the trial balance of the business as on 31 December 19X1:

		Dr £	Cr £
Purchases:	Poultry	216	
	Feeding stuffs	3,072	
	Sprays and fertilizers	1,451	
	Spraying machine	460	
Wages		2,908	
General expenses (not apportionable)		842	
Sales:			
	Fruit		6,022
	Poultry		558
	Eggs		5,843
	Motor mower (cost £90 written down to £50)		46
Capital accounts:	A. Cherry		6,450
	Tom		3,340
	Leo	840	
Drawings—A. Cherry		930	
Equipment at 1 January 19X1 at cost		3,420	
Equipment at 1 January provision for depreciation			1,510

Stocks on hand were as follows:

	31 Dec 19X0	31 Dec 19X1
Sprays and fertilizers	310	289
Poultry	320	154
Feeding stuffs	363	412

The following additional information is given to you:

1. Drawings by Tom and Leo have been £15 and £14 per week respectively, which amounts have been included in the wages account. Of the wages, one quarter is to be charged to the fruit department and three quarters to the poultry department.
2. The father and son Tom live in the farmhouse and are to be charged jointly per annum £30 for fruit, and £68 for eggs and poultry, such charges being shared equally. Leo is to be charged £38 for fruit and £62 for eggs and poultry.
3. Independent of the partnership, Leo kept some pigs on the farm and in respect of this private venture he is to be charged £140 for feeding stuffs and £40 for wages.
4. A. Cherry is to be credited with £360 for rent of the land (to be charged as to two thirds to the fruit and one third to the poultry departments), and Tom is to be credited with £84 by way of salary for packing eggs and dressing poultry.
5. Eggs sold in December 19X1 and paid for in January 19X2 amounted to £243 and this sum was not included in the trial balance.
6. An account to 31 December 19X1 for £24 was received from a veterinary surgeon after the trial balance had been prepared. This account included a sum of £14 in respect of professional work as regards Leo's pigs, which he himself paid.
7. Annual provision was to be made for depreciation on equipment at 10 per cent on cost at the end of the year.

You are required to prepare:

(a) a trading account (showing separately the trading profit on the fruit and poultry departments) and profit and loss and appropriation accounts for the year ended 31 December 19X1, and
(b) the partners' capital accounts in columnar form showing the balances as on 31 December 19X1

(CACA)

17. Field, Green and Lane are in partnership making up accounts annually to 31 March. Due to staff difficulties proper records were not maintained for the year ended 31 March 19X9, and the partners request your assistance in preparing the accounts for that year.

The balance sheet on 1 April 19X8 was as follows:

Capital accounts	£	£	Fixed assets	Cost £	Depn. £	Net £
Field	10,000		Fixed plant	15,000	6,000	9,000
Green	10,000		Motor vehicles	4,000	1,000	3,000
Lane	2,500		Fixtures and fittings	500	250	250
		22,500		£19,500	£7,250	12,250

Current accounts	£	£	Current assets		£	
Field	5,000		Stock in trade		19,450	
Green	2,000		Debtors		10,820	
Lane	500		Prepayments		250	
		7,500	Cash in till		75	30,595
		30,000				

Current liabilities	£					
Trade creditors	5,350					
Accruals	1,125					
Bank overdraft	6,370					
		12,845				
		£42,845				£42,845

The accruals in the balance sheet comprised: audit fee £600, heat and light £400, and advertising £125.
The prepayment of £250 was in respect of rates.
A summary of the bank statement provides the following information for the year to 31 March 19X9.

	£
Takings banked	141,105
Purchases	111,805
Wages	6,875
Rates and water	6,850
Heat and light	1,720
Delivery and travelling	3,380
Repairs and renewals	1,475
Advertising	375
Printing and stationery	915
Sundry office expenses	215
Bank charges	1,100
Audit fee	600

The following items were paid from the takings before they were banked:

Wages: cleaner £5 per week; van driver's mate £10 per week
Casual labour for the year: £555
Paraffin for shop heating: £445
Advertising: £75
Sundry office expenses: £515
Purchases for resale: £12,635
Hire of delivery vehicle: £20 per week
Partners' drawings per week: Field £40, Green £30, Lane £30

You ascertain the following additional information:

1. The partners are allowed interest of 5 per cent per annum on their capital accounts.
2. Profits and losses are shared in the ratio Field 5, Green 3, Lane 2; with the proviso that Lane is guaranteed by Field an income of £3,000 per annum, excluding his interest on capital.
3. Certain goods had been appropriated by the partners during the year. The selling price of these goods was £460, allocated as follows:
    Field £235, Green £110, Lane £115.
4. Depreciation on fixed assets is to be provided at the following rates: fixed plant 5 per cent, motor vehicles 25 per cent and fixtures and fittings 10 per cent, using the straight line method.
5. Accrued charges for heat and light at 31 March 19X9 were £450.
6. Rates of £750 were prepaid at 31 March 19X9.
7. Your charges for the 19X8/X9 audit were estimated at £650.
8. At 31st March 19X9, Stocks were £22,345, Debtors £11,415, trade creditors £5,920 and cash in till £100.

You are required to prepare:

(a) the partnership's trading and profit and loss account and profit and loss appropriation account for the year ended 31 March 19X9, and
(b) the balance sheet as at 31 March 19X9. (Movements in the partners' current accounts should be shown on the face of the balance sheet.)   (CACA)

25. Changes in partners: revaluations and goodwill

When a partner leaves a partnership due to, for example, retirement or death, and whenever a new partner is admitted, it has the effect of bringing the old partnership to an end and transferring the business to a new partnership. The retiring partner(s) will want to take out their share of the business assets and any new partner(s) may be expected to introduce capital. Furthermore, a new profit sharing agreement must be made. The situation would be relatively simple, in accounting terms, if three conditions could be met:

1. the separate assets and liabilities of the business are all included in the accounts at values the partners agree to be current;
2. no account is taken of 'goodwill';
3. the change occurs at the end of the year.

The difficulties which arise when these conditions do not apply will be discussed later in this chapter. The term goodwill has special significance in accounting and explanation of this is also introduced later.

Retirement of a partner

This can be considered initially using the simplifying assumptions 1, 2 and 3 set out above. The first step in dealing with the retirement of a partner is to ensure that the accounts are complete at the date of retirement, including crediting the partner's current account with the partner's share of profit and debiting the current account with the partner's drawings to this date. The retiring partner's share of the partnership assets are then represented by the sum of the balances on his or her current and capital accounts. As soon as the individual ceases to be a partner, that person no longer has capital invested in the partnership and must thus be treated as a loan creditor. The balances on the former partner's current and capital accounts are, therefore, transferred to a loan account in the individual's name. This loan is eliminated either by one payment, or alternatively there may be a clause in the partnership agreement to make repayment by instalments over time. Since the person is no longer a partner, any interest payable on this loan is an expense of the partnership to be charged in the profit and loss account and not an appropriation of profits as in the case of interest on loans made by partners.

The accounting entries relating to the retirement of a partner are illustrated in Example 25.1.

Example 25.1
Britten, Edwards and Howe are partners sharing profits equally after interest on partner's

loans of 5 per cent per annum. Edwards retires on 1 January 19X9 and is to be repaid one year later. Interest on money due to her is to be at 8 per cent per annum.

The balance sheet at 31 December 19X8 was summarized as below, before the appropriation of profit:

Capital accounts

	£	£
Britten		10,000
Edwards		6,000
Howe		5,000
		21,000

Current accounts

	£	£
Britten	1,000	
Edwards	1,500	
Howe	1,100	3,600
Profit and loss account — profit for year		1,000
		25,600
Partner's loan from Edwards		2,000
		27,600
Sundry net assets		27,600

First the appropriation of profits should be carried out as follows:

	B £	E £	H £	Total £
Profit for year				1,000
Interest on loan @ 5 per cent		100		(100)
				900
Balance shared equally	300	300	300	(900)
	300	400	300	—

The journal and ledger entries in respect of Edward's share of profits will be as follows:

		£	£
Profit and loss appropriation account	Dr	400	
Current Account — Edwards			400

This produces a balance on Edwards' current account of £1,500 + £400 = £1,900. The balances on the retiring partner's capital, current and loan accounts are then transferred to a new loan account as shown by the following journal entries:

		£	£
Capital Account — Edwards	Dr	6,000	
Current Account — Edwards	Dr	1,900	
Partners' Loan Account — Edwards	Dr	2,000	
Loan Account — Edwards			9,900
		9,900	9,900

After crediting the other partner's current accounts with their share of profits the balance sheet on the 1 January 19X9 after Edward's retirement will be as follows:

	£	£
Capital accounts		
Britten		10,000
Howe		5,000
		15,000
Current accounts		
Britten	1,300	
Howe	1,400	
		2,700
		17,700
Sundry net assets		27,600
Less: Loan — Edwards		9,900
		17,700

The revaluation of assets on changes in partners

The values of assets and liabilities shown in the ledger and the balance sheet (i.e. the book values) are not normally the current values. Therefore, when a new partner is admitted to a business or an existing partner dies or retires it is usually necessary to revalue all the assets and liabilities. The reason for this revaluation is that since assets are normally shown in the accounts at their historic cost there will be unrealized holding gains and losses which have not been recorded in the books (e.g. arising from an increase in the market value of property since the date of purchase). These must be taken into account by means of a revaluation, and each partner's capital account credited with their share of the unrealized gains (or debited with their share of any unrealized losses).

Thus when an existing partner dies or retires, the revaluation ensures that the former partner received his or her share of any unrealized holding gains. Similarly when a new partner is admitted the revaluation is necessary to ensure that the old partners receive recognition of their shares of the unrealized holding gains. If this was not done the new partner would be entitled to a share of these gains when they were eventually realized despite the fact they arose prior to the partner's admission to the partnership.

An illustration of the ledger entries relating to the revaluation of assets on changes in partners is given in Example 25.2.

Example 25.2

Bill and Harry are in partnership sharing profits equally. On the 1 July 19X1 Harry retired and Jane was admitted as a partner who is to contribute cash of £9,000 as capital. Future profits are to be shared, Bill three fifths and Jane two fifths.

The balance sheet at the 30 June 19X1 was as follows:

Capital accounts		£	Fixed assets	Cost £	Dep. £	WDV £
Bill		17,000	Plant	13,500	3,300	10,200
Harry		17,500	Fixtures	10,500	2,700	7,800
		34,500		24,000	6,000	18,000
Current accounts						
Bill	4,800					
Harry	2,100	6,900	Current assets			
			Stock		13,800	
			Debtors		9,450	
Current liabilities			Cash		3,900	27,150
Creditors		3,750				
		45,150				45,150

It was decided that stock is to be valued at £12,000 and fixtures at £13,050 (before deducting depreciation). Of the trade debtors, £1,350 are considered doubtful debts.

The ledger entries relating to the above revaluation and change of partners are required.

It is necessary to first set up a revaluation account in the ledger and enter the increases and decreases in value of all the assets. The resulting profit or loss on revaluation must then be shared between the old partners in their old profit sharing ratio and entered in their capital accounts. The cash introduced by the new partner is simply credited to her capital account. This is shown below.

Fixtures

Balance b/d	10,500	
Revaluation a/c	2,550	
	13,050	

Stock

Balance b/d	13,800	Revaluation a/c		1,800
		Balance c/d		12,000
	13,800			13,800
Balance b/d	12,000			

Provision for bad debts

	Revaluation account	1,350

Revaluation account

Write down of stock	1,800	Write up of fixtures		2,550
Provision for bad debts	1,350	Loss on revaluation —		
		Capital Bill	300	
		Capital Harry	300	600
	3,150			3,150

Capital

	Bill	Harry	Jane		Bill	Harry	Jane
				Balance b/d	17,000	17,500	—
Revaluation a/c	300	300					
				Bank			9,000
Balance c/d	16,700	17,200	9,000				
	17,000	17,500	9,000		17,000	17,500	9,000
				Balance b/d	16,700	17,200	9,000

Finally, the transfers in respect of Harry's capital and current accounts must be made, which would involve the following journal entry:

Capital Account — H	Dr	17,200	
Current Account — H	Dr	2,100	
Loan Account — H			19,300
		19,300	19,300

So far, consideration has been given to situations where any deceased or retiring partners' capital accounts have had credit balances and the remaining partners are required to make payments to them. If there is a debit balance on a capital account, a retiring partner will be due to pay this to the partnership. However, if the retiring partner is unable to make this payment, there will be a deficiency to be shared among the remaining partners. The partnership agreement may specify how this sharing is to take place. In the absence of such an agreement, then the precedence of a court ruling in the case of *Garner v. Murray* will apply under English law. Under this rule, the deficiency is shared in proportion to the partners' credit balances on their capital accounts at the last balance sheet date before the retirement. Subsequent revaluations are not taken into account in calculating these proportions nor are profit sharing ratios.

The nature of goodwill

The precise nature of goodwill is difficult to define in a theoretically sound manner. However, it is generally recognized that goodwill exists, since a value is normally attached to it when a business is purchased. Goodwill usually arises in the accounts where another business has been purchased at some time in the past. The value frequently takes the form of the excess of the purchase price of the other business over the market value of its net assets. The existence of this excess shows that the purchaser of a business is prepared to pay for something in addition to the net assets. Goodwill is the label given to that something. Thus in Statement of Standard Accounting Practice 22 — Accounting for Goodwill, goodwill is defined as 'the difference between the value of a business as a whole and the aggregate of the fair values of its separable net assets'. Clearly, therefore, goodwill cannot be bought and sold separately from the other assets of a business. When one business is taken over by another business, the excess of the purchase price over its net asset value is referred to as *purchased goodwill*.

It follows from the above that purchased goodwill represents the advantages which arise from taking over an existing business rather than building up a new business from scratch. However, goodwill also exists where another business has not been taken over. This is referred to as *non-purchased goodwill*. Any ongoing business is normally worth more as a going concern than is shown by the value of its net tangible assets. Otherwise it would probably be better to shut the business down and sell the separate assets. From this standpoint, goodwill may be said to represent the present value of the future profits accruing from an existing business (net of the value of its separable assets). Thus goodwill arises from a number of attributes that an ongoing business possesses such as the following:

1. The prestige and reputation attaching to the name of a business or its products and thus the likelihood that present customers will continue to buy from the business in future (e.g. Rolls Royce cars, Levi jeans, Marks & Spencer quality).
2. Existing contracts for the supply of goods in the future (e.g. construction, aerospace, defence equipment etc).
3. The location of the business premises (e.g. a newsagent next to a railway station) and other forms of captive customers (e.g. a milk distributor's clientele).
4. The possession of patents, trademarks, brand names and special technical knowledge arising from previous expenditure on research and development. However, some of these may be valued as separate assets.
5. The existence of known sources of supply of goods and services including the availability of trade credit.
6. The existing staff including particular management skills. The costs of recruiting and training present employees gives rise to an asset that is not recorded in the balance sheet but nevertheless represents a valuable resource to the business. Furthermore, these costs would have to be incurred if a business was started from scratch.
7. Other set-up factors. An existing business has the advantage of having collected together the various items of equipment and other assets necessary for its operations. Obtaining and bringing together these assets usually involves delay and expense, and avoiding this is an advantage of an ongoing business.

It should be observed that a business might be expected to make future losses arising from a poor reputation, etc. This can result in the purchase price of a business being lower than its net asset value. The difference between these two amounts is referred to as *negative goodwill*.

The recognition of goodwill in accounts

As explained above, all businesses possess either positive or negative goodwill. However, this may or may not be recorded in the books and thus appear on the balance sheet as an intangible fixed asset. SSAP22 prohibits goodwill being recorded in the books of companies unless it has been purchased; that is, unless the company has at some time in the past taken over another business and the purchase price exceeded the net asset value of that business. The main reason for this is that the valuation of non-purchased goodwill is regarded as not being sufficiently accurate to meet the objectivity concept. Although the accounts of sole traders and partnerships do not have to be prepared in accordance with Statements of Standard Accounting Practice, it is nevertheless highly unlikely that these will include goodwill except possibly when another business has been purchased. In the case of a partnership this includes where a new partner is admitted or an existing partner retires or dies. The law states that in each instance the old partnership is dissolved, and thus effectively taken over by the new partnership. The accounts of the new partnership may therefore include goodwill acquired from the purchase of the old partnership. This is examined in detail later in the chapter.

The current established thinking is that the value of goodwill declines with the passage of time. It therefore has a finite life. Thus, like most other fixed assets, when purchased goodwill is recorded in the accounts it should be amortized (i.e. depreciated) over its useful economic life. An alternative approach is to write it off immediately against the partners' capital (or reserves in the case of companies) at the time of purchase. This procedure will be described later. However, there is a school of thought that the value of goodwill can be perpetuated by, for example, expenditure on advertising, training, etc. and thus has an infinite life. It is therefore sometimes argued that it is not necessary to depreciate goodwill.

The valuation of goodwill

As explained previously, the cost of purchased goodwill is deemed to be the excess of the purchase price of a business over the market/fair value of its net assets. In the case of company accounts the value of goodwill is usually computed in precisely this manner. However, in the case of sole traders and partnerships the purchase price of a business is frequently arrived at by valuing the net tangible assets (often at market prices) and, as a separate item, goodwill. This is particularly common where a new partner is admitted or an existing partner leaves.

There are a number of methods of valuing goodwill. These reflect the customs/conventions of businesses generally and certain trades and professions in particular. It should be emphasized that in practice the amount arrived at using one of these methods is frequently regarded as a starting point in negotiating a final value for goodwill. The most common methods are as follows:

1. A given multiple of the annual, monthly or weekly turnover/sales/fees. The multiple is intended to represent the number of years' future sales that are likely to result from the goodwill presently attaching to the business. The turnover may be an estimate of future sales, or more likely an average of a given number of past periods. This method is common in the case of retail businesses and professional firms such as accountants, solicitors etc.

2. A given multiple of the annual profit. Again the multiple is intended to represent the number of years' future profits that are likely to be generated from the existing goodwill. The annual profit may be either an estimate of the future profit or more likely an average of a given number of past years. The profits used in the computation may be those shown in the audited accounts or alternatively what is termed the abnormal or super profit. This refers to the profit shown in the accounts minus a notional charge for interest on capital and proprietors' salaries. The super profit is intended to represent the return from risking money in a business over and above what could be earned by depositing that money elsewhere at a fixed rate of interest and taking employment with a guaranteed salary. This method of valuing goodwill may be particularly appropriate in riskier industries with fluctuating profits such as engineering and building construction.

3. The excess of the capitalized value of the (past or forecasted) annual (average) profit (or super profit) over the current (market) value of the net tangible assets of the business. The capitalized value is normally computed by multiplying the annual profit by the average price–earnings (P–E) ratio of similar size companies in the same industry whose shares are listed on the stock exchange. The capitalized value is intended to reflect the total value of the business as a going concern. This method may be most appropriate in the case of a large business that is not a company or whose shares are not quoted on a stock exchange. It is a common method of valuing unquoted companies such as for inheritance tax purposes.

Each of these methods is illustrated in later examples.

The admission of a new partner and the treatment of goodwill

When a new partner is admitted to a partnership the value of the assets introduced into the business will be debited to the relevant asset accounts and credited to the new partners' capital account. Furthermore, an adjustment to the old partners' capital accounts is necessary to recognize the value of goodwill which they have created and therefore belongs to them. The principle is exactly the same as with the revaluation of assets except that the asset has not previously been recorded in the books. There are six possible ways of dealing with this, each of which is described below and illustrated using Example 25.3.

Example 25.3
A and B are in partnership sharing profits in the ratio 3 : 2. The balances on their capital accounts are: A £15,000 and B £20,000.

On 31 December 19X8 they decide to admit C as a partner who is to bring in £10,000 as her capital and receive half of all future profits. The old partners profit sharing ratio will continue to be 3 : 2.

Goodwill is to be calculated at twice the average super profits of the last three years. The super profits are after charging interest on capital of 5 per cent per annum and partners' salaries of £12,500 per annum each.

The profits transferred to the profit and loss appropriation account are as follows:

	£
Year ended 31/12/X6	28,560
Year ended 31/12/X7	29,980
Year ended 31/12/X8	32,210

It may be assumed that any premium payable by C is equal to the amount of the original goodwill she would receive if this were realized during the time she was a partner.

The value to be ascribed to goodwill would first be calculated as follows:

Year ended	Net profits	Salaries	Interest on capital	Super profits
31/12/X6	28,560	25,000	1,750	1,810
X7	29,980	25,000	1,750	3,230
X8	32,210	25,000	1,750	5,460
				10,500

$$\text{Goodwill} = 2 \times \frac{£10,500}{3} = £7,000$$

Note that the new profit sharing ratio will be A3 : B2 : C5. Since C is to receive one half of all future profits, A's share will be 3 divided by 3 + 2 multiplied by the remaining one half. Similarly B's share will be $\frac{2}{5} \times \frac{1}{2} = \frac{2}{10}$.

The different methods of treating goodwill on the admission of a new partner can now be shown as follows:

1. The value of goodwill is debited to a goodwill account and credited to the old partner's capital accounts in their old profit sharing ratio. This results in the new partner not being charged for her share of goodwill because she will not get a share of it when it is realized or when she leaves.

Goodwill

19X8
31 Dec   Capital A   4,200
31 Dec   Capital B   2,800
                                   ——————
                          7,000

Capital

		A	B	C
19X8				
31 Dec	Balance b/d	15,000	20,000	
31 Dec	Bank			10,000
31 Dec	Goodwill	4,200	2,800	

2. The value of goodwill is debited to a goodwill account and the old partners withdraw on equivalent amount of money in their old profit sharing ratio. Again this results in no charge being made to the new partner because she will not receive a share of goodwill when it is realized, or when she leaves.

Capital

		A	B	C
19X8				
31 Dec	Balance b/d	15,000	20,000	
31 Dec	Bank			10,000

Goodwill

19X8			
31 Dec	Bank — A	4,200	
31 Dec	Bank — B	2,800	7,000

Bank

19X8			19X8			
31 Dec	Capital C	10,000	31 Dec	Goodwill — A	4,200	
				Goodwill — B	2,800	7,000

3. The value of goodwill is credited to the old partners' capital accounts in their old profit sharing ratio and debited to the new partner's capital account in their new profit sharing ratio. This has the effect of charging the new partner for her share of goodwill. She will get this back when it is eventually realized, or when she leaves. It also means that no goodwill account is maintained in the books.

Capital

19X8		A	B	C	19X8		A	B	C
31 Dec	Goodwill				31 Dec	Balance b/d	15,000	20,000	
	contra	2,100	1,400	3,500	31 Dec	Bank			10,000
					31 Dec	Goodwill			
						contra	4,200	2,800	—

4. The new partner pays into the busines a premium as payment for her share of goodwill. It is computed by multiplying the value of goodwill by the new partners' share of profits. This is credited to the capital accounts of the old partners in their old profit sharing ratio. Again no goodwill account is maintained in the books.

Premium payable by C = £7,000 × $\frac{1}{2}$ = £3,500

Capital

19X8		A	B	C	19X8		A	B	C
31 Dec	Premium contra	—	—	3,500	31 Dec	Balance b/d	15,000	20,000	
					31 Dec	Bank			10,000
					31 Dec	Premium			
						contra	2,100	1,400	

5. The new partner pays into the business a premium as in point 4 above and the old partners withdraw the same amount in their old profit sharing ratio. Again there is no goodwill account.

Capital

19X8		A	B	C	19X8		A	B	C
31 Dec	Premium contra	—	—	3,500	31 Dec	Balance b/d	15,000	20,000	
31 Dec	Bank —								
	drawings	2,100	1,400		31 Dec	Bank			10,000
					31 Dec	Premia			
						Contra	2,100	1,400	—

6. The new partner pays privately to the old partners a premium as in point 4 above. The old partners divide this between them in their old profit sharing ratio. There are no entries in the books of the partnership.

   C pays privately to A £2,100 and to B £1,400 and no entries relating to goodwill or the premium are made in the books.

   The most common methods are 1 and 3 above.

An outgoing partner and the treatment of goodwill

When a partner leaves, the balances on his or her capital and current accounts are repaid. However, it is necessary first to make an adjustment to the partners' capital accounts in recognition of the value of goodwill that has been created, some of which belongs to the outgoing partner. There are a number of ways of dealing with this as follows:

1. The value of goodwill is debited to a goodwill account and credited to the old partners' capital accounts in their old profit sharing ratio.
2. The value of goodwill is credited to the old partners' capital accounts in their old profit sharing ratio and debited to the remaining partners' capital accounts in their new profit sharing ratio. This effectively results in the remaining partners purchasing the outgoing partner's share of goodwill. No goodwill account is maintained in the books.
3. The outgoing partner's share of goodwill is credited to his or her capital account and debited to the remaining partners' capital accounts in their new profit sharing ratio. Again no goodwill account is maintained in the books.

   It should be noted that these involve the same principles as methods 1, 3 and 4 respectively in the case of the treatment of goodwill where there is an incoming partner.

Incoming and outgoing partners and goodwill

We have thus far dealt with the revaluation of assets on changes in partners and the treatment of goodwill where there is either an incoming or outgoing partner. The final step is to combine all of these and examine the situation where there is both an incoming and outgoing partner. This is a fairly simple step since the treatment of goodwill involves exactly the same principles whether there is an incoming or outgoing partner. An illustration is given in the following example.

Example 25.4
Beech and Oak are in partnership, sharing profits and losses in the ratio 3 : 5 respectively. The balance sheet drawn up on 31 December 19X9 showed the following position:

	£		£	£
Capital accounts:		*Fixed assets*:		
Beech	11,000	Premises	16,000	
Oak	14,000	Fixtures	6,000	22,000
	25,000	*Current assets*:		
Creditors	9,000	Stock	4,000	
		Debtors	3,000	
		Cash	5,000	12,000
	34,000			34,000

Beech retired as from 1 January 19X0 and at the same date Maple was admitted to the partnership. For the purpose of these changes, the premises were revalued at £19,500, fixtures at £4,500, stock at £5,800 and goodwill was agreed at £10,000. A provision for bad debts of £200 is also to be created. The new valuations are to be included in the business books but no account for goodwill is to be maintained. In the new partnership, profits and losses will be divided in the proportions 3:2 between Oak and Maple respectively. Maple will introduce cash of £15,000 and Beech is to receive payment for his capital in cash, but no other cash is to change hands between partners in implementing the change.

You are required to show the above changes in the revaluation account and the partners' capital accounts.

Revaluation account

Fixtures		1,500	Premises	3,500
Provision for bad debts		200	Stock	1,800
Profit on revaluation —				
Beech	1,350			
Oak	2,250	3,600		
		5,300		5,300

Capital accounts

	Beech	Oak	Maple		Beech	Oak	Maple
Goodwill contra	—	6,000	4,000	Balance b/d	11,000	14,000	—
Cash	16,100			Profit on			
Balance c/d	—	16,500	11,000	revaluation		1,350	2,250
				Goodwill contra	3,750	6,250	—
				Cash	—	—	15,000
	16,100	22,500	15,000		16,100	22,500	15,000

Notes

1. The double entry for the items in the revaluation account will be in the respective asset accounts and the provision for bad debts account.
2. The goodwill is credited to the old partners' capital accounts in their old profit sharing ratio (Beech $\frac{3}{8}$ × £10,000 = £3,750; Oak $\frac{5}{8}$ × £10,000 = £6,250) and debited to the new partners' capital accounts in their new profit sharing ratio (Oak $\frac{3}{5}$ × £10,000 = £6,000; Maple $\frac{2}{5}$ × £10,000 = £4,000).
3. The cash paid to Beech of £16,100 is the balance on his capital account after the revaluation of assets and adjustments for goodwill.

Changes in partners' profit sharing ratio

Sometimes partners decide to change the proportions in which they share profits and losses. This may occur when the partners agree that one partner is to spend more (or less) time on partnership business, or alternatively one partner's skills have become more (or less) valuable to the partnership.

If a change in the profit sharing ratio occurs at some time during the accounting year, it will be necessary to divide the profit before appropriations into the periods prior to and after the change. This is usually done on a time basis. The interest on capital, salaries and shares of profit are then computed for each period separately. It should be noted that this procedure also has to be followed when a new partner is admitted and/or a partner leaves during the accounting year.

When there is a change in the profit sharing ratio it is also necessary to revalue the assets including goodwill. As in the case of changes in partners, the profit or loss on revaluation is computed in a revaluation account and transferred to the partners' capital accounts. An adjustment must also be made in respect of goodwill, using the principles already described. A simple illustration is given in Example 25.5.

Example 25.5

X and Y are in partnership sharing profits and losses equally. They have decided that as from 1 October 19X8 the profit sharing ratio is to become X three fifths and Y two fifths.

The accounts are made up to 31 December each year. The profit for the year ended 31 December 19X5 was £60,000. The balance sheet at 31 December 19X5 prior to sharing profits is as follows:

		£
Net assets		210,000
Capital X		80,000
	Y	70,000
Profit for the year		60,000
		210,000

It was, decided that the impact of the change in profit sharing ratio on each partners' share of the assets would be effected at 31 December 19X5 when the net assets were valued at £250,000. The goodwill was valued at £25,000 but no goodwill account is to be maintained in the books.

You are required to show the entries in the partners' capital accounts and a balance sheet at the 31 December 19X5.

	Total	£ 1 Jan — 30 Sept	£ 1 Oct — 31 Dec
Profit for the year apportioned on a time basis	60,000	45,000	15,000
Shares of profit — X	31,500	22,500	9,000
— Y	28,500	22,500	6,000
	60,000	45,000	15,000

Revaluation account

Profit on revaluation —			Net assets	40,000
Capital X	20,000		(250,000 − 210,000)	
Capital Y	20,000	40,000		
		40,000		40,000

Capital accounts

	X	Y		X	Y
Goodwill contra	15,000	10,000	Balance b/d	80,000	70,000
Balance c/d	129,000	121,000	Shares of profit	31,500	28,500
			Profit on revaluation	20,000	20,000
			Goodwill contra	12,500	12,500
	144,000	131,000		144,000	131,000
			Balance b/d	129,000	121,000

X and Y

Balance sheet as at 31 December 19X5

	£
Net assets	250,000
Capital X	129,000
Y	121,000
	250,000

Reference

1. Accounting Standards Committee (1989). *Statement of Standard Accounting Practice 22 — Accounting for Goodwill* (ICAEW).

Exercises

1. (a) Explain the nature of goodwill.
   (b) Describe the business attributes that are thought to give rise to goodwill.

2. (a) What is the difference between positive and negative goodwill?
   (b) What is the difference between purchased goodwill and non-purchased goodwill?

3. (a) Explain the circumstances in which goodwill might appear in the books of a partnership.
   (b) Describe how it would be treated in the balance sheet.

4. A member of the board of Shoprite Enterprises plc has suggested two accounting policies for consideration by the financial director in preparing the latest set of accounts. These have been summarized as follows:

   (i) The incorporation of goodwill in the accounts as a permanent fixed asset in recognition of the favourable trading situations of several of the business's outlets and also to reflect the quality of management experience in the business.

   (ii) No depreciation to be provided in future on the buildings owned by the company, because their market value is constantly appreciating and, in addition, this will result in an increase of the profit of the company.

   Required:
   (a) Briefly explain your understanding of each of the following:
       (i) goodwill;
       (ii) depreciation.
   (b) Discuss the acceptability of each of the above suggested accounting policies, highlighting any conflict with accounting concepts.   (AEB)

5. Describe three different methods of valuing goodwill where the purchase price is unknown.

6. Al and Bert are in partnership, sharing profits equally. At 30 June, they have balances on their capital accounts of £12,000 (Al) and £15,000 (Bert). On that day they agree to bring in their friend Hall as a third partner. All three partners are to share profits equally from now on. Hall is to introduce £20,000 as capital into the business. Goodwill on 30 June is agreed at £18,000.
   Required:
   (a) Show the partners' capital accounts for 30 June and 1 July on the assumption that the goodwill, previously unrecorded, is to be included in the accounts.
   (b) Show the additional entries necessary to eliminate goodwill again from the accounts.
   (c) Explain briefly what goodwill is. Why are adjustments necessary when a new partner joins a partnership?   (CACA)

7. Brown and Jones are in partnership, sharing profits and losses equally. The balance sheet drawn up on 31 March 19X5 showed the following position:

	£		£	£
Capital accounts		*Fixed assets*		
Brown	110,000	Premises	80,000	
Jones	87,000	Fixtures	60,000	140,000
	197,000	*Current assets*		
Sundry creditors	98,000	Stock	40,000	
		Debtors	30,000	
		Cash	85,000	155,000
	295,000			295,000

   Brown retired as from 1 April 19X5 and at the same date Smith was admitted to the partnership. For the purpose of these changes, the premises were revalued at £115,000, fixtures at £68,000, stock at £36,000 and goodwill was agreed at £90,000. A provision for bad debts of £3,000 is also to be created. The new valuations are to be included in the business accounts, but no account for goodwill is to be maintained. In the new partnership, profits and losses will be divided in the proportions 3:2 between Jones and Smith respectively. Smith will introduce cash of £100,000 and Brown is to receive payment for his capital in cash but no other cash is to change hands between partners in implementing the change.
   You are required to show the above changes in the revaluation account and partners capital accounts.

8. Blackburn, Percy and Nelson are in partnership sharing profits equally. On 1 January 19X9 Nelson retired and Logan was admitted as a partner. Nelson has agreed to leave the amounts owing to her in the business as a loan until 31 December 19X9. Logan is to contribute £6,000 as capital. Future profits are to be shared, Blackburn one half and Percy and Logan one quarter each.
   A goodwill account is to be opened and kept in the books. The goodwill should be valued at the difference between the capitalized value of the estimated super profits for the forthcoming year and the net asset value

of the partnership at 31 December 19X8 after revaluing the assets. The capitalized value of the expected super profits is to be computed using the price–earnings ratio, which for this type of business is estimated as 8. The super profits are after deducting notional partners' salaries but not interest on capital. The net profit for 19X9 is estimated as £48,750 and it is thought that the partners could each earn £15,000 a year if they were employed elsewhere.

The balance sheet at 31 December 19X8 was as follows:

Capital			*Fixed assets*	*Cost*	*Depn.*	*WDV*
Blackburn		10,000	Plant	9,000	2,200	6,800
Percy		8,000	Vehicles	7,000	1,800	5,200
Nelson		5,000				
		23,000		16,000	4,000	12,000
Current accounts						
Blackburn	1,300		*Current assets*			
Percy	1,900		Stock		9,200	
Nelson	1,400	4,600	Debtors		6,300	
Current liabilities			Cash		2,600	18,100
Creditors		2,500				
		30,100				30,100

It was decided that stock is to be valued at £8,000 and vehicles at £8,500 (before deducting depreciation). Of the trade debtors £900 are considered doubtful debts.

You are required to show the ledger entries relating to the above revaluation and change of partners.

9. Gupta, Richards and Jones are in partnership sharing profits and losses in the ratio 5:4:3. On 1 January 19X0 Richards retired from the partnership and it was agreed that Singh should join the partnership, paying a sum of £30,000. From this date, profits are to be shared equally between the three partners and, in view of this, Jones agrees to pay a further £10,000 into the partnership as capital.

The balance sheet at 31 December 19X9 showed:

	£	£
Fixed assets		
Property		60,000
Fixtures		30,000
		90,000
Current assets		
Stock	30,000	
Debtors	15,000	
Bank	5,000	
	50,000	
Creditors	10,000	40,000
		130,000
Capital accounts		
Gupta	60,000	
Richards	40,000	
Jones	25,000	
		125,000
Current accounts		
Gupta	1,000	
Richards	2,500	
Jones	1,500	5,000
		130,000

It was agreed that in preparing a revised opening balance sheet of the partnership on 1 January 19X0 the following adjustments should be made:

1. Property is to be revalued at £70,000 and fixtures are to be revalued at £32,000.
2. Stock is considered to be shown at a fair value in the accounts. A provision for doubtful debts of £1,200 is required.
3. Professional fees of £600 relating to the change in partnership structure are to be regarded as an expense of the year to 31 December 19X9, but were not included in the profit and loss account of that year. They are expected to be paid in March 19X0.
4. Goodwill of the partnership as at 31 December 19X9 is estimated at £30,000. No account for goodwill is to be entered in the books, but appropriate adjustments are to be made in the partners' capital accounts.
5. On retirement, Richards is to be paid a sum of £40,000. The balance owing to her will be recorded in a loan account carrying interest of 12 per cent, to be repaid in full after two years.
6. All balances on current accounts are to be transferred to capital accounts. All balances on capital accounts in excess of £20,000 after this transfer are to be transferred to loan accounts carrying interest at 12 per cent.

You are required to:

(a) compute the balances on the loan accounts of Richards and the new partners on 1 January 19X0, following completion of these arrangements;
(b) prepare an opening balance sheet for the partnership on 1 January 19X0, following completion of these arrangements;
(c) explain briefly *three* factors to be taken into account when establishing profit sharing arrangements between partners.   (JMB adapted)

10. Street, Rhode and Close carried on business in partnership sharing profits and losses, Street 5/12, Rhode 4/12 and Close 3/12.

Their draft balance sheet as on 31 March 19X9 was as follows:

	£	£		£	£
Capital accounts			Leasehold premises	8,000	
Street	8,500		*Less* Amount written off	800	7,200
Rhode	6,000		Plant and machinery	——	
Close	4,500		at cost	9,200	
	——	19,000	*Less* Provision for depn.	2,700	6,500
Current accounts					
Street	850		Stock on hand		5,400
Rhode	1,300		Sundry debtors	4,200	
Close	1,150		*Less* Provision for		
	——	3,300	doubtful debts	750	3,450
Loan: Street		4,000	Cash at bank	——	8,000
Sundry creditors		4,250			
		£30,550			£30,550

Street retired from the partnership on 31 March 19X9 and Rhode and Close decided to carry on the business and to admit Lane as a partner who is to bring in capital of £10,000. Future profits are to be shared equally between Rhode, Close and Lane.

By agreement, the following adjustments were to be incorporated in the books of account as at 31 March 19X9:

1. Plant and machinery to be increased to £6,900, in accordance with a valuer's certificate.
2. Stock to be reduced to £4,860, since some items included therein were regarded as unsaleable.
3. The provision for doubtful debts to be increased to £830.
4. Provision to be made for the valuer's charges, £140.

The partnership deed provided that on the retirement of a partner the value of goodwill was to be taken to be the amount equal to the average annual profit of the three years ending on the date of retirement. The profits of such three years were:

Year ended 31 March 19X7   £7,800
Year ended 31 March 19X8   £9,400
Year ended 31 March 19X9   £11,600

The partners agreed that, in respect of the valuing of goodwill, the profits should be regarded as not being affected by the revaluation.

It was decided that an account for goodwill should not be opened in the books, but that the transactions between the partners should be made through their capital accounts.

£3,000 was repaid to Street on 1 April 19X9 and she agreed to leave £12,000 as a loan to the new partnership. Rhode, Close and Lane promised to repay the balance remaining due to Street within six months.

You are required to prepare:

(i)   the revaluation account;
(ii) the partner's capital accounts (in columnar form);
(iii) Street's account showing the balance due to her; and
(iv) the balance sheet of Rhode, Close and Lane as on 1 April 19X9.   (CACA adapted)

11. Matthew, Mark and Luke were in partnership sharing profits and losses in the ratio 5 : 3 : 2, accounts being made up annually to 30 June. Fixed capitals were to bear interest at the rate of 5 per cent per annum, but no interest was to be allowed or received on current accounts or drawings. Any balance on current accounts was to be paid at each year end.

Luke left the partnership on 30 September 19X6, but agreed to leave his money in the business until a new partner was admitted, provided interest at 5 per cent was paid on all amounts due to him.

John was admitted to the partnership on 1 January 19X7, providing capital of £2,000. It was agreed that the new profit sharing ratio be Matthew 5, Mark 4, John 1, but Mark was to guarantee John an income of £3,000 per annum in addition to his interest on capital.

At 1 July 19X6 each partner had a fixed capital of £4,000.

Drawings during the year 19X6/19X7 were as follows:

Matthew	£750
Mark	£600
Luke	£220 (to 30 September 19X6)
John	£80

The profit for the year to 30 June 19X7 was £20,000 which may be assumed to have accrued evenly over that period.

You are required to show:

(a) the profit and loss appropriation account, and
(b) the partner's current account for the year ended 30 June 19X7.   (CACA)

12. Hawthorn and Privet have carried on business in partnership for a number of years, sharing profits in the ratio of 4 : 3 after charging interest on capital at 4 per cent per annum. Holly was admitted into the partnership on 1 October 19X4, and the terms of the partnership from then were agreed as follows:

1.   Partner's annual salaries to be: Hawthorn £1,800, Privet £1,200, Holly £1,100.
2.   Interest on capital to be charged at 4 per cent per annum.
3.   Profits to be shared: Hawthorn four ninths, Privet three ninths, Holly two ninths.

On 1 October 19X4, Holly paid £7,000 into the partnership bank and of this amount £2,100 was in respect of the share of goodwill acquired by her. Since the partnership has never created, and does not intend to create, a goodwill account, the full amount of £7,000 was credited for the time being to Holly's capital account at 1 October 19X4.

The trial balance of the partnership at 30 June 19X5, was as follows:

	Dr £	Cr £
Cash at bank	3,500	
Stock at 1 July 19X4	11,320	
Purchases	102,630	
Sales		123,300
Wages and salaries	6,200	
Rates, telephone, lighting and heating	2,100	
Printing, stationery and postage	530	
General expenses	1,600	
Bad debts written off	294	
Capital accounts: Hawthorn		22,000
Privet		11,000
Holly		7,000
Current accounts: Hawthorn	2,200	
Privet	1,100	
Holly	740	
Debtors and creditors	27,480	13,744
Freehold premises	12,000	
Furniture, fixtures and fittings at 1 July 19X4	5,800	
Bad debts reserve		450
	£177,494	£177,494

After taking into account the following information and the adjustment required for goodwill, prepare trading and profit and loss accounts for the year ended 30 June 19X5, and a balance sheet as on that date. On 30 June 19X5:

1. Stock was £15,000.
2. Rates (£110) and wages and salaries (£300) were outstanding.
3. Telephone rental paid in advance was £9.
4. Provision for bad debts is to be adjusted to $2\frac{1}{2}$ per cent of debtors.
    Depreciation to be provided on furniture, fixtures and fittings at 10 per cent.
    Apportionments required are to be made on a time basis.   (CACA)

26. The nature of limited companies and their capital

There are a large number of different legal forms of organization. However, these can be all grouped into two categories, known as bodies sole and bodies corporate. Bodies sole consist of sole traders and partnerships. All other forms of organization are bodies corporate. A key feature of bodies corporate is that they are recognized by law as being a legal entity separate from their members.

A body corporate is one which is created either by Royal Charter, such as The Institute of Chartered Accountants in England and Wales, or by act of Parliament. The act of Parliament may relate to either the creation of a specific organization, such as the British Broadcasting Corporation, or alternatively permit the creation of a particular form of legal entity by any group of individuals. The most common forms of legal entity which can be created under such acts of Parliament include building societies, charities, clubs and companies.

A company can thus be defined as a legal entity which is formed by registration under the Companies Acts, the main one being the Companies Act 1985 as modified by the Companies Act 1989. There are four types of companies, which consist of companies whose liability is limited by shares, companies with unlimited liability, companies whose liability is limited by guarantee and companies limited by shares and guarantee. Companies limited by guarantee include organizations such as some professional bodies where the liability of its members is limited to the amount of their annual subscription. The remainder of this chapter deals with companies whose liability is limited by shares. These are commonly known as limited companies.

The characteristics of companies limited by shares

1. A company is a legal entity separate from its shareholders (owners). This means that companies enter into contracts as legal entities in their own right. Thus creditors and others cannot sue the shareholders of the company but must take legal proceedings against the company. This is referred to as not being able to lift the veil of incorporation.
2. A company has perpetual existence in that the death of one of its shareholders does not result in its dissolution. This may be contrasted with a partnership where the death of a partner constitutes a dissolution.
3. The liability of a company's shareholders is limited to the nominal value of their shares. This means that if a company's assets are insufficient to pay its debts the shareholders cannot be called upon to contribute more than the nominal value of their shares towards paying those debts.
4. The shareholders of a company do not have the right to take part in its management as such. They appoint directors to manage the company. However, a shareholder may also be a director (or other employee).

5. Each voting share carries one vote at general meetings of the company's shareholders (e.g. in the appointment of directors). There may be different classes of shares, each class having different rights and, possibly, some being non-voting.
6. A limited company must have at least two shareholders but there is no maximum number.

The classes of companies limited by shares

There are two classes of companies limited by shares, namely public and private. Under the Companies Act a public limited company must be registered as such and is required to have a minimum authorized share capital of £50,000. The principal reason for forming a public limited company is to gain access to greater amounts of capital from investment institutions and members of the public. The shares of many, but not all, public companies in the UK are therefore quoted on the International Stock Exchange, London.

All other limited companies are private companies. These are not allowed to offer their shares for sale to the general public and thus do not have a stock exchange quotation. One of the main reasons for forming a private rather than a public company is that it enables its owners to keep control of the business, for example, within the family.

The name of a public company must end with the words 'public limited company' or the abbreviation 'PLC'. The name of a private company must end with the word 'limited' or the abbreviation 'Ltd'. A business which does not have either of these descriptions after its name is not a limited company even if its name contains the word company (the only exception being certain companies which have private company status, such as charities, who are permitted under licence to omit the word limited from their name).

The legal powers and duties of limited companies

A company is formed by sending to the Registrar of Companies certain documents and the appropriate fee. The most relevant of these documents are the Memorandum and Articles of Association. These define a company's powers and duties. The *Memorandum of Association* contains:

1. The name of the company, which must end with the words 'public limited company' or 'limited'.
2. The address of the company's registered office.
3. A statement that the ordinary shareholders' liability is limited to the nominal value of their shares.
4. The objects of the company. These refer to the type of trade or industry in which the company will operate and are usually stated in very broad terms. A company must not engage in any trade or business that is not specified in its Memorandum of Association. If it does so the company is said to be trading *ultra vires*, that is beyond its powers, and any such contract is void.
5. The authorized/nominal capital of the company. That is, the types, nominal value and maximum number of shares the company can offer for sale. This differs from the issued/allotted share capital, which refers to the actual number of shares that have been sold.

6.   A statement that the company is either a public limited company or a private limited company.

Any of the above can be subsequently changed by a special resolution passed at a general meeting of the company's shareholders. Such a resolution requires at least 75 per cent of the votes cast.

The *Articles of Association* can best be described as a rule book which sets out the rights of a company's shareholders between themselves. It contains regulations relating to the issue of shares, conduct of meetings, borrowing powers, the appointment of directors etc. The Companies Acts have provided a model set of articles known as Table A. A company may either make up its own articles or alternatively adopt those in Table A. Furthermore, where there is nothing in a company's articles relating to a particular matter, Table A will apply.

When a company is registered it is issued with what might be described as a birth certificate by the Register of Companies. This is called a *Certificate of Incorporation*. However, before a public limited company can commence trading it must satisfy the Registrar that certain regulations relating to its capital structure have been complied with. When this is done the Registrar issues a *Trading Certificate* on receipt of which the company can commence trading.

The costs of forming a company, including the above documents, are referred to as *preliminary*, *promotion or formation expenses*.

The nature and types of shares and loan capital

Companies are financed predominantly by the issue (sale) of shares, loan stock and debentures, and by retaining part of each year's profit. In the UK all shares, loan stock and debentures have a fixed face or nominal value. This is often £1 or 25 pence in the case of shares and £100 for debentures and loan stock. There are a number of different types of shares and loan capital, each of which is described below.

Ordinary shares

Possession of an ordinary voting share represents part ownership of a company and it entitles the holder to one vote in general meetings of the company's ordinary shareholders. This gives shareholders the power to appoint and dismiss a company's directors. The holder of an ordinary share is also entitled to a share of the company's annual profit in the form of a dividend. The amount of the dividend per share is decided each year by the company's directors and varies according to the amount of profit. In years when the company earns high profits the ordinary shareholders normally receive a large dividend. However, ordinary shareholders run two risks. Firstly, when profits are low they may receive little or no dividend. Secondly, should the company go bankrupt (into liquidation is the correct legal term) the ordinary shareholders are not entitled to be repaid the value of their shares until after *all* the other debts have been paid. Often, where a company has made substantial losses, there is little or nothing left for ordinary shareholders after the company has paid its other debts.

It should also be noted that a company cannot normally repay its ordinary shareholders the money they have invested except in the event of liquidation (or by court order). If an ordinary shareholder wishes to sell his shares a buyer must be found. In the case of public companies whose shares are quoted on the International Stock Exchange, London, the seller may use this as a means of disposing of shares. Similarly, a prospective buyer may acquire 'second-hand' shares through the stock exchange.

Preference shares

Unlike ordinary shares, preference shares carry no voting rights. Preference shareholders are entitled to a fixed rate of dividend each year based on the nominal value of the shares. for example, 8 per cent preference shares with a nominal value of £1 each carry an annual dividend of eight pence per share. A company may make several issues of preference shares each of which can carry a different rate of dividend. Preference shareholders have priority over the ordinary shareholders in that their dividends are a prior claim against profit. The preference dividends are thus deducted before calculating the profit available for distribution to ordinary shareholders as dividends. Like ordinary dividends, the dividend on preference shares is classified as an appropriation of profit which means that the dividend may be waived (but not varied). However, the directors of companies usually try to avoid such drastic action, since it would be an indication of financial weakness.

In the event of a company going into liquidation, the preference shareholders are normally entitled to be repaid the nominal value of their shares before the ordinary shareholders. However, if no money is left after paying the other debts they would get nothing.

As in the case of ordinary shares, companies are not normally allowed to repay preference shareholders the money they have invested except in the event of liquidation. Should a preference shareholder wish to dispose of shares he or she must find a buyer or sell them through the International Stock Exchange, London, if the company has a quotation for the preference shares.

There are two advantages of preference shares from the point of view of a company. One is that, since the rate of dividend is fixed, the company knows in advance what its future annual commitment is in respect of preference dividends. The second advantage is that preference shares are a permanent source of long-term capital which does not have to be repaid. However, since the introduction of the corporation tax system in 1965 it has become unpopular to issue preference shares because the dividend is not an allowable charge against income for tax purposes, while interest on debt is allowable. This makes debt a relatively more attractive source of fixed return finance for most companies. Small companies may be able to take advantage of the tax rules applicable to them to offset this difference.

There are a number of different types of preference shares with rights which vary from those described above. These include:

1. *Cumulative preference shares*
    As explained above, if there is insufficient profit in any year a preference shareholder may receive no dividend. However, in the case of cumulative preference shares the holders will receive any such arrears of dividends (before any other shareholder gets a dividend) in the first subsequent year that there is sufficient profit to cover the dividend. Most of the preference shares quoted on the London stock exchange are cumulative.
2. *Participating preference shares*
    In addition to receiving a fixed rate of dividend, holders of participating preference shares are entitled, along with the ordinary shareholders, to a share of the profit remaining after deducting preference dividends.

3. *Redeemable preference shares*

    These differ from other preference shares in that they are repayable by the company on a date fixed when the shares are issued. Because such a reduction in capital may endanger the creditors' interests, the Companies Act states that when a redemption takes place the company must either make a new issue of shares with the same total nominal value, or capitalize an equivalent amount of profits. Capitalization refers to a transfer of retained profits to a capital reserve. This means that the amount transferred cannot be distributed as dividends.

Debentures/loan stock

Debentures and loan stock are not shares and have no voting rights. They represent a loan to the company and carry a fixed rate of interest per annum based on the nominal value. For example, 10 per cent debentures with a nominal value of £100 each carry annual interest of £10 per debenture. A company may make several issues of debentures or loan stock, each of which can have a different rate of interest. Debenture holders are entitled to their interest before the preference and ordinary shareholders get their dividends, and it must be paid even if there is a loss. The interest on debentures is thus referred to as a charge against profit whereas dividends constitute an appropriation of profit.

In the event of a company going into liquidation the debenture holders are entitled to be repaid the nominal value of their debentures before the preference and ordinary shareholders. Such debentures are usually referred to as *unsecured* in that although they rank before the shareholders they are not entitled to be repaid before the other creditors. However, some issues of debentures are secured on certain of the company's assets by either a *fixed charge* or *floating charge*. A fixed charge is usually on specified assets such as property, plant or vehicles, and means that the company cannot dispose of those assets. A floating charge is usually on assets such as stock. In this case the company can sell the assets but must replace them with similar assets of an equivalent value.

When debentures are secured, an accountant or solicitor may be appointed by the company to act as a trustee for the debenture holders. It is the trustee's responsibility to ensure that the value of the assets is always sufficient to repay the debenture holders. If this is not the case, or that the company may not be able to pay the annual interest on the debentures, the trustee may take legal possession of the assets, sell them and repay the debenture holders. Such drastic action usually results in the company going into liquidation.

Debentures and loan stock are usually repayable at some future date, which is specified when they are issued. This date is often several decades after they are issued. Should a debenture holder wish to dispose of their debentures they must find a buyer or sell them through the International Stock Exchange, London, if the company has a quotation for the debentures.

The main advantage of debentures to a company is that the annual interest on debentures is an allowable charge against income for tax purposes.

A comparatively recent variation on debentures that has proved popular is *convertible loan stock*. These are debentures with a fixed annual rate of interest that also carry the right, at the holders' option, to convert them into a specified number of ordinary shares within a given time period, which is fixed when they are issued. The attraction of convertible loan stock is that the holder hopes to make a capital gain on conversion at some time in the future by virtue of the conversion rate being such that the ordinary shares can be acquired at an effective cost which is lower than the market price at the date of conversion. Suppose,

Ordinary/equity shares	*Preference shares*	*Loan stock/debentures*
1. Owners of the company who are normally entitled to vote at general meetings of the company's shareholders (e.g. to elect directors)	1. No voting rights	1. No voting rights
2. Receive a dividend the rate of which is decided annually by the company's directors. It varies each year depending on the profit and is an appropriation of profit	2. Receive a fixed rate of dividend each year which constitutes an appropriation of profit	2. Receive a fixed rate of interest which constitutes a charge against income in computing the profit
3. Last to be repaid the value of their shares in the event of the company going into liquidation	3. Repaid before the ordinary shareholders in the event of liquidation	3. Repaid before the ordinary and preference shareholders in the event of liquidation
4. Non-repayable except on the liquidation of the company	4. All but one particular type are non-repayable except on liquidation	4. Normally repayable after a fixed period of time
5. Rights specified in Articles of Association	5. Rights specified in Articles of Association	5. Rights specified in the terms of issue
6. Dividends non-deductible for tax purposes	6. Dividends non-deductible for tax purposes	6. Interest deductible for tax purposes

Figure 26.1 A summary of the characteristics of shares and loan stock.

for example, a company issues £100 convertible loan stock at a price of £108, the rate of conversion being 90 ordinary shares for every £100 loan stock. At the date of the issue the ordinary shares are quoted on the stock exchange at a price of £1 each. If at some future date the market price of the shares rises to, say, £1.50 it is beneficial to convert, since the shares would effectively cost £1.20 each (i.e. £108 ÷ 90 shares) compared with a market price of £1.50. Where the effective cost is more than the current market price of £1.50. Where the effective cost is more than the current market price it would not be beneficial to convert and so the debentures should be retained.

A summary of the characteristics of shares and loan stock is given in Figure 26.1. A more detailed summary of the different types of preference shares and loan stock is shown in Figure 26.2.

The issue of shares and debentures

Shares can be, and usually are, issued (sold) by the company at a price in excess of their nominal value. The amount by which the issue price exceeds the nominal value is referred to as a *share premium*. In the case of a public limited company whose shares are listed on the stock exchange, the price at which the shares are quoted is usually different from both the nominal value and the issue price. The market price may be either above or below the issue price and the nominal value.

Debentures can be issued by the company at a price that is either greater or less than their nominal value. The latter is referred to as a debenture discount.

Types of preference shares
(1) Non-cumulative—do not receive arrears of dividends
(2) Cumulative—if the dividend on these shares is not paid in any year the holders are entitled to it in the next year that there is sufficient profit before any other shareholder receives a dividend.
(3) Redeemable—the only type of preference share that is repaid by the company after the expiration of a period specified when they were issued
(4) Participating—in addition to receiving a fixed annual rate of dividend they are also entitled to a further dividend which is in the nature of a dividend on ordinary shares

Advantages: (a) non-repayable (except (3) above); (b) the annual cost/dividend is known thus facilitating planning; (c) in extreme circumstances the annual dividend can be waived.

Disadvantages: the dividends are not deductable for tax purposes.

Types of loan stock/debentures
(1) Unsecured/naked—in the event of the company going into liquidation these are repaid before the share-holders, but after other creditors.
(2) With a fixed charge—secured on assets that the company cannot dispose of without the trustee for the debenture holders permission. In the event of the security being in jeopardy, or the company not paying the annual interest, the trustee can take legal possession of the asset(s), sell them and repay the debenture holders.
(3) With a floating charge—the same as debentures with a fixed charge except that the asset(s) on which the debentures are secured can be sold by the company but must be replaced with asset(s) of an equivalent value.
(4) Convertible loan stock—carry the right, at the holders option, to convert them into ordinary shares within a given time period fixed when they are issued. The rate of conversion is usually such that the holder obtain ordinary shares at a price which is lower than the market price of the shares at the date of conversion.

Advantages: (a) the annual cost/interest is known; (b) the interest is deductible for tax purposes.

Disadvantages: (a) they have to be repaid after the expiration of the period specified when they were issued; (b) the interest must be paid before the shareholders receive any dividend. This can be a burden when the proceeds of the issue have been used to finance expansion that may not result in revenue during the early years, or where there is a reduction in the annual profit or high interest rates.

Figure 26.2 A summary of the types of preference shares and loan stock.

When shares and debentures are issued the price may be payable by instalments. These consist of amounts payable: (a) on application; (b) on allotment/allocation of the shares by the company; and (c) any number of further instalments, referred to as calls.

Public limited companies offer shares, loan stock and debentures for sale to members of the public by means of a document known as a *prospectus*. This usually takes the form of a booklet sent by the company to anyone who expresses an interest in the issue. It may also consist of a full page advertisement in a national newspaper, such as the *Financial Times*. The contents of a prospectus include: (a) the total number of shares the company wishes to issue and the minimum subscription (i.e. the smallest number for which the applicant can apply); (b) the price of each share, stating the amounts payable on application, allotment and any calls; (c) details of the rights attaching to all classes of shares; and (d) a report by the company's auditors on the profits and dividends of the last five years, and the assets and liabilities at the end of the previous accounting year.

Interim and final dividends

Most large companies pay both interim and final dividends on their ordinary shares. An interim dividend is paid halfway through the year, when the profit for the first six months is known. The amount is decided by the directors. The final dividend is additional to the interim dividend and, although it relates to the same accounting year, is paid just after the end of the year. This is because the final dividend has to be approved by the ordinary shareholders at the annual general meeting (AGM), and this is always held after the end of the accounting year when the profit for the year is known. Thus the final dividend is always outstanding at the end of the year, and referred to as a proposed final ordinary dividend.

Dividends on preference shares and interest on loan stock and debentures are also often paid in two instalments, one halfway through the year and the other at the end of the year. However, the amount relating to the last half of the year may be outstanding at the end of the accounting year.

The books of account and published accounts

Companies are required by law to keep proper books of account, and each year to prepare a set of published accounts (i.e. a profit and loss account and balance sheet) which conform with the books of account. The 'books' of account need not necessarily actually be in the form of books, but there must be some set of records of the business transactions (e.g. a computerized system). A copy of the annual final accounts must be sent to each ordinary shareholder and the Registrar of Companies. The latter are available for inspection by the general public at Companies House.

The auditors' report

Limited companies are required by law to have their books and annual final accounts audited by an independent qualified accountant. The accounts covered by the audit consist of the profit and loss account and balance sheet.

Although paid by the company, the auditors act on behalf of the ordinary shareholders and are appointed by them at the annual general meeting (AGM). The auditors' function is to ascertain, or rather form an opinion of, whether or not the *accounts give a true and fair view of the stae of affairs and the profit of the company and have been properly prepared in accordance with the Companies Act*. Their opinion is given in the auditors' report, which is attached to the final accounts, and uses wording similar to that in italics in the last sentence. If the accounts are considered not to give a true and fair view or do not comply with the Companies Acts in some other way, the nature of the departure is usually stated in the auditors' report. This is referred to as a 'qualified' audit report.

It is important to appreciate that the auditor does not guarantee that no fraud or errors have taken place. In the UK, shareholders and loan creditors would be unlikely to expect damages from the auditors if a company subsequently went into liquidation or discrepancies were discovered, unless the auditors are shown to have been negligent. Furthermore, the auditors' report is not intended to be interpreted as passing an opinion on how efficiently and effectively the directors have used the company's assets.

Statutory books

Companies are obliged by law to maintain certain records relating to their capital and directors. These are known as statutory books and consist of the following:

1. Register of Members, containing the name, address and number of shares held by each shareholder.
2. Register of Debenture Holders, containing the name, address and number of debentures/ loan stock held by each debenture holder.
3. Register of Directors and Company Secretary, stating the name, address and occupation of each.
4. Register of Directors' Shareholdings, showing the number of shares held by each director.
5. Register of Mortgages and Other Charges secured on the company's assets, showing the name and address of the lender and the amount of each loan.
6. Minute Book of General Meetings of the company's ordinary shareholders, containing details of the proceedings and resolutions.
7. Minute Book of Directors' Meetings, containing details of the resolutions.

Companies are also required by law to submit to the Registrar of Companies each year an annual return, showing changes in the entries in the statutory books during that year. This information is available for inspection by the general public at Companies House. The statutory books (except the Minutes of Directors' Meetings) are also required by law to be available for inspection by members of the public at the company's registered office.

The annual general meeting

The law demands that companies hold an annual general meeting (AGM). This is a meeting of the ordinary/equity shareholders at which they are entitled to vote on a number of matters. These include the following:

1. To receive and adopt the report of the directors and the published accounts for the year. This provides shareholders with an opportunity to question the directors on the contents of the accounts. The accounts are usually adopted, but if shareholders think that the accounts are inaccurate or misleading they may vote not to accept the accounts. If the shareholders vote not to adopt the accounts this does not mean that another set has to be prepared.
2. To declare and adopt a proposed final dividend for the year on the ordinary shares. The amount of the final dividend is proposed by the directors. The shareholders cannot propose some other figure. Thus if the shareholders vote not to adopt the proposed dividend they will get no final dividend for that year.
3. To elect directors. This is a source of shareholders' power, in that if they are dissatisfied with the accounts, the dividend, or the company's performance they may vote not to re-elect the existing directors. Shareholders also have the right to nominate other people as directors.
4. To appoint auditors and fix their remuneration. The directors normally suggest a specific firm of auditors, and the power to fix their remuneration is often delegated to the directors by the shareholders at the AGM. Large companies usually appoint a reputable national or international firm of accountants to act as auditors.

Exercises

1. Describe the characteristics of companies limited by shares.

2. How does a public limited company differ from a private limited company?

3. Describe the contents of the Memorandum and Articles of Association. What are the purposes of these documents?

4. What are preliminary expenses?

5. Explain the main differences between ordinary shares, preference shares and debentures/loan stock.

6. Explain how each of the following arises:

    (a)   a share premium;
    (b)   a debenture discount.

7. Outline the main contents of a prospectus.

8. What is the difference between an interim dividend and a final dividend?

9. What is an auditors' report? How useful do you think this is in its present form and with its current legal standing in the UK?

10. Describe the contents of the statutory books. What is the purpose of each of these books?

11. What is the annual general meeting of a company? Describe the proceedings at such a meeting.

27. The preparation of the final accounts of limited companies

The Companies Act requires companies to send their ordinary shareholders a copy of the annual final accounts. These are referred to as the annual report (or published accounts) and include a profit and loss account and balance sheet. There are detailed legal requirements relating to the content and format of annual final accounts. These are beyond the scope of this book, which is confined to the preparation of company final accounts prior to putting them in a form suitable for publication.

As in the case of sole traders and partnerships, it is now common practice for companies to prepare final accounts in vertical form. Furthermore, it is usual to combine the trading and profit and loss accounts into a single profit and loss account. The entries are the same as where there are two accounts.

The differences between the final accounts of companies and those of sole traders are explained below.

The profit and loss account

The contents of the profit and loss account of companies are the same as that for sole traders and partnerships, with the following exceptions:

1. In arriving at the net profit, certain items not found in the accounts of sole traders and partnerships must be included. These consist of share transfer fees received, directors' emoluments/remuneration (e.g. fees, salaries, pensions, compensation for loss of office etc.), auditors' fees and expenses, interest on debentures, and preliminary/formation/promotion expenses. The latter refers to the costs incurred in forming a company, such as registration fees, preparation of the Memorandum and Articles of Association etc. They must not be retained in the accounts as an asset.

2. After the net profit has been computed, various appropriations are made in a section of the profit and loss account, sometimes referred to as the profit and loss appropriation account. These occur in the following order:

   (a) *Corporation tax.* Since a company is a separate legal entity, it is liable for the taxation on its annual profit, which is referred to as corporation tax. This is a debit entry in the profit and loss appropriation account with a corresponding credit to an account in the name of the Inland Revenue. The latter is a sundry creditor which is shown on the balance sheet as a current liability because the law dictates that corporation tax is payable nine months after the end of the accounting year to which it relates. Where the profit and loss appropriation account is prepared in vertical form the corporation tax is deducted from the net profit to give a subtotal referred to as the net profit after taxation.

(b) *Preference share dividends*. Where the profit and loss appropriation account is prepared in vertical form, these are deducted from the net profit after tax. This is because they are an appropriation of the profit after tax and not a charge against income (like debenture interest). The preference dividends comprise any interim dividend paid plus the final dividend. The interim dividend paid will have been debited to the preference share dividends account in the ledger and thus shown in the trial balance. The final dividend may be outstanding at the end of the accounting year, in which case it is necessary to create an accrual in the preference dividends account and to show the amount owing on the balance sheet as a current liability. The total of the interim and final dividends are then debited to the profit and loss appropriation account with a corresponding credit in the preference share dividends account.

(c) *Ordinary share dividends*. These are entered in the profit and loss appropriation account after the preference dividends because the latter have a prior claim against profits. The ordinary dividends comprise any interim dividend paid plus the proposed final dividend. The interim dividend paid will have been debited to the ordinary share dividends account and thus shown in the trial balance. The proposed final dividend will always be outstanding at the end of the accounting year and thus it is necessary to create an accrual in the ordinary share dividends account and show the amount owing on the balance sheet as a current liability. The total of the interim and proposed final dividends are then debited to the profit and loss appropriation account and credited to the ordinary share dividends account.

(d) *Transfer to reserves*. The profit remaining after deducting dividends is the undistributed or retained profit for the year and is carried down as a credit balance on the profit and loss appropriation account. Note that it is not transferred to the capital account, as in the case of sole traders and partnerships. However, sometimes companies transfer a part of their undistributed profit to a reserve account. The reason for this is to indicate to shareholders that the directors do not intend to distribute it as dividends but rather to earmark it for some other use, such as expansion of the business by purchasing additional fixed assets. The entry for a transfer to a reserve is to debit the profit and loss appropriation account and credit the reserve account. There is a difference of opinion in the literature regarding whether the debit entry in the profit and loss appropriation account should appear before or after the preference and ordinary dividends. However, since transfers to reserves are no longer common, the issue is really only academic. Reserves are discussed further below.

The balance sheet

The contents of the balance sheet of companies is the same as that of sole traders and partnerships with the following exceptions:

1. The current liabilities of companies also usually include corporation tax on the annual profit, accrued debenture interest, and the outstanding final dividends on preference and ordinary shares.

2. The long-term liabilities of companies also often include the nominal value of loan stock and debentures.

3. The capital and profits of a company are shown separately under two headings comprising the nominal value of the share capital and the reserves. The share capital may take a number of forms. As explained in the previous chapter, when shares are issued the price may be payable by instalments. Thus at the end of any given accounting year the proceeds of sale may be at a number of possible stages of collection. Each of these is given a particular label in the balance sheet of companies as follows:

   (a) *Authorized/nominal share capital.* This refers to the types, nominal value and maximum number of shares that the company is permitted by its Memorandum of Association to issue.

   (b) *Allotted share capital.* This refers to the total nominal value of the number of shares that have actually issued at the date of the balance sheet.

   (c) *Called-up share capital.* This refers to that part of the allotted share capital which the company has required the shareholders to pay. It will consist of the amounts payable on application and allotment plus any calls that have been made by the company up to the date of the balance sheet.

   (d) *Paid-up share capital.* This refers to that part of the called-up share capital which the shareholders have actually paid. In principle the called-up and paid-up share capital should be the same. However, in practice a few shareholders default, resulting in non-payment of calls.

The figure for share capital that enters into the total of the balance sheet is the paid up ordinary and preference share capital. This is frequently the same as the allotted and called-up share capital. However, if these are different from the paid-up capital they must be shown as memorandum figures (i.e. not entering into the total of the balance sheet). The authorized capital must always be disclosed as a memorandum amount.

Reserves may be of two sorts, either distributable or non-distributable. These are also frequently referred to as revenue and capital reserves respectively. Distributable/revenue reserves are those which can be distributed to shareholders as dividends. These include general reserves and the balance on the *profit and loss account*, both of which consist of retained profits of the current and previous accounting years.

Non-distributable/capital reserves cannot be distributed as dividends. These may take a number of forms. The most common is the balance on a *share premium* account. This arises from shares having been issued at a price in excess of their nominal value. The excess is credited to a share premium account. Another common non-distributable reserve is a *revaluation reserve*. This arises if a fixed asset (usually land and buildings) is revalued and shown in the balance sheet at an amount which exceeds its historic cost. The excess is credited to a revaluation reserve account. A third form of non-distributable reserve is a *capital redemption reserve* (CRR). This is a statutory reserve, being identified in the Companies Acts. It arises when shares are redeemed or purchased back from shareholders. Attention is given to the CRR and share repurchase in the next chapter.

The total amount of reserves is added to the paid-up share capital and shown on the balance sheet as the 'shareholders' interests'.

An illustration of the final accounts of limited companies is given in Example 27.1.

Example 27.1

The following is the trial balance of XYZ Ltd at 31 March 19X9:

	£	£
Ordinary shares of £1 each, fully paid		100,000
5 per cent preference shares of £1 each, fully paid		20,000
8 per cent debentures		30,000
Share premium		9,500
Revaluation reserve		10,000
General reserve		2,000
Retained profit from previous years		976
Motor vehicles at revaluation	210,000	
Depreciation on vehicles		19,000
Stock	14,167	
Debtors/creditors	11,000	8,012
Provision for doubtful debts		324
Bank balance	9,731	
Purchases/sales	186,000	271,700
Wages and salaries	16,362	
General expenses	3,912	
Directors' remuneration	15,500	
Preliminary expenses	1,640	
Debenture interest	1,200	
Ordinary dividend (interim)	2,000	
	471,512	471,512

You are given the following information:

1. Stock at 31 March 19X9 is valued at £23,487.
2. Depreciation of motor vehicles is to be provided at the rate of 10 per cent per annum on the fixed instalment method.
3. The provision for doubtful debts is to be made equal to per cent of the debtors at 31 March 19X9.
4. Debenture interest of £1,200 and preference share dividends of £1,000 are outstanding at 31 March 19X9.
5. Provision is to be made for taxation on the year's profit amounting to £9,700.
6. There is a proposed final ordinary dividend of 5 pence per share.
7. The directors have decided to increase the general reserve by a further £3,000.
8. The authorized share capital consists of: (a) 200,000 ordinary shares of £1 each; and (b) 50,000 per cent preference shares of £1 each.

You are required to prepare in vertical form the profit and loss account for the year ended 31 March 19X9 and a balance sheet at that date.

Workings–for clarity, these are shown by presenting the relevant ledger accounts.

Provision for doubtful debts

Balance c/d	550	Balance b/d	324
(5 per cent × 11,000)		Profit and loss a/c	226
	550		550
		Balance b/d	550

Provision for depreciation

Balance c/d	40,000	Balance b/d	19,000
		Profit and loss a/c	21,000
	40,000		40,000
		Balance b/d	40,000

Debenture interest

Bank	1,200	Profit and loss a/c	2,400
Accrual c/d	1,200		
	2,400		2,400
		Accrual b/d	1,200

Preference dividend

Balance c/d	1,000	Profit and loss a/c	1,000
	1,000		1,000
		Balance b/d	1,000

Ordinary dividends

Bank	2,000	Profit and loss a/c	7,000
Balance c/d	5,000		
(100, 000 × 5 p)			
	7,000		7,000
		Balance b/d	5,000

Corporation tax

		Profit and loss a/c	9,700

General reserve

Balance c/d	5,000	Balance b/d	2,000
		Profit and loss a/c	3,000
	5,000		5,000
		Balance b/d	5,000

XYZ Ltd

Balance sheet as at 31 March 19X9

	£	£	£
Fixed assets			
Motor vehicles at revaluation			210,000
Less: Aggregate depreciation			40,000
			170,000
Current assets			
Stock		23,487	
Debtors	11,000		
Less: provision for doubtful debts	550	10,450	
Bank		9,731	
		43,668	
Less: Current liabilities			
Creditors	8,012		
Dividends (1000 + 5000)	6,000		
Corporation tax	9,700		
Debenture interest	1,200	24,912	
Net current assets			18,756
Total assets less current liabilities			188,756
Less: Long-term liabilities			
8 per cent debentures			30,000
Net assets			158,756
Authorized share capital			
200,000 ordinary shares of £1 each			200,000
50,000 5 per cent preference shares of £1 each			50,000
			250,000

	£	£
Allotted share capital		
100,000 ordinary shares of £1 each		100,000
20,000 5 per cent preference shares of £1 each		20,000
		120,000
Reserves		
Share premium	9,500	
Revaluation reserve	10,000	
General reserve	5,000	
Profit and loss account	14,256	
		38,756
Shareholders' interests		158,756

XYZ Ltd
Profit and loss account for the year ended 31 March 19X9

	£	£
Sales		271,000
Less: Cost of sales		
Stock at 1 April 19X8	14,167	
Add: Purchases	186,000	
	200,167	
Less: Stock at 31 March 19X9	23,487	
		176,680
Gross profit		95,020
Less: Expenditure		
Wages and salaries	16,362	
General expenses	3,912	
Provision for depreciation	21,000	
Provision for doubtful debts	226	
Directors' remuneration	15,500	
Preliminary expenses	1,640	
Debenture interest	2,400	
		61,040
Net profit before tax		33,980
Less: Corporation tax		9,700
Profit after tax		24,280
Less: Dividends–		
preference	1,000	
ordinary	7,000	
		8,000
Undistributed profit		16,280

Undistributed profit (from page 276)	16,280
Less: Transfer to general reserve	3,000
Retained profit for the year	13,280
Add: Retained profit of previous years	976
Retained profits at end of year	14,256

Notes

1. The workings for this example are shown in the form of ledger accounts to help students understand the double entry. In examinations it is usually sufficient to state the necessary additions and subtractions.
2. The amount of the proposed final dividend on ordinary shares is computed by multiplying the dividend per share by the number of shares that have been issued/allotted as shown in the trial balance (i.e. 5p × 100,000 = £5,000). Sometimes the dividend per share is expressed as a percentage. In this case the percentage is applied to the nominal value of the issued/allotted ordinary share capital (e.g. 5 per cent × £100,000 = £5,000).
3. It is important to ensure that the amounts entered in the profit and loss account in respect of debenture interest and preference share dividends are the amounts paid plus any which is outstanding at the end of the year. Sometimes in examination questions students are not told how much is outstanding or even that anything is outstanding. In these circumstances the total amount to be entered in the profit and loss account is ascertained using the information given in the question relating to the rates of debenture interest and preference dividends as follows:

    8 per cent debentures £30,000
    ∴ Annual interest = 8 per cent preference shares £2,400
    5 per cent preference shares £20,000
    ∴ Annual dividend = 5 per cent × 20,000 = £1,000

    The amounts to be entered as current liabilities in the balance sheet can then be found by subtracting the amounts paid as shown in the trial balance as follows:

    Debenture interest outstanding = 2,400 − 1,200 = £1,200
    Preference dividends outstanding = 1,000 − 0 = £1,000

4. It is generally accepted practice to prepare the final accounts of companies in vertical form. However, the profit and loss account (and appropriation account) must also be prepared in the ledger by transferring all the balances on the income and expense accounts to this account in the normal manner. Unlike the profit and loss accounts of sole traders and partnerships, the profit and loss account of companies will always contain a balance brought down from the previous year. The retained profit of the current year is added to this balance and the resulting figure is carried forward to the next year. It should also be remembered that journal entries are supposed to be made for all the above entries in the ledger.

5. As explained earlier in this chapter, the law allows revenue reserves such as the general reserve and the balance on the profit and loss account at the end of the previous year to be distributed to shareholders as dividends. This is not common in practice or in examination questions because it is undesirable for economic/commercial reasons. However, a description of the accounting entries may help students to appreciate the nature of reserves. When a dividend is to be distributed from revenue reserves, this will be apparent from the profit and loss appropriation account because the profit after tax will be lower than the amount of the dividends for that year. In this case the retained profit of the previous year (i.e. the balance on the profit and loss account at the end of the previous year) should be added to the profit after tax and before dividends instead of being entered at the bottom of the profit and loss appropriation account. If the profit after tax plus retained profit of the previous year is still less than the dividends, a transfer back from the general reserve must be made of an amount necessary to cover the dividened. The double entry for this transfer is to debit the general reserve and credit the profit and loss appropriation account. In the vertical format this will be an addition to the profit after tax and before dividends.

6. As explained earlier in this chapter, preliminary expenses must not be retained in the accounts as an asset. There are two possible ways of dealing with these. One is to charge them to the profit and loss account as in the above example. However, this reduces the profit, which most companies wish to avoid if possible. The alternative, and preferred treatment, is to charge preliminary expenses against the balance on the share premium account, the double entry being to credit the preliminary expenses account and debit the share premium account. The amount entered on the balance sheet in respect of the share premium account will then be the difference between the balance shown in the trial balance and the preliminary expenses, that is, the balance on the share premium account after entering the preliminary expenses.

Exercises

1. Explain the difference between the authorized share capital, allotted share capital, called up share capital and paid up share capital of companies.

2. Explain the difference between distributable reserves and non-distributable reserves, giving two examples of the latter.

3. Explain the difference between a reserve and a provision.

4. Set out below is the capital section of a company's balance sheet.

	31 March 19X8	31 March 19X7
	£'000	£'000
Ordinary share capital	140,000	140,000
Preference share capital	–	30,000
Share premium	20,000	20,000
Capital redemption reserve	30,000	–
Revaluation reserve	9,700	7,200
General reserve	27,000	20,000
Profit and loss account	84,900	70,300
	311,600	287,500

You are required to explain the five different reserves that are shown on this company's balance sheet, including in your answer the possible reasons for their existence.

(JMB)

5. (a) The following terms usually appear in the final accounts of a limited company:
        (i)   interim dividend,
        (ii) authorized capital,
        (iii) general reserve,
        (iv) share premium account.
        Required:
        An explanation of the meaning of each of the above terms.
    (b) The following information has been obtained from the books of Drayfuss Ltd:

Authorized capital	100,000 8 per cent £1 preference shares
	400,000 50p ordinary shares
Profit and loss account balance	
1 April 19X8 Cr	£355,000
General reserve	£105,000
Issued capital	80,000 8 per cent £1 preference shares
	(fully paid)
	250,000 50p ordinary shares
	(fully paid)
Net trading profit for the year	
to 31 March 19X9	£95,000

The preference share interim dividend of 4 per cent had been paid and the final dividend of 4 per cent had been proposed by the directors.

No ordinary share interim dividend had been declared, but the directors proposed a final dividend of 15p per share.

The directors agreed to transfer to general reserve £150,000.

Required:

The profit and loss appropriation account for the year ended 31 March 19X9. Ignore taxation. (AEB)

6. The trial balance of Northfield Ltd at 31 December 19X9 appeared as follows:

	£	£
Ordinary shares of £1–fully paid		50,000
Purchases	220,000	
Retained profit		30,000
Freehold property–cost	80,000	
Fixtures–cost	15,000	
Fixtures–accumulated depreciation		9,000
Rates	3,000	
Motor vehicles–cost	28,000	
Motor vehicles–accumulated depreciation		14,000
Insurance	2,000	
Stock	40,000	
Debtors	30,000	
Trade creditors		24,000
Sales		310,000
Bank	12,100	
12 per cent debentures		40,000
Debenture interest	2,400	
Wages and salaries	34,000	
Heat and light	4,100	
Professional fees	3,900	
General expenses	1,200	
Motor expenses	2,000	
Provision for bad debts		1,000
Bad debts	300	
	478,000	478,000

Additional information:

1. During the year a motor vehicle purchased on 31 March 19X6 for £8,000 was sold for £3,000. The sale proceeds were debited to the bank account and credited to the sales account, and no other entries have been made in the accounts relating to this transaction.
2. Depreciation has not yet been provided for the year. The following rates are applied on the straight line basis, with an assumption of no residual value:
   Fixtures and fittings   10 per cent
   Motor vehicles   20 per cent
   The company's policy is to provide a full year's depreciation in the year of acquisition and no depreciation in the year of disposal.
3. Stock at 31 December 19X9 amounted to £45,000.
4. Rates paid in advance amount to £400. Insurance includes £200 paid in advance. An electricity bill covering the quarter to 31 December 19X9 and amounting to £320 was not received until February 19X0. It is estimated that the audit fee for 19X9 will be £1,500. An accrual also needs to be made in relation to debenture interest.
5. A general provision for bad debt of 4 per cent is to be carried forward.
6. The directors propose a dividend of £10,000.

You are required to:

(a) prepare a profit and loss account and balance sheet on the basis of the above information.
(b) explain the meaning of the terms 'provision' and 'reverse', giving *one* example of *each* from the balance sheet you have prepared.   (JMB adapted)

7. The trial balance of Queue plc at 31 December 19X8, before any of the items noted below, is as follows:

	Dr £	Cr £
Issued share capital (£1 ordinary shares)		30,000
Freehold properties–at cost	40,000	
Motor vehicles		
–at cost	10,000	
–depreciation to 31 December 19X7		4,000
Expenses	11,000	
Stock at 31 December 19X7	12,000	
Purchases	70,000	
Sales		100,000
Debentures (10 per cent)		15,000
Debenture interest	750	
Bank overdraft		1,000
Bank interest	250	
Debtors and creditors	25,000	15,000
Dividend paid	1,500	
Profit and loss balance 31 December 19X7		5,500
	170,500	170,500

The following notes are to be incorporated as appropriate:

1. Closing stock is £10,000.
2. The debentures were issued on 1 April 19X8.
3. The bank statement received does not agree with the cash book as at 31 December 19X8 because of the following differences:

   (a) cheque in cash book not on bank statement £600;
   (b) standing order included on bank statement but not in cash book £200;
   (c) credit transfer from a debtor, on bank statement but not in cash book £500.

4. All the motor vehicles were purchased in 19X6. Depreciation has been, and is still to be, provided at the rate of 25 per cent per year on cost. On 31 December 19X8 one vehicle, purchased on 1 January 19X6 for £4,500, was sold for £2,750. This sale was accepted in part settlement of the price of £4,000 for a new van. No entries have been made in the books with regard to these transactions, and no money has been paid or received.
5. The corporation tax liability for the year to 31 December 19X8 is estimated at £5,000.
6. A final dividend of 6p per share on the existing shares is proposed.
7. By agreement, 10,000 new £1 ordinary shares are issued at 125p per share and the proceeds transferred immediately to the company bank account.

Required:
Prepare final accounts in good order for internal use. Show necessary workings clearly.   (CACA)

8. The following is the trial balance of D. Cooper Ltd as at 30 September 19X9:

	£	£
Authorized and allotted share capital–		
100,000 ordinary shares of £1 each		100,000
50,000 7 per cent preference shares of 50p each		25,000
Leasehold premises at valuation	140,000	
Goodwill	20,000	
Plant and machinery (cost £80,000)	66,900	
Loose tools (cost £13,000)	9,100	
Stock	9,400	
Debtors/creditors	11,200	8,300
Bank overdraft		7,800
Purchases/sales	49,700	135,250
Directors' salaries	22,000	
Rates	4,650	
Light and heat	3,830	
Plant hire	6,600	
Interest on debentures	1,200	
Preliminary expenses	1,270	
10 per cent debentures		24,000
Provision for bad debts		910
Share premium		25,000
Profit and loss account		2,580
Revenue reserve		10,200
Interim dividend on ordinary shares	3,250	
Audit fees	1,750	
Revaluation reserve		9,860
Bad debts	700	
Listed investments	8,000	
Investment income		650
	359,550	359,550

The following additional information is available:

1. Stock at 30 September 19X9 is valued at £13,480.
2. Rates include a payment of £2,300 for the six months from 1 July 19X9.
3. Depreciation on plant is 15 per cent per annum of cost and the loose tools were valued at £7,800 on 30 September 19X9.
4. The provision for bad debts is to be adjusted to 10 per cent of the debtors at the end of the year.
5. The preference share dividends are outstanding at the end of the year and the last half year's interest on the debentures has not been paid.
6. The corporation tax on this year's profits is £6,370.
7. The directors propose to declare a final dividend on the ordinary shares of 13 pence per share and transfer £2,500 to the revenue reserve.

You are required to prepare in vertical form a profit and loss account for the year ended 30 September 19X9 and a balance sheet at that date.

9. The following is the trial balance of L. Johnson Ltd at 31 December 19X8.

	£	£
Authorized capital–		
200,000 ordinary shares of £1 each		200,000
90,000 5 per cent preference shares of £1 each		90,000
Issued capital–		
80,000 ordinary shares		80,000
50,000 5 per cent preference shares		50,000
Freehold buildings (at cost)	137,000	
Motor vehicle (cost £35,000)	20,400	
Plant and machinery (cost £40,000)	32,950	
Development costs (cost £10,000)	6,600	
Interim dividend on preference shares	1,250	
Provision for bad debts		860
Wages and salaries	5,948	
Bad debts	656	
Discount allowed/received	492	280
Goodwill	10,000	
Listed investments	4,873	
Purchases/sales	78,493	130,846
Capital redemption reserve fund		10,000
Capital reserve		12,500
Formation expenses	250	
Directors' emoluments	13,000	
Returns inwards/outwards	1,629	1,834
Rates	596	
Dividends received		300
Profit and loss account		3,126
Share transfer fees received		126
Light and heat	1,028	
Audit fee	764	
Revenue reserve		8,400
Share premium		5,600
10 per cent debentures		30,000
Stock	9,436	
Debtors/creditors	11,600	8,450
Bank overdraft		3,643
	345,965	345,965

You are given the following additional information:

1. Corporation tax of £2,544 will be payable on the profits of 19X8.
2. Rates include £200 for the half year ended on 31 March 19X9.
3. Electricity for the quarter to 31 Jaunary 19X9 of £330 is not included in the trial balance.
4. The provision for bad debts is to be adjusted to 5 per cent of the debtors at the end of the year.
5. Annual depreciation on the reducing balance method is 20 per cent of plant, 25 per cent of vehicles and 10 per cent of development costs.
6. Formation expenses are to be written off against the share premium account.
7. Stock at 31 December 19X8 was £12,456.
8. It is proposed to pay a final dividend on the ordinary shares of 6.25 pence per share.
9. The directors have decided to transfer £4,000 to the revenue reserve this year.
10. The debenture interest for the year and the final dividend on the preference shares are outstanding at the end of the year.

You are required to prepare in vertical form a profit and loss account for the year ended 31 December 19X8 and a balance sheet at that date.

10. The following is the trial balance of Oakwood Limited as at 30 June 19X5:

	Debit £	Credit £
Authorized capital:		
150,000 ordinary shares of £1 each		150,000
70,000 5 per cent preference shares of £1 each		70,000
Allotted capital:		
125,000 ordinary		125,000
60,000 5 per cent preference shares		60,000
Freehold buildings at cost	165,000	
Development costs (cost £12,000)	5,400	
Goodwill	8,000	
Delivery vehicles (cost £28,000)	18,700	
Plant and machinery (£34,000)	31,900	
Listed investments	3,250	
10 per cent debentures		20,000
Share premium		9,000
Revenue reserve		6,100
Interim dividend on ordinary shares	2,000	
Interim dividend on preference shares	1,500	
Provision for bad debts		730
Administrative salaries	6,370	
Bad debts	740	
Discount allowed/received	290	310
Purchases/sales	81,230	120,640
Audit fee	390	
Preliminary expenses	200	
Directors' remuneration	14,100	
Returns inwards/outwards	230	640
Carriage inwards	310	
Rates	600	
Interest received		400
Profit and loss account		7,700
Share transfer fees received		140
Light and heat	940	
Postage and telephone	870	
Stock	8,760	
Debtors/creditors	10,400	7,890
Bank overdraft		2,630
	361,180	361,180

Additional information:

1. Corporation tax of £1,080 will be payable on the profit of this year.
2. Rates include a prepayment of £150.
3. Gas used in May and June 19X5 of £270 is not included in the trial balance.
4. Stock at 30 June 19X5 was £11,680.
5. The provision for bad debts is to be adjusted to 5 per cent of debtors at 30 June 19X5.
6. Annual depreciation on the reducing balance method is 20 per cent of plant, 10 per cent of vehicles, 25 per cent of development costs.
7. Sales includes goods on sale or return at the 30 June 19X5 which cost £500 and were invoiced to debtors at a price of £1,000.
8. Included in plant and machinery are consumable tools purchased during the year at a cost of £300.
9. The preliminary expenses are to be written off against the share premium account balance.
10. It is proposed to pay a final dividend on the ordinary shares of 3.2 pence per share.
11. The directors have decided to transfer £3,000 to the revenue reserve.

You are required to prepare in vertical form a profit and loss account for the year ended 30 June 19X5.

11.   The Cirrus Company Ltd has the following balances on its books at 31 December 19X0.

	£	£
50p ordinary shares		20,000
£1 6 per cent preference shares		14,000
Purchases	240,000	
Sales		310,000
Stock at 1 January 19X0	20,000	
Directors' fees	6,000	
Undistributed profit at 1 January 19X0		35,700
10 per cent debentures		20,000
Debentures interest paid	1,000	
Discounts allowed	500	
Administrative expenses	18,400	
Sales staff salaries	18,500	
Selling and distribution expenses	4,000	
Heating and lighting	2,500	
Rent and rates	1,700	
Debtors	14,000	
Provision for doubtful debts at 1 January		300
Creditors		9,700
Land and buildings at cost	65,000	
Vans at cost less depreciation	19,800	
Cash in hand	400	
Bank balance		2,100
	£411,800	£411,800

The following information is also given:

1.   The stock at 31 December 19X0 has been valued at £32,000. Further investigation reveals that this includes some items originally purchased for £3,000 which have been in stock for a long time. They need modifications, probably costing about £600, after which it is hoped they will be saleable for between £3,200 and £3,500. Other items, included in the total at their cost price of £5,000, have been sent to an agent and are still at his premises awaiting sale. It cost £200 for transport and insurance to get them to the agent's premises and this amount is included in the selling and distribution expenses.

2.   The balance on the vans account (£19,800) is made up as follows:

	£
Vans at cost (as at 1 January 19X0)	30,000
Less: Provision for depreciation to	
1 January 19X0	13,800
	16,200
Additions during 19X0 at cost	3,600
	£19,800

Depreciation is provided at 25 per cent per annum on the diminishing balance method. The addition during the year was invoiced as follows:

	£
Recommended retail price	3,000
Signwriting on van	450
Undersealing	62
Petrol	16
Number plates	12
Licence (to 31 December 19X0)	60
	3,600

3. The directors, having sought the advice of an independent valuer, wish to revalue the land and buildings at £80,000.
4. The directors wish to make a provision for doubtful debts of 2½ per cent of the balance of debtors at 31 December 19X0.
5. Rates prepaid at 31 December 19X0 amounted to £400, and salesmen's salaries owing at that date were £443.
6. The directors have proposed an ordinary dividend of 5p per share and the 6 per cent preference dividend.
7. Ignore VAT.

Required:
(a) Explain carefully the reasons for the adjustments you have made in respect of items 1, 2 and 3 above.
(b) Prepare a trading and profit and loss account for the year ended 31 December 19X0, and a balance sheet as at that date.
(c) Briefly distinguish between your treatment of debenture interest and proposed dividends.

(CACA)

28. Changes in share capital

A feature distinguishing companies from other forms of business organization is the use of equity finance through the issue of shares. Chapter 26 drew attention to the characteristics of company capital. In this chapter we shall focus on the special accounting procedures which are used to record expansion in the number of shares through issues, and reductions through redemptions.

Share issues to the public

Often share issues involve very large sums of money and, given that a series of actions needs to be taken, are complex matters. Since, in addition, this money is being paid in by members of the public, great care must be taken in the procedures which record the various actions.

It may be useful, before considering the accounting procedures themselves, to review the whole process it must record. A number of methods may be used to issue shares to the public, but the accounting procedures are similar and, for these can be presented most appropriately by considering an Offer for Sale.

First an offer is made to the public to apply for shares. At this time the price to be paid for the share is set. This price may be the same as the par value, or nominal value, of the share. However, under the Companies Acts shares may not be issued at below their par value. Thus a £1 share may be issued at £1 or any price above £1, say £3. The additional amount included in the price is the share premium, which must be recorded as one of the special capital reserves as considered in the previous chapter.

It is usual for applicants to be required to send money representing part but not all of the price of the shares for which they apply. Once the closing date for applications is reached the number of shares applied for must be compared with the number on offer. If applications are lower than the number on offer, the issue is undersubscribed and the company will either be required to cancel the offer and refund the application money or to call upon the underwriters to take up the remaining shares. If the issue is oversubscribed, then a basis for allotting shared must be established. Some applications may be rejected and the application money must be refunded; some may get a reduced allocation and their application money used as further payment towards the price of the shares.

Having established the basis for allocation, shares can then be issued to those who are to get them—an action known as allotment. The balance of the price is, typically, payable in instalments, perhaps some on allotment (and known as 'allotment money') and some at a later date (known as 'call money'). There may be more than one instalment, so there would be a first call, second call, etc. Anyone failing to pay on call is liable to forfeit their partly paid shares and once forfeited, these may be reissued to others on terms agreed for this purpose.

The major stages may be summarized:

	STAGE				
	Application	Allotment	Calls	Forfeit	Reissue
Cash effects on company	Application money received	(*shares issued*) Some application money refunded	Call money received	—	Reissue money received

The double entry to reflect the stages can now be explained.

	Transaction	Debit	Credit
1. Application	money received	cash	application and allotment account
2. Allotment	refund application money	application and allotment account	cash
	allotment money received	cash	application and allotment account
	issue of shares partly paid	application and allotment account	share capital
	any share premium included	application and allotment account	share premium

Note that any share premium is immediately identified and amounts are transferred to this special reserve

3. Call	call made	call account	share capital

Shareholders become due to pay and share capital is immediately increased

4. Forfeit	forfeited shares are identified as called	share capital	forfeited shares account
	premium included in called up value (if any)	share premium	forfeited shares account
	balance on the call account relating to arrears on forfeit shares	forfeited shares account	call account

Forfeited shares are removed from other shares and the arrears are excluded from the capital they represent so that the call account can be closed

| 5. Reissue | paid up value of shares reissued | reissues (forfeited shares reissued) account | share capital |

Share capital is reinstated; forfeited shares reissued account is used as a temporary account to coordinate the entries

	money received	cash	reissues account
	amount in forfeit shares account relating to reissues	forfeit shares account	reissues account
	balance on reissues account	reissues account	share premium

Any excess of total payments for the reissued shares from both original and subsequent issues is a share premium

An example can be used to show how these entries will be reflected in the various ledgers.

Example 28.1

The issued share capital of Stag plc was £100M being 100M ordinary shares of £1 each fully paid with no share premium account. Since the company wished to expand but had a bank balance of only £1M it decided to issue more shares. On 2 January 19X1 the company offered 40M shares to the public at £1.25 each, payable 40p on application, 30p on allotment and 55p on call at 30 June 19X1.

Applications closed on 31 January when applications had been received for 65M shares. On 4 February, 15M were rejected and money returned and allotments were made pro rata to the remaining applicants.

Note that since 50M share applications were not rejected, allotments were on the basis of four shares 50p paid for every five shares applied for each with 40p application money; a balance of only 20p per share will be payable on allotment.

The amounts due on allotment were received in full by 28 February.

By 4 July, call money for 32M shares had been received. The remaining shares (8M) were forfeited.

On 18 July 4M forfeited shares were reissued at 75p each. Ignore any other transactions that may have occurred.

For the initial issue, shares are to be issued at a premium of £1.25 less £1 equals 25p per share.

The entries to record the new application and allotment will appear in the relevant ledgers as shown below (all amounts shown in £M).

Bank

2/1	b/fwd	1	4/2	Appln. and Allotment	6
31/1	Appln. and Allotment	26			
28/2	Appln. and Allotment	8		c/fwd	29
		35			35
	b/fwd	29			

Application and allotment

4/2	cash (refund 15M @ £0.4)	6	31/1	cash (65M @ £0.4)	26
4/2	share capital	18	28/2	cash (40M @ £0.2)	8
4/2	share premium (40M @ £0.25)	10			
		34			34

Share capital

			2/1	b/fwd	100
			4/2	Appln. and Allotment	18
				c/fwd	118

Share premium

			4/2	Appln. and Allotment	10
				c/fwd	10

The call and forfeiture can then be entered in the ledgers

Bank

b/fwd	29	
call	17.6	
c/fwd	46.6	

Share capital

4/7	Forfeited shares	8		b/fwd	118
	c/fwd	132	30/6	Call	22
		140			140
				b/fwd	132

Share premium

4/7	Forfeited shares	2		b/fwd	10
	c/fwd	8			
		10			10
				b/fwd	8

Call

30/6	Share capital (40M @ 55p)	22	4/7	Cash (32M @ 55p)	17.6
			4/7	Forfeited shares	4.4
		22			22

Forfeited shares

4/7	Call		4.4	4/7	Share capital	
	c/fwd		5.6		(8M @ £1.00)	8
					Share premium	2
			10			10
					b/fwd	5.6
					(being 8M @ £0.70)	

Finally the amounts can be entered for the reissue of 4M shares.

Bank

	b/fwd	46.6	
18/7	Reissues		
	(4M @ £0.75)	3	
	c/fwd	49.6	

Share capital

		b/fwd	132
	18/7	Reissues	4
		c/fwd	136

Share premium

		b/fwd	8
	18/7	Reissues	1.8
		c/fwd	9.8

Forfeit shares

18/7	Reissues			b/fwd	5.6
	(4M @ 70p)	2.8			
	c/fwd	2.8			
		5.6			5.6
				b/fwd	2.8

Reissues

18/7	Share capital		18/7	Cash	3
	(4M @ £1)	4	18/7	Forfeit shares	2.8
	Share premium	1.8			
		5.8			5.8

The balances can be interpreted. The share capital represents the original shares plus 36M shares issued at £1 par value. The forfeited shares account balance of £2.8M is the remaining 4M shares not reissued at the 70p application and allotment amounts; the share premium is £9M premium at 25p on the 36M shares issued plus the additional premium of £800,000 on the reissue—in the case of the 4M reissued shares, 75p rather than just the call money of 55p was raised, giving 4M × 20p = £800,000.

Bonus issues

By contrast with issues to the public, the accounting for bonus issues is relatively straight-forward. No cash is involved and the issue represents 'converting' capital or revenue reserves into shares and distributing these to existing shareholders. While some reserves may have a range of uses, shares are regarded as a particularly permanent form of capital. The effect of making a bonus issue is to adjust the capital structure portrayed in accounts. The increased permanence of capital this presents may be taken as an indicator of increased security. The double entry may make use of a temporary bonus account so that credit amounts can be transferred from reserves to the bonus account and from these to share capital on the issue of the shares. For example, the capital structure of XS plc at 1 May 19X1 may be:

	£000
Share capital 2M ordinary shares of £1 each	2,000
General reserves	1,800
Share premium	3,000
Sundry net assets	6,800

It may be decided to make a bonus issue of two bonus shares for every existing share (this is a very large bonus in relation to the current number of shares, but serves to illustrate the change clearly). Since general reserves represent revenue reserves, while share premium is a capital reserve for which the law permits only limited uses, it will probably be more attractive to the company to utilize the share premium first. The double entry will be

	£	£
Dr Share premium	3,000,000	
General reserves	1,000,000	
Cr Bonus account		4,000,000

and then

	£	£
Dr Bonus account	4,000,000	
Cr Share capital		4,000,000

so that the balance sheet would indicate a revised capital structure as:

	£000
Share capital 6M shares of £1	6,000
General reserves	800
Sundry net assets	6,800

The same shareholders own the same assets but their ownership is represented by more shares. In theory, they should be in just the same position as before the issue.

Rights issues

These have some features of both of the above types of issue. Issuing to the public in response to an offer of shares is an expensive and potentially risky process. Costs can be saved by offering shares to existing shareholders at below the current market price. The shareholders are being offered this special price and failure to take up their rights to the issue would mean that they had given up these benefits. As a result, all shareholders can be expected either to take up the issue (providing it is priced sufficiently below the existing market price) or to sell their rights to someone who will. The success of the issue is much less risky.

If the full subscription price is payable upon issue, the entries are simple. Recognition must be given to any premium included in the price. Thus, for a company with 15 million shares of £1 which decides to make a 1 for 5 rights issue at a price of £1.80 (when the market price is £2.50 say) the entries must reflect the 80p per share premium.

	£	£
Dr Cash 3M × £1.80	5,400,000	
Cr Share capital		3,000,000
Share premium		1,400,000

Purchase and redemption of shares

By contrast to issuing new shares, we now turn to accounting for buying them back. The law identifies two types of buying back shares, purchase and redemption. Apart from the words that are used to describe the transactions and the change of name in account headings, the accounting procedures are identical for both types. The difference arises from the time the shares are originally issued. Some shares are issued as 'redeemable shares'. This may be on specific terms during a specifically defined period or merely at the discretion of the company or even the shareholder. Purchase takes place when shares which are not identified as 'redeemable' are purchased by the company.

In both cases, important legal restrictions are applicable. Some of these restrictions are to ensure the company cannot buy all its shares, so that it would have no shareholders. Companies may only issue redeemable shares provided it has, in issue, some shares that are not redeemable. After any purchase of shares a company must have in issue shares such that at least two shareholders remain owning shares that are not redeemable. Only fully paid shares may be redeemed or purchased and all shares bought back by the company must be cancelled so they are not available for resale. The law does not restrict the classes of shares which may be redeemed, although most examples have tended to deal with preference shares. The illustrations tend to show redemption of preference shares, but purchase or redemption of ordinary shares could equally well be used.

A particular concern embodied in the law is to maintain the paid-in capital. This is intended as a protection for creditors. While shareholders may be entitled, under the Companies Acts, to receive payments from distributable profits, paid-in capital cannot be freely distributed. If a company is wound up, creditors must be paid before shareholders get any capital repayment. The preferred position of the creditors would have been severely undermined if any earlier capital repayments had been made. The law restricts companies from using borrowing to make payments to shareholders beyond any profits made, since this may leave nothing for the creditors. The idea of maintenance of capital, introduced in accounting as a basis for measurement (see Chapter 2), is being utilized here, in restricting dividends to distributable profits, as a legal principle.

The legal considerations relating to the nominal value of shares are separated from those dealing with premiums, so initially this section will address redemption (or purchase) at nominal values first and then introduce the treatment of premiums.

Redemption (or purchase) at nominal value

The legal requirements for maintenance of capital when a redemption is made can be achieved by:

1. Setting aside distributable profits equal to the nominal value of capital redeemed by transferring that amount to a non-distributable reserve known as 'capital redemption reserve'. To enable this to be carried out, there must have been distributable profits sufficient to redeem the capital repaid and the transfer 'freezes' those profits in a capital form.
2. Issuing new shares explicitly for the purpose of providing funds for the redemption with nominal value not less than that of the shares redeemed. This effectively replaces the capital redeemed by new capital.
3. A combination of new issues and transfers to capital redemption reserve which, in total, amount to the nominal value of capital redeemed.

Examples will illustrate how these are applied.

The following is the summarized balance sheet of J plc as at 30 June 19X1.

	£000
Sundry assets	280
Cash	160
	440
Preference share capital (issued at par)	80
Ordinary share capital	200
Share premium	20
Unappropriated profit and loss	140
	440

If the company decided to redeem all the preference capital at par (i.e. the nominal value) without any new issue of shares, then the double entry would be:

	£	£
Dr Preference share capital	80,000	
Cr Cash		80,000

to reflect the repayment, and

	£	£
Dr Unappropriated profit and loss	80,000	
Cr Capital redemption reserve		80,000

to transfer distributable profits to the capital redemption reserve to maintain paid in capital.

The maintenance of capital can be readily identified:

	Before £000		After £000
Preference share capital	80	Capital redemption reserve	80
Ordinary share capital	200		200
Share premium	20		20
Non-distributable capital	300		300

Suppose the company had only £60,000 cash and £380,000 sundry assets. It might wish to raise money to contribute to the redemption through the issue of shares. If a rights issue of £50,000 ordinary shares was made, at par, as part of the scheme of redemption the entries would be

	£	£
Dr Cash	50,000	
Cr Ordinary share capital		50,000
Dr Preference share capital	80,000	
Cr Cash		80,000
Dr Unappropriated profit and loss	30,000	
Cr Capital redemption reserve		£30,000

The amount transferred is the excess of the shares redeemed over the nominal value of the capital issued.

Again the maintenance of non-distributable capital can be demonstated:

	Before £000		After £000
Preference share capital	80	Capital redemption reserve	30
Ordinary share capital	200		250
Share premium	20		20
	300		300

Redemption (or purchase) at a premium

Shares will often be bought back at a price above the nominal value, the excess representing a premium. Unless the shares were originally issued at a premium, the premium paid must be transferred from distributable profits. Even where the shares were originally issued at a premium, there are limitations on the extent by which the transfer may be reduced. The amount is restricted to the smaller of:

1. the premium on the original issue of the shares;
2. the sum of the balance on the share premium account plus the premium on the new issue used to fund (in part) the redemption.

Consider the following illustration, extracted from the balance sheet of K plc as at 31 December 19X0.

	£
Isued share capital	
100,000 ordinary A shares of £1 each fully paid	100,000
20,000 ordinary B shares of £1 each fully paid	20,000
Share premium on ordinary shares	3,000
Revenue reserves	50,000
	173,000

The ordinary B shares were originally issued at a premium of 25 per cent. The company purchased the 20,000 B shares for £29,000, issuing £12,000 A shares at £1.40 to contribute to the funding of the purchase. The relevant entries would be:

Dr B shares	20,000	
Dr Redemption premium	9,000	
Cr Cash		29,000

to record the redemption,

Dr Cash	16,800	
Cr Ordinary A shares		12,000
Cr Share premium		4,800

to record the new issue,

Dr Revenue reserves	8,000	
Cr Capital redemption reserve		8,000

to record the transfer in respect of the nominal value of the shares redeemed in excess of the nominal value of the new shares issued, and

Dr Share premium	5,000	
Cr Redemption premium		5,000

which is the maximum amount that can be set against the share premium, being the lower of:

(i)   the original premium on the issue, i.e. 25 per cent of £20,000 = £5,000, and
(ii) the sum of the balance on share premium account   £3,000
      and the premium on the new issue   4,800   7,800

Finally:

Dr Revenue reserves	4,000	
Cr Redemption premium		4,000

This transfers the balance of the redemption premium. These entries produce the following change:

	After
A shares	112,000
Share premium	2,800
Capital redemption reserves	8,000
	122,800
Revenue reserves	38,000
	160,800

The next example brings together many of the matters considered in this chapter.

The following items are extracted from the balance sheet of Weaver (Ropes) plc at 31 December 19X1:

	£
Issued share capital	
250,000 ordinary shares of £1 each fully paid	250,000
75,000 6 per cent redeemable preference shares	75,000
Share premium	5,000
Revenue reserves	70,000
	400,000

The preference shares were originally issued at a premium of 12 per cent.

On 1 January 19X4 the company resolved:

1. to issue 50,000 ordinary shares of £1 each at a premium of 10 per cent, payable 40 per cent on application and the balance on allotment; the issue is to be made to finance in part the redemption of preference shares;
2. to redeem the preference shares at a premium of 20 per cent; and
3. to make a bonus issue of one ordinary share for £1 each for every five ordinary shares.

These actions were duly taken by the company consecutively in the order shown. Applications were received for 54,000 ordinary shares, the application monies for 4,000 shares being returned.

You are required to present the relevant ledger accounts to record the above transactions and to show how the items appear in Weaver's balance sheet after the transactions have been carried out.

The ledger accounts would appear as below (all figures in £s).

Ordinary shares

	brought forward	250,000
	Application and allotment	50,000
	CRR	25,000
	Revenue reserves	35,000
		360,000

Preference shares

Redemption	75,000	brought forward	75,000

Share premium

Premium on redemption	10,000	brought forward	5,000
		Application and allotment	5,000

Revenue reserves

Premium on redemption	5,000	brought forward	70,000
CRR	25,000		
Ordinary shares	35,000		
c/fwd	5,000		
	70,000		70,000
		brought forward	5,000

Application and allotment

Cash	1,760	Cash	23,760
Ordinary shares	50,000	Cash	23,760
Share premium	5,000		
	56,760		56,760

Capital redemption reserve

Share	25,000	Revenue reserves	25,000

Premium on redemption

Redemption	15,000	Share premium	10,000
		Revenue reserves	5,000

Redemption account

Cash	90,000	Preference shares	75,000
		Premium on redemption	15,000
			90,000
	90,000		

The maximum amount that can be set off against the share premium is the lower of 14 per cent of £75,000 = £10,500 and £5,000 balance brought forward plus £5,000 on the new issue, i.e. £10,000.

Balance sheet extract	£
Issued ordinary shares	360,000
Revenue reserves	5,000
	365,000

Exercises

1. The summarized balance sheet for Turner plc at 1 May 19X7 showed:

	£
Authorized capital	1,000,000
Issued share capital:	
800,000 shares of 50p each fully paid	400,000
Revenue reserves	350,000
Sundry assets	750,000

On 1 June 19X7, 200,000 shares were offered to the public at 60p, 20p payable on application, 20p on allotment and 20p on call at 31 December 19X7.

Applications were received for 300,000 shares. Those relating to 50,000 shares were returned, the balance of the excess application money being retained to reduce amounts due on allotment. All shares allotted were taken up, but call money on 10,000 shares remained unpaid at 31 January 1988. These shares were forfeited and reissued as fully paid at 40p per share on 1 February 1988.

On 29 February 1988, Turner plc made a 1 for 4 bonus issue.

You are required to show the ledger accounts to record the above transactions, minimizing any reduction in revenue reserves.

2. At 31 July 19X2, the balance sheet of Winder Engineering plc showed the following position:

	£
Issued share capital:	
80,000 10 per cent redeemable cumulative preference	
shares of £1 each issued at par	80,000
200,000 ordinary £1 shares	200,000
Share premium	20,000
Unappropriated profit and loss	140,000
	440,000
Sundry assets	380,000
Cash	60,000
	440,000

The preference shares are redeemable at a premium of 5 per cent at any time during 19X2 and the company decided it would redeem the preference shares as follows:

1 August: 40,000 preference shares redeemed for cash.
1 September: 25,000 ordinary £1 shares be offered for sale at £1.20 per share, 70p on application, the balance on allotment, the issue being made to provide some of the funds for redeeming the remaining preference shares.
15 September: Application lists closed, applications for 30,000 shares having been received. Applications for 5,000 shares were unsuccessful and the cash received in respect of these applications was returned.
20 September: The balance due on allotment was received in full.
29 September: The remaining 40,000 preference shares were redeemed.

Required:
(a) Prepare the necessary journal entries to record the above transactions:
(b) Prepare a balance sheet at 30 September 19X2 which incorporates these changes. (Assume that no other transactions take place between 1 August and 30 September 19X2.)

3. Stafford plc has an issued share capital of 2 million redeemable preference shares of £1 each and 14 million ordinary shares of 50p. The preference shares which were issued at a premium of 10 per cent are redeemable at 7.5 per cent premium on 1 May 19X4.
   On 30 April 19X4, the company's balance sheet was as presented below:

Share capital	£
Preference shares	2,000,000
Ordinary shares	7,000,000
Profit and loss	1,330,000
Sundry creditors	1,720,000
	12,050,000
Sundry assets	10,375,000
Investments	775,000
Balance at bank	900,000
	12,050,000

In order to carry out the redemption of the preference shares, the following were carried out:

1. The investments were sold realizing £695,000.
2. Company funds were utilized such that a balance of £330,000 was left on the profit and loss account.
3. Ordinary shares were issued at a premium of 25 per cent to raise the balance of the funds required.

The preference shares were redeemed on the due date, and the issue of ordinary shares was fully subscribed. You are required to:

(a) prepare the journal entries required to record the above transactions;
(b) present the resulting balance sheet.

29. The appraisal of company accounts using ratios

The main function of published company final accounts is to provide information that will enable shareholders and loan creditors to evaluate the performance and financial position of a company. However, the absolute amount of profit, or assets and liabilities, shown in the accounts is not usually a particularly meaningful criterion for evaluating the performance or financial position of a business.

For example, if Company A has a profit of £200,000 and Company B has a profit of £1 million, one cannot conclude that B is more profitable than A. Company B may have used net assets of £10 million to generate this profit whereas Company A may have only used net assets of £0.5 million. Thus A is said to be more profitable than B because the profit is 40 per cent of the value of its net assets compared with only 10 per cent in the case of B. Similarly, if Company B had a profit of £900,000 last year, one cannot conclude that it is more profitable this year. The value of the net assets last year may only have been £8 million, which gives a return of 11.25 per cent.

Indeed the terms 'profitability' and 'return' are taken as referring to the relationship between the profit and the value of the net assets/capital used to generate that profit. Thus in order to evaluate a company's performance and financial position over time, or in relation to other companies, it is necessary to compute various accounting ratios. These are primarily intended for the use of external groups of users such as shareholders, loan and trade creditors etc., whose only source of accounting information is that contained in published accounts.

It is important to appreciate at the outset that accounting ratios have a number of limitations. One of these stems from the aggregate nature of information in published accounts. Companies are not required to disclose all the items which enter into the computation of profit or values of assets and liabilities in the balance sheet. As a result the information needed to compute some ratios may not be available. This necessitates the use of surrogate data in the calculation of some ratios. Furthermore, comparisons of ratios over time and between companies can be misleading when economic conditions change and/or where the companies concerned are operating in substantially different industries. Ratios must therefore always be interpreted in the light of the prevailing economic climate and the particular circumstances of the company or companies concerned. The limitations of ratio analysis will be discussed in the context of each ratio and are summarized at the end of the chapter.

There are a large number of ratios that can be calculated from the information contained in published accounts. These ratios may be grouped under four main headings, each heading reflecting what the ratios are intended to measure: (1) measures of return on investment and risk; (2) measures of a company's performance; (3) measures of solvency and liquidity; and (4) measures of the control of working capital. The most common ratios in each of these four classes are described on the following pages and illustrated using the information in Example 29.1.

Example 29.1

The following is an extract from the published accounts of A. Harry plc, for the year ending 31 January 19X8.

Profit and loss account	£'000
Turnover	5,280
Cost of sales	(3,090)
Gross profit	2,190
Distribution costs	(560)
Administrative expenses	(230)
Interest payable on loan stock	(400)
Profit on ordinary activities before taxation	1,000
Corporation tax	(250)
Profit on ordinary activities after taxation	750
Proposed dividend on ordinary shares	(300)
Retained profit for the year	450

Balance sheet	£'000	£'000
Fixed assets at cost		9,470
Aggregate depreciation		(2,860)
		6,610
Current assets		
Stocks	850	
Trade debtors	1,070	
Bank and cash	1,130	
	3,050	
Amounts falling due within one year		
Trade creditors	1,030	
Proposed dividends	300	
Advance corporation tax	100	
Corporation tax	250	
	1,680	
Net current assets		1,370
Total assets less current liabilities		7,980
Amounts falling due after more than one year:		
10 per cent loan stock of £100 each		(4,000)
Net assets		3,980
Capital and reserves		
Allotted share capital: 2,000,000 ordinary shares of £1 each		2,000
Profit and loss account		1,980
Shareholders' interest		3,980

Further information: the ordinary shares and loan stock are currently quoted on the International Stock Exchange, London, at £4 and £90 respectively. Assume the basic rate of income tax to be 25 per cent.

Measures of return on investment and risk

This group of ratios is primarily intended for the use of shareholders, although a company's management will probably monitor these ratios as a guide to how investors view the company. There are a number of investment ratios some of which are published in the *Financial Times*. These include the following

The dividend yield

This is calculated as:

$$\frac{\text{annual ordinary dividend (gross)} \times 100}{\text{current market value of the ordinary shares}}$$

The dividend yield is usually expressed in terms of the gross yield, that is, before deduction of income tax. The dividends shown in companies' profit and loss accounts exclude income tax. Thus to arrive at the gross dividend before deduction of income tax it is necessary to add the income tax to the dividend shown in the accounts. However, since this is not given, another method of arriving at the gross dividend is used, as follows:

$$\text{Dividend shown in profit and loss account} \times \frac{100}{100 - \text{Basic rate of income tax}}$$

For Example 29.1 this will give:

$$£300,000 \times \frac{100}{100 - 25} = £400,000$$

The income tax is therefore £400,000 − £300,000 = £100,000 (or 25 per cent × £400,000). This is often shown as a current liability in the balance sheet which is referred to as advance corporation tax.

The dividend yield can now be computed as follows:

$$\frac{£400,000}{2,000,000 \times £4} \times 100 = 5 \text{ per cent}$$

The same principle can be used to calculate the interest yield on debentures and loan stock.

The dividend yield is said to measure the ordinary shareholders' annual return on investment, and may be compared with what could be obtained by investing in some other company. However, such comparisons can be misleading for two main reasons. Firstly, companies have different risk characteristics. A comparison of the dividend yields of, for example, a steel company and a utility company would be misleading because the former is a riskier investment than the latter. Secondly, companies have different dividend policies, in that some distribute a greater proportion of their annual profit than others. Put slightly differently, the annual dividend is only part of an investor's total return, in that the investor will also expect to make a capital gain in the form of an increase in the market price of shares. This partly results from companies retaining a proportion of their annual profits. The dividend yield is often about 5 per cent, but varies between companies for the reason outlined above.

Some investors regard the dividend yield as important because they are primarily interested in maximizing their annual income (e.g. retired persons). However, for other investors the dividend yield may only be of limited importance because they are more interested in capital gains (e.g. for tax reasons).

Dividend cover

This is calculated as:

$$\frac{\text{profit after corporation tax and preference dividends}}{\text{annual ordinary dividends (gross)}}$$

For Example 29.1 this will give:

$$\frac{£750,000}{£400,000} = 1.875$$

The profit after corporation tax and preference dividends is used in the calculation of this ratio because it represents the profit available for distribution as dividends to ordinary shareholders.

The dividend cover indicates how likely it is that the company will be able to maintain future dividends on ordinary shares at their current level if profits were to fall in future years. It is thus a measure of risk. The amount by which the dividend cover exceeds unity represents what might be called the margin of safety. Thus a company with a high dividend cover would be more likely to be able to maintain the current level of ordinary dividends than a company with a low dividend cover. The average dividend cover for companies whose shares are listed on the International Stock Exchange, London, is about 2 but clearly this depends on a company's dividend policy.

Earnings per share (EPS)

This is calculated as:

$$\frac{\text{profit after corporation tax and preference dividends}}{\text{number of ordinary shares in issue}}$$

For Example 29.1 this will give:

$$\frac{£750,000}{2,000,000} = £0.375$$

The profit after corporation tax and preference dividends is used in the calculation of this ratio because it represents the profit available for distribution as dividends to ordinary shareholders.

This is referred to as the earnings. There are complex rules for acertaining the number of ordinary shares but these are beyond the scope of this book. The rules are applied where the issued share capital has changed during the year, because, for example, there has been an issue of shares during the year. The calculation involves determining an average number of shares for the year.[1]

EPS is not strictly a measure of return on investment. However, as will be discussed below, it is included in the calculation of another widely used accounting ratio. Furthermore, EPS is generally regarded as an important consideration in investment decisions; it was the subject of one of the first accounting standards (SSAP3) which requires that it be disclosed in published profit and loss accounts for all listed and USM companies. As explained earlier, the absolute amount of profit (in this context, available for distribution as dividends) is not usually a satisfactory measure of performance because it ignores the amount of net asset/capital which has been used to generate that profit. However, EPS takes this into consideration in the form of the number of ordinary shares and thus provides a useful means of evaluating performance (where performance is defined from the shareholders' point of view as relating to the profit available for distribution as dividends). The trend in EPS over time indicates growth or otherwise in the profit attributable to each ordinary share. Inter-firm comparisons of EPS are not advisable.

The price–earnings (P–E) ratio

This is calculated as

$$\frac{\text{current market price of each ordinary share}}{\text{earnings per share}}$$

For example 29.1 this will give:

$$\frac{£4}{£0.375} = 10.67$$

The P–E ratio varies considerably between different industries and companies in the same industry. Many authors shy away from explaining the P–E ratio because its meaning is somewhat ambiguous, despite the fact that this is probably the mostly widely cited accounting ratio. The P–E ratio is a reflection of risk in that it represents the number of years' earnings that investors are prepared to buy at their current level. This is probably better explained in terms of what is essentially a payback period. The P–E ratio shows the number of years it will take to recoup the current price of the shares at the present level of EPS (the share price being recouped in the form of dividends and retained profits). Where an investment is risky, investors will want to get their money back relatively quickly, whereas if an investment is comparatively safe a longer payback period will be acceptable. Thus companies in risky industries such as mining and construction tend to have a low P–E ratio, whereas companies in relatively safe industries such as food retailing and utilities, and those which are diversified, tend to have a high P–E ratio.

The P–E ratio also varies between companies in the same industry.

If investors think that a company's earnings are going to decline, the P–E ratio will tend to be lower than the average for the industry. Conversely if profits are expected to rise, the P–E ratio will tend to be higher (both of which occur because of decreases and increases in the share price respectively). The P–E ratio is therefore also a reflection of the expected earnings growth potential of a company. This means that sometimes industries which one would expect to have a high P–E ratio, since they are relatively safe, in fact have a low P–E ratio because the earnings are expected to decline (e.g. the banking industry in the early 1990s).

It appears that the P–E ratio is sometimes also used in practice to identify shares which are over- or under-priced. A share is said to be over-priced if its P–E ratio is higher than the norm for the industry or other similar companies, and under-priced if the P–E ratio is lower than the norm for the industry or other similar companies. However, as explained above, this is probably an over-simplification because the intrinsic/real value of a share will depend on the expected future earnings of the particular company.

Another way of looking at the P–E ratio is to invert the formula and express the result as a percentage. This is referred to as *the earnings yield*. For Example 29.1 this will give:

$$\frac{£0.375}{£4} \text{ or } \frac{£750,000}{2M \text{ @ } £4} \times 100 = 9.375 \text{ per cent}$$

The earnings yield is not really a yield in the same sense as the dividend yield, since not all of the earnings are distributed as dividends. However, it is often referred to as a measure of return on investment. As in the case of EPS, the earnings yield is a useful means of evaluating performance (where performance is defined from the shareholders' point of view as relating to the profit available for distribution as dividends). The trend in the earnings yield over time indicates how efficiently and effectively a company has utilized the amount of money the shareholders have invested in the company in terms of the current share price. It can also be used to compare the performance of different companies.

The return on equity/shareholders' interests

This is calculated as:

$$\frac{\text{profit after corporation tax and preference dividends} \times 100}{\text{shareholders' interests (excluding preference shares)}}$$

For Example 29.1 this will give:

$$\frac{£750,000}{£3,980,000} \times 100 = 18.8 \text{ per cent}$$

The return on equity is essentially the same as the earnings yield. The difference is that, instead of expressing the earnings as a percentage of the market price/value of the ordinary shares, this is expressed as a percentage of the book value of the ordinary shares in the form of the shareholders' interests. Since the latter is not the 'real' (i.e. market) value of the shareholders' investment this ratio can be said to be inferior to the earnings yield.

However, the return on equity, like the earnings yield, is a common measure of return on investment which is used to evaluate profitability (where profitability is defined from the shareholders' point of view as relating to the profit available for distribution as dividends). It is said to indicate how efficiently and effectively a company's management has utilized the shareholder's funds/interests. The ratio may be used to compare the profitability of different companies and/or to examine trends over time.

The gearing ratio

Gearing, or leverage as it is called in the USA, refers to the relationship between the amount of fixed interest capital (i.e. loan stock, debentures, preference shares etc.) and the amount of equity capital (i.e. ordinary shares). In discussions of gearing the fixed interest capital is frequently referred to as the debt capital, which is taken to include preference shares. As a broad generalization, where the value of fixed interest capital is less than the value of equity, a company is said to have low gearing. Where the value of debt capital is more than the value of equity, a company is said to have high gearing.

The gearing ratio may be expressed in a number of ways, as follows:

(a) *Using the nominal values* of the fixed interest capital and ordinary share capital thus:

$$\frac{\text{nominal value of debt capital} \times 100}{\text{nominal value of debt capital} + \text{nominal value of ordinary shares}}$$

The debt capital refers to the preference shares, loan stock, debentures, bank loans, mortgages and any other long-term borrowing, such as an overdraft for more than one year. An illustration of the calculation of the gearing ratio using this formula is given in Example 29.2. This also highlights the difference between low gearing and high gearing.

Example 29.2

	Company with low gearing	Company with high gearing
	£	£
Ordinary shares of £1 each	400,000	100,000
10 per cent preference shares of £1 each	30,000	150,000
10 per cent debentures of £100 each	70,000	250,000
	500,000	500,000
Gearing ratio	20 per cent or 1 : 4	80 per cent or 4 : 1

(b) *Including the reserves and retained profits as part of the equity capital thus*:

$$\frac{\text{nominal value of debt capital} \times 100}{\text{nominal value of debt capital} + (\text{nominal value of ordinary shares} + \text{reserves} + \text{retained profits})}$$

Returning to the data in Example 29.1 this would be calculated as follows:

$$\frac{\pounds 4,000,000 \times 100}{\pounds 4,000,000 + (\pounds 2,000,000 + \pounds 1,980,000)} = 50 \text{ per cent}$$

This method of expressing the gearing ratio is considered to be superior to the first because reserves and retained profits constitute part of the shareholders' interests and thus the capital which they provide. The logic behind this is perhaps more obvious when the gearing ratio is calculated in terms of the book value of the assets, thus:

$$\frac{\text{nominal value of debt capital} \times 100}{\text{total assets less current liabilities}} = \frac{\pounds 4,000,000}{\pounds 7,980,000} \times 100 = 50 \text{ per cent}$$

This formula highlights that the gearing ratio shows the proportion of the assets which are financed by fixed interest capital.

(c) *Using the current market prices* of a company's ordinary shares and debt capital, thus:

$$\frac{\text{market value of debt capital} \times 100}{\text{market value of debt capital} + \text{market value of ordinary share capital}}$$

Using the data in Example 29.1 this would be calculated as follows:

$$\frac{40{,}000 \text{ @ } \pounds90 \text{ (or } \pounds4M \times \pounds90/\pounds100) \times 100}{(40{,}000 \text{ @ } \pounds90) + (2{,}000{,}000 \text{ @ } \pounds4)} = 31 \text{ per cent}$$

This is generally regarded as being a more theoretically sound method of expressing the gearing ratio because market prices are said to represent the 'real' value of the debt capital and shareholders' interests as distinct from the nominal or book values.

There are a number of other ways of expressing gearing, which show the relationship between the annual amount of interest on debt capital and the profit for the year. However, these are not used very often.

The gearing ratio is a measure of the 'financial risk' attaching to a company's ordinary shares which arises because of the prior claim that fixed interest capital has on the annual income and assets (in the event of liquidation). This financial risk is additional to the 'operating risk' that is associated with the particular industry(ies) in which a company is trading.

Companies are said to engage in gearing because it usually produces substantial benefits for the ordinary shareholders. In crude terms the money provided by loan creditors is used to generate income in excess of the loan interest that the tax deductability of interest contributes to this benefit. In technical terms, gearing usually increases the profit available for distribution as dividends to ordinary shareholders and thus the earnings per share, (EPS), although it does have an impact on the riskiness of these earnings. These effects are illustrated numerically, as shown in Example 29.3. The data are taken from Example 29.2. These two companies are assumed to be identical in all respects except their gearing. Both have a profit after tax (but before interest) of £50,000 and an EPS of 10 pence in year 1. Although this example is clearly unrealistic, it illustrates the impact of gearing vividly. In the case of the company with low gearing, a 100 per cent increase in the profit after tax (but before interest) in year 2 results in a 125 per cent increase in the profit available for distribution as dividends to ordinary shareholders. By contrast, in the case of the highly geared company, a 100 per cent increase in the profit after tax in year 2 results in a 500 per cent increase in the distributable profit. Similarly, a 100 per cent increase in the profit after tax results in a 125 per cent increase in the EPS of the low-geared company, compared with a 500 per cent increase for the company with high gearing. This can be summarized in the form of a general rule as follows: any increase in profit (before charging interest) will result in a *proportionately greater* increase in the profit available for distribution (and the EPS) of a highly geared company compared with an equivalent increase for a company with low gearing.

Example 29.3

Year 1	Company with low gearing		Company with high gearing	
	£	£	£	£
Profit before interest		50,000		50,000
Preference dividends	3,000		15,000	
Interest	7,000	10,000	25,000	40,000
		40,000		10,000
Earnings per share		10p		10p

Year 2

Profit before interest		100,000		100,000
Preference dividends	3,000		15,000	
Interest	7,000	10,000	25,000	40,000
		90,000		60,000
Earnings per share		22.5p		60p

However, gearing is a double-edged sword, in that the same occurs in reverse when there is a decrease in profit. Imagine that the chronological sequence in Example 29.3 is reversed giving profit before interest £100,000 in Year 1 and 50,000 in Year 2 representing a 50 per cent decrease in the profit after tax (but before interest). This results in a reduction in the distributable profit and EPS of 56 per cent in the case of the low-geared company, compared with 83 per cent for the company with high gearing. This can also be summarized in the form of a general rule as follows: any decrease in the profit (before charging interest) will result in a proportionately greater reduction in the profit available for distribution (and the EPS) of a highly geared company compared with an equivalent decrease for a company with low gearing.

Furthermore, the level of gearing affects a company's break-even point. A company with high gearing will have a larger break-even point than an equivalent company with low gearing. This is because the interest charges of a highly geared company are greater than for an equivalent company with low gearing. In Example 29.3 the break-even point of the highly geared company is £30,000 (i.e. £40,000 − £10,000) higher than that of the low-geared company. This means that a company with high gearing has to earn a greater profit (before interest) before it can declare a dividend compared with an equivalent company that has low gearing. Thus if the profit after tax of these companies fell to, say £20,000, the company with low gearing would still be able to declare an ordinary dividend from the current year's trading profit whereas the highly geared company could not.

To sum up, the ordinary shareholders in a highly geared company benefit from gearing when profits are relatively large. However, they run two risks. Firstly, when profits are small the dividends will be less than would be the case with low gearing. Secondly, if the company goes into liquidation they will not be repaid the value of their shares until after all the fixed interest capital has been repaid. Usually very little or nothing is left for the ordinary shareholder. Thus the tendency to assume that gearing is advantageous may be a misconception because while it frequently results in a proportionately greater increase in the distributable profit it also makes the ordinary shares riskier. To use an analogy, one should not bet on an outsider in a horse race merely because the winnings would be greater than betting on the favourite. One must weigh up the possible return in relation to the perceived risk.

Measures of a company's performance

The main function of published company final accounts is to provide information that will enable shareholders and loan creditors to evaluate the performance and financial position of a company. Performance may relate to a number of things, such as productivity, energy conservation, pollution control, etc. From the ordinary shareholders' point of view, performance is usually equated with the profit available for distribution as dividends, or the earnings per share. However, the term 'performance' is normally associated with an entity view of business enterprises. This section therefore examines various measures of a company's performance from the point of view of it being an economic entity separate from the shareholders, and irrespective of the way in which its assets are financed (i.e. the proportion of debt to equity capital).

A number of accounting ratios are used to measure different aspects of performance. Many of these are derived from a single ratio known as the *return on capital employed*. This is ascertained as follows:

$$\frac{\text{profit before tax and interest on long term loans}}{\text{net capital employed}} \times 100$$

Net capital employed refers to the shareholders' interests + long term liabilities. Using the data in Example 29.1 this is calculated thus:

$$\frac{£1,000,000 + £400,000}{£3,980,000 + £4,000,000} \times 100 = 17.5 \text{ per cent}$$

The logic behind this ratio is perhaps more obvious when it is calculated as the return on assets as follows:

$$\frac{\text{profit before tax and interest on long term loans}}{\text{total assets less current liabilities}} \times 100$$

$$\frac{£1,000,000 + £400,000}{£7,980,000} \times 100 = 17.5 \text{ per cent}$$

Some authors advocate expressing the return on capital employed in terms of the gross capital employed. This refers to the shareholders interests + long term liabilities + current liabilities. A somewhat easier way of calculating this is fixed assets + current assets. Clearly the return on gross capital employed/total assets will be different from the return on net capital employed/total assets less current liabilities. The latter is more common in practice.

Whatever method is used there is a problem concerning the point in time at which the capital employed should be measured. In the above computation this was taken as being the end of the accounting year, for simplicity. However, this is not really justifiable because the capital employed includes the retained profit for the year and any additional capital raised during the year. The retained profit for the year was not available to generate the profit throughout this year, and it is unlikely that any capital raised during the year provided a significant contribution to the profit for the year. Given the time lags between capital expenditure and assets becoming productive, it may be more appropriate to use the capital employed at the start of the accounting year. Alternatively, if the additional capital is known to have generated profit during the year, the average capital employed for the year would be used. The same considerations apply to the return on equity discussed earlier. The return on capital employed is a measure of profitability that is used to indicate how efficiently and effectively a company has utilized its assets during a given accounting period. It is a common means of evaluating a company's profitability over time, and comparing the profitability of different companies.

However, the use of historical cost data in the calculation of this ratio can give a distorted view of the profitability for two reasons. Firstly, during times of rising prices the denominator in the formula comprises a mixture of assets acquired at various points in time when the prevailing level of prices were different. In times of rising prices, the denominator is understated by historical cost. Secondly, the numerator tends to be overstated, since the historical cost profit is calculated by matching current selling prices with historic costs. Thus the effect of historical cost accounting in both the denominator and the numerator is to inflate the return on capital.

The return on capital employed can be broken down into two further ratios as follows:

$$\text{Return on capital employed} = \frac{\text{profit}}{\text{turnover}} \times \frac{\text{turnover} \times 100}{\text{total assets less current liabilities}}$$

Using the data in Example 29.1 these are calculated thus:

$$\frac{\text{profit}}{\text{turnover}} \times 100 = \frac{£1,000,000 + £400,000}{£5,280,000} \times 100 = 26.5 \text{ per cent}$$

$$\frac{\text{turnover}}{\text{total assets less current liabilities}} = \frac{£5,280,000}{£7,980,000} = 0.66$$

The first of these two ratios is referred to as the profit margin. It is often described as a measure of profitability that shows what percentage of sales revenue is profit. Different products have different profit margins. Jewellery and greengrocery, for example, usually have a higher profit margin than electrical goods and clothing. Also, different sized businesses have different profit margins. Small shops, for example, have a higher profit margin than supermarkets. Interfirm comparisons of profit margins should therefore only be made between companies in the same industry and of a comparable size.

The Companies Act requires the disclosure of an analysis of profit and turnover for each class of business. It is therefore possible to calculate the profit margin for each class of business. These could be used in inter-firm comparisons of performance. However, this can be misleading because the profit margin constitutes an average for all the products comprising one particular class of business, and few firms sell exactly the same combination of products (i.e. product mix). Time series analysis of profit margins is likely to be more meaningful. Variations in the profit margin over time can be due to a number of factors relating to changes in the product mix, selling prices and costs.

The second of the above ratios is referred to as the asset turnover ratio. This shows the amount of sales revenue that has been generated per £ of capital employed. It is a measure of the level of activity and productivity. Different industries have different asset turnover ratios primarily because of differences in technology. Labour intensive industries usually have a high asset turnover ratio, whereas capital intensive industries tend to have a lower asset turnover ratio. Inter-firm comparisons of asset turnover ratios should therefore only be made between companies in the same industry. Time series analysis of asset turnover ratios is likely to be more meaningful. Changes in the asset turnover ratio over time can be due to a number of factors, such as producing at under capacity, labour inefficiency, overstocking etc.

There is an important relationship between the asset turnover ratio and the profit margin. In order to achieve a satisfactory return on capital employed, a company with a low asset turnover ratio (e.g. capital intensive) will need a high profit margin on its products. Conversely a company with a high asset turnover ratio (e.g. labour intensive) will only require a low profit margin on its products.

The profit margin and asset turnover ratio may be broken down into a number of other ratios in order to pinpoint more precisely the reasons for changes in performance over time.

These are as follows:

Profit margin:

$$\frac{\text{cost of sales}}{\text{turnover}} \times 100$$

$$\frac{\text{gross profit}}{\text{turnover}} \times 100$$

$$\frac{\text{distribution costs}}{\text{turnover}} \times 100$$

$$\frac{\text{administrative expenses}}{\text{turnover}} \times 100$$

Asset turnover ratio:

$$\frac{\text{turnover}}{\text{fixed assets}}$$

$$\frac{\text{turnover}}{\text{net current assets}}$$

The last ratio can be further subdivided into a number of other ratios relating to each constituent of net current assets. These are discussed in a later section on the appraisal of working capital.

Measures of solvency and liquidity

The main function of published accounts is to provide information that will enable shareholders and loan creditors to evaluate the performance and financial position of a company. The phrase 'financial position' is normally taken as including whether or not a company will be able to pay its debts as and when they become due. A business that is unable to do so is said to be insolvent, and will usually be forced into compulsory liquidation by its creditors. Sometimes profitable businesses face financial crisis, frequently because of overtrading. This broadly means that a company has invested too much in fixed assets and stock but too little in liquid assets and is thus short of cash.

Solvency does not mean that at any point in time a business must have enough money to pay its liabilities. These will fall due at various dates in the future. Solvency therefore refers to whether or not liabilities are covered by assets which will be realized as the liabilities fall due. Thus if the value of current assets is less than the amount of current liabilities a business may be insolvent.

However, even if current assets are equal to or greater than current liabilities this is no guarantee of solvency, since some current assets are less liquid than others. Liquidity refers to the ease with which an asset can be turned into cash without loss. Cash in hand and money in a bank current account are the most liquid types of asset, followed by listed investments, trade debtors and stock. Current assets are usually presented in published accounts in what is referred to as a reverse order of liquidity.

Two fairly crude but common ratios used to measure liquidity are as follows.

The working capital/current ratio

This is calculated thus:

$$\frac{\text{current assets}}{\text{current liabilities}}$$

Using the data in Example 29.1 this gives:

$$\frac{£3,050,000}{£1,680,000} = 1.8$$

This is a measure of the extent to which current liabilities are covered by current assets. As a generalization, the current ratio should be between 1.5 and 2 although this depends on the type of industry and the prevailing economic climate. A ratio of lower than 1.5 may indicate a poor liquidity position and thus future insolvency. At the other extreme a business can have too much working capital, which normally means that its assets are not being used as profitably as they otherwise might.

The working capital ratio has a serious limitation as a measure of liquidity, which is that some current assets are less liquid than others. In particular, stocks and work in progress are not easily realized without loss in the short term. A better criterion for measuring a company's ability to pay its debts as and when they become due is the liquidity ratio. In this ratio stocks and work in progress are excluded from current assets.

The liquidity/quick ratio or acid test

This is calculated thus:

$$\frac{\text{current assets} - \text{stocks and work in progress}}{\text{current liabilities}}$$

Using the data in Example 29.1 this gives:

$$\frac{£3,050,000 - £850,000}{£1,680,000} = 1.3$$

Bank overdrafts are frequently excluded from the current liabilities in the calculation of this ratio because, although an overdraft is usually legally repayable at short notice, in practice it is often effectively a long-term liability.

The liquidity ratio indicates whether a company is likely to be able to pay creditors, current taxation, dividends and other current liabilities from its cash at bank, the proceeds of sale of listed investments, and the amounts collected from debtors, that is, without having to raise additional capital or sell fixed assets. As a generalization, the liquidity ratio should therefore be at least one. However, this criterion cannot be applied to all types of businesses. Large retailing companies, for example, often have a liquidity ratio of less than one. They buy goods on credit, sell them for cash, and turn over their stock rapidly. This stock is a relatively liquid asset. It is therefore only necessary for the working capital ratio be at least one.

A poor liquidity position usually arises from continual losses, but can be the result of overtrading. At the other extreme a business can have too much liquidity. Where this is not temporary, the excess should be invested in fixed assets (assuming that there are profitable investment opportunities).

The working capital and liquidity ratios are, at best, crude conventional measures of liquidity. Most users of published accounts are interested in liquidity as an indicator of whether a company will be able to pay its debts, or alternatively if it is likely to go into liquidation in the near future. There is empirical research which demonstrates that the working capital and liquidity ratios are not particularly good predictors of insolvency. However, certain other ratios have been found to be useful in predicting corporate failure. The two most often cited studies of bankruptcy are by Altman[2] in the USA and Taffler[3] in the UK. They each identify a set of five accounting ratios which provide successful predictions of company failure. These are as follows:

Altman	*Taffler*
$$\frac{\text{profit before interest and tax}}{\text{total assets}}$$	$$\frac{\text{profit before interest and tax}}{\text{opening total assets}}$$
$$\frac{\text{working capital}}{\text{total assets}}$$	$$\frac{\text{working capital}}{\text{net worth}}$$
$$\frac{\text{sales}}{\text{total assets}}$$	$$\frac{\text{sales}}{\text{average stock}}$$
$$\frac{\text{retained earnings}}{\text{total assets}}$$	$$\frac{\text{quick assets}}{\text{total assets}}$$
$$\frac{\text{market value of equity}}{\text{book value of total debt}}$$	$$\frac{\text{total liabilities}}{\text{net capital employed}}$$

Both of these studies make use of a statistical technique known as multiple discriminant analysis. This involves taking several ratios together in a multiple regression model. The set of five ratios in Altman's model enabled him to correctly classify as bankrupt or non-bankrupt 95 per cent of the cases in a sample of failed and non-failed US companies. He further claims that these ratios can be used to predict bankruptcy up to two years prior to actual failure. Similarly, Taffler correctly classified all but one company in a sample of UK companies, and asserts that his model exhibits predictive ability for about three years prior to bankruptcy.

However, there are doubts about the validity of the results of studies such as these for a number of reasons. Firstly, the research is not based on a theory which explains why particular ratios should provide successful predictions of insolvency. Secondly, these studies make use of historical cost data, the deficiencies of which have already been explained. Finally, there are several problems involved in the use of statistical techniques such as discriminant analysis which make the results questionable.

The appraisal of working capital

The phrase 'working capital' has two slightly different meanings. In computational terms it relates to the amount of the net current assets. However, it is also used in a general sense to refer to the current assets and current liabilities. In this section the phrase 'working capital' is intended to be interpreted in the latter sense.

One way of looking at the appraisal of working capital is in terms of the interrelationship between a company's performance and liquidity position. As regards performance, the analysis of working capital is an extension of the asset turnover ratio (or more precisely the ratio of turnover to net current assets) which shows how effective a company's management have been in utilizing the various constituents of working capital. This in turn affects a company's liquidity position.

If there has been a significant change in the working capital and/or liquidity ratios one would want to try to pinpoint the cause(s). In crude terms, the appraisal of working capital reveals whether too much or too little is invested in, for example, debtors and stock relative to a company's level of activity (i.e. turnover). In theory there is an optimal level of working capital. However, in practice all that users of published accounts can do is to identify changes in the relative level of debtors and stock. These are taken as *prima facie* indicators of the effectiveness of credit control and stock control respectively.

There are a number of ratios that can be calculated relating to those items which make up the working capital. Each of these must be considered in the light of the particular circumstances of the company, the type of industry, and the prevailing economic climate. The most common ratios used in the appraisal of working capital are as follows.

The average period of credit taken by trade debtors

This is calculated thus:

$$\frac{\text{trade debtors}}{\text{turnover}} \times \text{the number of days in a year}$$

Using the data in Example 29.1 this gives:

$$\frac{£1,070,000}{£5,280,000} \times 365 = 74 \text{ days}$$

Instead of using the debtors at the end of the accounting year in the numerator some authors compute the average trade debtors as follows:

$$\frac{\left(\begin{array}{c}\text{debtors at the end of} \\ \text{the previous year}\end{array}\right) + \left(\begin{array}{c}\text{debtors at the end of} \\ \text{the current year}\end{array}\right)}{2}$$

The argument for using this method of computation is that it gives a more representative figure for the 'normal' level of debtors. However, the important point is that the ratio should be computed on a consistent basis, otherwise comparisons will be misleading. Another method of expressing this ratio is referred to as the debtors turnover ratio. It is calculated by inverting the fraction (and excluding the number of days in a year).

As the title above suggests, this ratio shows the average number of days credit taken by trade debtors. The most common terms of credit in the UK is that an invoice is due for payment by the end of the calendar month following the calendar month in which the goods are delivered/invoiced. The minimum average period of credit is thus approximately 45 days (i.e. $1\frac{1}{2}$ months). However, many debtors take a longer period than this if they can, since it is obviously beneficial for them to do so. An average period of credit of around 75 days (i.e. $2\frac{1}{2}$ months) is therefore not uncommon.

However, when this ratio is calculated from the information in published accounts it may be nothing like any of these figures. This occurs if a company has both cash and credit sales. Since trade debtors arise because of credit sales, the denominator in the ratio should obviously comprise only the credit sales. However, these are not disclosed separately in published accounts. Consequently, the aggregate of cash and credit sales has to be used in the computation, which results in a lower figure than if the denominator comprises only the credit sales. This is therefore clearly not the 'real' average period of credit, and a change in the proportion of cash to credit sales can distort the ratio over time.

The average period of credit taken by trade debtors varies between industries and according to the economic situation. Retailers, for example, usually grant little or no credit whereas wholesalers and manufacturers often allow a considerable period of credit. Comparisons should therefore really only be made between businesses in the same industry and for a particular company over time. Where the period of credit is high compared with other firms (or with the average for the industry), and/or increasing over time, this is normally taken as indicating inadequate credit control procedures.

The average period of credit received from trade creditors

The basic principle used in the calculation of the ratio for trade debtors can also be applied to trade creditors in order to ascertain the average period of credit taken by the reporting entity. This is calculated as follows:

$$\frac{\text{trade creditors}}{\text{purchases for the year}} \times 365$$

As in the case of debtors, the figure of trade creditors used in the computation of this ratio may be the average of those at the end of the previous year and the end of the current year. Another method of expressing this ratio is referred to as the creditors turnover ratio. It is calculated by inverting the fraction (and excluding the number of days in a year).

The amount of purchases is not normally disclosed in published accounts and thus a surrogate has to be used, such as the cost of sales. Alternatively if the company publishes a statement of value added, the figure for bought-in materials and services shown therein can be used as the denominator in this ratio.

Using the data in Example 29.1 this will give:

$$\frac{£1,030,000}{£3,090,000} \times 365 = 122 \text{ days}$$

It is obviously beneficial to delay paying creditors for as long as possible. However, this may adversely affect the company's credit rating, and creditors may refuse to supply further goods on credit. Also, where the period of credit is high compared with other firms (or with the average for the industry) and/or increasing over time, this may be an indication of financial weakness.

The stock turnover ratio

This is calculated thus:

$$\frac{\text{cost of sales}}{\text{stock of finished goods}}$$

Using the data in Example 29.1 this will give:

$$\frac{£3,090,000}{£850,000} = 3.64$$

As in the calculation of the average period of credit for debtors and creditors, there is an argument for using an average of the stock at the end of the previous year and the current year as the denominator in this ratio. Once again the important point is that a consistent basis of computation should be used to ensure meaningful comparisons. Another method of expressing this ratio is referred to as the number of days sales from stock. It is calculated by inverting the fraction and multiplying the answer by 365.

The stock turnover ratio shows the number of times that a business 'turns over'/sells its average/normal level of stock during the accounting year. In very simple terms, a greengrocer who goes to market once a week and sells all of these goods during that week would have a stock turnover ratio of 52 (because there are 52 weeks in a year). Stock turnover ratios vary between industries. Food retailers, for example, have a relatively high stock turnover ratio whereas jewellery retailers normally have a much lower ratio. Comparisons should therefore really only be made between firms in the same industry and for a particular company over time. Where the stock turnover ratio is low compared with other firms (or with the average for the industry), and/or decreasing over time, this is normally taken as indicating a lack of adequate stock control.

The limitations of ratio analysis

Example 29.1 was deliberately kept simple for the purpose of illustration. In particular, it contains no comparative figures for the previous year. Thus no time series analysis was possible. Also, in the calculation of some ratios (e.g. earnings per share, return on equity, return on capital employed) the amount at the end of the accounting year was used when it would have been more appropriate to take the figure at the beginning of the year or an average for the year. Companies are required by law to include comparative figures for the previous year in their published accounts. These would therefore usually be available and should be used where appropriate.

Ratio analysis has a number of limitations. Most of these have already been explained in the context of particular ratios but can be summarized as follows:

1. Comparisons between companies in the same industry and for a particular company over time may be misleading if different accounting policies are used to calculate profits and value assets.
2. Many ratios have to be calculated using historical cost data since few companies publish a current cost profit and loss account and balance sheet. These ratios will therefore be distorted and thus comparisons may be misleading.
3. The data needed to compute some ratios is not disclosed in published accounts and thus surrogates have to be used (e.g. the aggregate cash and credit sales in the calculation of the average period of credit taken by trade debtors). This may also mean that comparisons are misleading.
4. The general yardsticks or performance criteria which may be applied to particular ratios (e.g. a liquidity ratio of at least one) are not appropriate for all types of industry.

5. Changes in a given ratio over time and differences between companies must be considered in the light of the particular circumstances of the reporting entity, the type of industry, and the general economic situation. They may also be due to deliberate policy decisions by management such as a build up of stocks prior to a sales promotion compaign.

6. A single ratio may have limited information value by itself, but a number of different ratios taken together should give a general picture of the company's performance or financial position (e.g. in the prediction of insolvency).

References

1. Accounting Standards Steering Committee (1974). *SSAP3—Earnings per Share* (ICAEW).
2. Altman, E. A. (1968). Financial ratios, discriminant analysis and the prediction of corporate bankruptcy, *Journal of Finance* (September).
3. Taffler, R. J. (1982). Forecasting company failure in the UK using discriminant analysis and financial ratio data, *Journal of the Royal Statistical Society* **145**, Part 3.

Exercises

1. Explain what each of the following is intended to measure: (a) dividend yield; (b) dividend cover; (c) earnings per share; (d) price–earnings ratio; and (e) return on equity.

2. (a) Explain what is meant by capital gearing/leverage.
    (b) Why might this influence a prospective investor's decision concerning whether or not to buy ordinary shares in a company?

3. Explain what each of the following is intended to measure:

    (a) return on capital employed;
    (b) profit margin;
    (c) asset turnover ratio;
    (d) working capital and liquidity ratios;
    (e) average period of credit taken by debtors;
    (f) stock turnover ratio.

4. Examine the empirical evidence relating to the predictive ability of accounting ratios with regard to insolvency.

5. Explain the limitations of using accounting ratios in time series analysis and inter-firm comparisons, giving examples where appropriate.

6. Dale is in business as a sole trader. You are presented with the following summarized information relating to his business for the year to 31 October 19X8:

    Trading, profit and loss account for the year to 31 October 19X8

	£000	£000
Sales: cash	200	
credit	600	800

Less: cost of goods sold—		
opening stock	80	
purchases	530	
	610	
Less: closing stock	70	540
Gross profit		260
Expenses		205
Net profit for the year		55

Balance sheet at 31 October 19X8

	£000	£000
Fixed assets		
Plant and machinery at cost	1,000	
Less: accumulated depreciation	450	550
Current assets		
Stocks	70	
Trade debtors	120	
Cash	5	
	195	
Less: current liabilities		
Trade creditors	130	65
		615
Capital		
As at 1 November 19X7		410
Net profit for the year	55	
Less: drawings	50	5
		415
Loan		200
		615

Required:
(a) Based on the above information, calculate *eight* recognized accounting ratios; and
(b) list what additional information you would need in order to undertake a detailed ratio analysis of Dale's business for the year to 31 October 19X8.

  Note that in answering part (a) of the question, each ratio must be distinct and separate. Marks will *not* be awarded for alternative forms of the same ratio.   (AAT)

7. The following is an extract from the published accounts of Blue Light plc for the year ended 31 March 19X8.

Proft and loss account

	£000	£000
Turnover		4,230
Cost of sales		(2,560)
Gross profit		1,670
Distribution costs		(470)
Administrative expenses		(380)
Interest payable on debentures		(240)

Profit on ordinary activities before taxation	580
Corporation tax	(270)
Profit on ordinary activities after taxation	310
Proposed dividend on ordinary shares	(150)
Retained profit for the year	160

Balance sheet

Fixed assets at cost		7,240
Aggregate depreciation		(2,370)
		4,870
Current assets		
Stocks	480	
Trade debtors	270	
Bank and cash	320	
	1,070	
Amounts falling due within one year		
Trade creditors	260	
Proposed dividends	150	
Advance corporation tax	50	
Corporation tax	270	
	(730)	
Net current assets		340
Total assets less current liabilities		5,210
Amounts falling due after more than one year:		(3,000)
8 per cent debentures of £100 each		
Net assets		2,210
Capital and reserves		£'000
Called up share capital: 500,000		500
ordinary shares of £1 each		
Profit and loss account		1,710
Shareholders' interest		2,210

Further information: The ordinary shares and debentures are currently quoted on the London stock exchange at £5 and £110 respectively. Assume the basic rate of income tax is 25 per cent.

You are required to calculate the ratios that you would include in a report to a prospective investor relating to measures of return on investment and risk, performance, liquidity, and the appraisal of working capital. Comment briefly on the results and the limitations of your analysis.

8. The following is a summary of some of the accounting ratios of two companies in the same industry and of a comparable size for the year ended 30 June 19X5.

	Small plc	Large plc
Dividend yield	4 per cent	7 per cent
Dividend cover	3.6	2.1
Earnings per share	17p	23p
P–E ratio	14	8
Return on equity	22 per cent	27 per cent

Return on capital employed	18 per cent	15 per cent
Profit margin	20 per cent	25 per cent
Asset turnover ratio	0.9	0.6
Gearing ratio	28 per cent	76 per cent

You are required to write a report to a prospective investor on the comparative return on investment, risk and performance of these two companies.

9.   B. Beasley Ltd manufactures components for the motor vehicle industry. The following is a summary of some of its accounting ratios as at 30 April 19X3 and 30 April 19X4:

	19X3	19X4
Working capital ratio	1.5	1.7
Liquidity ratio	1.1	0.8
Stock turnover	6.3	5.9
Debtors ratio	52 days	63 days
Creditors ratio	71 days	78 days

You are required to write a report to one of the company's major shareholders on the change in its liquidity and working capital position over the year ended 30 April 19X4.

10.   White and Black are sole traders. Both are wholesalers dealing in a similar range of goods. Summaries of the profit calculations and balance sheets for the same year have been made available to you, as follows:

Profit and loss accounts for the year

	White £000	£000	Black £000	£000
Sales		600		800
Cost of goods sold		450		624
		150		176
Administrative expenses	64		63	
Selling and distribution expenses	28		40	
Depreciation—equipment and vehicles	10		20	
Depreciation—buildings	—	102	5	128
Net profit		48		48

Balance sheets as at end of year

	White £000	£000	Black £000	£000
Buildings		29		47
Equipment and vehicles		62		76
Stock		56		52
Debtors		75		67
Bank balance		8		—
		230		242
Creditors	38		78	
Bank balance	—	38	4	82
Capital		192		160

Required:
Compare the performance and financial position of the two businesses on the basis of the above figures, supporting your comments where appropriate with ratios and noting what further information you would need before reaching firmer conclusions.   (CACA)

11. Two retailers show the following accounts for the year to 31 December 19X9.

Balance sheets as at 31 December 19X9

	A. Ltd.		B. Ltd.	
	£000	£000	£000	£000
Fixed assets				
Premises		5,000		8,000
Fixtures		500		1,000
		5,500		9,000
Current assets				
Stock	800		900	
Debtors	50		60	
Bank	330		720	
	1,180		1,680	
Current liabilities	850		980	
		330		700
		5,830		9,700
Long-term loans		800		5,000
		5,030		4,700
Share capital—				
ordinary shares of £1		3,000		2,000
Retained profits		2,030		2,700
		5,030		4,700

Profit and loss accounts for the year ended 31 December 19X9

	£000	£000	£000	£000
Turnover		13,360		16,020
Cost of sales		8,685		10,090
		4,675		5,930
Distribution	2,300		2,870	
Administration	1,375		1,670	
		3,675		4,540
Operating profit		1,000		1,390
Interest		65		400
Net profit		935		990
Dividend		300		400
Retained profit for year		635		590

You are required to:

(a) compute for each of the two companies:
   (i) one ratio relevant to an assessment of liquidity;
   (ii) one ratio relevant to an assessment of gearing;
   (iii) three ratios relevant to an assessment of profitability and performance.
(b) summarize briefly the overall strengths and weaknesses of Company A, using each of the ratios you have computed.

                                                     (JMB)

12. The outline balance sheets of the Nantred Trading Co. Ltd were as shown below:

Balance sheets as at 30 September

	19X5 £	£	19X6 £	£
Fixed assets (*at written down values*)				
Premises	40,000		98,000	
Plant and equipment	65,000		162,000	
		105,000		260,000
Current assets				
Stock	31,200		95,300	
Trade debtors	19,700		30,700	
Bank and cash	15,600		26,500	
	66,500		152,500	
Current liabilities				
Trade creditors	23,900		55,800	
Corporation tax	11,400		13,100	
Proposed dividends	17,000		17,000	
	52,300		85,900	
Working capital		14,200		66,600
Net assets employed		119,200		326,600
Financed by				
Ordinary share capital	100,000		200,000	
Reserves	19,200		26,600	
Shareholders' funds		119,200		226,600
7 per cent debentures		—		100,000
		119,200		326,600

The only other information available is that the turnover for the years ended 30 September 19X5 and 19X6 was £202,900 and £490,700, respectively, and that on 30 September 19X4 reserves were £26,100.

Required:
(a) Calculate, for each of the two years, six suitable ratios to highlight the financial stability, liquidity and profitability of the company.
(b) Comment on the situation revealed by the figures you have calculated in your answer to (a) above.

13. You are given below, in summarized form, the accounts of Algernon Ltd for 19X6 and 19X7.

Balance sheets

	19X6 Cost £	Depn £	Net £	19X7 Cost £	Depn £	·Net £
Plant	10,000	4,000	6,000	11,000	5,000	6,000
Building	50,000	10,000	40,000	90,000	11,000	79,000
			46,000			85,000
Investments at cost			50,000			80,000
Land			43,000			63,000
Stock			55,000			65,000
Debtors			40,000			50,000
Bank			3,000			—
			237,000			343,000

Ordinary shares £1 each	40,000	50,000
Share premium	12,000	14,000
Revaluation reserve	—	20,000
Profit and loss account	25,000	25,000
10 per cent debentures	100,000	150,000
Creditors	40,000	60,000
Proposed dividend	20,000	20,000
Bank	—	4,000
	237,000	343,000

Profit and loss accounts

	19X6	19X7
	£	£
Sales	200,000	200,000
Cost of sales	100,000	120,000
	100,000	80,000
Expenses	60,000	60,000
	40,000	20,000
Dividends	20,000	20,000
	20,000	—
Balance b/f	5,000	25,000
Balance c/f	25,000	25,000

(a) Calculate for Algernon Ltd, for 19X6 and 19X7, the following ratios:

Return on capital employed;
Return on owners' equity (return on shareholders' funds);
Debtors turnover;
Creditors turnover;
Current ratio;
Quick assets (acid test) ratio;
Gross profit percentage;
Net profit percentage;
Dividend cover;
Gearing ratio.

(b) Using the summarized accounts given, and the ratios you have just prepared, comment on the position, progress and direction of Algernon Ltd. (CACA)

14. Delta Limited is an old-established light engineering company. The key performance data for the company between 19X3 and 19X7 are given below.

	19X3	19X4	19X5	19X6	19X7
Profit before tax and interest/sales (per cent)	3.6	0.5	0.6	8.1	9.8
Sales/fixed assets (times)	4.6	3.4	3.3	3.5	3.7
Sales/net current assets (times)	2.2	2.5	2.9	3.7	5.1
Cost of sales/stock (times)	1.9	2.0	2.4	2.7	2.9
Debtors/ave. days sales (days)	80	77	75	67	64
Creditors/ave. days sales (days)	58	57	61	64	71
Cost of sales/sales (per cent)	71	73.7	75	71	69.5
Selling and distribution/sales (per cent)	19	18.7	18.5	16	15.6
Administrative/sales (per cent)	6.4	7.1	5.9	4.9	5.1
Current ratio	4.9	2.8	3.3	2.1	1.8

You are required to examine the above data and write a report to the directors of Delta Limited analysing the performance of the company between 19X3 and 19X7. (JMB)

30. Cash and funds flow statements

The nature of cash flow statements

The term 'funds' can be interpreted in two ways. The first, and simplest, equates funds with cash and money in a bank current/cheque account. This interpretation may be referred to as cash funds, and forms the basis of cash flow statements.

In simple terms, the purpose of a cash flow statement is to show the reasons for the change in the cash and bank balance over the accounting year. It might be thought that this is relatively straightforward, since it could be done in the form of a summarized cash book or receipts and payments account. Unfortunately, however, it is usually not done in this way but rather in the form of changes in the value of the items in the balance sheet between the end of the previous year and the end of the current year.

These changes are often classified as either sources or applications of cash funds. Sources essentially relate to receipts and applications to payments. However, in terms of changes in the items in the balance sheet, sources of cash funds comprise the following:

1. The net profit for the year. Any loss for the year is an application of funds.
2. Capital introduced and money borrowed during the year in the form of loans received.
3. Proceeds from the sale of fixed assets and investments.
4. Increases in current liabilities and decreases in current assets.

Applications of cash funds comprise the following:

1. Drawings.
2. Any capital or loans repaid during the year.
3. Purchases of fixed assets and investments.
4. Increases in current assets and decreases in current liabilities.

Probably the most confusing aspect of cash flow statements is the changes in current assets and liabilities. Some simplified examples may thus be helpful. An increase in creditors is a source of funds because the money that would otherwise have been used to pay these creditors is available for other purposes. A decrease in debtors is also a source of funds since this results in an inflow of additional money. Similarly a decrease in stock is a source of funds because the proceeds of sale result in more money being available. Conversely an increase in stock is an application of funds since money will have been used to pay for it. Similarly an increase in debtors is an application of funds because allowing debtors additional credit is like giving them a loan. A decrease in creditors is also an application of funds since money will have been paid out to them. Frequently, certain sources of funds have corresponding applications. For example, an increase in stock may be 'financed' by an increase in creditors.

A simple cash flow statement might consist of the above list of sources and applications of cash funds including a breakdown of the changes in current assets and current liabilities between creditors, debtors and stock. This is illustrated in Example 30.1.

Example 30.1

The following are the balance sheets of A. Cash as at 30 September 19X4 and 30 September 19X5:

	30 Sept 19X4			30 Sept 19X5
	£	£	£	£
Fixed assets				
at cost	85,000			97,000
Current assets				
Stock		13,600	10,800	
Debtors		8,400	9,700	
Cash and bank		2,500	3,600	
		24,500	24,100	
Current liabilities				
Creditors		(7,300)	(6,100)	
Net current assets	17,200			18,000
Total assets less				
current liabilities	102,200			115,000
Long term liabilities				
Bank loan	(20,000)			(15,000)
Net assets	82,200			100,000
Capital				
At start of year	77,700			82,200
Add: capital				
introduced	2,800			4,300
profit for the year	21,600			34,200
	102,100			120,700
Less: drawings	(19,900)			(20,700)
At end of year	82,200			100,000

You are required to prepare a cash flow statement for the year ended 30 September 19X5.

A. Cash

Cash flow statement for the year ended 30 September 19X5

	£	£
Sources of cash funds:		
Profit for the year		34,200
Capital introduced		4,300
Decrease in stock (13,600 − 10,800)		2,800
		41,300

Total sources		41,300

Applications of cash funds

Drawings	(20,700)	
Repayment of bank loan (20,000 − 15,000)	(5,000)	
Purchase of fixed assets (97,000 − 85,000)	(12,000)	
Increase in debtors (9,700 − 8,400)	(1,300)	
Decrease in creditors (7,300 − 6,100)	(1,200)	
		(40,200)
Increase in cash and bank balance		1,100
Cash and bank balance at 1 Oct 19X4		2,500
Cash and bank balance at 30 Sept 19X5		3,600

Advantages of cash flow statements

The advantages of cash flow statements are often presented as arguments for a system of cash flow reporting and are frequently expressed in terms of the deficiencies of profit and loss accounts and balance sheets. This should not be interpreted to mean that cash flow statements are an alternative to profit and loss accounts. The profit and loss account and balance sheet have a number of limitations, and cash flow statements provide useful additional information for the following reasons:

1. Most readers and potential readers (e.g. private shareholders) appreciate the meaning and importance of cash and will therefore find cash flow statements easier to understand and more relevant. In contrast the nature of profit and capital, and the contents of the profit and loss acccount and balance sheet are more difficult to understand.
2. Cash flow statements are more objective in that cash received and paid are observable events. In contrast the profit and loss account and balance sheet are based on the accruals, matching and prudence concepts which involve subjective allocations, valuations, etc.
3. Cash flow statements therefore permit more meaningful comparisons of performance over time, and between actual performance and forecasts.
4. Profit is only a symbol or measure of performance. The ultimate success and survival of an enterprise depends on its ability to generate and use cash in the most efficient manner. The cash flow statement provides information that facilitates an evaluation of the efficiency with which cash has been generated and used.
5. Future dividends, the repayment of loans and payments to trade creditors depend primarily on the availability of cash and not profits. Cash flow statements provide information which allows users of company published accounts to make more accurate predictions of future dividends, insolvency, etc.

Few accountants would quarrel with the assertion that cash (or funds) flow statements provide useful additional information. However, most would be opposed to the idea that they should replace the profit and loss account for the following reasons:

1. A statement which is easier to understand is not necessarily more relevant or useful.
2. Cash flow statements also involve subjective judgements.

3. The use of cash flow statements in making comparisons and the evaluation of performance can be misleading. The pattern of cash flows over time are often erratic and therefore not indicative of an enterprise's long-term performance.
4. Cash flow statements focus on the financing activities of an enterprise rather than the economic or trading activities. They therefore do not provide meaningful information on either past or future economic performance.

The nature of funds flow statements

There is a second, more common and more complex interpretation of the term 'funds' which is broader than simply equating funds with cash. In this case funds is taken as referring to the current assets and current liabilities. This interpretation may be labelled working capital (WC) funds, and forms the basis of funds flow statements, which until recently have been presented in company published accounts as a statement of source and application of funds.

This interpretation of the term funds usually causes great confusion in the minds of students. A simple analogy may therefore be helpful. A friend informs you that it is your turn to buy a round of drinks. You reply that you are short of funds. He interprets this to mean short of cash because you left your money at home and therefore offers to lend you some money. You decline because what you meant was that you not only do not have any cash but you do not anticipate receiving any money in the near future and will thus be unable to repay his loan. In short, your friend interpreted the term funds to mean cash whereas you used the term funds to mean working capital, in that not only do you not have any cash you also have no current assets, such as debtors from which you anticipate receiving cash in the near future.

In simple terms, the purpose of a WC funds flow statement is to show the reasons for the change in working capital over the accounting year. In slightly different terms, the purpose of a statement of source and application of funds is said to be to 'show the manner in which the operations of a company have been financed and in which its financial resources have been used'.

Sources of cash and WC funds	Working capital funds			Applications of cash and WC funds
	Sources of cash funds	Cash funds	Applications of cash funds	
Profits Capital introduced	Increase in creditors	Change in cash	Decrease in creditors	Losses Drawings
Loans received Sale of fixed assets	Decrease in debtors Decrease in stock	and bank balance	Increase in debtors Increase in stock	Loans repaid Purchase of fixed assets

Figure 30.1 Sources and applications of cash and working capital funds.

As in the case of cash flow statements, it is usual for the funds statement to be presented in the form of changes in the value of the items in the balance sheet between the end of the previous year and the end of the current year. These changes are normally classified as either: (1) sources of WC funds; (2) applications of WC funds; or (3) increases/decreases in working capital. The items that fall into each of these categories are shown in Figure 30.1 which also highlights the difference and relationship between cash funds and working capital funds. A numerical illustration is given in Example 30.2 which is based on the data in Example 30.1.

Example 30.2

A. Cash
Statement of source and application of funds for the year ended 30 September 19X5

	£	£
Source of funds:		
Profit for the year		34,200
Total funds generated from operations		34,200
Funds from other sources:		
Capital introduced		4,300
		38,500
Application of funds:		
Drawings	(20,700)	
Repayment of bank loan	(5,000)	
Purchase of fixed assets	(12,000)	
		(37,700)
		800
Increase in working capital:		
Increase in debtors	1,300	
Increase in cash and bank	1,100	
Decrease in creditors	1,200	
Decrease in stock	(2,800)	
		800

Advantages of funds flow statements

The main reason for conceptualizing funds in terms of working capital, and the principal advantage of funds flow statements, is to focus attention on the change in the working capital. Any change in the cash and bank balance is regarded as of only secondary importance. Similarly changes in the composition of specific items such as stock, debtors and creditors are also of only secondary importance. The composition of WC is usually continually changing, which is why these are sometimes referred to as circulating assets. A shift of funds between, say, cash and stock, or a shortage of cash, is often only a temporary phenomenon and therefore of limited interest. However, a change in the total WC is a significant, relatively permanent event since it will involve an increase or decrease in capital and/or a shift of funds between WC and fixed assets. A funds flow statement is intended to highlight this event and show the sources of any increase in the WC or the way in which any decrease has been applied.

The disadvantages or limitations of funds flow statements are usually presented in terms of the advantages of cash flow statements. These were explained earlier in this chapter.

Preparation of cash and funds flow statements

The preparation of cash and funds flow statements of companies involves some additional considerations as follows.

Sources of funds include:

1. The profit for the year before taxation and dividends. This is because these two items are shown separately as applications of funds.
2. Capital introduced will comprise the amount received from any issues of shares and debentures during the year.

Applications of funds include:

1. Corporation tax paid during the year. In most cases this will be the taxation on the previous year's profit since corporation tax is payable nine months after the end of the accounting year.
2. Instead of drawings, the amounts paid during the year in respect of preference and ordinary share dividends. This will normally comprise the interim dividend plus the final dividend of the previous accounting year.
3. Capital repaid will consist of any shares and debentures redeemed during the year.

The preparation of cash and funds flow statements for both sole traders and companies involves some further complications with regard to the figure for profit (or loss) which is included in the statement. This should reflect the funds generated from a business's operating activities. However, the amount of profit shown in the profit and loss account is after deducting (and adding) certain items which do not involve the movement of funds. These consist of:

1. Provisions for depreciation on fixed assets
2. Profits and losses on the sale of fixed assets
3. Increases and decreases in provisions for bad debts

All of these items are purely accounting adjustments which arise from the preparation of the profit and loss account using the accruals and matching concept. They do not represent movements of cash or WC funds. It is therefore necessary to adjust the figure of profit shown in the profit and loss account in respect of these items to arrive at the funds generated from operations that is entered in the cash or funds flow statement as follows:

Profit per profit and loss account
Add: provisions for depreciation
       losses on sale of fixed assets
       increase in provision for bad debts
Less: profits on sale of fixed assets
       decrease in provision for bad debts
=   Funds generated from operations

This is illustrated in Example 30.3.

Example 30.3
The following are the balance sheets of C. F. Flow Ltd as at 31 March 19X1 and 31 March 19X2:

	31 Mar 19X1 £	£	31 Mar 19X2 £	£
Fixed assets at cost	173,000			165,000
Less: aggregate depreciation	(46,000)			(52,000)
	127,000			113,000
Current assets				
Stock		48,400	56,700	
Debtors		39,100	36,200	
Less: provision for bad debts		(1,700)	(1,400)	
Cash and bank		37,400	34,800	
		8,600	17,300	
		94,400	108,800	
Current liabilities				
Creditors		(31,400)	(32,800)	
Corporation tax		(15,700)	(18,500)	
Proposed dividends		(26,200)	(29,600)	
		(73,300)	(80,900)	
Net current assets	21,100			27,900
Total assets less current liabilities	148,100			140,900
Long-term liabilities				
10 per cent debentures	(52,000)			(20,000)
Net assets	96,100			120,900
Called-up share capital				
Ordinary shares of £1 each	50,000			60,000
Reserves				
Share premium		18,000	26,000	
Profit and loss account		21,700	25,300	
General reserve		6,400	9,600	
	46,100			60,900
Shareholders' interests	96,100			120,900

Notes

1. Fixed assets which cost £8,000 and had a written down value of £4,200 were disposed of during the year ended 31 March 19X2 at a price of £3,500. There were no other acquisitions or disposal of fixed assets during the year.
2. The total depreciation on fixed assets for the year was £9,800.
3. The corporation tax outstanding at 31 March 19X1 of £15,700 was paid on 31 December 19X1.
4. The proposed ordinary dividend at 31 March 19X1 of £26,200 was paid on 1 May 19X1. In addition an interim ordinary dividend of £8,600 was paid on 1 October 19X1.
5. During the year 10,000 ordinary shares were issued at a price of £1.80 each.

You are required to prepare a cash flow statement for the year ended 31 March 19X2.

Computation of profit before taxation and dividends

	£	£
Increase in balance on profit and loss account— (25,300 − 21,700)		3,600
Transfer to reserve (9,600 − 6,400)		3,200
Ordinary dividends—		
Interim	8,600	
Proposed final	29,600	38,200
Corporation tax		18,500
		63,500

C. F. Flow Ltd
Cash flow statement for the year ended 31 March 19X2

	£	£
Sources of cash funds		
Profit for the year before tax and dividends	63,500	
Add (Less): Adjustments for items not involving the movement of funds—		
Provision for depreciation	9,800	
Loss on sale of fixed assets (4,200 − 3,500)	700	
Decrease in provision for bad debts (1,700 − 1,400)	(300)	
Funds generated from operations		73,700
Issue of shares (10,000 × £1.80)		18,000
Proceeds of sale of fixed assets		3,500
Increase in creditors (32,800 − 31,400)		1,400
Decrease in debtors (39,100 − 36,200)		2,900
		99,500

Applications of cash funds

Tax paid	(15,700)
Dividends paid (26,200 + 8,600)	(34,800)
Repayment of debentures	(32,000)
(52,000 − 20,000)	
Increase in stock (56,700 − 48,400)	(8,300)
	(90,800)
Increase in cash and bank balance	8,700
Cash and bank balance at 1 April 19X1	8,600
Cash and bank balance at	
31 March 19X2	17,300

Notes

1. The proceeds from the issue of shares of £18,000 should correspond with the increase in ordinary share capital (60,000 − 50,000) and share premium account (26,000 − 18,000) shown in the balance sheet (i.e. 10,000 + 8,000).
2. The information given in the notes to the accounts should correspond with the changes in fixed assets and aggregate depreciation shown in the balance sheet as follows:

Fixed assets

19X1	Balance b/d	173,000	19X2		
1 Apr			31 Mar	Bank	3,500
			31 Mar	Provision for depreciation (8,000 − 4,200)	3,800
			31 Mar	Profit or loss on sale	700
			31 Mar	Balance c/d	165,000
		173,000			173,000

Provision for depreciation

19X2			19X1		
31 Mar	Fixed assets (8000 − 4200)	3,800	1 Apr	Balance b/d	46,000
31 Mar	Balance c/d	52,000	19X2 31 Mar	Profit and loss	9,800
		55,800			55,800

The reason for understanding how the information given in the notes in respect of issues of shares and fixed assets corresponds with changes in the balance sheet is that sometimes not all the information required is given as notes to the accounts (e.g. acquisitions of fixed assets, issues of shares, revaluations of assets). The student will then have to ascertain the missing information by examining the changes in the balance sheet. A useful way of doing this is in terms of the ledger accounts.

3.   A funds flow statement in respect of this example is shown below.

C. F. Flow Ltd
Statement of source and application of funds for the year ended 31 March 19X2

	£	£
Source of funds		
Funds generated from operations		73,700
show computation)		
Funds from other sources:		
Issue of shares		18,000
Proceeds of sale of fixed assets		3,500
		95,200
Application of funds		
Tax paid	(15,700)	
Dividends paid	(34,800)	
Repayment of debentures	(32,000)	
		(82,500)
		12,700
Increase in working capital		
Increase in stock	8,300	
Increase in cash and bank	8,700	
Decrease in debtors	(2,900)	
Increase in creditors	(1,400)	
		12,700

In the preparation of either a cash or funds flow statement, investments held as a fixed asset are treated in the same way as other fixed assets. However, investments held as a current asset are treated in the same way as cash and bank. Any change in the amount of current asset investments is added to or subtracted from the change in the cash and bank balance and shown on cash flow statements as 'cash and cash equivalents' or on funds flow statements as 'movements in net liquid funds'. Net liquid funds are defined as 'cash at bank and in hand and cash equivalents (e.g. investments held as current assets) less bank overdrafts and other borrowings repayable within one year of the accounting date'.

Relationship between cash/funds flow statements, profit and loss accounts and balance sheets

Cash and funds flow statements are intended to complement the profit and loss account and balance sheet. The difference between a cash/funds flow statement and a profit and loss account lies in the observation that profit is not the same as the increase in cash over a given accounting period, but rather is only one source of funds. The relationship between a cash/funds flow statement and a balance sheet is that the former 'identifies the movements in assets, liabilities and capital which have taken place during the year and the resultant effect on net liquid funds' shown on the latter. It also provides a link between the balance sheet at the beginning of the period, the profit and loss account for the period, and the balance sheet at the end of the period.

Reference

1. Accounting Standards Steering Committee (1978). *Statement of Standard Accounting Practice 10—Statements of Source and Application of Funds* (ICAEW).

Exercises

1. (a) Explain the meaning of the term 'funds' in the context of cash flow statements.
    (b) Explain the purpose(s) of a cash flow statement.

2. Describe the advantages and limitations of cash flow statements.

3. (a) Explain the meaning of the term funds in the context of statements of source and application of funds.
    (b) Explain the purpose(s) of a statement of source and application of funds.

4. Describe the advantages and limitations of funds flow statements.

5. Compare and contrast the nature of cash funds and working capital funds.

6. Explain how cash and funds flow statements differ from: (a) profit and loss accounts; and (b) balance sheets.

7. Explain the meaning of each of the following in the context of funds flow statements:
    (a) funds generated from operations;
    (b) cash equivalents;
    (c) net liquid funds.

8. J. White, a sole trader, has produced the following balance sheets for the years ended 31 March 19X6 and 31 March 19X7.

Balance sheet at 31 March 19X6

	£	£	Fixed assets:	Cost £	Depn. £	Net £
J. White—Capital			Freehold premises	10,000		10,000
account		15,000	Shop fittings	1,000	750	250
Current account	3,000		Motor vehicle	800	400	400
Profit for the year	5,400					
	8,400			11,800	1,150	10,650
Less drawings for						
the year	3,200	5,200	Current assets			
			Stock	11,000		
Trade creditors		12,000	Debtors	1,000		
			Cash at bank	9,500		
			Cash in till	50		21,500
		£32,200				£32,200

Balance sheet at 31 March 19X7			Fixed assets:	Cost	Depn.	Net
J. White—Capital						
account		15,000				
Current account			Freehold premises	10,000	—	10,000
Balance at	5,200		Shop fittings	1,200	870	330
1 April 19X6			Motor vehicle	800	600	200
Profit for the year	5,800					
	11,000			12,000	1,470	10,530
Drawings for	4,500	6,500	Current assets:			
the year			Stock	15,400		
Trade creditors		8,000	Debtors	540		
			Cash at bank	3,000		
			Cash in till	30		18,970
		£29,500				£29,500

He is unable to understand why, after he has made a profit for the year ended 31 March 19X7 of £5,800, his bank balance has fallen by £6,500.

You are required to prepare a report explaining how this has occurred.   (CACA)

9. Prepare a statement of source and application of funds (or funds flow statement) using the information in Question 8 above.

10. The following are the balance sheets of A. Brooks as at 30 June 19X6 and 30 June 19X7:

	30 June 19X6		30 June 19X7	
	£	£	£	£
Fixed assets		65,000		72,000
at cost				
Aggregate depn.		(13,000)		(14,500)
		52,000		57,500
Current assets				
Stock	6,700		7,300	
Debtors	5,400		4,100	
Cash and bank	—		900	
	12,100		12,300	
Current liabilities				
Creditors	(4,800)		(6,200)	
Bank overdraft	(1,300)		(—)	
	(6,100)		(6,200)	
Net current assets		6,000		6,100
Total assets less current liabilities		58,000		63,600
Bank loan (5 years)		(15,000)		(10,000)
Net assets		43,000		53,600

Capital			
At start of year		38,500	43,000
Capital introduced		2,700	20,000
Profit for the year		14,100	—
		55,300	63,000
Loss for the year	(—)		(1,800)
Drawings	(12,300)		(7,600)
		(12,300)	(9,400)
At end of year		43,000	53,600

There were no disposals of fixed assets during the year.

M A. Brooks cannot understand how there can be a loss for the year when there has been an increase in the cash and bank balance. You are required to explain this by preparing a cash flow statement for the year ended 30 June 19X7.

11. Prepare a statement of source and application of funds (or funds flow statement) using the information in Question 10 above.

12. The balance sheets of Antipodean Enterprises at the end of two consecutive financial years, were:

Balance sheets

	31 December 19X2		31 December 19X3	
	£	£	£	£
Fixed assets at written down value				
Premises	38,000		37,000	
Equipment	17,600		45,800	
Cars	4,080		18,930	
		59,680		101,730
Investments (long-term)		17,000		25,000
Current assets				
Stocks	27,500		19,670	
Debtors and prepayments	14,410		11,960	
Short-term investments	3,600		4,800	
Cash and bank balances	1,800		700	
	47,310		37,130	
Current liabilities				
Creditors and accruals	20,950		32,050	
Bank overdraft	—		28,200	
	20,950		60,250	
Working capital		26,360		(23,120)
Net assets employed		£103,040		£103,610
Financed by:				
Opening capital	67,940		75,040	
Capital introduced (withdrawn)	4,000		(6,500)	
Profit/(loss) for year	15,300		25,200	
Drawings	(12,200)		(15,130)	

Closing capital	75,040	78,610
Long-term liability		
Business development loan	28,000	25,000
	£103,040	£103,610

Profit for year ended 31 December 19X3 (£25,200) is after accounting for:

	£
Depreciation—premises	1,000
—equipment	3,000
—cars	3,000
Profit on disposal of equipment	430
Loss on disposal of cars	740

The written down value of the assets at date of disposal was:

	£
Equipment	5,200
Cars	2,010

Required:

(a) Prepare a statement of sources and applications of funds for Antipodean Enterprises for the year ended 31 December 19X3.
(b) Comment on the financial position of the business as revealed in your answer to (a) and by the balance sheet as at 31 December 19X3.   (CACA)

13. The directors of J. Kitchens Ltd were pleased when their accountants informed them that the company has made a profit of £24,000 during the year ended 31 December 19X3. However their pleasure was turned into confusion when the cashier showed them a letter he had received from their banker. This indicated that he had reviewed Kitchens' account and was concerned to note the deterioration in their bank position. During 19X3 a small overdraft of £500 had reached £9,800 and was nearing the limit of their security. The directors would like to see an explanation of this increased overdraft, particularly as they had declared lower dividends than for the previous year. You are given the balance sheets at 31 December 19X2 and 31 December 19X3:

	19X2		19X3	
Fixed assets	£	£	£	£
Leasehold premises—cost	30,000		30,000	
—depn.	6,000	24,000	9,000	21,000
Plant—cost	41,000		48,000	
—depreciation	7,000	34,000	9,500	38,500
		58,000		59,500
Current assets				
Stock	14,900		22,500	
Debtors	11,300	26,200	16,400	38,900
		84,200		98,400
Share capital and reserves				
Share capital		20,000		20,000
Reserves		35,000		51,000
Current liabilities				
Creditors		19,700		17,600
Overdraft		500		9,800
Dividends payable		9,000		—
		£84,200		£98,400

Notes

		19X2	19X3
1.	Dividends:		
	Interim	3,000	8,000
	Final	9,000	—
		£12,000	£8,000

2. During the year plant costing £10,000 with a net book value of £6,000 was sold for £6,400.
3. The amount included for debtors at 31 December 19X3 is after making a provision for bad debts of £600 (19X2: £400).

You are required to prepare a cash flow statement showing why the overdraft has increased.

14. Prepare a statement of source and application of funds (or funds flow statement) using the information in Question 13 above.

15. The following are the balance sheets of L. Tyler Ltd as at 31 May 19X8 and 31 May 19X9:

	31 May 19X8		31 May 19X9	
	£	£	£	£
Fixed assets at cost		143,000		131,000
Aggregate depreciation		(28,000)		(37,000)
		115,000		94,000
Current assets				
Stock	21,600		19,400	
Debtors	11,800		14,200	
Less: provision for bad debts	500		700	
	11,300		13,500	
Investments	3,900		17,100	
Cash and bank	4,600		12,800	
	41,400		62,800	
Current liabilities				
Creditors	(8,400)		(6,700)	
Corporation tax	(5,800)		(7,200)	
Proposed dividends	(19,600)		(21,800)	
	(33,800)		(35,700)	
Net current assets		7,600		27,100
Total assets less current liabilities		122,600		121,100
Long-term liabilities				
8 per cent loan stock		(30,000)		(5,000)
Net assets		92,600		116,100
Called up share capital				
Ordinary shares of 50p each		60,000		70,000
Reserves				
Share premium	25,000		34,000	
Revenue reserve	4,200		6,900	
Profit and loss account	3,400		5,200	
		32,600		46,100
Shareholders' interests		92,600		116,100

Notes

1. Fixed assets which cost £12,000 and had a book value of £7,500 were sold during the year ended 31 May 19X9 for £8,100. There were no other purchases or sales of fixed assets during that year.
2. The amounts of corporation tax and proposed dividends shown in the balance sheet as outstanding at 31 May 19X8 were paid during the year ended 31 May 19X9. In addition an interim dividend of £6,400 was paid on 1 January 19X9.

You are required to prepare a cash flow statement for the year ended 31 May 19X9.

16. Prepare a statement of source and application of funds (or funds flow statement) using the information in Question 15 above.

17. The balance sheet of Euston Ltd as at 31 December 19X8, with corresponding amounts, showed the following.

	19X8		19X7	
	£000	£000	£000	£000
Freehold property at cost		2,000		2,000
Plant and machinery:				
Cost	3,500		3,000	
Depreciation	1,300		1,000	
		2,200		2,000
		4,200		4,000
Current assets:				
Stock	470		400	
Debtors	800		600	
Prepayments	60		50	
Bank	20		150	
	1,350		1,200	
Current liabilities:				
Creditors	230		200	
Taxation	100		80	
Dividends	50		30	
Accruals	70		90	
	450		400	
Net current assets		900		800
		5,100		4,800
12 per cent debentures		1,000		800
		4,100		4,000
Share capital		2,500		2,500
Retained profit		1,600		1,500
		4,100		4,000

Notes relevant to 19X8

1. An item of plant costing £100,000 with a written down value of £60,000, was sold at a profit of £15,000 during the year. This profit has been included in the profit and loss account for the year.
2. No interim dividend was paid during the year.
3. Tax paid during the year was £76,000.
4. Sales were £4,800,000 (19X7: £4,000,000). The gross profit percentage has remained steady.

You are required to prepare a cash flow statement for the year to 31 December 19X8.   (JMB adapted)

18. The following are the balance sheets of Waterloo plc for the last two financial years ended on 30 September:

	19X8		19X7		Notes
Fixed assets	£000	£000	£000	£000	
Intangible					
Goodwill		200		200	1
Tangible					
Buildings	970		720		2
Plant and machinery	350	1,320	370	1.090	2
		1,520		1,290	
Current assets					
Stocks	420		300		
Trade debtors	220		120		
Balance at bank	—		20		
	640		440		
Creditors, less than one year					
Bank overdraft	120		—		
Trade creditors	190		200		
Proposed dividends	60		45		3
	(370)		(245)		
Net current assets		270		195	
		1,790		1,485	
Creditors, more than one year					
9 per cent debentures		(360)		(400)	
		1,430		1,085	
Capital and reserves:					
Ordinary shares, of 50p each, fully paid		750		500	4
Share premium	100		350		4
Revaluation reserve	300		—		
Retained profit	280	680	235	585	
		1,430		1,085	

Explanatory notes to the balance sheets:
1. Goodwill arising from the purchase of a business on 1 November 19X6 was valued at £200,000. It is the policy of the company to hold purchased goodwill as a permanent asset in the books of account.
2. The movement during the year to 30 September 19X8 in fixed tangible assets was as follows:

	Buildings		Plant and machinery	
	£000	£000	£000	£000
Cost a 1 October 19X7	820		600	
Surplus on revaluation	300		—	
Additions	—		100	
Disposals	—		*(50)	
		1,120		650
Provision for depreciation at 1 October 19X7	100		230	
Depreciation on disposal	—		*(40)	
Depreciation for year	50	(150)	110	(300)
30 September 19X8		970		350

*The plant and machinery disposed of during the year was sold for £5,000.

3. Apart from the final proposed dividends shown in each balance sheet, interim dividends were paid in each of the years as follows:

19X8	*19X7*
£25,000	£15,000

4. There was a bonus issue during the year to 30 September 19X8 of one new ordinary share for every two held.

Required:
(a) A sources and applications of funds statement for the year ended 30 September 19X8, together with a statement showing the movement in working capital.
(b) An examination of the accounting treatment adopted by Waterloo plc for:
   (i) goodwill,
   (ii) buildings,
   and a statement as to how the valuation of each of these assets may be affected if the company ceased to be regarded as a 'going concern'.   (AEB)

19. The summarized balance sheets as at 31 March 19X8 and 19X9 of Higher Limited are as follows:

	19X9		*19X8*		*Additional*
	£000	£000	£000	£000	*information*
Fixed assets; at net book value		175		150	1
Current assets	90		80		2
Creditors, less than one year	(70)		(50)		
		20		30	
		195		180	
Creditors, more than one year		(30)		(30)	
		165		150	
Capital and reserves					
Ordinary shares of £1 each		90		80	3
8 per cent redeemable preference shares of 50p each		—		30	3
Share premium account		25		20	3
Capital redemption reserve		15		—	
Proft and loss account		35		20	
		165		150	

Additional information:

1. Fixed assets

	Cost	*Depn.*	*Net book value*
	£000	£000	£000
Balance at 31 March 19X8	200	50	150
Additions	60	—	60
Disposals	(40)	(25)	(15)
Depreciation for the year to 31 March 19X9	—	20	(20)
	220	45	175

Fixed assets disposed of during the year were sold for £22,000.

2. Current assets at 31 March for each of the two years comprise the following:

	19X9	19X8
	£000	£000
Stocks	35	27
Debtors	22	28
Bank	24	22
Cash	9	3
	90	80

3. The preference shares were redeemed during the year ended 31 March 19X9. This redemption was funded by a new issue of ordinary shares at a premium.
4. A transfer of £15,000 from the profit and loss account was made to the capital redemption reserve.

Required:
(a) Prepare a source and application of funds statement for Higher Limited for the year ended 31 March 19X9, showing clearly the change in the working capital.
(b) Explain the purpose and uses of the source and application of funds statement.   (AEB)

20. You are given below, in summarized form, the accounts of Algernon Ltd for 19X6 and 19X7.

Balance sheets

	19X8			19X7		
	Cost	Depn.	Net	Cost	Depn.	Net
	£	£	£	£	£	£
Plant	10,000	4,000	6,000	11,000	5,000	6,000
Building	50,000	10,000	40,000	90,000	11,000	79,000
			46,000			85,000
Investments at cost			50,000			80,000
Land			43,000			63,000
Stock			55,000			65,000
Debtors			40,000			50,000
Bank			3,000			—
			237,000			343,000
Ordinary shares £1 each			40,000			50,000
Share premium			12,000			14,000
Revaluation reserve			—			20,000
Profit and loss account			25,000			25,000
10 per cent debentures			100,000			150,000
Creditors			40,000			60,000
Proposed dividend			20,000			20,000
Bank			—			4,000
			237,000			343,000

Proft and loss accounts

	£	£
Sales	200,000	200,000
Cost of sales	100,000	120,000
	100,000	80,000
Expenses	60,000	60,000
	40,000	20,000
Dividends	20,000	20,000
	20,000	—
Balance b/f	5,000	25,000
Balance c/f	25,000	25,000

Required:
(a) Prepare a source and application of funds statement for Algernon Ltd for 19X7, to explain as far as possible the movement in the bank balance.
(b) Using the summarized accounts given, and the statement you have just prepared, comment on the position, progress and direction of Algernon Ltd. (CACA)

31. Value added tax and columnar books of prime entry

Value added tax

Value added tax is a sales tax that is ultimately borne by the consumer. Most businesses charge their customers with (output) VAT and buy goods and services which are subject to (input) VAT. However, these businesses do not usually suffer VAT as a cost of inputs, in that the input VAT is set off against the output VAT and periodically the difference is paid to HM Customs & Excise or a refund obtained. Consequently none of the items shown in the accounts normally include VAT. The only exceptions to this are debtors and creditors. Furthermore, there may be a current liability for VAT at the end of an accounting year that represents the difference between output and input VAT which has not been paid to HM Customs & Excise at that date.

A number of rates of VAT have existed at various times. For some time the standard rate was 15 per cent but in 1991 this was raised to 17.5 per cent. Some products are zero rated, i.e. bear no VAT; some businesses are exempt so that they do not charge VAT on their outputs but do have to pay VAT on their inputs.

The accounting entries for VAT are relatively straightforward in principle. When goods which are subject to VAT are purchased for cash, the price including VAT is credited in the cash book. The corresponding debit consists of two entries—the cost excluding VAT is debited to the purchases account, and the amount of VAT is debited to a VAT account. Similarly when goods that are subject to VAT are purchased on credit, the price including VAT is credited to the the creditors account. The corresponding debit consists of two entries—the cost excluding VAT is debited to the purchases account, and the amount of VAT is debit to a VAT or HM Customs & Excise account which is essentially a personal account. Conversely, when goods which are subject to VAT are sold on credit, the price including VAT is debited to the debtors account. The corresponding credit consists of two entries—the price excluding VAT is credited to the sales account, and the amount of VAT is credited to the VAT account. A simple illustration is given in Example 31.1 below.

Example 31.1

A. Ltd buys goods on credit from B. Ltd at price of £200 plus 17.5 per cent VAT. A. Ltd then sells these goods to C. Ltd for £320 plus 17.5 per cent VAT. Show the ledger entries in the books of A. Ltd.

B. Ltd

	Purchases	235

Purchases

B. Ltd	200	

Value added tax

| B. Ltd | 35 | C. Ltd | 56 |

C. Ltd

| Sales | 356 |

Sales

| C. Ltd | 320 |

Periodically the VAT account is balanced and the difference between the two sides paid to HM Customs & Excise where this is a credit balance, or a refund obtained where there is a debit balance.

A further complication with VAT is that some businesses are classed as either zero rated or exempt. This means that they do not have to charge their customers with VAT. In the case of zero rated businesses, they obtain a refund of the VAT that they have paid on goods and services purchased. Thus input VAT is debited to the VAT account, and the only credit entry in this account is a cheque received from HM Customs & Excise as a refund. However, businesses that are classed as exempt do not get a refund. In this case there is no VAT account in the ledger because the cost of goods and services purchased including VAT is simply debited to the relevant nominal accounts.

Columnar books of prime entry

A columnar book of prime entry is one which contains analysis columns. The use of analysis columns in the petty cash book was described in Chapter 8. In practice most of the other books of prime entry, namely the day books and cash book, also frequently contain analysis columns. Each is described below.

The simplest is the sales day book and sales returns day book. This often contains analysis columns relating to the different departments or types of products that the business sells. This makes it possible to compute the gross profit of each department in departmental trading accounts. The sales and returns day books also usually contain an analysis column in respect of value added tax.

The purchases day book and purchases returns day book also often contain analysis columns. These may relate to the different departments or types of products. However, a more common form of columnar purchases day book contains not just credit purchases of goods for resale, but also expenses incurred on credit (e.g. the purchase of stationery) and the purchase of fixed assets on credit. Indeed any invoice received in respect of goods or services purchased on credit is often recorded in the columnar purchases day book. The purchases and returns day books also usually contain an analysis column relating to value added tax.

Lastly, the cash book frequently also contains memorandum analysis columns on both the debit and credit sides. Those on the credit side are much the same as in the petty cash book. The columns on the debit side are used in the same way but obviously relate to different types of receipts. The cash book also usually contains an analysis column on each side relating to value added tax.

As explained in the context of columnar petty cash books, the purpose of having analysis columns in books of prime entry is to facilitate the posting of the ledger. Each column relates to a particular type of income or expenditure such as stationery, motor expenses etc. Every transaction is entered in a total column and an appropriate analysis column. At the end of each calendar month the total of each column is posted to the relevant account in the ledger. Thus instead of posting each transaction to the ledger separately, income and expenditure of the same type is collected together in analysis columns and the total for the period posted to the relevant ledger account.

Illustrations of the use of columnar day books and cash books are given in Examples 31.2 and 31.3 respectively.

Example 31.2

A Singh is in business as a builders' merchant. The following credit transactions took place during August 19X5:

2 Aug   Purchased goods for resale from AB Ltd for £560 plus 17.5 per cent VAT.
5 Aug   Bought stationery from CD Ltd for £120 plus 17.5 per cent VAT.
10 Aug   Purchased fixtures and fittings for the shop from EF Ltd for £2,000 plus 17.5 per cent VAT.
18 Aug   Sold goods to YZ Ltd for £1,000 plus 17.5 per cent VAT.
23 Aug   Sold some old loose tools previously used in the shop to WX Ltd for £1,600 plus 17.5 per cent VAT.
25 Aug   Returned goods costing £200 + VAT to AB Ltd and received a credit note.
29 Aug   Returned stationery costing £40 + VAT to CD Ltd and received a credit note.

You are required to make the necessary entries in the relevant columnar books of prime entry and the ledger.

Purchases day book (PDB)

Date	Name of creditor	Total	VAT	Purchases	Stationery	Misc.
2 Aug	AB Ltd	658	98	560		
5 Aug	CD Ltd	141	21		120	
10 Aug	EF Ltd	2,350	350			2,000
		3,149	469	560	120	2,000

Sales day book (SDB)

Date	Name of debtor	Total	VAT	Sales	Misc.
18 Aug	YZ Ltd	1,175	175	1,000	
23 Aug	WX Ltd	1,880	280		1,600
		3,055	455	1,000	1,600

Purchases returns day book (PRDB)

Date	Name of creditor	Total	VAT	Purchases	Stationery	Misc.
25 Aug	AB Ltd	235	35	200		
29 Aug	CD Ltd	47	7		40	
		282	42	200	40	—

The ledger

Purchases

31 Aug	Total per PDB	560

Stationery

31 Aug	Total per PDB	120	31 Aug	Total per PRDB	40

Fixtures and Fittings

10 Aug	EF Ltd	2,000

VAT

31 Aug	Total per PDB	469	31 Aug	Total per SDB	455
			31 Aug	Total per PRDB	37

AB Ltd

25 Aug	Returns + VAT	235	2 Aug	Purchases + VAT	658

CD Ltd

29 Aug	Stationery + VAT	47	5 Aug	Stationery + VAT	141

EF Ltd

			10 Aug	Fixtures + VAT	2,350

Purchases returns

			31 Aug	Total per PRDB	200

Sales

			31 Aug	Total per SDB	1,000

Loose tools

23 Aug	WX Ltd	1,600

YZ Ltd

31 Aug	Sales + VAT	1,175

WX Ltd

23 Aug	Loose tools + VAT	1,880

Notes

1. The amount of each invoice (including VAT) shown in the total columns of the day books is posted individually to the debtors and creditors personal accounts in the normal way. The total of the VAT column in each day book is posted to the VAT account. Similarly the total of each of the other analysis columns in the day books is posted to the relevant ledger account. The only exception to this is the miscellaneous column where each entry would have to be posted separately because they normally involve more than one ledger account.

Example 31.3 (continuation of Example 31.2)
A. Singh had the following cheque receipts and payments during September 19X5:

1 Sept	Balance at bank £8,000.
3 Sept	Introduced additional capital of £900.
7 Sept	Sold goods for £400 plus 17.5 per cent VAT.
12 Sept	Received a cheque from YZ Ltd for £1,140 after deducting £35 cash discount.
20 Sept	Drawings £250.
22 Sept	Purchased goods for resale costing £230 plus VAT.
23 Sept	Bought stationery costing £200 plus 17.5 per cent VAT.
25 Sept	Purchased a motor vehicle for £5,000 plus 17.5 per cent VAT.
27 Sept	Paid AB Ltd £398 after deducting £25 cash discount.
29 Sept	Paid HM Customs & Excise the VAT outstanding at the end of July 19X5 of £21.

You are required to make the necessary entries in a columnar cash book and the ledger.

The columnar cash book (debit side) (CB)

Date	Details	Total	VAT	Debtors	Discount Allowed	Sales	Misc.
19X5							
1 Sept	Balance b/d	8,000					8,000
3 Sept	Capital	900					900
7 Sept	Sales	470	70			400	
12 Sept	YZ Ltd	1,140		1,140	35		
		10,510	70	1,140	35	400	8,900

The columnar cash book (credit side)

Date	Details	Total	VAT	Creditors	Discount received	Purchases	Stationery	Misc.
19X5								
20 Sept	Drawings	250						250
22 Sept	Purchases	356	56			320		
23 Sept	Stationery	235	35				200	
25 Sept	Motor vehicles	5,875	875					5,000
27 Sept	AB Ltd	398		398	25			
29 Sept	HM Customs & Excise							
	Totals	7,135	987	398	25	320	200	5,250
30 Sept		3,375						
	Balance c/d	10,510						

The ledger

Capital

	19X5		
	3 Sept	Bank	900

Sales

	31 Aug	Total per SDB	1,000
	30 Sept	Total per CB	400

YZ Ltd

31 Aug	Sales + VAT	1,175	12 Sept	Bank	1,140
			12 Sept	Discount allowed	35
		1,175			1,175

Discount Allowed

30 Sept	Total per CB	35

Drawings

20 Sept	Bank	250

Purchases

| 31 Aug | Total per PDB | 560 | | | |
| 30 Sept | Total per CB | 320 | | | |

Stationery

| 31 Aug | Total per PDB | 120 | 31 Aug | Total per PRDB | 40 |
| 30 Sept | Total per CB | 200 | | | |

Motor vehicles

| 25 Sept | Bank | 5,000 | | | |

AB Ltd

25 Aug	Returns + VAT	235	2 Aug	Purchases + VAT	658
27 Sept	Bank	398			
27 Sept	Discount received	25			
		658			658

Discount received

| | | | 30 Sept | Total per CB | 25 |

VAT

31 Aug	Total per PDB	469	31 Aug	Total per SDB	455
31 Aug	Balance c/d	23	31 Aug	Total per PRDB	37
		492			492
30 Sept	Total per CB (credit)	987	1 Sept	Balance b/d	23
			30 Sept	Total per CB (debit)	70
			30 Sept	Balance c/d	894
		987			987
1 Oct	Balance b/d	894			

Notes

1. The total of all the analysis columns on the debit side of the cash book except the discount allowed column should equal the total of the total column. Similarly the total of all the analysis columns on the credit side of the cash book except the discount received column should equal the total of the total column.
2. The total of each analysis column in the cash book is posted to the relevant ledger

account. The exceptions to this are the miscellaneous, debtors and creditors columns where each item has to be posted to the ledger individually.

3. Where cheques are received from debtors and paid to creditors, the VAT included in these amounts is not shown in the VAT column of the cash book. This would result in double counting because the VAT has already been entered in the VAT account in the ledger via the VAT columns of the day books when the goods were purchased/sold. The total amount of the cheque is therefore entered in the debtors and creditors columns and posted to the personal accounts.

Exercises

1. (a) Briefly explain the nature of value added tax (VAT) and how this is collected by businesses.
    (b) Describe how this affects the items shown in the final accounts of businesses.
    (c) What does it mean when a business is classified as: (i) zero rated; and (ii) exempt for VAT purposes?
2. (a) Explain the main purpose of columnar day books.
    (b) Describe the possible format of: (i) a columnar purchases day book; and (ii) a columnar cash book. Your answer should include reference to value added tax.
3. Mudgee Ltd issued the following invoices to customers in respect of credit sales made during the last week of May 19X7. The amounts stated are all net of value added tax. All sales made by Mudgee Ltd are subject to VAT at 15 per cent.

Invoice No.	Date	Customer	Amount
			£
3045	25 May	Laira Brand	1,060.00
3046	27 May	Brown Bros	2,200.00
3047	28 May	Penfold's	170.00
3048	29 May	T. Tyrell	460.00
3049	30 May	Laira Brand	1,450.00
			————
			5,340.00

On 29 May Laira Brand returned half the goods (in value) purchased on 25 May. An allowance was made the same day to this customer for the appropriate amount.

On 1 May 19X7 Laira Brand owed Mudgee Ltd £2,100.47. Other than the purchases detailed above, Laira Brand made credit purchases of £680.23 from Mudgee Ltd on 15 May. On 21 May Mudgee Ltd received a cheque for £2,500 from Laira Brand.

Required
(a) Show how the above transactions would be recorded in Mudgee Ltd's sales book for the week ended 30 May 19X7.
(b) Describe how the information in the sales book would be incorporated into Mudgee Ltd's double entry system.
(c) Reconstruct the personal account of Laira Brand as it would appear in Mudgee Ltd's ledger for May 19X7.   (AAT)

4. Kwella Ltd received the following invoices from suppliers during the week commencing 23 November 19X7. All purchases made by Kwella Ltd are subject to value added tax at 15 per cent. The following list gives the *gross* value of each invoice received.

Date received	Invoice No.	Date of invoice	Supplier	Gross amount
				£
23 Nov	GL 788	18 Nov	Glixit plc	506.00
24 Nov	899330	19 Nov	Moblin Ltd	115.00

25 Nov	G 1101	17 Nov	S & G Gates	724.50
26 Nov	AX 1256	23 Nov	Goldrins Glues	1,115.50
27 Nov	CS 772	25 Nov	Wixit Wires Ltd	1,794.00

On 25 November Kwella Ltd rejected all the goods invoiced on 24 November by Moblin Ltd (invoice no 899330) because they were not what had been ordered. The goods were returned to Moblin Ltd along with Kwella Ltd's debit note (D 56) for the full invoice amount.

On 26 November Kwella Ltd had to return some of the goods purchased on 17 November from S & G Gates (invoice no. G 1101) because they were sub-standard. A debit note (D 57) for a gross value of £241.50 was returned with the goods.

Required:

(a) Write up Kwella Ltd's purchases book and purchases returns book for the week commencing 23 November 19X7 totalling the columns off as at 28 November 19X7.

(b) Describe how the information in the purchases book and purchases returns book would be incorporated into Kwella Ltd's ledger.

(c) The balance brought forward on S & G Gates' account at 1 November 19X7 was £920.00 which Kwella Ltd settled in full by cheque on 13 November after deducting 5 per cent discount. There were no other transactions with S & G Gates during the month of November other than those detailed above.

Reconstruct Kwella Ltd's ledger account for S & G Gates for the month of November 19X7 balancing off the account as at the 30 November 19X7.   (AAT)

5. A business commenced trading for the week commencing 28 May 19X0 with £79 in cash and a bank overdraft of £515.

The following receipts and payments occurred during the week ending 3 June 19X0.

28 May   Paid travelling expenses of £37 in cash.

29 May   Paid a telephone bill of £115 (including £15 value added tax) by cheque.

29 May   Grant Degan, a credit customer settled an invoice for £90 paying £81 in cash and receiving £9 discount for prompt settlement.

30 May   Made cash sales totalling £460 including £60 value added tax. The amount was received by cheque and was immediately banked.

31 May   Paid an invoice for £100 from Gaga Ltd by cheque for £92. £8 discount was received for prompt settlement.

1 June   Made cash purchases totalling £115 including value added tax of £15 paying by cheque.

1 June   Made cash sales of £230 inclusive of value added tax of £30.

2 June   Paid staff wages of £300. This was partly paid by cheques totalling £230, the balance being paid in cash.

2 June   Paid £200 from the till into the business bank account.

Required:

(a) Draw up a cash book with separate columns for dates, narrations, folios, discount, VAT, bank and cash. Enter the opening balances and record the transactions for the week commencing 28 May 19X0. Balance the cash book as at 3 June 19X0.

(b) Describe how the totals for the Discount and VAT columns will be entered into the ledger.

(AAT)

6. After completing a training course at a technical college, Michael Faraday set up in business as a self-employed electrician on 1 January 19X5.

He was very competent at his job, but had no idea how to maintain proper accounting records. Sometime during 19X5 one of his friends asked Michael how well his business was doing. He replied 'All right . . . I think . . . but I'm not quite sure'.

In the ensuing conversation his friend asked whether he had prepared accounts yet, covering his first quarter's trading, to which Michael replied that he had not. His friend then stressed that, for various reasons, it was vital for accounts of businesses to be prepared properly.

Shortly afterwards Michael came to see you to ask for your help in preparing accounts for his first quarter's trading. He brought with him, in a cardboard box, the only records he had, mainly scribbled on scraps of paper.

He explained that he started his business with a car worth £700, and £2,250 in cash of which £250 was his savings and £2,000 had been borrowed from a relative at an interest rate of 10 per cent per annum. It was his practice to pay his suppliers and expenses in cash, to require his customers to settle their accounts in cash and to bank any surplus in a business bank account. He maintained lists of cash receipts and cash payments, of supplies obtained on credit and of work carried out for customers and of appliances sold, and credit.

The list of credit suppliers comprised:

Date supplied 19X5	Supplier	Amount owed £	Date paid 19X5	Amount paid £	Remarks
January	Dee & Co.	337.74	March	330.00	Received discount £7.74
	AB Supplies	528.20	March	528.20	
February	Simpson	141.34	March	138.00	Received discount £3.34
	Cotton Ltd	427.40	March	130.00	Payment on account
			April	297.40	Remainder
	Dee & Co.	146.82	March	140.00	Received discount £6.82
March	AB Supplies	643.43	April	643.43	
	Simpson	95.60			Not yet paid

The purchase in January from Dee & Co. was of tools and equipment to enable him to carry out electrical repair work. All the remaining purchases were of repair materials, except for the purchase in February from Cotton Ltd, which consisted entirely of electrical appliances for resale.

In addition to the above credit transactions, he had bought repair materials for cash, as follows:

19X5	£
January	195.29
February	161.03
March	22.06

Other cash payments comprised:

19X5		£
January	Rent of premises for January to June 19X5	400.00
	Rates of premises for January to March 19X5	150.00
	Stationery	32.70
	Car running expenses	92.26
February	Sundries	51.54
	Car running expenses	81.42
March	Sundries	24.61
	Car running expenses	104.52
	Transfer to bank	500.00

He had also withdrawn £160.00 in cash at the end of each month for living expenses.

The list of credit customers comprised:

Date of sale 19X5	Customer	Amount owed £	Date received 19X5	Amount received £	Remarks
January	D. Hopkins	362.80	February	357.00	Allowed discount £5.80
	P. Bolton	417.10	March	417.10	
February	G. Leivers	55.00	March	55.00	
	M. Whitehead	151.72	April	151.72	
	N. John Ltd	49.14	April	49.14	
	A Linneker	12.53	March	12.53	
March	E. Horton	462.21	April	462.21	
	S. Ward	431.08	March	426.00	Allowed discount £5.08
	W. Scothern & Co.	319.12			Not yet received
	N. Annable	85.41			Not yet received

The above amounts relate to charges for repair work which he had carried out, except that the amounts shown in February for G. Leivers, N. John Ltd and A. Linneker are for sales for electrical appliances.
In addition to the above credit transactions, he had cash takings, as follows:

19X5		£
January	Repair work	69.44
February	Repair work	256.86
March	Repair work	182.90
	Appliances	112.81

He estimated that, at the end of March 19X5, his stock of electrical repair materials was £691.02 and of electrical appliances for resale was £320.58, his tools and equipment were worth £300.00 and his car, £600.00. Apart from loan interest, the only accrual was for heating and lighting, £265.00.

Required:
(a) Prepare:
   (i) purchase day book with analysis columns for type of purchase, and
   (ii) sales day book with analysis columns for class of business undertaken.
(b) Open, post to 31 March 19X5 only, and balance a columnar cash book suitably analysed to facilitate ledger postings.
(c) Open, post to 31 March 19X5 only, and balance a creditors ledger control account and a debtors ledger control account. Use the closing balances in your answer to (g) below. (NB: Individual accounts for creditors and debtors are *not* required.)
(d) Open, post and balance sales and cost of sales accounts, each with separate columns for 'Repairs' and 'Appliances'.
(e) Prepare M. Faraday's trading account for the quarter ended 31 March 19X5, distinguishing between gross profit on repairs and on appliance sales.
(f) Prepare M. Faraday's general profit and loss account for the quarter ended 31 March 19X5.
(g) Prepare M. Faraday's balance sheet as at 31 March 19X5.   (CACA).

7. M. Essex is in business as a wholesale coal merchant. The following transactions took place during December 19X7:

1 Dec Balance at bank £5,000.
3 Dec Purchased goods on credit from English Coal for £400 plus VAT.
4 Dec Received an invoice for £240 plus VAT from Solihull Garage in respect of vehicle repairs on credit.

5 Dec   Bought stationery costing £240 plus VAT and paid by cheque.
6 Dec   Sold goods on credit to Black for £600 plus VAT.
7 Dec   Bought goods on credit from Scottish Coal for £320 plus VAT.
8 Dec   Paid wages by cheque of £350.
10 Dec Sold goods for £520 plus VAT and received a cheque for this amount.
11 Dec Purchased goods costing £720 plus VAT and paid by cheque.
12 Dec Sold goods on credit to White for £800 plus VAT.
13 Dec Received an invoice for £360 plus VAT from Solihull Garage relating to motor expenses incurred on credit.
14 Dec Bought goods for resale costing £480 plus VAT and paid by cheque.
15 Dec Purchased a motor vehicle on credit from Solihull Garage costing £4,000 plus VAT.
16 Dec Received telephone bill from English Telecom for £560 plus VAT.
17 Dec Sold a motor vehicle on credit to Solihull Garage for £2,000 plus VAT.
18 Dec Sold goods for £640 plus VAT and received a cheque.
19 Dec Paid insurance premium on vehicles of £720 by cheque.
20 Dec Purchased stationery for £160 plus VAT by cheque.
23 Dec Sold an old motor vehicle for £3,000 plus VAT and received a cheque for this amount.
28 Dec Received a cheque from Black for £680 after deducting £25 cash discount.
29 Dec Received a cheque from White for £905 after deducting £35 cash discount.
30 Dec Paid English Coal £450 by cheque after deducting cash discount of £20.
31 Dec Paid Scottish Coal £346 by cheque after deducting cash discount of £30.

You are required to:
(a) Write up the sales and purchases day books and the cash books using appropriate analysis columns where there is more than one transaction of the same type.
(b) Make the necessary entries in the ledger.
 Assume the rate of VAT to be 17.5 per cent.

32. The use of computers in accounting

Some basic computer concepts

Computers come in all shapes and sizes. In recent years, there has been a massive growth in the use of *personal computers*, small enough to sit on a desk, but powerful enough to carry out a wide range of accounting functions. A large organization will often use a *mainframe computer* for its accounting: mainframes work faster than personal computers, and can handle much bigger data files. In between come the *mid-range* or *minicomputers*. Prices vary in accordance with the processing power—from a few-hundred pounds for a cheap personal computer, to two or three million pounds for a large mainframe.

All these machines work on the same basic principles. Information must be fed into the computer, either from a keyboard or a more specialized device like a bar code reader. The computer must be able to store this information, and the most common method is to write data on to *magnetic disks*, from which data can be retrieved very rapidly. Data which are only used occasionally, or which are needed for archiving, are stored on *magnetic tapes*. The computer contains a *central processing unit*, which is the 'brain' of the machine, performing all the logical functions and calculations. The computer must be able to communicate its results back to its users, usually via a *display screen* (usually associated with a *keyboard*, and sometimes referred to as *monitor* or *terminal*) or via a 'hard copy' device such as a *printer* or a microfilm machine. All these components comprise the *hardware* of the system.

In order to carry out a specialized function, like accounting, the computer must be provided with a *program* designed for this purpose. The program instructs the computer on how it should organize its data (e.g. in the various ledgers), how values are to be processed (e.g. adding up debits or credits), and how data should be transmitted to and from the input and output devices. Programs are generally known as *software*. The same computer can run a wide variety of programs—so it could be processing accounts at one moment, and graphic design work the next. When reference is made to something which has been done 'by the computer', it is often more accurate to regard it as something achieved 'by the software': indeed, the reliability and ease of use of a system will usually owe more to the quality of writing of the software than to anything in the design or manufacture of hardware.

Software can be designed to allow just one user to interact with it at a time, or it can support *multiple* users. Multiple user systems are very common on mainframes and mid-range machines, and are increasingly being built from personal computers linked together locally. Many companies like to be in a situation where several members of staff can all gain access to the accounts simultaneously. If so, the software must be able to handle this, by maintaining the one set of accounts, but allowing different users to update or query them, via their keyboards and displays. This adds to the complexity of the software, since checks must be built in to ensure that users always see the latest, correct, version of the information in the accounts.

Specialized software is also needed to support long-distance communications between

356

users and the computer. A large organization may wish to hold all its accounts on a mainframe at its head office, but with access made available to staff at regional offices. In this case, communication lines and software must be installed to enable the remote users to 'see' all the same facilities as their colleagues at the head office.

The development of computerized accounting

Computers are adept at following logical rules and working out the results of numerical calculations. This has made them particularly useful in many areas of accounting, and their use has grown dramatically in recent years.

In the early days, fully-fledged systems were confined to large organizaitons, who tended to design and write their own programs for their computers. To do this, it was necessary for their staff to have quite detailed expertise in many aspects of computer programming and operation. The systems were based on *batch operations*: information had first to be keyed in, transferred to magnetic discs or punched cards, and then processed by having a series of programs process all the data in a single batch run.

Since then, a number of technological improvements have brought computer-based systems within the grasp of every organization, large and small. Most obviously, the computers themselves have shrunk in size and cost, while offering much better reliability and faster processing speeds. Less obviously, the techniques for preparing programs (or software) have become more sophisticated and error-free, and the quality of display screens has improved, so that software can be designed to communicate with the user in a variety of ways. These may include combinations of colours, panels, diagrams and charts, and 'question-and-answer' screens laid out in much the same way as ordinary paper forms. In the hands of a good software designer, these facilities make computing attractive and easy to use.

It is now commonplace for computers to be used *interactively*, rather than in batch mode, giving users instant access to the information held on the computer, and allowing information to be entered directly into the computer's files. Laser printers have also transformed the quality of output which can be provided, by giving high resolution printing of a wide variety of layouts and type styles.

Increasingly, suppliers are taking advantage of all these developments, to offer 'user friendly' screen displays which guide the user through every transaction. More and more software is also being sold in ready-to-use 'packages', rather than being developed specially for every individual requirement. An accounts package will typically be provided with detailed instructions on how it should be installed and operated, leaving the user with little more to do than choose from among a number of standard options. At this point the system is capable of being fully operational. Such a system is, however, just like any other accounting system: it calls for careful planning of the way the different accounts are set up and operated, the clerical staff need to understand how to use the system, and the input and output of data must be properly controlled. The fact that the software can be up and running within just a few minutes should not be allowed to obscure this.

Other more general purpose packages can be used in accounting, notably *spreadsheets*. These offer much greater flexibility, but are less attractive for most routine accounting, since more time has to be spent in designing the system, and it is usually difficult to provide adequate audit and security facilities. More commonly, the accounts package will be a source of statistical data to be fed into a spreadsheet, for use in management accounting or financial analysis.

The advantages of computerized accounting systems

The emergence of a mass market for accounts packages has meant that sophisticated software can be acquired at relatively low prices (usually well below the price of the hardware on which the software will be used). But what are the incentives for using computerized accounting? It is not simply because of the speed with which computers can calculate: individual cases can be worked out just as quickly on a pocket calculator. Nor do computers invariably save staff time, since a great deal of information still has to be collected and keyed in, and forms and reports have to be printed out and distributed. The key advantages offered by the computer derive from its enormous capacity for storing data, and its ability to retrieve or analyse all or any of that data at a moment's notice. Typical reasons for moving to a computerized system are described below.

Improved detail

Computer storage is not confined in the same way as the pages of a book. It can handle a more or less indefinite number of columns and rows. This makes it possible to keep track of a variety of useful details about each and every transaction—for example, for every sale, one could identify the salesman, the sales area, the product category, and the industrial classification of the customer. Details for many hundreds of customers can be kept in this way in just one file.

Reduced data capture

Once entered, data can be retrieved by the computer in many different contexts. If it 'knows' a customer's address, for example, it can be asked to put that address on an invoice or a reminder letter: the address does not have to be re-entered in each case. Similarly, if a clerk is entering orders, the computer may 'volunteer' some ready made entries for prices,

Order No. **10025**			Thomas Tanks plc, 15, Railway Cuttings, Birmingham B15 2TT
Customer code	**T009**		
Date received	**25 09 92**		
Date required	**9 10 92**		Credit Limit **4000.00**
Product code	Quantity	Description	Value
PR5544	**20**	**A4 paper**	**216.20**
PR5592	**12**	**markers, black**	**15.24**

Figure 32.1 A simplified screen layout for order entry. The operator only needs to enter the shaded values—the computer can generate a new order number, provide today's date, and retrieve details such as the customer's address and the price and description of each product.

discounts, standard product descriptions, and so on: in a few cases, the clerk may wish to overrule these 'default' entries, but for most of the time he or she need only confirm that the default value is correct, thereby saving having to type in all the details.

Multiple access

It is difficult for more than a handful of people to look at a set of books simultaneously. However, a computer system can allow simultaneous access to all its files for large numbers of users. This does not merely avoid possible bottlenecks and queues in the accounts department, but opens up the possibility for people to work on the accounts via terminals located in different buildings, cities or even countries.

Greater accuracy

No computer offers protection against the operator who keys in erroneous data (although it may be able to carry out some immediate checks, for example to see whether a discount is within permissible limits). From this point on, though, the computer should not introduce any errors of calculation or logic. A reputable software package will have been put through stringent testing to ensure that amounts are posted and balanced correctly. As a result, the kinds of errors which are shown up by a typical trial balance and control accounts should simply never occur on a computer system.

Historical information

As well as storing a wide range of current information, the computer can retain large amounts of data relating to past events. This can range from detailed audit trails, to summarized information which is useful to managers trying to look at long-term shifts and trends.

Report generation

A package will typically generate several standard reports at each period-end. These can be prepared very rapidly, and so this reduces some of the pressure on the accounts department in having to gather together and process all the information as the end of the period approaches. A well-constructed package will also permit data to be extracted and used as raw material for other means of analysis (for example, based on spreadsheets), or it may incorporate report design facilities of its own. In either case, managers can expect to carry out rapid analysis of any pressure points in the company finances, and perhaps convert the figures into easily interpreted charts or graphs. An example is given in Figure 32.2.

SALES LEDGER: ACCOUNT BALANCES (AGED)						
CUST CODE	CUST NAME	CREDIT LIMIT	BALANCE	Current Period	30 Days	Over 30 Days
T009	T. Tanks	4000	1760.15	1203.45	556.70	0.00
T011	B. Timms	5000	4516.25	4020.15	324.10	172.00
T016	N. Todd	1500	1035.65	1035.65	0.00	0.00
T023	M. Tubbs	2500	519.23	380.12	98.56	40.55

Figure 32.2 Part of a typical computer-generated report. It enables customers with large or long-standing debts to be quickly identified.

Two further advantages can be added, although these are not experienced quite so widely at present. They are likely to be of increasing importance in the future:-

Intercommunication

Data can be exchanged almost instantaneously between computers linked by telecommunications lines. As more and more organizations acquire computers, they are beginning to explore ways of conducting business via telecommunications networks. A growing number of orders and invoices are now exchanged using electronic data interchange (EDI). This eliminates the need for the receiving organization to re-key the data into its own computer system, and reduces the turn-round time associated with conducting business through the mail. See Fig. 32.3.

Integration

Many suppliers offer options whereby the basic accounting software can be linked to other functions, such as the control of stock, or costing. This can enable an organization to be much more responsive to the outside world, and to improve the overall management of its activities. For example, an order entry clerk can be given the facility to check the stock control files, to see whether or not a requested item is available from stock. Managers can also be provided with timely end-of-period statistics, which relate accounting issues to performance in areas such as stock levels or work in progress. As more and more activities within an organization become computerized, and many of these activities generate accounting information as a by-product, it become feasible to link the systems together and give members of the workforce much improved access to information which is useful to them.

Figure 32.3 Intercommunication alternatives

The design of computerized accounting systems

It can be seen that computerization involves a great deal more than merely automating the traditional methods of bookkeeping. Software package designers invariably adhere to the terminology and conventions of bookkeeping, and software sometimes mimics traditional methods in the way it presents reports, or requests for data input: all this helps the accountant get to grips with the system quickly. However, some of the facilities made possible by computing cannot be implemented simply by 'putting ledgers on a screen'. New concepts have therefore to be introduced. These may involve adding new options when carrying out the traditional accounting tasks, or making subtle changes to the roles of the reports, ledgers and journals created by the system.

For example, traditional methods often centre around day books, which are a convenient place to gather together the records of a series of similar items, such as credit sales. Much of the information may need to be transcribed to other books, subsequently. Day books are a way of dividing up the process of data capture, so that manageable amounts of the work are carried out by different members of the accounting team. As we have seen, the computer systems designer does not have to worry about such constraints, since large numbers of people can all be given concurrent access to the same file. Nor is there any need for anyone to re-enter the data in any other file, since the computer can be programmed to do this automaticaly. While the options open to the designer are, in technical terms, very powerful, they have nevertheless to be used with discretion: it is still useful to ensure, for example, that different aspects of carrying out a transaction are done by different people, as a way of preventing fraud. A good computer system will therefore provide a means of identifying each authorized user (usually by requesting the entry of a *personal password*), and confining that user to a pre-defined range of activities. The designer has also to provide for the possibility that the computer may be part of a 'hybrid' system, in which both manual and computerized methods are used side by side. Most packages therefore provide for data to be entered up from journals, with screens tailored to accept a long batch of entries. All this militates against introducing radical changes in the view of the accounting data which is presented to the user.

When it comes to the interrogation of files, the designer will usually be more innovative. If, for example, a customer complains of non-delivery of goods, this may call for reference to two or three different books in a manual system. When were the goods ordered? Was the customer's credit satisfactory? Has despatch been requested? What were the terms of the sale? Such queries can require a lot of hunting around, particularly if the customer happens to have lost the reference number, or has forgotten that delivery was requested to a different location. Instead of searching through the books, and maybe making phone calls to other departments, the computer user should be able to request a summary of the current status of the order, together with any other relevant details of the background to the sale. Furthermore, if this can be done quickly while the customer is still on the phone, there is every chance that some kind of corrective action can be agreed on the spot, thus both saving time *and* improving customer relations.

Of course, not every accounting procedure needs to be carried out instantly. An organization which starts out with this ambition will quickly find that this adds considerably to the expense of computerization, not least because it will need a large and expensive computer to handle all the activity which results. There are many situations where the older, 'batch' approach is more appropriate. for example, if several clerks are all working on the creation of invoices, it may be desirable to store up all the output for printing towards the end of the day. This means that the invoices can all be printed and posted in one operation, rather than being produced sporadically at the end of each individual transaction. If special stationery is required on the printer, this can be set up just for the duration of the print run. If some kind of sorting operation is desirable (for example, printing first the UK and then the overseas customers), this can be done prior to printing. Batch runs may also be used to post entries between ledgers, or to carry out housekeeping jobs, such as reorganizing account codes, or making back-up copies of information from the system. Many of these activities are best done outside normal working hours, when no other transactions are taking place, and everything is 'pinned down' in the system, while copies are taken or any far-reaching changes are made.

The management and operation of computerized accounting systems

Responsibility for the maintenance and housekeeping of the system needs to be assigned to a system manager, who is qualified to oversee both the technical and accounting aspects of the system. This role differs markedly from that of a more traditional accounts department head or supervisor. The system manager will usually have a password which allows access to every facility of the system, including powerful facilities which are available to no-one else. The system manager will be able to set, and alter, options such as the following:

the dates and durations of accounting periods
the codes to be used for accounts, discounts, sales areas, etc.
the format of standard reports
the organization or location of data on disk files
the routing of routine output to different printers
the accounting facilities available to all *other* users of the system

As can be seen, such options affect every aspect of the system. The responsibilities of system management do not belong with a junior technician: an organization assigns then there at its peril.

Probably the most important responsibility of the system manager relates to the last area mentioned, namely system security. The access controls must be applied in such a way that they match closely with the operating procedures of the organization. In some cases, this may simply mean that a purchase order clerk is only permitted to have access to purchase order menus. In other areas, there may need to be further refinements—for example, in specifying that only a supervisor can alter certain values, such as prices, or override restrictions on credit.

The system manager should also ensure that back-up copies are taken regularly, so that the system can be re-created if necessary. This protects the organization against the risk of a disaster, such as vandalism or fire, rendering the system unusable. For a small system, it may be feasible to make a copy of its entire contents. In the case of larger systems, it is more common to begin with a total copy of this kind, and then to back up only the changes for the following periods. In either case, the back-up data needs to be moved to a separate, secure location for storage.

Finally, the system manager will also need to ensure that proper audit trails are being maintained, and that these, too, are available on back-up copies. Reputable packages will create detailed, secure trails automatically, and will provide batch programs (which are usually made accessible only to authorized users) for searching and analysing the trails. As the number of paper records tends to decrease (particularly with the advent of EDI), the computer-generated audit trail assumes more and more importance.

Some limitations of computer systems and the effects of new technology

Thus far, it may seem that computers have brought unremitting benefits to accounting. However, they have also thrown up a number of recurring problems for users. No software designer can anticipate the user's every need, and a 'standard' package, if it fails to provide all the facilities the user wants, can be very difficult to add to or modify. It is also vital that the hardware on which the system is running can offer consistently good performance: there is no point in having a first-rate facility for handling customer queries if the system needs two minutes to find the answer. In such circumstances, the customer on the end of the phone is very likely to get fed up with waiting, and hang up.

Perhaps the greatest minefield lying in wait for users of computerized systems has to do with standards. Every package tends to store data in its own particular way. In order to retrieve data for analysis by other packages (such as wordprocessing of spreadsheet software), it is essential that the accounts package can 'translate' its data into a format which the receiving package will understand. Similar problems can attend the transfer of data between compters, whether on magnetic tapes and disks, or via telecommunications lines. These problems come to the fore whenever organizations merge, or different departments try to cooperate in their accounting activities, since the parties may have started off with entirely different equipment and software.

Nor can it be said that the world of computerized accounting has in any sense 'settled down'. New technologies are appearing all the time. In future, we can expect to see cheap and sophisticated scanning systems, capable of recording and interpreting documents automatically. More 'intelligent' software will be able to offer advice and guidance on complex or infrequently used transactions. More powerful tools will be provided to help with the work of analysing accounts. Much of the outward appearance of accounting will continue to change: but this is unlikely to apply to any of its underlying rules.

Exercises

1. Explain the difference between (a) hardware and software; (b) 'batch' and 'interactive' processing; (c) the roles of magnetic disks and magnetic tape as storage media.

2. A new, computerized accounting system is to be introduced into an accounts department which has hitherto used only traditional bookkeeping. Six people work in the department. What advantages might they hope to see from the new system?

3. Give an example of *one* way in which a computerized accounting system might:
   reduce errors
   improve customer service
   improve the quality of accounting reports.

4. 'Good accounting software has the look and feel of traditional bookkeeping methods'. Explain the benefits which might follow from such an approach. Identify *one* accounting function where this approach might not

be the best one, and describe how a different approach might be implemented, taking advantage of some of the new possibilities of computing technology.

5. A 'system manager' will normally be appointed to take charge of a computerized accounting system. Draw up a brief job description, outlining the duties with such an appointment.

6. Information technology and computerized systems are rapidly increasing in importance in data recording.
   Do you consider that this trend will eventually remove the need for control accounts to be incorporated in the design of accounting systems? Explain your answer briefly. (CACA adapted)

33. Theoretical review of basic accounting procedures

The foundations of financial accounting were introduced in Chapters 1 and 2 and were extended in Chapter 10 to consider the fundamental accounting concepts, bases and policies. Having looked at how these are used in a range of accounting applications, it is now possible to review the accounting processes from a theoretical perspective. It may be helpful, at this stage, to re-read the material in Chapters 2 and 10 and to consider how they have contributed to the various accounting procedures that have been covered in this book.

The major considerations can be briefly restated.

1. Definition of the accounting entity is used to determine the boundaries of the subject to be reported upon. The accounting entity is created as an artificial construct and as such cannot own itself. The external owner's interest is identified as capital in the accounting equation.
2. The life of a business is divided into accounting periods usually of a year, each seen as a separate entity. Accounts are produced to show the results relating to a particular period. Division into periods is reflected by the emphasis given to periodic reporting and periodic income.
3. Income can be defined in terms of changes in capital represented in the balance sheets at the start and end of the period. A parallel approach is that of net production. Here, revenues are recognized in the period when they are realized and the matching principle identifies the costs to be traced to the appropriate period. Critical in this process is the classification of expenditure as either capital or revenue. Costs which are capitalized are capable of being carried forward from period to period as balance sheet items. Assets in the balance sheet are carried forward in anticipation of providing benefits to future periods and this may then lead to matching in those periods.
4. In measuring the values to be included in accounting reports three concepts have been set down in accounting standards and in particular SSAP2—Disclosure of Accounting Policies. In addition to the accruals concept and matching principle this stresses the concepts of prudence, going concern and consistency.
5. Other measurement properties were also considered in Chapter 10 including objectivity, verifiability and freedom from bias.
6. Any system of accounting for profit has to define either explicitly or implicitly three basic dimensions. These are the units of measurements, the valuation model and the concept of capital maintenance.

Some of the fundamental roles these ideas have played in accounting procedures can be readily identified. The compatibility between double entry bookkeeping and the view of the accounting entity as an artificial construct has the broadest implications. Accruals and matching are strongly represented in depreciation and provisions with more specific examples in the cases of stock valuations, periodic income on investments and periodic interest reporting for hire purchase transactions.

Recording transactions and historical cost in the measurement of income

The fundamental ideas of profit introduced in Chapter 2 were based on the accounting definition that profit was the maximum amount that could be withdrawn from a business while leaving the capital intact. This approach as a measure of performance has considerable appeal. As residual beneficiaries the owners' benefits from the business are not fixed but are entirely dependent on the success of the business. Such success can be readily assessed in terms of what can be taken out of the business while leaving it no worse off than it was at the start of the period. When this is also seen in the more dynamic terms of being the amount by which the revenue earned exceeds the cost of producing those revenues, it is also seen as a measure of operating efficiency—increasing the value over outputs as represented by revenues, while achieving a relative decrease in the inputs measured as the costs matched against that revenue.

It was again in Chapter 2 that the measurement approach utilized by historic cost accounting was described in terms of recording transactions. Subsequent chapters have illustrated this time and again. As an approach to measurement, the transaction basis contributes well to the objectivity and verifiability attributes. In the historical cost balance sheet, assets are represented by the capitalized expenditures which have not yet been matched against revenue through depreciation for example. In the profit and loss account, revenues and costs have all been quantified on the basis of transactions.

However, it would be wrong to deduce that the historical cost basis is entirely objective and verifiable. Subjectivity has entered in deciding whether an expenditure was capable of being capitalized or not, i.e. whether or not it represented an asset. Choice of methods of depreciation and the determination of provisions both involve substantial judgement. Similar scope exists in the allocation of indirect costs to stock values.

When considered in relation to other measurement attributes, historical cost may stand up less well, particularly when price changes are prevalent either in general, due to inflation, or for specific items arising as a result of changes in technology, tastes or other factors. The level of expenditures and asset values will be dependent upon timing so that the same asset may have a different value depending only upon when it is purchased. This promotes neither consistency nor comparability and we are likely to get varying mixtures of ages of expenditures both between businesses and between periods for the same business. If prices are generally rising then, although asset values may be regarded as prudent, matching older expenses based on correspondingly lower prices may understate cost relative to revenues and thus overstate profit. Understating asset values and overstating profit cannot be considered free from bias let alone prudent.

The historical cost convention has adopted particular approaches to the three basic dimensions. The unit of measurement is the currency unit, i.e. the pound sterling in the UK. Even if the purchasing power of the pound changes, there is no response in this dimension by the historical cost convention. As implied above, the valuation model used measures asset values at the original transaction price modified by provisions and write downs due to depreciation etc. The capital maintained is the money value of the shareholders' contributed capital plus accumulated profits.

Price change considerations

Price change has two broad impacts on the accounting approaches which have been described. First general price change through inflation undermines the stability of the value of the currency unit. Reducing the purchasing power of the pound through inflation means that comparison of amounts measured in pounds at different times is distorted.

One response to the problems of price change is to restate the accounts produced on a total cost basis by adjusting for changes in purchasing power. The procedure is to restate opening and closing balance sheets by indexing all items in the opening balance sheet and all non-monetary items including owners' capital in the closing balance sheet using general price level indices. Monetary items in the closing balance sheet would require no adjustments as they are already stated in current terms. The capital increase shown between the restated balance sheets would be the current purchasing power profit. This approach involves only limited adjustment from historical cost and, since these can be based on publicly available indices such as the retail price index, properties of objectivity and verifiability are not substantially reduced.

The unit of measurement that would then be employed would be the pound of current purchasing power at the year end. The purchasing power of the owners' capital would be maintained since it is restated in these terms. However the valuation model which adjusts asset values for general changes in prices may result in asset values that are considered to be an entire fiction. Assets do not all change price in line with inflation. In addition the increase that is being reported would be a combination of realized and unrealized gains, since the upward revaluation of assets by indexing them would be, increasingly, a value without the external evidence that would meet the needs of prudence and realization. A version of this approach known as CPP accounting was put forward in the UK but, given the limitations identified and others, it has been largely rejected.

The second major aspect of price change is the specific changes in asset values. The historic cost approach, which recognizes revenues only when they are realized, will produce periodic profits which represent both the results of current year's operations and gains made in previous periods which are only realized in the current period (although gains which are unrealized in the current period are excluded).

A response which can be made to this problem is to recognize unrealized gains in the period to which they relate but to treat these not as part of operating profit. Instead they can be regarded as holding gains, i.e. gains from continuing to own assets during price rises. Measuring profit in relation to opening and closing capital restated to include holding gains of the period produces a physical concept of capital maintenance, i.e. identifying the gains that can be withdrawn whilst permitting a business to own the same physical assets. Profit would be restated by eliminating holding gains. This is aptly described as operating profit, showing the ability of a business to produce revenues over and above the current cost of producing them through operating activities. Any adjustments necessary to eliminate holding gains from profit would be those necessary to re-state historic costs, included in the profit and loss account, to current costs.

Current cost accounting included such adjustments in three components. These were a depreciation adjustment, modifying depreciation to one based on the current cost of assets rather than the historical cost; a cost of sales adjustment, adjusting stocks values and purchases to current costs; a monetary working capital adjustment, adjusting for the price change of purchases during the creditor period and sales during the debt collection period. Considerable subjectivity is involved in identifying suitable indices for each of the possible specific price changes. The resulting reduction in objectivity and verifiability together with the costs of implementing the approach with all its complexities were considered to outweigh the advantages, particularly where the period of holding assets was relatively short and hence the impact of the adjustments was small. Current cost accounting has been widely abandoned as a result.

Index